BETTY ROSBOTTOM'S
COOKING SCHOOL COOKBOOK

BETTY ROSBOTTOM'S
COOKING SCHOOL COOKBOOK

BY BETTY ROSBOTTOM
ILLUSTRATIONS BY RODICA PRATO

WORKMAN PUBLISHING, NEW YORK

For Ronny and Michael
who both know well the recipes
for patience and love

———

Library of Congress Cataloging-in-Publication Data
Rosbottom, Betty.
Betty Rosbottom's cooking school cookbook.
Includes index.   1. Cookery.   I. Title.
TX715.R833 1987   641.5   87-42746
ISBN 0-89480-526-6   ISBN 0-89480-525-8 (pbk.)

Cover and book design: Susan Aronson Stirling
Cover photographs: Paul Elson

Workman Publishing Company, Inc.
1 West 39th Street
New York, NY 10018

Manufactured in the United States of America

First printing October 1987
10 9 8 7 6 5 4 3 2 1

ACKNOWLEDGMENTS

This cookbook, for so long a dream, has become a reality because of the help and support of many friends and colleagues. Mary Rogers, Brenda Brienza, Sally Thomson, and Marsha Cox were invaluable in organizing and preparing the manuscript. More than forty volunteers tested recipes week after week, carefully recording their impressions and comments for me. I am grateful to them, particularly Betty Ann Litvak, Bob Corea, and Wendy Gabriel, for sharing their time and talents so willingly. And the staff at La Belle Pomme—Sheri Lisak, Sue Peterson, June McCarthy, and our teachers—have been part of my culinary family and have contributed immeasurably to this book.

My admiration could not be greater for the wonderful people at Workman Publishing—Peter Workman, Bert Snyder, Kathie Ness, Susan Aronson Stirling, Barbara Scott-Goodman, Shannon Ryan, Andrea Bass, Janet Harris, and most especially Suzanne Rafer. As my editor she tirelessly guided me, a first-time author, through the frustrations and exhilarations of putting together a book. Judith Weber, my literary agent, whose initial enthusiasm for this book has never waned, and whose encouragement and good counsel I have come to count upon daily, has been a constant source of inspiration.

My gratitude to the management of Lazarus Department Stores for providing me with one of the finest teaching kitchens anywhere, and for their wholehearted support for this book.

Many of my recipes in this book have appeared in *Bon Appétit Magazine,* and I would like to thank that publication for their generous permission to reprint them here.

My thanks to *The Columbus Dispatch,* which gave me my first opportunity to write about food.

I owe a debt I'll never be able to repay to the talented cooks who have given classes at La Belle Pomme. From Jacques Pépin, Paula Wolfert, Maida Heatter, Perla Meyers, Giuliano Bugialli, Bernard Clayton, Julie Dannenbaum, Anne Willan, Madeleine Kamman and others, I have learned to recognize that cooking is an art that should be taught. A very special thanks must go to two distinguished teachers, Sheila Lukins and Bert Greene, without whose help this book would not have come to print.

To the students who have attended my classes over the past decade, I am grateful for your loyalty to the school, for your curiosity about all things culinary, and for your friendship.

Finally, I would like to thank my family, who have supported this work from conception to completion with only occasional complaint. My husband and son have sampled and critiqued dish after dish for this collection; they have helped clean stacks of dirty pots and pans; they have eaten countless meals out on nights when I was too tired to cook; and they have offered advice and made suggestions about the manuscript. Their patience, kindness, and understanding have been more than I deserved, but never less than I knew I could expect.

Betty Rosbottom
September 1987

CONTENTS

NOTES FROM A TEACHER

If anyone had asked me twenty years ago what my profession would be today, teaching cooking would never have entered my mind. After graduating from college in the 1960s, I moved to the East Coast, where my husband was to begin his graduate studies, while I taught French to seventh- and eighth-graders. Despite my enthusiasm for cooking our meals, I had few culinary skills to call on in our small apartment kitchen. My first efforts were modest, occasionally bordering on disaster: breakfasts of burnt scrambled eggs and soggy toast; dry tuna salad for lunch; uninspired fried chicken, overcooked vegetables, and sticky rice at dinner. Unpropitious beginnings indeed!

The route from fledgling home chef to cooking teacher has been somewhat circuitous. Obviously, as these early attempts imply, I did not grow up in front of a stove. But the foundations for my interest in food were laid early in my life. I was raised in the South, a region rich with culinary traditions, and was surrounded by relatives who adored food. Inveterate entertainers, they always centered our family gatherings around memorable home-cooked meals. And when they weren't eating, they were having lively discussions about food. I remember visiting my grandmother, a "make-from scratch" cook, in southern Mississippi. As a youngster, I would watch while she grated coconut for fresh coconut cream cake or scraped kernels from ears of corn for frying or used just-picked figs to concoct her locally famous preserves. My mother, who never considered herself a serious cook, definitely inherited some of the family talent; her vegetables, simmered slowly, Southern style, and her superb cornbread are still favorite memories from my childhood. But throughout my youth I only observed cooking from the sidelines. The emphasis was always on eating and talking about delicious food, not on learning how to prepare it.

Later, as a college student, I spent a year in France. Before that trip abroad, I had never known the food of another country, and like countless others, I was seduced by the flavors of French cuisine. During the first weeks of my stay, I lived with a French family in Dijon. Edith Paquet was my surrogate mother and a *cuisinière* of extraordinary versatility. Even foods I thought I didn't like tasted delicious when prepared in her simple kitchen.

I lived for the better part of that year in Paris, where I continued

my food experience—I spent as much time sampling the goods in the *pâtisseries* as I did studying in the libraries, and I became as familiar with *crème fraîche,* Normandy butter, and *chanterelles* as I did with the works of Molière, Baudelaire, and Sartre.

So, though my technical expertise was rather limited, I was learning to judge and savor food. Gradually, during the first years of my marriage, I compiled a substantial library of cookbooks and cooked my way through each one. When I wasn't preparing food, I was reading about it. I spent evenings, while my husband was studying for this Ph.D exams, surrounded by cookbooks, food magazines, and recipes clipped from newspapers. The books soon had tattered pages and broken spines as I practiced the techniques they described. Eventually my cooking skills improved and I began to develop my own culinary style. I wanted to cook and taste everything! Then I discovered cooking lessons and took session after session, month after month, addicted to the infinite possibilities of the world of cuisine.

When we moved to Ohio in the 1970s, I wanted to teach what I had learned, but being a newcomer to the Midwest, I wondered if Ohioans would share my interest in the culinary arts. In 1974 I decided to find out by placing a small, unassuming advertisement in the weekly *Upper Arlington News.* Buried between the garage sales and used-furniture ads, mine was easy to miss, but one woman saw it and called to inquire about classes. She signed up not only herself, but three other friends as well. On a cool spring night, the students of this first class arrived at my house. Their excitement that evening pervaded the kitchen, and at the end of the session I realized that no work I had done before was as satisfying as teaching others about food and its preparation. I had found my calling.

For two years I continued to give cooking classes in my home, but the groups were becoming far too big for my kitchen. The time seemed right to open a professional school in larger quarters. Named La Belle Pomme, it opened in a small suburban shopping center in Columbus, the first such school in the area. Columbusites responded overwhelmingly and filled the classes repeatedly. In 1981, with the school still growing, La Belle Pomme moved once again, this time to a beautiful large teaching kitchen in Lazarus Department Store in downtown Columbus. This is where I continue to teach today, supported by a staff of ten other professionals.

Often during the past decade I thought about writing a cookbook—a very special volume filled with the best and most unusual dishes taught at the school. Students told me the recipes they hoped I would include. They asked for a wide range in every category, rather than a specialized or narrowly focused cookbook. They encouraged me to give as many make-ahead tips as possible, and they urged me to offer menu accompaniments to the dishes. Finally, they suggested that the book be personal, reflecting what I often talked about in my classes. "Don't forget to tell how you got the recipe for Old-Fashioned Peach Custard Pie, or the origin of the word 'julep,' or how to use dental floss to slice cheesecake."

And throughout all the planning, organizing, testing, writing, and the myriad other activities that go into the composition of a cookbook, I have remembered these requests. This is a book that is broad in scope. It begins with a selection of special hors d'oeuvres, soups, and first courses, all fresh and innovative creations that have been among the most popular dishes taught in our classes. The section on main courses is composed of several chapters, including one on homemade pastas, with dishes as varied as the hearty Lasagne With Artichokes, Leeks, and Prosciutto and the elegant Fettuccine with Lobster and Scallops. The seafood selections include recipes for baking, broiling, and deep-frying all manner of fish, and the meat chapter deals with veal, lamb, pork, and beef prepared as sautés, roasts, and ragoûts. There's also a group of special grilled and smoked entrées.

I love vegetables, an important and often overlooked part of every meal, so there are many tempting and unusual vegetable recipes. There's a chapter for salads—both as main courses and as accompaniments—for each season of the year, and in the breads chapter there are directions for interesting muffins, rolls, and loaves. Since desserts are my specialty, it is appropriate that they form one of the largest sections of the book. Can anyone resist the creamy Espresso Cheesecake, the Coconut Cream Mousse Pie, or the dramatic Chocolate Ribbon Cake? The final section of the book reveals some other popular interests of my students, including a chapter of breakfast and brunch offerings and another for "chic sandwiches" and special drinks.

A few words about the dishes: I have tested and retested the recipes in this book many times, with the hope that the final versions will be clear, easy to follow, and successful. In some cases the recipes may seem lengthy, but read through them and you will see that this is because I have given detailed directions for each procedure and technique so that nothing is left to chance. Wherever make-ahead instructions are appropriate, I have included them. I have also mixed and matched recipes in menu suggestions to help readers see how

dishes can work together as part of a whole. All the recipes reflect what I think cooks want today—food that is simple but sophisticated, lighter but well balanced, new but with a sense of tradition.

Cooking is a great joy for me, and I hope that these recipes reflect this sentiment. Cooking is also an art, but one that all of us can enjoy. The French family I stayed with in Dijon would often say that *la meilleure conversation est toujours à table*—the best conversation is always at mealtime. Conviviality and a sense of well-being are natural responses to a table set with delicious food and wine. Good food encourages good company, and I hope that this collection of recipes will provide you with an abundance of both.

GREAT BEGINNINGS

The opening dish of a meal sets the scene. And since first impressions are the most lasting ones, the food should reflect extra care and thoughtfulness.

When planning a menu opener, I always opt for preparations that are made with the freshest seasonal offerings. Nothing is nicer than going to an early spring dinner party and tasting the season's first young asparagus in some original creation, or sampling a dish made with garden tomatoes at a summer fête.

This section is divided into three chapters. There are hors d'oeuvres for every occasion—try the Cajun Cashews as a starter for a tailgate meal, the Shrimp and Pistachio Pâté at an important dinner party, or the Baked Chèvre with Tomatoes and Garlic Toasts before an informal Sunday supper.

Soups—rich and creamy, light and delicate, for both cold weather and warm—make up the second chapter. And a selection of very special appetizers, some served hot, others cold, concludes the section.

HORS D'OEUVRES

The first appetizer I remember making was onion dip surrounded by potato chips. But it didn't take long for me to discover how much more inventive the hors d'oeuvre tray could be. During the past decade at La Belle Pomme, I have prepared countless appetizers, finding inspiration in various ethnic cuisines and inventing new dishes from America's regional foods. The recipes in this chapter are a sampling of the most popular inventions that have come from our kitchen.

A COOK'S REFLECTIONS

The dough used in these fritters is a basic French preparation called *pâte à choux*. The name translates as "cabbage pastry" and derives from the fact that when baked, the pastry puffs out like the leaves of a cabbage. Made with water, butter, flour, and eggs, the dough has many uses.

Mounded in rounds and baked, the pastry makes wonderful puffs perfect for filling with savory mixtures. When sugar is added to the dough, it can be used for cream puffs or éclairs. The Burgundian specialty called *gougère* is a mixture of choux pastry flavored with cheese and almonds and baked in a large ring.

In this recipe the dough is combined with cheese, shaped into balls, and deep-fried until golden and crisp.

Smoked Mozzarella Fritters

This is one of my favorite hors d'oeuvres to serve before a dinner party. The batter can be prepared well in advance and the fritters deep-fried to a golden crispness just before serving. No matter how many I make, I never have enough—and there are never any leftovers!

1 cup water
6 tablespoons (¾ stick) unsalted butter, cut into small pieces
½ teaspoon salt
Several sprinklings of cayenne pepper
1 cup all-purpose flour
4 large eggs
1 cup grated smoked mozzarella cheese (rind removed if present)
2 tablespoons chopped flat-leaf parsley
Vegetable oil for deep-frying
Sprigs of flat-leaf parsley, for garnish

1. Combine the water, butter, salt, and cayenne pepper in a heavy 2-quart saucepan over medium-high heat. When the water starts to boil, remove from the heat and add the flour to the pan all at once. Stir vigorously until thick. Return the pan to the heat and stir constantly for several minutes, until the dough leaves the sides of the pan. Remove the pan from the heat.

2. Leaving the dough in the pan, make a well in the center of the dough and break 1 egg into it. Beat until the egg is completely incorporated into the dough. Add the remaining eggs, one at a time, in the same way. With each addition, you will have to beat a little harder to mix the egg into the dough. The dough should be smooth when all the eggs have been added. Stir in the cheese and chopped parsley. (This dough can be used immediately, or you can make the dough several hours ahead, cover and refrigerate it, bring it back to room temperature, and then fry the fritters.)

3. To fry the fritters, heat oil for deep-frying to 325° F in a wok or a medium-size heavy saucepan. (Use a deep-frying thermometer to make certain the oil is at the correct temperature.)

4. Use a teaspoon to scoop out about a teaspoonful of dough. With a second teaspoon, shape the dough into a ball. Add seven or eight balls of dough to the hot oil, and cook until the fritters are puffed

THE RIGHT EQUIPMENT

A good deep-frying thermometer is essential in this recipe. I like the ones that have a face with clear markings and that clip onto the side of the pan.

AS A VARIATION

Although smoked mozzarella gives a special assertive taste to these fritters, other smoked cheeses (smoked Cheddar, smoked Gruyère, smoked gouda, for example) could be substituted.

AT THE MARKET

Saga Bleu is a creamy cheese with a rind; it resembles Brie in appearance. It has a distinctive bleu taste and is easier to spread than most other bleu varieties. If not available, French Roquefort or Maytag Bleu (from the U.S.) can be substituted.

and golden, 5 to 8 minutes. (Avoid crowding the fritters when frying because they expand while cooking.) Drain on paper towels. Repeat until all the dough has been used.

5. As you fry each batch of fritters, transfer them to a baking sheet and keep them in a warm oven (150° to 200° F) until all the fritters are done.

6. Serve the hot fritters in a basket or bowl lined with a napkin, garnished with the sprigs of parsley.

Makes 24 to 30 fritters

Saga Bleu and Ham Spirals

These pinwheels are made with a flaky pastry similar to—but easier to prepare than—puff pastry and are filled with a mixture of bleu cheese, sherry, and thin slices of ham. The spirals can be made in advance and frozen, and then baked to a golden brown.

2 cups all-purpose flour
½ teaspoon salt
1 cup (2 sticks) unsalted butter, well-chilled and cut into ½-inch cubes
1 large egg
1 tablespoon heavy or whipping cream
⅔ pound Saga Bleu cheese, well-chilled and rind removed
2½ tablespoons dry sherry
⅓ pound paper-thin slices baked ham
2 large egg whites, beaten to blend
Several clusters of lemon leaves, for garnish (optional)

1. To make the pastry, combine the flour and salt in a large bowl. Cut in the butter using a pastry blender or two knives, until the mixture resembles oatmeal flakes. Blend the egg and cream together, and stir into the dough. Gently knead the dough on an unfloured surface just until a smooth ball forms. Flatten to a rectangle, wrap the dough in plastic wrap, and refrigerate until firm, about 1 hour.

2. Roll the dough out on a lightly floured surface to form a 16 x 8-inch rectangle. With a short side nearest you, fold it into thirds as for a business letter. Lift the dough off the work surface, scrape the surface clean, and reflour. Return the dough to the work surface

with a short side nearest you. Repeat rolling and folding two more times. Wrap the dough tightly and refrigerate it for at least 1 hour or overnight.

3. Using an electric mixer, beat the cheese until light. Mix in the sherry.

4. Cut the chilled dough in half. Roll one piece out on a lightly floured surface to form a 12 x 10-inch rectangle. Spread half of the cheese mixture evenly over the dough, leaving a ½-inch border. Cover the cheese with half of the ham. Starting at one long side, roll the dough up very tightly, jelly roll fashion. Repeat this with the remaining dough, cheese, and ham. Place the rolls seam side down on a baking sheet, and press down lightly on the rolls. Cover with plastic wrap and freeze until firm, at least 45 minutes. (The spirals can be prepared to this point and frozen, tightly wrapped, up to one week ahead. Soften slightly in the refrigerator before continuing.)

5. Position a rack in the center of the oven and preheat to 400° F.

6. Lightly grease two baking sheets. Cut both dough rolls, seam side down, into ½-inch-thick slices. Arrange the slices flat on the prepared sheets, and brush with the egg whites. Bake until the cheese is bubbly, 12 to 15 minutes. Turn the baking sheets back to front and continue baking until the spirals are light brown, 8 to 10 minutes more. Transfer the spirals to a platter, and let cool at least 5 minutes. Serve in a napkin-lined basket or mounded on a serving tray, garnished with several clusters of lemon leaves.

Makes about 40 spirals

AT THE MARKET

Try to hand-pick mushrooms of equal size for this dish rather than buying the prepackaged variety. Fresh mushrooms should be light in color with no blemishes, and the caps tightly closed over the gills.

Bay scallops vary in size. For this recipe scallops approximately ½ to ¾ inch in diameter are preferable. If larger scallops are used, cut them into pieces about ½ to ¾ inch in diameter.

Mushrooms Stuffed with Scallop Cream

My students love these scallop-stuffed mushrooms. They are simple and easy to prepare, and guests always want seconds.

Special equipment: Flameproof baking sheet or pan

Mushroom Caps
2 tablespoons unsalted butter, plus more if needed
2 tablespoons vegetable oil, plus more if needed
36 large mushroom caps, 1½ to 2 inches in diameter

A COOK'S REFLECTIONS

When cleaning mushrooms never immerse them in water since these fungi act like sponges and absorb liquids quickly. I've found that the best way to clean mushrooms is to place them in a colander, rinse them quickly under cold running water, and then pat dry with a kitchen towel.

Scallop Filling

2 tablespoons unsalted butter
6 tablespoons finely chopped shallots
8 ounces tiny bay scallops, rinsed and patted dry
1 cup heavy or whipping cream
1¾ cups grated Gruyère cheese
½ cup grated imported Parmesan cheese
¾ cup dry bread crumbs
¼ teaspoon salt, plus more if needed
Freshly ground pepper to taste
Several sprigs of watercress, for garnish

1. To cook the mushroom caps, heat the butter and oil in a large heavy skillet over medium heat. Add enough mushroom caps, hollow side up, to fit comfortably in one layer in the pan. Sauté the caps for about 2 to 3 minutes, then turn them hollow side down and sauté until golden, another 2 minutes. Remove the mushrooms from the pan and drain on paper towels. Continue in the same manner with the remaining caps. Add additional butter and oil if needed.

2. To prepare the filling, melt the butter in a heavy medium-size skillet and add the shallots. Cook until softened, about 2 minutes. Then add the scallops and cook 2 minutes more. (Do not overcook or the scallops will become tough.) Remove the scallops and shallots with a slotted spoon to a side dish and reserve.

3. Place the cream in a medium-size saucepan and heat over medium heat until it is quite hot. Then gradually, a little at a time, stir in 1½ cups of the Gruyère and all the Parmesan. Add the reserved scallops and shallots. Then stir in the bread crumbs and the salt. Add more salt if necessary, and remove from the heat.

4. Salt and pepper the cavities of the mushroom caps. Then mound each cap with a tablespoon or more of the filling. When all the caps are filled, sprinkle each top with a little of the remaining Gruyère. (Depending on the size of the mushrooms, you may have some filling left over.) Place the filled caps on a generously buttered baking dish or pan that can withstand the heat of the broiler. (The mushrooms may be prepared several hours in advance, covered with plastic wrap, and refrigerated. Bring them to room temperature before broiling.)

5. When ready to serve, preheat the broiler and place the mushrooms under it for about 2 minutes. Watch carefully and remove the pan when the mushrooms have browned slightly on top and are heated through.

AS A VARIATION

Although I usually offer these stuffed mushrooms as an hors d'oeuvre, I sometimes serve them as a first course. For each serving, I place three large caps on a salad plate and garnish with several sprigs of watercress.

6. To serve, place the hot mushrooms on a serving plate and garnish with watercress sprigs.

Makes 36 mushrooms

Artichokes with Brie Sauce

This is one way I love to serve artichokes as an hors d'oeuvre. Circles of overlapping artichoke leaves surrounding a small glass or earthenware bowl full of a creamy mixture of Brie and leeks makes a dramatic presentation.

8 ounces Brie, well-chilled and rind removed
2 tablespoons unsalted butter
½ cup minced leeks (white parts only)
2 tablespoons all-purpose flour
1 cup heavy or whipping cream
¼ cup dry white wine
¼ teaspoon crushed dried rosemary
⅛ teaspoon ground dried thyme
Salt to taste
⅛ teaspoon cayenne pepper
3 medium artichokes
1 lemon, cut in half

1. Cut the cheese into cubes.

2. Heat the butter over medium-high heat in a heavy 10- to 11-inch deep-sided skillet. Add the leeks and sauté, stirring, until softened, 3 to 4 minutes. Add the flour, stir, and cook for 2 minutes. Add the cream and wine and stir until hot. Add the herbs. Then add the cheese cubes, a few at a time, making certain each addition has melted before adding the next. When all the cheese has been added and the sauce is smooth, taste and add salt, if needed, and the cayenne pepper. (The sauce can be made in advance to this point and then reheated in the top of a double boiler, when ready to serve.)

3. To cook the artichokes, heat water in a large 3- to 4-quart saucepan. While the water is heating, cut the stems from the artichokes. Then place each artichoke on its side and with a sharp knife cut off about an inch from the top. Use scissors to trim the tips (from which sharp points protrude) from the leaves. Place the prepared artichokes in the boiling water, cover with a lid slightly

AT THE MARKET

When buying artichokes, select those that have firm leaves, preferably without brown spots. The underside of the stem should appear to be freshly cut. Older artichokes have dried leaves which are starting to curl, and the cut end of the stem is often blackened.

ajar, and cook 30 to 40 minutes or until the artichoke bases are tender when pierced with a knife. Drain the artichokes.

4. Remove the leaves from the artichokes and place them on a large round or oval platter (preferably one that can be placed in a low oven), starting on the outside edge and arranging overlapping leaves in circles. Leave a small place in the center of the plate for the bowl of hot cheese sauce. Squeeze the lemon through a strainer over the artichoke leaves.

5. Remove the hairy chokes from the artichoke hearts, and trim the hearts with a knife so they have a smooth surface. Then slice the hearts into thin (¼-inch) slices. Place the heart slices in a circle just inside the last row of leaves. Squeeze some lemon juice over the hearts. (This dish may be prepared several hours in advance to this point, covered, and refrigerated.)

6. Ten minutes before serving time, place the plate with the leaves and hearts in a warm (200° F) oven to heat through.

7. Reheat the sauce and place it in a bowl in the center of the platter. Serve immediately. Eat by dipping the leaves into the hot sauce and eating the meaty bottom edge of the leaf.

Serves 6 to 8

THE RIGHT EQUIPMENT

A 1-cup porcelain or clear glass soufflé dish is a nice container to use when serving this at a fancy dinner party. For less formal occasions, an earthenware crock works well.

Mushroom Pâté

Of all the appetizers I have prepared over the years in my classes, this is the most popular with my students. Nothing could be easier to prepare or taste more delicious.

4 tablespoons (½ stick) unsalted butter, at room temperature
8 ounces mushrooms, cleaned and finely chopped
1½ teaspoons finely chopped garlic
¼ cup finely chopped scallions (green onions), white parts only
⅓ cup homemade chicken stock (see Index) or good-quality canned broth
4 ounces cream cheese, at room temperature
2 tablespoons finely minced fresh chives or green scallion tops
Salt and freshly ground pepper to taste
1 teaspoon chopped chives or green tops of scallions, for garnish
Toast points

1. Melt 2 tablespoons of the butter in a medium-size skillet over high heat. When it is hot, add the chopped mushrooms and sauté 2 to 3 minutes. Add the garlic and scallions and sauté 1 minute more. Add the chicken stock and cook over high heat until all liquid has evaporated, 4 to 5 minutes. Let the mushroom mixture cool to room temperature.

2. Combine the cream cheese and the remaining 2 tablespoons butter in a mixing bowl and stir to mix well. Add the mushroom mixture, minced chives, and salt and pepper. Mix well. Fill a 1-cup crockery bowl or an individual ramekin or soufflé dish with the mushroom mixture. Cover with plastic wrap and refrigerate until needed. (The pâté can be made a day in advance to this point.)

3. When ready to serve, sprinkle the pâté with chopped chives and garnish with toast points.

Serves 6

Pesto-Cheese Pâté with Parmesan Toasts

This is a dish I created after some good friends shared a bumper crop of basil with me one summer. The recipe makes two small pâtés but can be halved easily.

Special equipment: Clean unwaxed dental floss for slicing the cream cheese

Pâté
2 cups basil leaves (stems removed)
3 tablespoons pine nuts
3 medium cloves garlic
½ cup grated imported Parmesan cheese
Pinch of salt
2 tablespoons olive oil, plus more if needed
2 packages (8 ounces each) cream cheese, well chilled
12 paper-thin slices prosciutto
Basil sprigs, for garnish
Toasted pine nuts, for garnish (see Index)
Black olives, for garnish

Parmesan Toasts

18 slices best-quality white sandwich bread
1½ cups (3 sticks) unsalted butter
3 cups finely grated imported Parmesan cheese
1½ tablespoons coarsely ground black pepper

1. To make the pesto, place the basil, pine nuts, and garlic in a food processor or blender, or use a mortar and pestle, and purée. Add the cheese and salt and then gradually stir in the olive oil. Add only enough oil to make the pesto of spreading consistency. It should not be runny. Set aside.

2. Cut the two blocks of cream cheese horizontally into four slices. The best way to do this is to use a clean piece of dental floss and run it through each block of cream cheese three times (so that you get four thin slices from each block).

3. Lay one of the eight pieces of cream cheese flat on a work surface. Trim a slice of prosciutto to fit over the top of the cream cheese. Then spread 1½ tablespoons of the pesto over the prosciutto and top the pesto with another piece of trimmed ham. Place another piece of cream cheese on top and continue in this manner until you have a block composed of four pieces of cream cheese with filling between each layer. Make another cream cheese pâté with the remaining ingredients in the same manner. (The pâtés can be made a day in advance to this point, covered with plastic wrap, and refrigerated.)

4. Preheat the oven to 350° F.

5. Make the Parmesan Toasts: Stack six slices of bread together, and cut off the crusts. Cut the slices into four equal triangles. Roll each triangle flat with a rolling pin. Repeat with the remaining slices.

6. Melt the butter in a skillet. Mix the Parmesan cheese and black pepper together on a plate. Dip each triangle quickly into the melted butter, then dredge it in the Parmesan mixture and place it on a baking sheet.

7. Bake the triangles until golden and crisp, 5 to 7 minutes per side. Watch carefully, as they burn easily. After the toast points have baked 5 to 7 minutes per side, if they are brown but still not crisp, lower the temperature to 300° F and bake until firm, about 5 minutes more. Cool on paper towels and serve at room temperature. (The Parmesan Toasts can be baked early in the day on which they are to be served. They should be reheated for 5 to 10 minutes in a

300° F oven to make them crisp and then cooled slightly just before serving.)

8. To serve the pâtés, arrange each on a serving platter. Score the top of each pâté with a knife. Arrange a cluster of basil sprigs in one corner of the top of each pâté and put a few toasted pine nuts in the center of the leaves. Garnish the pâtés with black olives and serve with Parmesan Toasts.

Makes 2 pâtés, enough for 16 to 20 servings

Shrimp and Pistachio Pâté

This is a classic French-style recipe for a fish terrine and so takes some extra time to prepare. The results are well worth the effort, however. The flavor of the shrimp and pistachio nuts and the beautifully smooth texture of the pâté make it an irrestistible hors d'oeuvre or first course to begin a special dinner.

Special equipment: 8 x 4½-inch loaf pan; food processor

1 pound medium shrimp in the shell
4 tablespoons (½ stick) unsalted butter
⅓ cup chopped carrots
⅓ cup chopped onions
⅓ cup chopped celery
1 clove garlic, chopped
2 cups homemade chicken stock (see Index) or good-quality
    canned broth, plus more if needed
¾ cup dry white wine
½ teaspoon dried thyme
½ tablespoon fresh tarragon, or ½ teaspoon dried
2 tablespoons cognac
½ cup heavy or whipping cream
1½ tablespoons unflavored gelatin
¾ teaspoon salt
⅛ teaspoon cayenne pepper
1 to 3 teaspoons tomato paste (optional)
⅓ cup chopped unsalted pistachio nuts (skins removed)
2 tablespoons chopped fresh parsley
Several spinach leaves or watercress sprigs, for garnish
Toast points

A COOK'S REFLECTIONS

In order to flame a dish, the ingredients to which the liquor is being added should be warmed. If they aren't, then the liquor itself should be warmed. Use a long match and always stand back and avert your face when igniting a dish because sometimes the liquor produces very big flames.

GREAT ACCOMPANIMENTS

Used as a first course, this pâté could be followed by Sautéed Chicken Marinated in Lime and Honey, Carrot and Belgian Endive Sauté, and buttered new potatoes. The Apricot Sorbet completes the menu.

1. Shell and devein the shrimp. Set aside both the shells and the shrimp.

2. Melt 2 tablespoons of the butter in a medium-size skillet over medium heat. When it is hot, add the chopped vegetables and garlic and cook, stirring, until softened, about 4 minutes. Add the shrimp shells, stock, wine, thyme, and tarragon to the pan and simmer 30 minutes.

3. While the shells are cooking, melt the remaining 2 tablespoons butter in another medium-size skillet and, when it is hot, add the shrimp. Cook, stirring constantly, until the shrimp are pink and curled, 2 to 3 minutes. Add the cognac to the pan and flame. Cook, shaking the pan vigorously until the flame goes out. Remove the shrimp and pour all the juice from this pan into the pan with the shells and vegetables. Remove a single shrimp for the garnish. Purée the rest of the shrimp in a food processor. Add the heavy cream and process again. Leave the purée in the processor.

4. Remove the vegetable mixture from the heat. Strain it through a sieve, pressing down hard on the shells and vegetables with the back of a spoon to extract as much liquid as possible. You should have at least 1½ cups of stock. If you are short, add extra chicken stock to make this amount. Add the gelatin to the stock mixture and stir to dissolve well.

5. Add the stock to the shrimp in the processor and process until the mixture is smooth. Add the salt and cayenne pepper. If the purée looks pale, you can stir in 1 to 3 teaspoons of tomato paste to enhance the color.

6. Oil an 8 x 4½-inch loaf pan and line it with a sheet of waxed paper that extends several inches over the long sides of the pan. Line with another sheet of waxed paper that extends several inches over the short sides of the pan. Fill the pan with 1½ cups of the shrimp purée. Then chill the pan in the refrigerator until the mixture is slightly firmer, 20 to 30 minutes. (Leave the remaining shrimp purée at room temperature.)

7. Set aside 1 tablespoon chopped pistachios for the garnish. Toss the remaining nuts with the chopped parsley in a bowl. Remove the pâté from the refrigerator. Make a layer of the pistachio and parsley mixture over the chilled pâté. Pour the remaining shrimp purée into the pan. Refrigerate 6 hours or overnight, until very firm.

8. To serve the pâté, run a sharp knife between the paper and the sides of the pan. Unmold the pâté onto a serving platter and gently peel away the paper. Garnish the pâté with spinach leaves or watercress. Sprinkle the reserved chopped pistachios on the top, and butterfly the reserved shrimp and place it in the center. Keep the pâté refrigerated until needed. Serve with toast points.

Serves 12

Shrimp and Chèvre Canapés

These sophisticated appetizers look as if they take far more time to prepare than the few minutes actually required. Made by layering toasted crouton rounds with chèvre and marinated shrimp, they need only to be placed under the broiler to melt the cheese before serving.

Special equipment: 2-inch cookie cutter; clean unwaxed dental floss

12 slices good-quality white sandwich bread
2 tablespoons balsamic vinegar
½ teaspoon salt
6 tablespoons olive oil
12 large shelled, deveined, and cooked shrimp, halved lengthwise
8 ounces chèvre (in a long cylindrical shape, such as Montrachet without ash)
1½ tablespoons chopped fresh basil or flat-leaf parsley
Several sprigs of fresh basil or flat-leaf parsley, for garnish

1. Preheat the oven to 350° F.

2. Cut two rounds from each piece of bread with a 2-inch cookie cutter. (Use the scraps to make bread crumbs or save for another use.) Place the rounds on a baking sheet and bake, turning once, until light golden and crisp on both sides, about 15 minutes. Remove and reserve. (These croutons can be made several days in advance and stored in an airtight container.)

3. Combine the vinegar and salt in a mixing bowl and whisk in the olive oil. Place the shrimp halves in the vinaigrette and marinate 10 to 15 minutes. Then remove the shrimp and discard the sauce.

4. Cut the cheese into 24 thin rounds. The easiest way to get perfect slices is to use a piece of clean dental floss to cut through the cheese.

5. When ready to serve, preheat the broiler.

6. Place a slice of cheese on top of each crouton and put a marinated shrimp half on top of the cheese. Arrange on a baking sheet and place 5 to 6 inches below the broiler heat. Watch carefully. Broil only about 2 minutes, or until the cheese starts to soften and melt. Remove, and sprinkle each canapé with chopped basil.

7. To serve, place a bunch of fresh basil sprigs in a cluster in the center of a platter and arrange the canapés around the basil.

Makes 24 canapés, enough for 6

Baked Chèvre with Tomatoes and Garlic Toasts

Two close friends, who like good food as much as I do, took me to eat at a wonderful tapas bar, the Café Ba-Ba-Reeba, in Chicago several years ago. Everything we sampled that evening was superb, but the baked chèvre with tomatoes and garlic toasts was the unanimous favorite. Here is my version of this special dish.

3 tablespoons olive oil
1 cup chopped onions
4 cups peeled, seeded, chopped tomatoes, well drained (about 2½ pounds tomatoes)
1½ teaspoons finely chopped garlic
1 teaspoon salt
Freshly ground pepper to taste
¼ cup homemade chicken stock (see Index) or good-quality canned broth
8 ounces chèvre, at room temperature
1 tablespoon chopped fresh parsley or chives
Garlic Toasts (recipe follows)
¼ cup Spanish or Niçoise olives

1. Heat the oil in a heavy 10- to 11-inch skillet over medium heat. When it is hot, add the onions and sauté, stirring, 2 to 3 minutes.

2. Add the tomatoes and garlic and cook another 2 to 3 minutes.

3. Add the salt, pepper, and stock and simmer, uncovered, until all

GREAT ACCOMPANIMENTS

*I was so delighted when I duplicated
this delicious appetizer in my own
kitchen that I immediately planned
a whole dinner party around it. I
served Grilled Mustard-Glazed Cornish Hens and Asparagus, Carrots,
and Snow Peas with Prosciutto
as the main course, and Pink
Grapefruit Sorbet with Campari for
dessert.*

the liquid has evaporated and the tomatoes are tender but not mushy,
20 to 25 minutes or longer. Stir the mixture often. (The tomatoes
may be cooked a day in advance, covered, refrigerated, and reheated
before using.)

4. Preheat the oven to 400° F.

5. Mold the softened chèvre into a smooth round, 4 to 5 inches in
diameter and 1 to 1½ inches thick. Place the cheese in the middle of
a medium-size round or oval ovenproof dish. Spoon the warm
tomatoes in a border around the cheese.

6. Place the dish on the center shelf of the oven and bake until the
cheese just starts to melt but still holds its shape, 12 to 15 minutes.
Watch it carefully.

7. Place the baking dish on a serving platter or wicker tray. Sprinkle
the cheese with the fresh herb. Surround the dish with Garlic Toasts
and garnish with black olives.

Serves 8 to 10

GARLIC TOASTS

*1 loaf (20 to 24 inches) crusty French bread
½ cup olive oil
¾ cup (1½ sticks) unsalted butter, at room temperature
4 teaspoons very finely minced garlic
2 tablespoons chopped fresh parsley*

1. Preheat the oven to 300° F.

2. Split the bread lengthwise. Cut each half into 10 pieces and place
them on a baking sheet. Brush each piece generously on all sides
with olive oil.

3. Place the butter in a mixing bowl and add the garlic and parsley.
Mix well. Spread the top of each piece of bread with butter. Place
the buttered bread in the oven and bake until golden, about 20
minutes. (Toasts may be prepared several hours ahead and then
baked just before needed, or they may be assembled and baked
ahead, then reheated 3 to 4 minutes in a 300° F oven just before
serving.)

Cherry Tomatoes with Avocado Mousse

Since I can get good cherry tomatoes and ripe avocados almost all the time in central Ohio, this is an appetizer I offer year-round. However, I particularly like to serve these stuffed tomatoes in the summer when I am making a southwestern-style barbecue supper.

2 pints cherry tomatoes, cleaned and stems removed
3 ripe avocados
2 packages (3 ounces each) cream cheese, at room temperature
1 tablespoon plus 1 teaspoon very finely minced sweet red onion
1 clove garlic, very finely minced
2 teaspoons fresh lemon juice
¾ teaspoon chili powder
1 teaspoon salt, or to taste
¼ cup peeled, seeded, chopped tomato
½ cup sour cream
¼ cup slivered pitted black olives
1 head Boston lettuce, leaves separated and rinsed

1. Slice the tops off the cherry tomatoes. Using a small spoon (a grapefruit spoon works well), scoop out and discard the insides. Drain the tomatoes upside down on a kitchen towel.

2. To prepare the avocado mousse, remove the skin and pits from the avocados. Place the avocados and the cream cheese in the bowl of a food processor or blender. Add the red onion, garlic, lemon juice, chili powder, salt, and chopped tomato. Process just until you have a smooth, firm purée. Taste the mixture, and if desired, add more salt.

3. Turn the tomatoes upright and fill each with avocado mousse, mounding it slightly. (If you place the mousse in a pastry bag fitted with a medium star tip, it will be easy to pipe it into the tomatoes.)

4. Place the sour cream in another pastry bag and pipe a frill of sour cream on top of each filled tomato. Or spoon a dab of sour cream on each tomato by hand. Garnish each tomato with a sliver of olive.

5. To serve, arrange the tomatoes in diagonal rows on a serving tray, with several leaves of Boston lettuce at either end.

Serves 10 to 12

AS A VARIATION

Sometimes I buy six large tomatoes, peel them, take a slice off the top, hollow out the insides, and fill them with this mousse. I put the top slices back, slightly ajar, over the stuffed tomatoes and place them on a bed of lettuce greens. Napped with a little vinaigrette, this makes a wonderful first course or luncheon main course.

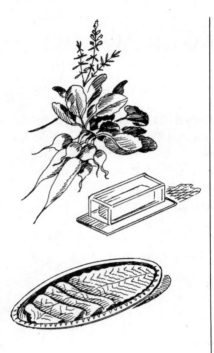

Smoked Salmon Butter

Because this dish takes only a few minutes to assemble, it has become a standard in the repertoire of many of my busy students. I have used it as an appetizer before countless dinner parties.

Special equipment: Food processor

6 ounces best-quality smoked salmon, such as Petrossian
¾ cup (1½ sticks) unsalted butter, at room temperature
1 teaspoon dried thyme (leaf, not powdered)
Salt to taste
¼ pound snow peas
6 scallions (green onions)
8 small red radishes, with leaves rinsed and roots cut off
8 white radishes, cleaned
Pumpernickel or rye bread

1. Combine the salmon and butter in the bowl of a food processor. Process until the mixture is a smooth purée, 30 to 40 seconds. Add the thyme and process just 5 to 10 seconds more. Taste the mixture and add salt if you want (the salmon is usually very salty). Place the salmon mixture in an attractive serving bowl such as a small soufflé dish, and smooth the top with a knife or spatula. Cover with plastic wrap and refrigerate. (The salmon butter can be made two to three days ahead to this point.)

2. String the snow peas and trim off the ends on the diagonal. Cook them in boiling water to cover for 2 minutes, then drain and rinse under cold running water. Pat dry. Wrap the snow peas in a clean kitchen towel and then in plastic wrap. (These can be prepared a day in advance.)

3. Rinse the scallions and cut off the roots. Leave about 2 inches of the green stems, trimming off the excess on the diagonal.

4. To serve, place the bowl of salmon butter in the center of a serving tray. Sprinkle a little extra thyme over the salmon. Arrange the snow peas, radishes, and scallions in a decorative pattern around the bowl. Serve with a basket of sliced pumpernickel or rye bread.

Serves 10 to 12

AT THE MARKET

You should buy the best-quality smoked salmon available for this recipe. I like Petrossian, which is now sold in many specialty markets around the country.

The white radishes I like to use as a garnish for this dish are called icicle radishes. Pale ivory in color and about 2½ to 3 inches long, they are usually available in supermarkets that have large produce areas. Clean the radishes under cold water, then dry them. Trim off the roots before using. If you have difficulty finding icicle radishes, they can be omitted from the recipe.

Smoked Salmon and Roquefort Croutons

Smoked salmon and bleu cheese are two foods I adore. In this dish they are paired in a surprisingly delicious union. The croutons can be completely assembled in advance and then broiled a few minutes before serving.

4 tablespoons (½ stick) unsalted butter, plus more if needed
4 tablespoons vegetable oil, plus more if needed
14 slices good French bread, about 2½ to 3 inches in diameter
*   and ⅓ inch thick*
4 ounces very thinly sliced best-quality smoked salmon, such as
*   Petrossian*
Freshly ground pepper to taste
4 ounces Roquefort cheese, at room temperature
Lemon leaves, for garnish

1. Place 2 tablespoons each of butter and oil in a heavy 10- to 11-inch skillet over medium-high heat. When the butter and oil are quite hot but not smoking, add enough bread slices to make a single layer. Sauté the bread slices, turning once or twice, until golden on both sides, 3 to 4 minutes total for both sides. Remove and drain on paper towels. As butter and oil are used up, add more of each in equal amounts until all the croutons have been sautéed.

2. Cut the salmon slices into small pieces about 2½ inches square, and place them on top of the sautéed bread slices. Grind pepper generously over the salmon. Then crumble the cheese and sprinkle it generously over the salmon. Arrange the croutons on a baking sheet. (Croutons can be assembled to this point up to an hour before baking.)

3. When ready to serve, preheat the broiler. Arrange a rack 3 to 4 inches from the heat source.

4. Broil the croutons, watching constantly, until the cheese has melted and a crust has started to form, about 2 to 3 minutes. Serve the croutons immediately, arranged on a plate decorated with lemon leaves.

Serves 4 to 6

AS A VARIATION

If Cheshire cheese is not available, you can substitute other varieties. Monterey Jack, Havarti, or even an American Cheddar could be used.

Cheshire Cheese and Watercress Crisps

I make these cheese rolls days in advance and store them in the freezer. A single recipe yields more than three dozen crisps, so they are especially good for large parties.

⅓ cup packed watercress leaves (no stems)
8 tablespoons (1 stick) unsalted butter, at room temperature
6 ounces English Cheshire cheese, grated
1 cup all-purpose flour
⅛ teaspoon cayenne pepper
⅛ teaspoon salt
Watercress sprigs, for garnish

1. Chop the watercress leaves very fine and set aside.

2. Place the butter and cheese in a bowl and blend with an electric mixer until smooth. With the mixer on slow speed, gradually blend in the flour. Then add the cayenne pepper, salt, and chopped watercress and mix until incorporated.

3. Remove the dough, which will be soft, from the bowl and shape it into a log approximately 2 inches in diameter and 8 inches long. Wrap the log in plastic wrap and put it in the freezer to firm, 1 hour. Then transfer it to the refrigerator. (If you wish to make the dough one to two days ahead, roll it into a log, cover with plastic wrap, and refrigerate. You will not need to freeze it. However, the dough can also be frozen for a week or more; bring it to refrigerator temperature a day before using.)

4. When ready to bake the crisps, preheat the oven to 400 ° F.

5. Remove the log from the refrigerator, unwrap, and cut it into thin slices, ⅛ to ¼ inch thick. Place them an inch apart on a baking sheet, and bake until lightly golden, about 10 minutes. Watch carefully. Remove the crisps with a spatula and let cool 2 to 3 minutes.

6. Serve the crisps in a napkin-lined basket with sprigs of watercress in the center. Eat the crisps with a little fresh cress.

Makes 36 to 42 crisps

AS A VARIATION

In addition to serving the cashews as an appetizer, I package them in decorative glass jars or tins and offer them as gifts to good friends.

Cajun Cashews

Having gone to college in New Orleans, I have been a longtime fan of Louisiana's spicy cuisine. These Cajun Cashews are my contribution to the Creole repertoire.

Special equipment: Jelly roll pan

1 tablespoon unsalted butter
2 teaspoons white vinegar or red wine vinegar
2 teaspoons Tabasco sauce
1 teaspoon cayenne pepper
½ teaspoon garlic salt
½ teaspoon salt
2 cups unsalted raw cashews

1. Preheat the oven to 350° F.

2. Line a jelly roll pan with a sheet of aluminum foil and set aside.

3. Place the butter, vinegar, Tabasco sauce, cayenne pepper, garlic salt, and salt in a medium-size heavy saucepan over medium heat and stir until the butter has melted and the seasonings are well incorporated. Add the cashews and toss until they are well coated with the mixture.

4. Pour the nuts onto the prepared baking pan and spread so they are in a single layer. Bake the nuts until dark golden brown, 10 to 15 minutes. Check the nuts after 10 minutes to make certain they are not browning too quickly. When the nuts are done, remove them from the oven and cool 5 minutes. Scrape the nuts and any dried seasonings on the bottom of the pan into a mixing bowl. Toss well.

5. Serve the nuts warm or at room temperature. (Nuts may be made several days in advance and stored in glass jars or other airtight containers.)

Makes 2 cups

A COOK'S REFLECTIONS

Phyllo Dough. Phyllo dough is the one dough I never make from scratch. You almost have to be raised with cooks who know the specialized technique of preparing and stretching this dough to learn the art. Luckily there are many good commercial brands of phyllo available and I encourage my students to use them. When buying prepared phyllo look to see if the dough is labeled "thin" or "thick." I find that the thick variety is easier to use, especially for cooks working with phyllo for the first time.

Spicy Phyllo Packages

Pam Park Curry, who teaches many of our classes on American cuisine of the Southwest, invented these addictive baked phyllo bundles filled with chiles and cheese and served with fresh salsa. Students love these appetizers and tell us repeatedly how much their guests have enjoyed them.

Special equipment: Jelly roll pan

2 tablespoons olive oil
1 cup chopped onions
1 tablespoon finely chopped garlic
2 cans (4 ounces each) mild green chiles, drained and chopped
½ teaspoon salt
⅛ teaspoon cayenne pepper
¾ teaspoon ground cumin
2 large eggs, lightly beaten
8 ounces Monterey Jack cheese, grated
2 tablespoons all-purpose flour
1 box thin phyllo sheets (approximately 18 x 14 inches each)
1 cup (2 sticks) unsalted butter, melted
2 tablespoons chili powder
Salsa Fresca (recipe follows)

1. Heat the olive oil in a medium-size heavy skillet over medium heat. When it is hot, add the onions and cook slowly, stirring, about 8 minutes. Do not let the onions brown. Add the garlic and cook 2 to 3 minutes more. Then add the green chiles, salt, cayenne pepper, and cumin and stir well. Cook the mixture until all liquid has evaporated, 4 to 5 minutes. Remove the pan from the heat and let the mixture cool to room temperature.

2. Add the eggs to the cooled onions and peppers. Then toss the cheese and flour together and add this to the mixture.

3. Unwrap the package of phyllo leaves but keep them covered with a slightly moistened kitchen towel. You will need approximately eight sheets of dough for this recipe. (Any unused dough should be tightly rewrapped and refrozen.)

4. Place a single sheet of phyllo dough on a work surface so that the long end is in front of you. Cut the dough in half so that you have two rectangles, 14 x 9 inches each.

5. Brush the rectangles with melted butter, then sprinkle them lightly with chili powder. Fold each of the rectangles in half so that you have two small rectangles, 14 x 4½ inches each. Place them so the shorter ends are in front of you.

6. Spread 2 tablespoons of the filling on each of the shorter ends in front of you. Fold in ½ inch along each long side, and roll into neat packages. Place seam side down on a jelly roll pan and brush with butter. Continue using sheets of phyllo in this way until all the filling is used. (The packages may be made one day in advance to this point. Cover with a slightly moistened clean kitchen towel and then cover with plastic wrap and refrigerate.)

7. When ready to bake, preheat the oven to 375° F.

8. Remove the packages from the refrigerator and bake until golden brown, 15 to 20 minutes. Serve on a platter accompanied by Salsa Fresca.

Makes 15 to 16 packages

AS A VARIATION

The fresh salsa can also be used as a dipping sauce for tortilla chips or as a sauce for grilled chicken or fish.

A COOK'S REFLECTIONS

A Hot Pepper Warning. The tissues around your eyes, nose, mouth, and ears are sensitive to the oils and fumes of hot peppers. If, by mistake, you rub any of these parts with pepper-coated fingers, you will feel a burning sensation. I always wear rubber gloves when working with hot peppers and remove them as soon as I have finished. Be sure to wash your rubber gloves to remove any remaining oils.

SALSA FRESCA

3 ripe medium tomatoes
2 jalapeño peppers, each about 2½ inches long
1 teaspoon finely chopped garlic
½ cup finely chopped onion
1 tablespoon chopped cilantro (fresh coriander leaves)
¼ teaspoon sugar
½ cup tomato juice
Salt to taste

1. Remove the stems, but don't peel the tomatoes. Cut them into ¼-inch dice.

2. Wearing rubber gloves (to keep from getting burned by the peppers), clean the peppers under cold water. Cut off the tops, slice them in half lengthwise, and scrape out the seeds. Chop finely.

3. Combine the tomatoes, chopped peppers, garlic, onion, cilantro, sugar, and tomato juice in a mixing bowl and mix well. Taste and add salt as desired. (Sauce may be made several hours in advance. Refrigerate, covered, but bring to room temperature before serving.)

Makes about 1½ cups

AT THE MARKET

Five-spice powder, hoisin sauce, and hot bean paste or sauce, are all available at Oriental markets and at some groceries.

Chinese Roast Pork Tenderloins with Dipping Sauce

My colleague Tom Johnson, a talented restaurant chef in Columbus, Ohio, created this delicious dish. The roast pork can be completely prepared and arranged on a serving platter in advance. It makes a marvelous addition to a buffet table at cocktail parties.

Pork
4 medium cloves garlic, crushed
1 piece fresh ginger (2 inches), peeled and grated
6 scallions (green onions), including 2 inches of green stems,
    chopped
1 tablespoon hot bean paste or hot bean sauce
¼ cup hoisin sauce
½ cup dry sherry
½ cup soy sauce
½ teaspoon salt
½ teaspoon five-spice powder
¼ cup honey
3 pork tenderloins (about 12 ounces each), all excess fat removed

Sauce and Garnish
Reserved marinade
1 tablespoon dry mustard
1 tablespoon soy sauce
1 cup toasted sesame seeds (see Index)
5 scallions (green onions)
1 orange, sliced

1. For the tenderloins, mix all ingredients except the pork in a shallow bowl or pan (not an aluminum one). Add the pork to the marinade, cover with plastic wrap, and marinate in the refrigerator at least 2 hours, turning frequently.

2. Preheat the oven to 350° F.

3. Remove the meat from the marinade. Strain and reserve the marinade. Place the tenderloins so that they are not touching on a rack in a roasting pan. (You may need more than one rack and pan to fit the roasts.)

4. Fill the pan with about 1 inch of water, making sure the water

A COOK'S REFLECTIONS

Five-spice powder is an interesting combination of star anise, fennel, cinnamon bark, cloves, and Szechuan peppercorns, all ground into a fine powder. It's extremely aromatic and flavorful and should be used sparingly.

AS A VARIATION

If available, kumquats with stems and leaves make a more unusual garnish than the orange slices.

does not touch the meat. Roast for 35 minutes. Increase the heat to 450° F and roast until the pork has an internal temperature of 170° F, 15 minutes more.

5. Remove the meat from the oven and let it cool completely. Refrigerate covered several hours or overnight.

6. For the sauce, measure 1 cup of the reserved marinade and strain. (Discard any extra marinade.) Place the dry mustard in a small bowl and whisk in the marinade. Add the soy sauce. Place the sauce mixture and the sesame seeds in separate serving bowls and reserve.

7. Cut the cooled pork tenderloins on a diagonal into ¼-inch slices and reserve.

8. For the garnish, make scallion "flowers": Cut off the root ends and all but 3 inches of the green stems of the scallions. With a sharp knife make 4 to 5 lengthwise slits along the white portion. Place the scallions in a bowl of ice water for 5 minutes, or until the white portion curls. Remove and drain.

9. Place the bowls of dipping sauce and sesame seeds on a platter. Arrange overlapping slices of pork on the platter and garnish with halved orange slices and the scallion flowers. To eat, dip a slice of pork into the dipping sauce and then into the sesame seeds.

Serves 12

SOUPS

According to my good friend Bernard Clayton, one of our country's best-known bread bakers and cookbook authors, "soups light the inner fires." And, I agree. Throughout the year I make soups at my house—sometimes fancy concoctions fashioned with imported cheeses, smoked fish, or exotic vegetables and on other occasions last-minute creations from simple leftovers. Whether it is a chunky, robust chowder or a silken, smooth potage, my family loves homemade soup. The dishes I create at home always wind up in my annual soup class at the school. These selections are among the favorites I have taught over the past few years.

HEARTY SOUPS

Corn and Gruyère Chowder

I created this soup after a generous friend brought me a bountiful harvest of late season corn.

6 thick strips bacon (4 to 5 ounces)
1½ cups chopped onions
4 cups fresh corn kernels (about 8 ears)
3½ cups homemade chicken stock (see Index) or good-quality
*   canned broth*
1 teaspoon salt
1 cup grated Gruyère cheese
1 cup heavy or whipping cream
Generous dash of cayenne pepper
Generous grating of fresh nutmeg
2 tablespoons chopped fresh chives

1. In a large heavy pot, cook the bacon over medium heat until it is crisp. Remove and drain on paper towels. Cool, then crumble the bacon and set aside. (If you are not serving the soup right away, wrap it in plastic wrap, and refrigerate. Spread the bacon on a baking sheet and reheat until crisp in a 300° F oven before using.)

2. Add the onions to the pot and cook, stirring often, for 3 minutes. Add the corn and cook, stirring often, for another 3 minutes. Add the chicken stock and salt and simmer, uncovered, 25 minutes.

3. Remove the soup from the heat and purée it well in a food processor, blender, or food mill. Return the soup to the pot, and over low heat, add the grated cheese, a small amount at a time, making certain each addition has melted before adding the next. Then gradually pour in the cream, stirring well.

4. Taste the soup and season with more salt if necessary. Then add the cayenne pepper and nutmeg to taste. (The soup can be prepared a day in advance. Cool, cover, and refrigerate.)

5. To serve, ladle the soup into bowls and garnish each serving with some crumbled bacon and chopped chives.

Serves 6

AS A VARIATION

I like to make this dish with fresh corn, but many of my students wanted to prepare it year-round and found they could substitute frozen corn with great success.

AS A VARIATION

In the summer, I make cold Scallop Vichyssoise from this recipe. After the chowder has been cooked, I chill it, then purée it, and finally stir in 4½ cups heavy or whipping cream. I serve the vichyssoise, garnished with chopped chives, in chilled bowls.

Scallop Chowder

When I discovered I was allergic to clams, it was the end of my days of enjoying clam chowder. As a substitute, I tried making that traditional New England soup with scallops instead—and loved the result.

Court Bouillon
1 carrot, peeled and sliced
1 small rib celery, coarsely chopped
4 sprigs parsley
1 bay leaf
10 black peppercorns
½ cup dry white wine
3 cups water

Chowder
1 slab (6 ounces) smoked bacon, partially frozen for easier cutting
1½ cups chopped leeks, white part only
3 tablespoons all-purpose flour
3½ cups milk, scalded
1 pound all-purpose potatoes, cut into ½-inch dice
1¼ pounds bay or sea scallops, cut into ½-inch-thick pieces
⅛ teaspoon cayenne pepper
¼ teaspoon freshly ground white pepper
½ teaspoon salt
1 cup heavy or whipping cream, plus more if needed
2 tablespoons chopped fresh parsley, for garnish

1. To make the court bouillon, combine all the ingredients in a large non-aluminum stockpot or saucepan. Bring the mixture to a simmer over medium heat. Simmer 30 minutes. Strain the stock and reserve. (You can make stock ahead and freeze it, or you can refrigerate it, covered, for 2 to 3 days.)

2. To prepare the chowder, cut the rind from the bacon and discard it. Cut the bacon into ¼-inch dice. Put the bacon in a large deep pot. Sauté until browned, about 3 to 4 minutes. Add the chopped leeks and sauté, stirring, 4 to 5 minutes. Add the flour and cook 2 minutes more. Then add the milk and potatoes and stir well. Bring to a simmer and cook until the potatoes are tender but not mushy, 15 to 20 minutes. Set aside.

3. Bring the reserved court bouillon to a simmer and add a handful of scallops. Poach the scallops just until opaque, 1 to 2 minutes. Remove the scallops with a slotted spoon, set aside, and continue the process until all the scallops have been poached. Then reduce the poaching liquid over high heat to 1½ cups. Add the reduced liquid to the leek, bacon, and potato mixture. (The soup and the poached scallops can be prepared a day in advance to this point. Cover each and refrigerate until needed.)

4. When you are ready to serve, heat the soup and add the cayenne pepper, white pepper, and salt. When the mixture is warm, whisk in the cream and continue cooking until the soup is hot. Add the poached scallops and cook only until they are heated through. Taste, and add more seasonings if necessary.

5. Serve in soup bowls garnished with chopped parsley.

Serves 8

Tomato and Corn Bisque

I created this soup several years ago to serve at a tailgate party. An easy dish to transport, it has a hearty flavor and tastes wonderful whether served indoors or outside on a crisp fall day.

5 tablespoons unsalted butter
1 cup chopped onions
1 teaspoon chopped garlic
¼ cup chopped green bell pepper
1½ cups fresh corn kernels (about 3 ears)
4 large tomatoes, stemmed and quartered
4 cups homemade chicken stock (see Index) or good-quality
*   canned broth*
1 tablespoon tomato paste
1 teaspoon chili powder
¾ teaspoon salt, or more to taste
1½ cups grated Monterey Jack cheese (about ⅓ pound)
1 cup sour cream
12 slices bacon, fried crisp and crumbled

1. In a large heavy pot, melt the butter. Add the onions, garlic, and green pepper and cook until just softened, 3 to 4 minutes. Add the corn and the tomatoes and cook, stirring, 3 minutes more.

GREAT ACCOMPANIMENTS

When I serve this soup as a main course, I usually offer a seasonal green salad garnished with black olives and sliced avocado, and a bowl of fresh tortilla chips.

2. Add the chicken stock, and stir in the tomato paste. Add the chili powder and salt. Stir to incorporate these ingredients into the soup. Bring the soup to a boil and cook at a simmer until all the vegetables are completely tender, 20 to 25 minutes.

3. Purée the soup in a food processor, blender, or food mill. (The soup can be prepared a day in advance to this point. Cool, cover, and refrigerate. Before proceeding, reheat, then continue with the recipe.)

4. Return the soup to the pot, and over low heat gradually add the cheese, about ¼ cup at a time. Make certain each addition has melted before adding the next. Check seasonings and add more salt if necessary.

5. Serve the soup in individual soup bowls and garnish each serving with a large dollop of sour cream and a generous sprinkling of bacon.

Serves 8

Best-Ever White Bean Chowder

I like to serve hot bean soup as a main course during cold winter weather. Of all the bean soups I have tried, this remains my favorite—the one I make over and over again for my family. Serve it with hot Southern Cornbread.

1½ cups white beans (Navy, Michigan, or Great Northern)
6 cups water
6 tablespoons (¾ stick) unsalted butter
1 teaspoon finely chopped garlic
¼ cup chopped onion
¼ cup chopped carrots
1 ham hock or ham bone
1 bouquet garni: ¼ teaspoon dried savory, ¼ teaspoon dried rosemary, 3 sprigs parsley, 1 bay leaf, all wrapped in cheesecloth and tied with string
5 cups homemade chicken stock (see Index) or good-quality canned broth
½ to ¾ cup heavy or whipping cream
Salt and freshly ground pepper to taste
3 tablespoons chopped fresh parsley, for garnish

A COOK'S REFLECTIONS

The word "chowder" is derived from the French *chaudière*, which means a large cooking cauldron. In today's vocabulary chowder has come to mean a hearty soup substantial enough to serve as a main dish.

1. Place the beans in a large pot and cover with the water. Bring the water to a boil and boil 2 minutes. Remove the pot from the heat, cover, and let the beans soak for 1 hour. Drain the beans well.

2. In a large heavy saucepan or pot, melt the butter. Add the garlic, onion, and carrots and sauté several minutes until softened. Add the drained beans, the ham hock, bouquet garni, and chicken stock. Bring the mixture to a simmer and cook, never letting the soup rise above a simmer, until the beans are tender, about 1 hour.

3. When the beans are tender, remove and discard the bouquet garni and ham hock. Spoon half the solids (beans, vegetables, etc.) into a blender, processor, or food mill and purée. Stir the puréed mixture back into the soup.

4. Slowly stir the cream into the soup and taste for seasoning. Add salt and pepper if needed. (The soup can be made a day in advance, covered, and refrigerated. Reheat when needed.) Serve in individual soup bowls and garnish with chopped parsley.

Serves 8

Pinto Bean Soup

This soup, created by my colleague Kathy Lane, is cooked for several hours on the stove and fills the kitchen with tempting aromas. It is a robust soup that guests always enjoy.

¾ pound dried pinto beans
½ pound sliced bacon, cut into ½-inch pieces
2 carrots, peeled and diced
1 medium-large sweet red onion, diced
2 tablespoons finely chopped garlic
5½ cups homemade chicken stock (see Index) or good-quality
   canned broth
1 teaspoon salt, or to taste
1 cup dark beer
1 cup sour cream
¼ pound sliced bacon, fried crisp and crumbled, for garnish
¼ cup chopped scallions (green onions), including part of the
   green stems, for garnish
¼ cup chopped fresh parsley, for garnish

GREAT ACCOMPANIMENTS

The Chili Cheese Corn Muffins are nice with this soup.

AT THE MARKET

A good dark Mexican beer such as Dos Equis is the best to use in this recipe.

A COOK'S REFLECTIONS

When I first started cooking I often avoided recipes that called for soaking dried beans; I was too busy to remember to start soaking the beans the night before I needed them. Now I'm still busy, but I've learned a quicker method: I place dried beans in a deep pot, cover them with water, bring them to a boil, and then remove them from the heat to soak, covered, 1 to 2 hours. This faster method is much more appealing to my students, whose schedules are often just as hectic as mine.

1. Place the beans in a large pot and cover with 3 inches of water. Bring the water to a boil and cook the beans 3 minutes. Turn off the heat and cover the pot. Let the beans stand for 2 hours. Drain the beans and discard the water.

2. In a 4- to 5-quart heavy pot, sauté the bacon pieces until almost crisp. Drain on paper towels. Pour off and discard all but 3 tablespoons of bacon fat in the pan. Reheat the fat, and when it is hot, add the carrots, onion, and garlic. Cook, stirring, until the vegetables have softened, 5 minutes. Add the reserved beans and bacon, the stock, salt, and beer to the pot. Bring the mixture to a simmer, then cover and simmer until the beans are tender, 2 hours.

3. With a slotted spoon, remove 3 cups of solids (beans, vegetables, and bacon) from the pot and purée in a food processor, blender, or food mill. Return the purée to the pot and stir well to thicken. Taste the soup and add more salt if needed. (The soup can be prepared a day in advance to this point. Cool, cover, and refrigerate. Before proceeding, reheat, then continue with the recipe.)

4. To serve the soup, ladle it into eight individual soup bowls. Garnish each serving with a generous dollop of sour cream, then sprinkle crumbled bacon over the sour cream. Finally, combine the scallions and parsley and sprinkle over the soup.

Serves 8

Winter Sausage and Leek Soup

This is a soup with a big robust taste that I like to make on cold days. It takes only a half hour to assemble and can be prepared a day in advance and reheated.

½ pound kielbasa or other good-quality cooked sausage
4 tablespoons (½ stick) unsalted butter
3 cups chopped leeks (5 or 6 small leeks), white parts only
1 teaspoon dried dill
3½ cups homemade chicken stock (see Index) or good-quality
  canned broth
1 cup heavy or whipping cream
½ cup grated imported Parmesan cheese
Salt to taste
Whole Wheat Toast Points (recipe follows)

GREAT ACCOMPANIMENTS

A salad of seasonal greens, julienned red bell pepper, thin wedges of Granny Smith apples, and walnuts, tossed with a mustard vinaigrette, is a colorful and appropriate side dish to serve with this soup. Fresh orange slices brushed with honey, then broiled, and served with scoops of vanilla custard ice cream make a simple dessert.

1. Cut 6 thin slices from the kielbasa sausage (for the garnish) and then cut the rest of the kielbasa into ½-inch dice.

2. Melt the butter in a heavy 3- to 4-quart saucepan or deep casserole and add the diced kielbasa and the slices. Cook over moderate heat, stirring, 4 to 5 minutes. Remove the 6 slices and reserve. Add the chopped leeks and sauté with the diced kielbasa, stirring, about 5 minutes. Sprinkle the dill over the mixture and toss well. Add the stock and bring the soup to a simmer. Simmer until the leeks are very tender and the soup has a good flavor, 25 to 30 minutes.

3. Remove the soup from the heat and purée in a food processor, blender, or food mill. Return the soup to the pan and place it over low heat. Stir in the cream. Add the cheese, about 2 tablespoons at a time, stirring well until each addition has melted before adding the next. (The soup can be prepared a day in advance to this point. Cool, cover, and refrigerate.)

4. To serve, reheat the soup and ladle it into individual bowls or into a soup tureen. Garnish with the reserved kielbasa slices and pass a bowl of Toast Points.

Serves 6

WHOLE WHEAT TOAST POINTS

6 slices good-quality whole wheat bread
6 tablespoons (¾ stick) unsalted butter, plus more if needed

1. Remove the crust from the bread slices, and cut each slice into four equal triangles.

2. Heat the butter in a medium-size heavy skillet over medium-high heat. When it is hot, add a few bread slices and cook until golden on both sides. Remove and drain on paper towels. Repeat with the remaining bread. (It may be necessary to use more butter, because the bread absorbs hot butter very rapidly.)

Tomato Soup Gratinée

For onion soup lovers here is another broth topped with toasted bread and melted cheeses. The crust covers a savory mixture of tomatoes, onion, and chicken.

THE RIGHT EQUIPMENT

One-cup (or larger) ovenproof earthenware bowls or individual soufflé dishes are perfect for this recipe.

GREAT ACCOMPANIMENTS

For a luncheon or light supper, Green Bean, Walnut, and Red Onion Salad is a nice side dish with this soup, and Chestnut Brownies make an excellent dessert.

4 cups homemade chicken stock (see Index) or good-quality canned broth
1 large whole chicken breast
¼ cup olive oil
2 cloves garlic, finely chopped
1 cup chopped onions
½ teaspoon dried basil, or 1 tablespoon chopped fresh basil leaves
2 cans (28 ounces each) Italian-style tomatoes, well drained
Salt and freshly ground pepper to taste
1 cup crème fraîche (see Index)
6 slices French bread, cut ½ inch thick and lightly toasted
½ cup grated imported Parmesan cheese
½ cup grated Gruyère cheese

1. Place the chicken stock in a large saucepan over medium heat and bring to a simmer. Add the chicken breast and simmer until tender, 30 to 40 minutes. Remove the breast, allow it to cool, and cut it into 1-inch cubes. Reserve the chicken cubes and stock.

2. Heat the oil in a large, heavy, deep pan over medium-high heat. Add the garlic and onions and sauté, stirring, until soft, 2 to 3 minutes. Add the basil and cook 1 minute more. Add the tomatoes and the reserved chicken stock. Simmer until the tomatoes are quite soft, 20 to 25 minutes.

3. Purée the soup in a food mill, blender, or food processor. Return it to the saucepan, and season with salt and pepper as needed. Add the chicken pieces and simmer 1 minute more.

4. Gradually whisk about ½ cup hot soup into the crème fraîche. Then gradually add the crème fraîche mixture to the soup. (The soup can be prepared a day in advance to this point. Cool, cover, and refrigerate until needed.)

5. When you are ready to serve, preheat the oven to 400° F.

6. Reheat the soup slowly on the stove, and then ladle it into individual ovenproof soup bowls. Float a slice of French bread on top of each, and sprinkle with the cheeses. Place the bowls on a baking sheet and bake until the cheeses melt, 5 to 7 minutes.

Serves 6

Russian Peasant Soup

Every February a group of our friends invites my husband and me to a "Beat the Blahs" party. We begin with champagne and stone crabs and then move on to a buffet of hot soups and salads. This hearty Russian soup, which was my contribution to the menu one year, was one of the most popular. Everyone asked for seconds.

2 heads cabbage, cored and cut into wedges
2 carrots, peeled and cut into ¼-inch slices
4 ribs celery, cut into ½-inch pieces
2 large turnips, peeled and quartered
12 cups homemade beef stock (see Index) or good-quality canned
    broth
2 cans (6 ounces each) tomato paste
Salt and freshly ground pepper to taste
6 tablespoons vegetable oil
4 onions, peeled, halved lengthwise, and sliced into ¼-inch slices
2 cloves garlic, finely chopped
6 medium baking potatoes, quartered
2 cups sour cream
½ cup chopped fresh dill or parsley

1. Put the cabbage, carrots, celery, turnips, and beef stock in an 8- to 10-quart deep stockpot. Bring to a simmer, then stir in the tomato paste and salt and pepper. Simmer, uncovered, until the vegetables are very tender, about 1½ hours.

2. Meanwhile, heat the oil in a medium-size heavy skillet. When it is hot, add the onions and sauté until softened, 3 to 4 minutes. Add the garlic and sauté 1 minute more. Remove from the heat and reserve.

3. When the vegetables in the stockpot are done, add the onion mixture and the potatoes. Cook until the potatoes are tender but not mushy, another 30 minutes. (The soup can be prepared a day in advance to this point. Cool, cover, and refrigerate until needed. It will actually improve in flavor.)

4. Serve the soup in a large tureen or in individual bowls. Garnish each serving with a large dollop of sour cream, and sprinkle chopped dill or parsley on top.

Serves 12

GREAT ACCOMPANIMENTS

Dark pumpernickel and a cucumber salad complement this dish nicely. Offer a plate of Lucy's Nanaimo Bars for something sweet.

A COOK'S REFLECTIONS

In Russia, this soup is known as *schi*. It can be the simplest of soups made with cabbage and such vegetables as potatoes, tomatoes, carrots, and onions, or it can be more elaborate and include smoked pork or boiled beef. It can be made in various ways: with just fresh cabbage, with a combination of sauerkraut and fresh cabbage, or with sauerkraut alone. It is always a hearty preparation.

GREAT ACCOMPANIMENTS

This soup is so filling that I often serve it as a main course. A salad of romaine lettuce tossed with a mustard vinaigrette, dark rye or pumpernickel bread, and a bowl of fruit served with Orange and Ginger Butter Cookies complete the menu.

Warming Beef and Lentil Soup

One cold winter evening, when heavy Ohio snows kept everyone housebound, neighbors invited our family to share this delicious soup with them. Its fragrance had permeated our hosts' home, tempting us even before we reached the table.

¼ cup vegetable oil
2 beef soup bones (about 3 pounds total)
2 beef shanks (1¾ to 2 pounds total)
4 cups coarsely chopped onions
1 tablespoon chopped garlic
3 quarts water
4 cups tomato purée
1 cup dry red wine
1 green bell pepper, cored, seeded, and coarsely chopped
2 bay leaves
1 teaspoon dried thyme
1 tablespoon salt, or to taste
Freshly ground pepper to taste
4 carrots, peeled and cut into ¼-inch slices
1 pound dry lentils, rinsed and drained
2½ teaspoons ground cumin
1½ cups sour cream

1. Heat the oil over medium-high heat in a large deep pot. Pat the soup bones and beef shanks dry with paper towels. When the oil is hot, add the bones and shanks to the pot and brown well on all sides. Remove the bones and meat from the pot and reserve.

2. Add the onions and garlic and cook until the onions have softened, about 5 minutes. Return the bones and meat to the pot. Add the water and tomato purée, red wine, green pepper, bay leaves, thyme, salt, and a generous grinding of pepper. Stir, and bring to a simmer. Cover, and simmer until the meat is tender, 3 to 4 hours.

3. Remove the meat and bones from the soup and place them on a work surface to cool. Meanwhile, skim and discard all fat from the surface of the soup. When the bones and meat have cooled so that you can handle them, cut the meat from the bones and shanks into small bite-size pieces and return the meat to the soup pot.

4. Add the carrots and lentils to the pot. Cook, uncovered, at a simmer until the vegetables and lentils are tender, about 2 hours. Taste, and add more salt if needed. Stir in the cumin. Cook, stirring over low heat, another 5 minutes. Remove the pot from the heat and let the soup cool 5 minutes. (The soup can be prepared 1 to 2 days in advance to this point. Cool, cover, and refrigerate.)

5. When ready to serve the soup, reheat until hot. Serve the soup in a large tureen with a bowl of sour cream as an accompaniment.

Serves 16

CREAM SOUPS

GREAT ACCOMPANIMENTS

This soup is especially nice to serve as a main course for an informal supper. Rosemary Savory Rolls and Belgian Endive and Spinach Salad with Lemon and Scallion Dressing work well with it. The Chocolate Walnut Caramel Tart is an excellent ending.

A COOK'S REFLECTIONS

Since leeks grow in sandy soil they are often covered with dirt or grit even when they reach the supermarket. To clean, cut off the root ends, then split the leeks, lengthwise. Rinse thoroughly under cold running water to remove all particles, then dry and use as needed.

Cream of Winter Vegetable Soup

Each of the root vegetables used in this soup has such a distinctive taste that no herbs or spices are necessary. The soup improves in flavor if made a day in advance.

8 tablespoons (1 stick) unsalted butter
2¼ cups chopped carrots
3 cups diced turnips
3 cups chopped leeks, white parts only
6 cups homemade chicken stock (see Index) or good-quality canned broth
¾ teaspoon salt, or to taste
1 cup heavy or whipping cream
Freshly ground white pepper to taste
4 tablespoons chopped fresh parsley, for garnish

1. In a large heavy casserole melt the butter and add the chopped carrots, turnips, and leeks. Cook over medium heat, stirring, until the vegetables have softened, 5 to 6 minutes. Add the chicken stock and salt and bring to a simmer.

2. Cook the soup at a simmer, uncovered, until the vegetables are completely tender, 25 to 30 minutes. Remove the soup from the heat and purée it in a food mill, food processor, or blender.

3. Return the soup to the casserole and stir in the cream. Heat until hot. Taste, and add salt and white pepper as needed. (The soup can be prepared a day in advance. Cool, cover, and refrigerate.)

4. When you are ready to serve, reheat the soup over low heat until it comes to a simmer. Serve in individual soup bowls and garnish with chopped parsley.

Serves 6

Cream of Butternut Squash and Leek Soup

This soup is thick and creamy—a wonderful first course for a fall or winter dinner. I have used this colorful dish many times to begin our Thanksgiving dinner.

4 pounds butternut squash
5 tablespoons unsalted butter
1¾ cups chopped leeks, white parts only
6 cups homemade chicken stock (see Index) or good-quality
    canned broth
¼ teaspoon dried thyme
1 teaspoon salt, or to taste
1 cup heavy or whipping cream, plus more if needed
1 cup milk, plus more if needed
Salt and freshly ground white pepper to taste
4 ounces good-quality smoked cured sausage, for garnish
Chopped fresh parsley or chives, for garnish
⅓ cup grated imported Parmesan cheese, for garnish

1. Cut the squash in half lengthwise. Scoop out the seeds with a spoon. With a sharp paring knife or peeler, remove the skin from the squash. Cut the squash into 1-inch cubes. You should have approximately 8 cups.

2. Melt the butter in a large 4- to 5-quart pot over medium-high heat, and add the leeks. Cook, stirring, for 3 to 4 minutes. Add the squash and stir to coat with butter; cook 1 to 2 minutes. Add the stock, thyme, and salt. Stir and bring to a boil. Reduce the heat and cook at a simmer, uncovered, until the squash is completely tender and mushy when pierced with a fork, 40 minutes or more. Remove the pan from the heat and purée the soup in a food processor, blender, or food mill. You will have a very thick purée.

3. Return the purée to the pan and add the cream and milk. Reheat

---

A COOK'S REFLECTIONS

If you've never cooked butternut squash, the pale orange-hued, bell-shaped winter squash, you might be surprised by how firm the skin is. To remove this tough outer layer, I cut the squash in half lengthwise, scoop out all the seeds and then I hold the squash half down with one hand and with a sharp paring knife in the other, I start at the base and remove the skin in long strips.

GREAT ACCOMPANIMENTS

If you serve this soup as a main course for a light supper or luncheon, offer the Green Bean, Walnut, and Red Onion Salad as a side dish and the Poached Pears with Blueberry Cassis Sauce for dessert.

AS A VARIATION

In place of the sausage, ½ cup pecan halves sprinkled over the soup makes a nice garnish.

over low heat, and if the soup is too thick, add more cream and milk in equal portions. Taste, and add salt and white pepper as desired. (Soup can be prepared a day in advance to this point. Cool, cover, and refrigerate. Reheat slowly, stirring, before serving.)

4. Cut the sausage into ⅛-inch-thick diagonal slices.

5. To serve, ladle the soup into individual bowls and garnish with three to four slices of sausage, the chives or parsley, and Parmesan cheese.

Serves 6 to 8

GREAT ACCOMPANIMENTS

Follow this soup with the Crown Roast of Pork with Mustard Herb Butter accompanied by the Barley with Leeks and Celery. You might also like to add the Green Bean, Walnut, and Red Onion Salad to the menu. The Chocolate Apricot Pecan Torte makes an excellent conclusion.

Cream of Apple, Carrot, and Caraway Soup

This is a rich and creamy soup flavored subtly with a hint of caraway. Although I serve it all through the cold weather months, I particularly like it during the holidays.

1 slab (8 ounces) bacon, partially frozen for easier cutting
2 tablespoons vegetable oil (optional)
1½ cups chopped leeks (white parts only)
1 pound Granny Smith apples, peeled and coarsely chopped
1 pound carrots, peeled and coarsely chopped
6 cups homemade chicken stock (see Index) or good-quality
*   canned broth, plus more if needed*
2 cups heavy or whipping cream
2 tablespoons caraway seeds
Salt and freshly ground pepper to taste
½ teaspoon salt
Pinch of sugar
3 tablespoons julienned carrot
3 tablespoons unsalted butter
6 tablespoons peeled and julienned Granny Smith apple

1. Cut the rind from the bacon and discard it. Cut the bacon into ¼-inch dice.

2. In a heavy Dutch oven, fry the bacon over medium-high heat until light brown. Add oil if necessary to prevent the bacon from sticking. Add the leeks and cook, stirring frequently, until they begin to soften, 3 to 4 minutes. Add the chopped apples and carrots and stir constantly for 3 minutes. Then add the stock and simmer, uncovered, until the apples and carrots are tender, 40 minutes.

3. Purée the soup in batches in a food processor or blender until very smooth. Strain the purée through a fine sieve and return it to the Dutch oven.

4. Bring the cream and caraway seeds to a boil in a small heavy saucepan and continue boiling until the cream is reduced by half, about 5 minutes. Strain the cream through a fine sieve and stir it into the soup. If necessary, thin the soup to the desired consistency by adding more stock. Season with salt and pepper. (The soup can be prepared 1 day ahead. Cool, cover, and refrigerate.)

5. When you are ready to serve the soup, reheat it over medium heat, stirring frequently. Bring 1 cup water with the ½ teaspoon salt and the sugar to a boil in a small saucepan. Add the julienned carrot and cook until just tender, 5 to 6 minutes. Drain.

6. Melt the butter in a medium-size heavy skillet over medium heat. Add the julienned apple and stir for 2 minutes. Add the cooked carrot and stir until heated through.

7. Ladle the soup into bowls. Garnish with the sautéed carrot and apple and serve.

Serves 8

Cream of Artichoke Soup

My students could not believe how easy this creamy soup is to prepare. This is one of those dishes that appear to be far more sophisticated than their simple preparations would imply.

2 to 3 leeks
6 tablespoons (¾ stick) unsalted butter
2 packages (10 ounces each) frozen artichoke hearts, thawed,
*   coarsely chopped*
5 cups homemade chicken stock (see Index) or good-quality
*   canned broth*
1 cup heavy or whipping cream
¼ cup freshly grated imported Parmesan cheese
Salt and freshly ground white pepper to taste

AT THE MARKET

Although I like to use fresh ingredients whenever possible, the frozen artichoke hearts, sautéed with leeks in butter and then simmered slowly in stock, produce a very good flavor in this soup.

1. Cut off the root ends of the leeks; cut the leeks in half lengthwise and rinse under cold running water to remove all dirt and grit. Chop the white parts coarsely (you should have 2 cups), and save the green stems for the garnish.

2. Melt the butter in a large heavy pot over medium heat. Add the chopped leeks and cook, stirring, 3 to 4 minutes. Add the artichoke hearts and cook another 2 minutes. Add the stock, bring to a simmer, and cook, uncovered, until the leeks and artichoke hearts are tender, about 25 minutes.

3. Meanwhile, cut the reserved green portions of the leeks into very thin julienne strips, enough to make ⅓ cup. Place the strips in a fine-mesh strainer and lower it into the simmering soup for about 1 minute or until the color is bright green. Remove, drain, and reserve the leeks.

4. When the vegetables are tender, remove the soup from the heat and purée it in a food processor, blender, or food mill. Then strain the soup, pushing with a scraper or spatula, through a large-mesh strainer to remove any fibers.

5. Return the soup to the pot; add the cream and reheat. Gradually stir in the cheese, and season to taste with salt and white pepper. (The soup and the leek garnish may be prepared a day in advance to this point. Cool, cover, and refrigerate the soup. Wrap the julienned leeks in a moistened paper towel and then in plastic wrap and refrigerate.)

6. To serve, reheat the soup and ladle it into individual bowls. Garnish each serving by floating a few of the blanched strips of leek in the center.

Serves 6

Cream of Jerusalem Artichoke Soup with Bacon Lardons

Cooks like nothing better than to discover a new ingredient. Jerusalem artichokes, or sunchokes as they are sometimes called, are one of my recent discoveries. The combination of this vegetable with leeks and bacon in this soup is enticing.

AT THE MARKET

Jerusalem artichokes, or sun-chokes, are knobby tubers resembling potatoes in appearance. They have light brown skin, a slightly sweet, smoky taste, and a crisp texture. Look for Jerusalem artichokes that are firm and have a smooth skin. Do not buy older ones that are dried out and shriveled. To prepare them for cooking, remove the skin using a vegetable peeler or a sharp paring knife.

GREAT ACCOMPANIMENTS

This soup is very rich and creamy and works nicely followed by the Filets of Salmon Baked with Lemons, Scallions, and Parsley; Wild Rice and Pine Nut Pilaf; and a seasonal salad with a vinaigrette dressing. For dessert, Honeydew Sorbet makes a light ending.

1 slab (8 to 10 ounces) smoked bacon, partially frozen for easier cutting
Vegetable oil, if needed
3 cups chopped leeks, white parts only, green stems reserved
3 pounds Jerusalem artichokes, peeled and cut into ¼-inch slices
6 cups homemade chicken stock (see Index) or good-quality canned broth
2 cups crème fraîche (see Index)
Salt and freshly ground pepper to taste

1. Cut the rind from the bacon and discard it. Cut the bacon into ¼-inch dice. In a large, heavy, deep pot, sauté the bacon cubes over medium heat until they are golden and the fat has been rendered. Remove the bacon cubes with a slotted spoon and drain on paper towels. Reserve. There should be enough fat left to coat the bottom of the pan generously. If not, add vegetable oil. If there is too much fat, discard the excess.

2. Heat the fat in the pot. When it is hot, add the leeks and cook over medium heat, stirring, for 4 to 5 minutes. Add the sliced Jerusalem artichokes, toss, and cook 2 to 3 minutes more. Add the stock and bring the soup to a simmer. Simmer, uncovered, until the vegetables are tender, 35 to 45 minutes.

3. Remove the pot from the heat and purée the soup in a food processor, blender, or food mill. The purée will be very thick. Return it to the pot and stir in the crème fraîche. Add salt and pepper to taste. Strain the soup through a sieve into another saucepan. (The soup can be prepared a day in advance to this point. Cool, cover, and refrigerate. Before proceeding, reheat the soup, stirring often, then continue with the recipe.)

4. While the soup is reheating, drop the reserved green leek stems into boiling water for a few seconds to set the color. Refresh them under cold water and pat dry. Use a sharp paring knife to cut the stems into very fine julienne.

5. Serve the soup in individual soup bowls. Garnish each serving with the julienned leeks and reserved bacon cubes.

Serves 8

Cream of Fennel Soup

When Perla Meyers was teaching at La Belle Pomme, a student, knowing how much Perla loves fresh ingredients, brought her some beautiful fennel bulbs. After the class, Perla quickly improvised this hearty soup and served it to our kitchen assistants. We all loved it!

7 tablespoons unsalted butter
4 cups chopped leeks (about 4 leeks), white parts only
8 cups chopped fennel (4 to 5 bulbs)
3 baking potatoes, peeled and diced
9 cups homemade chicken stock (see Index) or good-quality canned broth
¾ teaspoon salt, plus more if needed
Freshly ground pepper to taste
¾ cup heavy or whipping cream
4-ounce piece of prosciutto, cut into ¼-inch dice
8 leaves flat-leaf parsley

1. Melt 6 tablespoons of the butter in a heavy, deep 4- to 5-quart pot. When it is hot, add all but ⅓ cup of the chopped leeks. Sauté, stirring, 3 to 4 minutes. Add the chopped fennel. Stir, and sauté the fennel along with the leeks for 2 minutes more. Add the potatoes, chicken stock, and salt and pepper. Simmer, uncovered, until the vegetables are tender, 25 to 30 minutes.

2. Remove the pot from the heat and purée the soup in a food mill, food processor, or blender. Return the soup to the pot, add the cream, and stir well. Taste. Add more salt and pepper if needed. (The soup can be prepared a day in advance to this point. Cool, cover, and refrigerate. It actually improves in flavor when made ahead.)

3. When you are ready to serve, reheat the soup until hot. While the soup is reheating, melt the remaining tablespoon of butter in a small skillet over medium heat. Add the diced prosciutto and reserved ⅓ cup of chopped leeks and cook, stirring, 4 to 5 minutes.

4. To serve, ladle the soup into individual bowls. Garnish each serving with a little of the sautéed prosciutto, leeks, and a leaf of parsley. Serve immediately.

Serves 8

GREAT ACCOMPANIMENTS

If you are using this as a first course, follow it with Roast Lamb with a Pepper Coating, Peas with Rosemary and Pine Nuts, some buttered new potatoes, and for dessert, Cassis Walnut Tart.

Cream of Asparagus Soup

As soon as the first spring asparagus appears in the market, I buy some so I can make this soup. It is light and elegant—a perfect beginning for a special dinner.

2 pounds asparagus
4 tablespoons (½ stick) unsalted butter
1½ cups chopped leeks (about 2 medium leeks), white parts only
4 cups homemade chicken stock (see Index) or good-quality canned broth
2 large egg yolks
⅓ cup heavy or whipping cream
½ teaspoon curry powder
¼ teaspoon salt
Freshly ground pepper to taste
2 tablespoons chopped fresh chives
2 tablespoons chopped fresh mint

1. Cut off the tough lower portion of the asparagus stalks. With a vegetable peeler or paring knife, peel off the skin, starting just below the tip. Cut off the tips and set them aside. Cut the stalks into ½-inch pieces.

2. Melt the butter in a heavy 2-quart saucepan. Add the chopped leeks and sauté 1 to 2 minutes. Add the asparagus stalks and sauté 2 minutes. Then add the chicken stock and bring to a boil. Reduce the heat and simmer until the asparagus is very tender, 25 minutes. Add the asparagus tips and cook 10 minutes more. Remove six nice tips for the garnish.

3. Remove the soup from the heat and purée it in a food processor, blender, or food mill. If a processor or blender is used, strain the puréed soup through a wide-mesh sieve to remove any fibers. (The soup can be prepared a day in advance to this point. Cool, cover, and refrigerate. Before proceeding, reheat, then continue with the recipe.)

4. In a small bowl whisk the egg yolks and cream together. Gradually whisk ½ cup warm soup into the egg mixture. Return the egg mixture to the soup, stirring to prevent lumping. Add the curry powder, salt, and pepper. Cook over low heat, stirring constantly, until slightly thickened.

5. Serve the soup in individual bowls and garnish each serving with chopped chives, mint, and a reserved asparagus tip.

Serves 6

Cream of Brussels Sprouts Soup

This is an unusual and delicious soup to serve as a first course for a fall or winter dinner party.

6 slices good-quality bacon, cut into ½-inch pieces
2 tablespoons unsalted butter
2 cups chopped onions
3 cups Brussels sprouts (about 1¼ pounds), trimmed of stems, rinsed, and cut in half through the stem end
1 baking potato, peeled and cut into 1-inch dice
5 cups homemade chicken stock (see Index) or good-quality canned broth
2 cups crème fraîche (see Index)
Salt and freshly ground pepper to taste
Garlic Croutons (recipe follows)

1. In a heavy 4- to 5-quart pot, cook the bacon over medium-high heat until it is light golden but not browned and crisp. Pour off all but 2 tablespoons of the fat. Add the butter to the bacon and fat in the pan, and melt it over medium-high heat. Add the chopped onions and sauté until softened, 2 to 3 minutes.

2. Add the Brussels sprouts and the diced potato to the pot and cook, stirring the mixture well, for 1 minute. Add the chicken stock. Bring the soup to a simmer and cook until the Brussels sprouts are tender when pierced with a knife, 50 minutes.

3. Remove the pot from the heat and purée the soup in a food mill, food processor, or blender. Return the soup to the pot and over low heat gradually add the crème fraîche. Season to taste with salt and pepper. (The soup can be prepared a day in advance to this point. Cool, cover, and refrigerate.)

4. When you are ready to serve, reheat the soup until hot. Serve in individual bowls and garnish with Garlic Croutons.

Serves 6

GARLIC CROUTONS

4 tablespoons (½ stick) unsalted butter, at room temperature
1 clove garlic, very finely chopped
4 slices stale white bread with crusts

1. Preheat the oven to 300° F.

2. Combine the butter and garlic in a small bowl. Mix well and spread evenly on both sides of the bread slices. Cut the bread into ½-inch cubes and place on a baking sheet.

3. Bake the croutons, turning them several times to make certain they do not burn, about 15 minutes. Remove and cool.

Cream of Eggplant and Tomato Soup

A thick, creamy soup, with the eggplant flavor subdued by the abundance of tomatoes.

1 eggplant (1 to 1¼ pounds)
2½ pounds tomatoes (about 8), or 1 can (28 ounces) Italian-style
*   plum tomatoes*
2 tablespoons unsalted butter
2 tablespoons olive oil
1 cup chopped onions
1 large clove garlic, chopped
2 tablespoons chopped fresh basil or 2 teaspoons dried
1 tablespoon fresh oregano or 1 teaspoon dried
3 cups homemade chicken stock (see Index) or good-quality
*   canned broth*
1 teaspoon salt or to taste
½ to ¾ cup heavy or whipping cream
Freshly ground pepper to taste
6 sprigs fresh basil or flat-leaf parsley, or 1½ tablespoons
*   chopped fresh chives, for garnish*

1. Peel the eggplant and cut it into 1-inch cubes. You should have about 3 cups. Place the cubes in a colander and salt generously. Let the eggplant rest for 30 minutes. Pat dry and reserve.

GREAT ACCOMPANIMENTS

*For a luncheon, serve this soup as a
first course. The Wild Rice and
Shrimp Salad along with a basket of
hot French bread makes an excellent
entrée, and the Fresh Peach Halves
with Blueberries and Lemon Custard
Sauce are a fine ending.*

2. Peel, seed, and coarsely chop the fresh tomatoes or drain the canned tomatoes. Set aside.

3. Heat the butter and olive oil over medium heat in a large heavy pot. Add the onions, garlic, and eggplant cubes. Sauté, turning constantly, for 3 to 4 minutes. Reduce the heat if the mixture starts to brown.

4. Add the chopped basil, oregano, tomatoes, chicken stock, and salt, and bring to a simmer. Simmer, uncovered, until the eggplant is quite tender, 20 to 25 minutes.

5. Purée the soup in a food processor, blender, or food mill. Return the purée to the pot and add ½ cup heavy cream. If the soup is too thick, add the additional cream. Check the seasonings and add more salt if needed, and pepper. (The soup can be prepared one day in advance. Cool, cover, and refrigerate. Reheat when needed.) Serve the soup in individual bowls garnished with fresh basil.

Serves 6

SUMMER SOUPS

Crab and Escarole Soup

Tom and Peggy Turgeon, two of the most talented teachers at La Belle Pomme, created this unusual soup for one of their classes. It takes just fifteen minutes to make this dish.

2 small heads escarole lettuce, rinsed and dried
8 cups homemade chicken stock (see Index)
2 bottles (8 ounces each) clam juice
¼ teaspoon cayenne pepper
Salt to taste
1 pound cooked crabmeat, at room temperature
½ cup dry sherry
⅓ cup grated imported Parmesan cheese

AS A VARIATION

You can substitute small pieces of cooked lobster, bay scallops, or shrimp in this recipe.

1. Cut the escarole into ¼-inch-wide julienne strips and reserve.

2. Combine the chicken stock and the clam juice in a large heavy pot and bring to a simmer over medium heat. Add the escarole and cook until it is tender but still bright green, about 7 minutes. Add the cayenne pepper to the soup. Taste, and add salt if needed.

3. Divide the crabmeat among eight soup bowls. Pour 1 tablespoon of sherry over the crabmeat in each bowl, then ladle a cup of soup into each bowl. Sprinkle each serving with Parmesan cheese.

Serves 8

Summer Tomato and Watercress Soup

This is a soup to make in summer when the tomatoes are ripe, juicy, and in abundant supply. The watercress, a nice seasonal garnish to this dish, adds a peppery taste. I have served this soup as a first course and as an entrée along with a salad and hot buttered bread.

6 pounds ripe tomatoes
8 tablespoons (1 stick) unsalted butter
1½ cups chopped onions
1½ teaspoons dried thyme
2 cups homemade chicken stock (see Index) or good-quality
    canned broth
2 teaspoons salt, or to taste
¼ cup raw long-grain rice
½ cup heavy or whipping cream
1 cup chopped watercress leaves (no stems)

1. Dip each tomato into boiling water for 20 seconds. Then remove it with a slotted spoon and plunge it into cold water. After all the tomatoes have been blanched, use a sharp knife to peel off the skins. Remove the stems. Cut the tomatoes in half horizontally and squeeze each half to extract and discard the juice and seeds. Then chop the tomatoes coarsely.

2. Melt the butter in a large pot over medium-high heat. When it is hot, add the onions and cook, stirring, until softened, 3 to 4 minutes.

AS A VARIATION

This soup is also good served cold. Refrigerate it until chilled, then add the watercress. Check seasonings again, since cold food often needs additional salt.

3. Add the chopped tomatoes and the thyme, and cook, stirring several times so the mixture does not burn on the bottom, 5 to 7 minutes more.

4. Add the stock, salt, and rice, and bring the soup to a simmer over low heat. Cook until the tomatoes are tender and mushy, 25 to 30 minutes.

5. Remove the soup from the heat and purée it in a food processor, blender, or food mill. Stir in the cream. Check the seasoning and add more salt if needed. (The soup can be made a day in advance to this point. Cool, cover, and refrigerate.)

6. To serve, reheat the soup and add the watercress. Serve immediately.

Serves 8

Chilled Smoked Salmon Bisque

Using the best-quality smoked salmon is the most important thing to remember in preparing this soup. Although it is expensive, it will make the difference between an ordinary and an extraordinary dish. The bisque takes only a few minutes to assemble and makes a very sophisticated first-course offering for an elegant dinner.

3 tablespoons unsalted butter
⅓ cup finely chopped shallots
1 piece (8 ounces) smoked salmon, cut into small pieces
2 packages (3 ounces each) cream cheese, cut into chunks, at room temperature
1½ cups heavy or whipping cream
1 cup milk
½ cup plus 2 tablespoons sour cream
Dill sprigs, for garnish
Slices of pumpernickel

1. Melt the butter in a heavy 4-quart saucepan over medium heat. Add the shallots and cook until softened. Lower the heat and add the salmon pieces. Cook for about 1 minute. Add the cream cheese to the pan. Cook, stirring, until the cream cheese has melted. Remove the pan from the heat.

2. Purée the salmon mixture in a food processor or blender until

AT THE MARKET

Petrossian is an excellent brand of smoked salmon found in many specialty markets.

GREAT ACCOMPANIMENTS

Follow the bisque with Grilled Mustard-Glazed Cornish Hens, served with Wild Rice and Pine Nut Pilaf and Asparagus with Chive Butter. The Raspberry Mousse Pie with a Brownie Fudge Crust makes a fine dessert.

smooth. Leave the purée in the processor.

3. Whisk together the heavy cream, milk, and sour cream in a bowl. Then, with the processor or blender on, pour in the cream mixture and process until very smooth. Refrigerate several hours, until well chilled. (The soup can be prepared a day in advance to this point. Cover and refrigerate until needed.)

4. Ladle the soup into six small soup bowls. Garnish each serving with a sprig of fresh dill and serve slices of pumpernickel bread alongside.

Serves 6

Chilled Tomato Soup with Avocado Cream

It's hard to describe this soup except to say that it's delicious. Served well chilled, it is cool and refreshing—but since it is made with a generous seasoning of cayenne pepper, it has a spicy, piquant flavor as well.

Tomato Soup
¼ cup vegetable oil
2 cups chopped onions
¾ cup chopped carrots
1 tablespoon finely chopped garlic
1 teaspoon salt
½ teaspoon cayenne pepper
4 cups homemade chicken stock (see Index) or good-quality canned broth
4 pounds tomatoes, peeled, seeded, and chopped

Avocado Cream
2 very ripe avocados
⅔ cup sour cream
¼ cup heavy or whipping cream, plus more if needed
4 teaspoons fresh lemon juice
½ teaspoon salt
¼ cup chopped scallions (green onions), including green stems, for garnish

AS A VARIATION

This soup is delicious served hot on a chilly winter day. Use one 28-ounce can Italian-style plum tomatoes, drained and coarsely chopped, in place of the fresh tomatoes.

1. To make the soup, heat the oil in a heavy 4- to 5-quart saucepan over medium heat. Add the onions, carrots, and garlic and cook until the vegetables soften, stirring occasionally, 5 to 10 minutes. Mix in the salt and cayenne pepper.

2. Add the stock, bring to a boil, and simmer, uncovered, 30 minutes. Increase the heat to high, add the tomatoes, and cook until softened, about 10 minutes.

3. Remove the soup from the heat and purée it in a food processor or blender. Transfer the soup to a bowl, cool, cover, and refrigerate. (The soup can be prepared a day in advance to this point.)

4. When ready to serve, peel the avocados, remove the seeds, and place the avocados in the container of a food processor or blender. Add the sour cream, heavy cream, lemon juice, and salt. Process the mixture until very smooth, a minute or more. Transfer the avocado purée to a bowl, and if it seems too thick, whisk in 2 to 3 additional tablespoons cream to thin it.

5. Adjust the seasoning and ladle the soup into well-chilled bowls. Gently spoon 2 to 3 tablespoons Avocado Cream atop each. Garnish with scallions.

Serves 6

Carrot Soup with Coriander

Cold carrot soup may not be unusual anymore, but the addition of cilantro in this preparation makes it more special.

5 tablespoons unsalted butter
1½ cups chopped leeks, white parts only
3 cups chopped carrots (about 1¼ pounds)
5 cups homemade chicken stock (see Index) or good-quality canned broth
1 teaspoon salt, or to taste
Freshly ground pepper to taste
1 cup sour cream
1 cup light cream
1 tablespoon fresh lemon juice
¼ cup finely chopped cilantro (fresh coriander leaves)
6 cilantro sprigs, for garnish

A COOK'S REFLECTIONS

Coriander is one of the oldest herbs known to man. Its seeds have been found in Bronze Age ruins in the Aegean Islands and in the tombs of ancient pharaohs. Today fresh coriander is one of the world's most commonly used herbs.

AT THE MARKET
Cilantro (fresh coriander) looks like flat-leaf parsley. However, crushed coriander leaves (unlike parsley) release a strong, assertive smell, making them easy to identify. Often this fresh herb can be found in Oriental markets (where it may be labeled ''Chinese parsley'') or in Spanish markets.

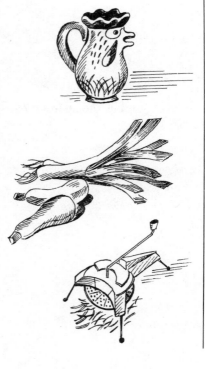

1. In a heavy 4- to 5-quart pot or saucepan, melt the butter over medium heat. Add the leeks and sauté, stirring, 4 minutes. Add the carrots, and cook and stir 5 minutes more. Add the stock, salt, and pepper and bring the mixture to a simmer. Cook, uncovered, until the vegetables are tender, about 25 minutes.

2. Remove the soup from the heat and purée it in a food processor, blender, or food mill. Cover, and refrigerate several hours until chilled. (The soup can be made a day in advance to this point.)

3. When you are ready to serve, whisk in the sour cream, light cream, lemon juice, and chopped cilantro. Taste, and if desired, add more salt (cold foods often need more seasoning).

4. To serve, ladle soup into individual bowls. Garnish each serving with a sprig of cilantro.

Serves 6

Chicken Soup with Three Peppers and Chèvre

After the holiday season my family always asks for lighter food to help shed recently acquired pounds. In response to their requests, I created this piquant and satisfying soup. It has become a welcome addition to our table, and I serve it year round.

6 cups homemade chicken stock (see Index)
1 red bell pepper
2 leeks
2 small yellow squash (about 4 ounces each)
3 tablespoons olive oil
½ teaspoon cayenne pepper
½ teaspoon coarsely ground black pepper
Salt to taste
1 log (6 ounces) chèvre, sliced into 6 rounds

1. Heat the chicken stock in a saucepan over low heat. Keep at a simmer.

2. Remove the stem, seeds, and membranes from the red pepper and then cut it into strips, 1½ inches by ¼ inch.

A COOK'S REFLECTIONS

Homemade chicken stock is essential to the success of this soup. The canned variety will not do it justice.

3. Cut the green stems and roots from the leeks and cut the white parts in half lengthwise. Rinse under cold water to remove dirt and grit, then cut into strips 1½ inches by ¼ inch.

4. Cut off the ends of the squash, quarter them lengthwise, and cut into strips 1½ inches by ¼ inch. Parboil in boiling water to cover for 2 minutes, drain, and pat dry.

5. Heat the olive oil in a medium-size heavy skillet over medium heat. When the oil is hot, add the red pepper slices and sauté 2 minutes. Then add the leeks and sauté another 2 minutes. Finally, add the squash and sauté until the vegetables are just tender, 3 to 4 minutes. Season with cayenne and black pepper.

6. To serve, fill six shallow soup bowls with 1 cup of hot chicken stock. Ladle ⅓ cup of the vegetable mixture into each bowl. Taste the soup, and add more salt if desired. Garnish each serving with a round of cheese and serve hot.

Serves 6

FIRST COURSES

First courses are usually a little more substantial than hors d'oeuvres. Savory tarts, served hot or at room temperature, shimmering soufflés, light fish and vegetable creations, are all good choices for this part of a meal. I have enjoyed serving the many dishes in this section—from the Summer Pesto Tart made with fresh basil to the elegant Shrimp and Scallop Timbales with a Tomato-Watercress sauce. All of these recipes make stellar beginnings for any meal.

AT THE MARKET

Medium-size stalks of asparagus are the best for this recipe. Look for ones that are ½ inch in diameter, with tender spears.

Hot Asparagus Soufflé

One of the most interesting classes ever taught at La Belle Pomme was a spring course entitled "The Asparagus Fête." Jim Budros was the teacher, and this was one of the tempting dishes he created for students to sample.

Special equipment: 6-cup soufflé dish; food processor

Soufflé
5 tablespoons unsalted butter, plus 1 more if soufflé is to be made
    ahead, at room temperature
5 tablespoons finely grated imported Parmesan cheese
1 pound fresh asparagus, cleaned and trimmed
1 teaspoon finely chopped shallots
¼ cup all-purpose flour
1½ cups light cream, warmed
5 large eggs, separated, at room temperature
½ teaspoon salt, or to taste

Lemon Butter Sauce
3 large egg yolks
1 tablespoon fresh lemon juice
¼ teaspoon salt
⅛ teaspoon cayenne pepper
8 tablespoons (1 stick) unsalted butter
½ cup heavy or whipping cream

1. To prepare the soufflé, first wrap the soufflé dish with a collar: Cut a sheet of aluminum foil long enough to wrap and overlap around the circumference of a 6-cup soufflé dish. Fold it in half lengthwise, and then wrap it around the dish so a collar is formed. Secure the foil by tying it in place with string. Use 1 tablespoon of the butter to butter the inside of the soufflé dish and the collar. Dust the inside of the dish and the foil lightly with 1 tablespoon of the Parmesan cheese.

2. Fill a heavy skillet with 1 inch of water and place it over medium-high heat. When the water comes to a boil, add the asparagus. Cook the asparagus at a boil until they are very tender when pierced with a knife, 4 to 5 minutes.

3. Remove the asparagus from the heat and place in a large sieve or colander. Refresh under cold running water to stop the cooking

One of the hardest things for me to master as a beginning cook was beating egg whites to the proper consistency for soufflés; I tended to overbeat them. Egg whites beat best if they are at room temperature with a pinch of salt added to help break up the gelatinous texture. For a soufflé, beat the whites until soft peaks form. They should have a smooth dense consistency but not be stiff or dry. I add the beaten whites to the soufflé base in thirds, using a rubber spatula to fold them in and turning the bowl a quarter of a turn every few seconds to help distribute the whites evenly.

process. Dry the asparagus well. Cut off and reserve the tips for the garnish. Process the stalks in a food processor until you have a smooth purée. Set aside.

4. Melt the remaining 4 tablespoons butter in a heavy saucepan over medium heat. Add the shallots and cook, stirring, until tender, 1 to 2 minutes. Add the flour and stir for 2 minutes; do not let the mixture brown. Stir in the cream and whisk until the mixture is smooth and thickened.

5. Remove the pan from the heat and add the egg yolks, one at a time, heating well after each addition. Fold in 2 tablespoons of the Parmesan cheese and the salt. Then add the asparagus purée. Taste, and if desired, add more salt. (The soufflé can be prepared several hours in advance to this point. Cut the extra tablespoon of butter into small pieces and dot the top of the soufflé with it. Cover lightly with waxed paper and leave at room temperature.)

6. When you are ready to bake the soufflé, preheat the oven to 400° F.

7. Beat the egg whites until stiff but still moist. Fold the whites into the soufflé base in three equal additions. Place the soufflé filling in the prepared mold and bake on the center shelf of the oven until puffed, 30 to 35 minutes.

8. While the soufflé is baking, prepare the sauce. Place the egg yolks, lemon juice, salt, and cayenne pepper in a food processor or blender. Melt the butter in a small heavy saucepan. Then gradually, with the machine running, pour the hot butter through the feed tube until all the butter is added and the sauce is smooth.

9. Remove the sauce to a bowl. Whip the cream until it is firm but not stiff, and fold it into the tepid sauce.

10. To serve, take the soufflé from the oven and carefully remove the collar. Sprinkle the top with the remaining 2 tablespoons Parmesan cheese. Serve the soufflé immediately, accompanied by a bowl of the sauce and a bowl of the reserved asparagus tips. As you offer each soufflé serving, ladle some of the sauce over it and garnish it with asparagus tips.

Serves 6

AS A VARIATION

*The tomato sauce for this dish is
quite chunky. If you prefer a
smoother texture, purée the sauce in
a food processor, blender, or food
mill and add an additional ½ cup
heavy cream.*

Early Autumn Soufflés

These are good individual cold-weather soufflés which I like to
serve to small groups. The sauce and the soufflé base can be
prepared ahead. Then you only need to beat the egg whites and
assemble the soufflés before baking.

Special equipment: Six 1-cup soufflé dishes, ramekins, or custard
cups

Tomato Ragoût

*1 slab (4 ounces) lean smoked bacon, partially frozen for easier
    cutting*
Vegetable oil, if needed
½ cup finely chopped onion
*1 can (14½ ounces) whole tomatoes, drained well and coarsely
    chopped*
1 tablespoon chopped fresh parsley
1 tablespoon chopped fresh chives
1½ teaspoons fresh thyme, or ½ teaspoon dried
⅓ cup dry vermouth
½ cup heavy or whipping cream, plus more if needed
Salt and freshly ground pepper to taste

Soufflé

*3 tablespoons unsalted butter, plus 1 tablespoon if soufflés are to
    be made ahead*
¼ cup all-purpose flour
1 cup milk
4 large eggs, separated, at room temperature
1¼ cups grated medium-sharp or sharp Cheddar cheese
½ teaspoon Dijon mustard
Generous sprinkling of cayenne pepper
Generous grating of fresh nutmeg
¼ teaspoon salt, or to taste
2 large egg whites, at room temperature

1. To make the Tomato Ragoût, cut the rind from the bacon and
discard. Cut the bacon into ¼-inch dice. In a heavy medium-size
skillet, sauté the bacon cubes over medium-high heat until lightly
browned. If the bacon does not give off 2 tablespoons fat, add enough
vegetable oil to make that amount in the skillet. If the bacon releases
excessive fat, pour off all but 2 tablespoons.

2. Add the onion to the skillet and cook, stirring, until golden but not browned, 2 to 3 minutes. Add the tomatoes and herbs and toss well. Then add the vermouth. Lower the heat and cook until the tomatoes are mushy and resemble a coarse purée, 10 to 15 minutes.

3. Add ½ cup cream to the tomato mixture and cook, stirring, about 4 minutes. Add salt and pepper to taste and remove from the heat. (The sauce can be made a day in advance. Cool, cover, and refrigerate.)

4. To make the soufflé base, melt the 3 tablespoons butter in a heavy saucepan over medium heat. Add the flour and cook, stirring constantly, for 2 minutes. Add the milk and whisk constantly until the mixture thickens and comes to a boil.

5. Remove the pan from the heat and add the egg yolks, one at a time, stirring well after each addition. Gradually, a little at a time, stir in 1 cup of the cheese. Add the mustard, cayenne pepper, nutmeg, and salt. (The soufflé base can be made several hours in advance. Cut the extra tablespoon of butter into small pieces, dot the soufflé base with it, and cover loosely with waxed paper. Leave at room temperature.)

6. When you are ready to prepare the soufflés, preheat the oven to 375° F. Butter six 1-cup soufflé dishes, ramekins, or custard cups.

7. Beat the 6 egg whites until they are firm and hold soft peaks. Then fold one third of the whites into the soufflé base. Fold in the remaining whites in two equal additions.

8. Fill the soufflé dishes about three-quarters full, mounding the soufflé mixture in the center. Sprinkle the soufflés with the remaining ¼ cup cheese.

9. Place the soufflé dishes on a baking sheet, put it on the center shelf of the oven, and bake until the soufflés are puffed and golden on top, about 15 minutes.

10. While the soufflés are baking, reheat the Tomato Ragoût over low heat and keep it warm. If desired, add cream to thin the sauce.

11. To serve, make a small hole in the top of each soufflé and ladle about 2 tablespoons sauce into each. Pass the remaining sauce separately. Serve immediately.

Serves 6

Spinach, Chèvre, and Walnut Tart

This rustic pie, made with a rich puff pastry crust, works well as a first course and is also filling enough to offer as an entrée for a luncheon or a light supper. The puff pastry does take more time to prepare than traditional tart pastry, but it is heaven to eat with its buttery, flaky texture and is certainly worth the effort.

Special equipment: Heavy-duty electric mixer; rimless baking sheet; 9½-inch springform pan

Pastry
1½ cups unbleached all-purpose flour
½ cup cake flour
1¾ cups (3½ sticks) well-chilled unsalted butter, thinly sliced
½ teaspoon salt
¼ to ½ cup ice water

Filling
¾ cup heavy or whipping cream
5 ounces creamy chèvre, such as Montrachet (without the ash), crumbled
10 ounces fresh spinach, trimmed
1 cup boiling water
3 tablespoons unsalted butter
¼ cup minced shallots
1 teaspoon minced garlic
½ cup chopped walnuts
Salt to taste
Freshly grated nutmeg to taste
Cayenne pepper to taste
2 large eggs
2 tablespoons fresh bread crumbs

1. To make the crust, refrigerate both flours 1 hour. Freeze the chilled butter for 15 minutes. Combine both flours and the salt in a bowl of a heavy-duty electric mixer. Top with the butter. Using the paddle attachment, beat until the butter is broken into pea-size pieces and is well coated with flour. Gradually mix in just enough ice water to bind the dough (it will still be lumpy).

GREAT ACCOMPANIMENTS

I like to use this tart as a first course to precede the Roast Lamb with a Pepper Coating or the Roast Capon Stuffed with Sausage, Onions, and Sweet Red Peppers. As a main course, this tart could be served with a green salad tossed in vinaigrette. Either way the Pink Grapefruit Sorbet with Campari makes a refreshing conclusion.

2. Roll the dough out on a well-floured surface to form a 12 x 8-inch rectangle, sprinkling the dough with flour as needed if it is very sticky. Lightly sprinkle the dough with flour, and fold it in thirds as for a business letter. Lift the folded dough off the work surface, scrape the surface clean, and reflour. Return the dough to the work surface with a short side nearest you. (If at any time the dough contracts and becomes difficult to roll, refrigerate it for 30 minutes or longer.) Repeat the rolling, folding, and turning three more times. Cover with plastic wrap and refrigerate 1 hour.

3. Roll, fold, and turn the dough two more times. Wrap it in plastic and refrigerate at least 20 minutes. (Pastry can be prepared two days ahead. Keep tightly covered in plastic wrap and refrigerated. Dough can also be frozen. Thaw in the refrigerator before using.)

4. Sprinkle a rimless baking sheet with water. Roll the dough out on a floured surface to form a ⅛-inch-thick round. Transfer it to the prepared baking sheet. Center the bottom of a 9½-inch springform pan over the dough and press down to mark an outline. Remove the pan and trim the dough to 1¾ inches beyond the outline. Roll the edge of the dough up to the outline. Squeeze this edge with your fingers to form 1¼-inch-high sides. Pierce the bottom of the pastry with a fork. Place the extended side of the springform pan around the pastry, carefully closing the side to encase it. Gently press the pastry against the pan side. Refrigerate at least 30 minutes to firm. (The pastry can be prepared up to 1 day ahead. Cover tightly with plastic wrap and refrigerate.)

5. For the filling, stir the cream and cheese together in a saucepan over low heat until smooth. Set aside.

6. Reserve 8 spinach leaves for garnish. Cook the remainder in a saucepan with the boiling water until just wilted. Drain the spinach, squeeze it dry, and chop.

7. Melt 2 tablespoons of the butter in a small heavy skillet over medium heat. Add the shallots and garlic and cook until soft, stirring occasionally, 3 minutes. Add the walnuts and stir 1 minute. Add the chopped spinach and season with salt, nutmeg, and cayenne pepper. Remove from the heat.

8. Mix the eggs into the cheese mixture and then add the spinach mixture. (The filling can be prepared 1 day ahead and refrigerated.)

9. To bake the tart, position a rack in the lower third of the oven and preheat to 375° F.

10. Pour the filling into the cold pastry shell. Sprinkle with the bread crumbs and dot with the remaining 1 tablespoon butter. Bake 10 minutes. Reduce the temperature to 350° F and bake 10 more minutes. Remove the pan sides and continue baking the tart until the crust is golden brown and the filling is firm to the touch, 25 to 35 minutes. Cover the edges of the tart with foil if the crust is browning too quickly.

11. Remove the pan from the oven and cool 10 minutes. Cut the tart into eight pieces. Place a reserved spinach leaf on each plate, and top it with a slice of the tart.

Serves 8

Summer Pesto Tart

This ricotta tart with a pesto topping is one of my favorite inventions.

Special equipment: 9-inch tart pan, 1½ inches high, with removable bottom

Pastry
1 cup all-purpose flour
Pinch of salt
4 tablespoons (½ stick) unsalted butter, well chilled and cut into small pieces
4½ teaspoons solid vegetable shortening, well chilled
3 tablespoons ice water

Filling
2 tablespoons unsalted butter
1 tablespoon olive oil
1 cup minced shallots (about 6 ounces)
1 container (15 ounces) ricotta cheese
4 large eggs, at room temperature
1¼ teaspoons salt
Freshly ground white pepper to taste ·
Freshly grated nutmeg to taste

Pesto (recipe follows)
Fresh basil sprigs, for garnish
1½ tablespoons pine nuts, for garnish

1. To prepare the dough by hand, combine the flour and salt in a bowl. Cut in the butter and shortening, using a pastry blender or two knives, until the mixture resembles oatmeal flakes. Gradually add the water, mixing just until the dough holds together. Transfer the dough to a lightly floured surface. Using the heel of your hand, smear ¼ cup of the dough at a time across the surface to form a 6-inch-long strip. Gather the dough together and repeat two more times. (Smearing the dough across a work surface in this way helps blend the fat and flour together.) Gather the dough into a ball and flatten it to a disk. Wrap it with plastic wrap and refrigerate at least 1 hour, or as long as overnight.

The pastry dough can also be made in a food processor: Place the dry ingredients in the bowl; add the butter and shortening. Process until the mixture resembles oatmeal flakes. With the machine still running, add the water through the feed tube until a ball of dough forms. Wrap the dough and refrigerate as in the hand method.

(The dough can be made 1 day in advance or it can be frozen. Thaw in the refrigerator before using.)

2. Preheat the oven to 375° F.

3. Roll the dough out on a lightly floured surface to form a ⅛-inch-thick round. Fit the round into a 9-inch tart pan. Trim and crimp the edges. Line the crust with parchment or foil, and fill it with pie weights or dried beans. Bake until the crust is set, about 10 minutes. Remove the lining and weights and continue baking until the crust is brown, about 15 minutes more. Remove the pastry from the oven. Leave the oven temperature at 375° F.

4. To make the filling, heat the butter with the oil in a small heavy skillet over low heat. Add the shallots and cook until they begin to soften, stirring frequently, about 5 minutes. Set aside to cool slightly. Combine the ricotta, eggs, salt, white pepper, and nutmeg in a large bowl. Add the shallots and beat until the filling is smooth.

5. Spoon the filling into the crust. Bake until a knife inserted in the center comes out clean, 25 to 30 minutes. Spread Pesto evenly over the tart and bake the tart 5 minutes longer. Cool slightly. Serve warm or at room temperature, garnished with basil sprigs and pine nuts.

Serves 8

PESTO

2 cups lightly packed fresh basil leaves
3 tablespoons pine nuts
3 cloves garlic
½ cup freshly grated imported Parmesan cheese
Pinch of salt
5 tablespoons olive oil

1. Purée the basil, pine nuts, and garlic in a food processor or blender. Mix in the cheese and salt.

2. With the machine running, gradually add the oil through the feed tube. (The pesto can be prepared 1 week ahead. Transfer it to a jar and cover the top with a thin film of olive oil. Seal the jar and refrigerate.)

Makes about 1 cup

Tomato, Cheese, and Basil Tart

This is one of the most attractive dishes in my repertoire. I can't wait to make it every summer when garden tomatoes and fresh basil start to appear in our local markets.

Special equipment: 9-inch tart pan with removable bottom

Pastry
1 cup all-purpose flour
Pinch of salt
4 tablespoons (½ stick) unsalted butter, well chilled and cut into small pieces
4½ teaspoons solid vegetable shortening, well chilled
3 tablespoons ice water

Filling
3 ripe tomatoes (about 6 ounces each)
8 ounces St. André cheese, well chilled
Olive oil
3 tablespoons chopped fresh basil leaves
1 tablespoon chopped walnuts

1. To prepare the dough by hand, combine the flour and salt in a

bowl. Cut in the butter and shortening, using a pastry blender or two knives, until the mixture resembles oatmeal flakes. Gradually add the water, mixing just until the dough holds together. Transfer the dough to a lightly floured surface. Using the heel of your hand, smear ¼ cup of the dough at a time across the surface to form a 6-inch-long strip. Gather the dough together and repeat two more times. (Smearing the dough across a work surface in this way helps blend the fat and flour together.) Gather the dough into a ball and flatten it to a disk. Wrap it with plastic wrap and refrigerate at least 1 hour, or as long as overnight.

The pastry dough can also be made in a food processor: Place the dry ingredients in the bowl; add the butter and shortening. Process until the mixture resembles oatmeal flakes. With the machine still running, add the water through the feed tube until a ball of dough forms. Wrap the dough and refrigerate as in the hand method.

(The dough can be made 1 day in advance or it can be frozen. Thaw in the refrigerator before using.)

2. Preheat the oven to 375° F.

3. Roll the dough out on a lightly floured surface to form a ⅛-inch-thick round. Fit the round into a 9-inch tart pan, and trim and crimp the edges. Line the crust with parchment or foil and fill it with pie weights or dried beans. Bake until the crust is set, about 10 minutes. Remove the lining and weights, and continue baking until the crust is brown, about 15 minutes more. Remove the pastry from the oven. (The tart shell can be baked several hours ahead and left at room temperature until needed.)

4. Remove the stems from the tomatoes and cut the tomatoes into ¼-inch-thick slices.

5. Remove the chalky rind from the cheese and cut the cheese into thin slices. Do not worry if the cheese breaks or crumbles. Arrange the tomato slices alternately with pieces of cheese, overlapping, in a single layer in the cooked pie shell. Brush the tomatoes and cheese with a thin coating of olive oil. Sprinkle the basil and walnuts over the tart. (The tart may be assembled 30 minutes in advance to this point.)

6. Preheat the broiler and arrange a rack 4 to 5 inches from the heat source. Broil the tart until the cheese is completely melted, 3 to 5 minutes. Watch carefully so it does not burn. Remove the pan rim from the tart and serve warm.

Serves 6

Torta di Verdura (Italian Vegetable Tart)

Several years ago, when Lazarus Department Stores planned a big retail celebration called "Inspiration Italy," I was asked to go to Florence to help plan the food events for this promotion. My mission was to work with the chefs from the Ciga Hotels, who had been invited to prepare the food during this fête. This was my favorite recipe of those I tasted. It is the creation of Faustino Monti, the executive chef of the Excelsior Hotel in Florence.

Special equipment: 8½-inch springform pan

Pastry
2 cups all-purpose flour
½ teaspoon salt
¾ cup (1½ sticks) unsalted butter, well chilled and cut into small
*   pieces*
1 large egg, lightly beaten
1 tablespoon ice water, if needed

Filling
2 small zucchini, cleaned and trimmed
Salt
2 tablespoons unsalted butter
½ cup chopped onion
1 large red bell pepper, cored, seeded, and cut into ¼-inch dice
1 baking potato, cut into ¼-inch dice
1 teaspoon finely chopped garlic
1 cup chopped spinach leaves
Salt and freshly ground pepper to taste
2 large eggs
1 cup heavy or whipping cream
4 ounces ricotta cheese
½ cup grated imported Parmesan cheese
Generous grating of fresh nutmeg

Glaze
1 large egg yolk
1 teaspoon water

1. To make the dough by hand, place the flour and salt in a mixing bowl and cut in the butter, using a pastry blender or two knives,

AS A VARIATION

Although the vegetables listed in the recipe are those I use most often, you could vary the offerings. Cooked sliced carrots, yellow squash, steamed broccoli, and cooked spring peas are all possibilities.

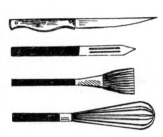

until the mixture resembles oatmeal flakes. Slowly add the beaten egg and mix (add water if needed). Shape the dough into a ball, wrap in plastic wrap, and refrigerate until firm, about 30 minutes.

To prepare the crust in a food processor, place the flour and salt in the work bowl. Add the chilled butter and process, pulsing for several seconds until the mixture resembles oatmeal flakes. Add the egg and process until a ball of dough is formed. (If needed, add the tablespoon of ice water to help the dough form a ball shape.) Remove the dough from the processor, wrap in plastic wrap, and refrigerate as in the hand method. (The dough can be made 1 day in advance to this point.)

2. For the filling, cut the zucchini into ¼-inch dice and place them in a colander over a mixing bowl. Salt them well and let them stand 30 minutes. Then pat the zucchini dry with a kitchen towel.

3. Melt the butter in a large skillet over medium-high heat. Add the onion and garlic and sauté 2 minutes. Then add the diced zucchini, red pepper, and potato and continue to stir and cook until the vegetables are soft but still retain some crispness, about 5 minutes. Add the spinach, stir well, and cook another 2 to 3 minutes. Taste the vegetables, and season the mixture generously with salt and pepper. Set aside.

4. Combine the eggs and cream in a bowl and mix well. Then stir in the cheeses and nutmeg. Add the vegetables to this mixture. Taste, and add more salt and pepper if desired.

5. Remove the dough from the refrigerator. Cut off one third and set it aside. Place the larger piece between two sheets of waxed paper and roll it into a 12-inch round ¼ inch thick. Using a bowl or a pan with a 12-inch diameter as a guide, cut the dough out to the exact size. Remove one sheet of paper and mold the dough, paper side up, into an 8½-inch springform pan. Carefully pull off the remaining waxed paper. Press the dough into the pan; the dough should extend slightly over the rim of the pan. Fill the crust with the filling.

6. Roll the remaining dough out between two sheets of waxed paper to form an 8½-inch round ¼ inch thick. Remove one sheet of waxed paper and place the dough, paper side up, on top of the filling. Peel off the remaining paper. Press the sides of the pastry down and crimp to form a seal between the top crust and the side. Cut several slits in the top of the dough for air vents.

7. Roll scraps of dough into a circle and cut out decorative shapes (leaves, hearts). Place the shapes around the edges.

8. To make the glaze, lightly beat the egg yolk with the water. Brush the top of the tart with the glaze. (The tart can be prepared several hours in advance to this point, covered, and refrigerated.)

9. When you are ready to bake the tart, preheat the oven to 400° F.

10. Bake the tart on the center shelf of the oven for 45 minutes. Lower the temperature to 375° F and bake 15 minutes more. Remove the pan from the oven and cool to room temperature.

Serves 6

Mushroom and Scallop Turnovers

When I was asked to create a special dinner for the governor of Ohio, Richard Celeste, I decided to serve this first course. I was delighted that the governor, as well as his guests, loved this dish.

Filling
6 tablespoons (¾ stick) unsalted butter
¾ pound mushrooms, cleaned and sliced thin through the stems
1 tablespoon finely chopped garlic
⅓ cup dry sherry
¾ pound bay scallops (if small, leave whole; if large, cut in half)
¾ cup toasted almonds (see Index)
¾ cup grated Gruyère cheese
2 tablespoons all-purpose flour
3 tablespoons sour cream
2 tablespoons heavy or whipping cream
1 tablespoon chopped fresh tarragon, or 1 teaspoon dried
2 tablespoons chopped fresh chives
Salt to taste
Cayenne pepper to taste
Freshly ground black pepper to taste

Phyllo
10 thick phyllo sheets, 14 x 18 inches each, thawed
1 cup (2 sticks) unsalted butter, melted
¾ cup dry bread crumbs
Watercress sprigs, for garnish

GREAT ACCOMPANIMENTS

To follow these turnovers, I often serve Marinated Roast Racks of Lamb, steamed fresh asparagus, and Wild Rice and Pine Nut Pilaf. Lemon Cassis Mousse then ends the menu.

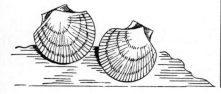

1. To prepare the filling, melt the butter in a large skillet over medium-high heat. When it is hot, add the mushrooms and garlic and sauté about 4 minutes. Stir in the sherry and cook, stirring, 3 to 4 minutes.

2. When most of the liquid has evaporated from the skillet, add the scallops and cook, stirring, until they are opaque, about 4 minutes. Then add the almonds, Gruyère, and flour, and toss and cook another 2 minutes.

3. Remove the skillet from the heat. Mix the sour cream and heavy cream together and add to the skillet. Stir in the tarragon and chives. Taste the mixture and season to taste with salt, cayenne pepper, and black pepper. Set aside. (The filling can be made several hours in advance, covered, and refrigerated.)

4. To assemble the phyllo turnovers, place the phyllo sheets on a work surface and cover with a lightly moistened kitchen towel. Place a single phyllo sheet on a work surface with the short side in front of you, and brush with melted butter. Sprinkle a tablespoon of bread crumbs over the phyllo sheet. Then fold the long sides toward the center so they slightly overlap. Brush with butter.

5. Place ⅓ cup of the filling on one corner of the dough. Then fold the dough diagonally, like a flag, so that the filling is enclosed in a triangle. Continue folding it up until all the dough is used. Trim any excess dough so you have a neat triangular package. Brush the turnover with butter. Place the turnover on a baking sheet. Continue in this manner until you have ten packages. (The turnovers can be made several hours in advance. Cover with a lightly moistened kitchen towel, then wrap in plastic wrap and refrigerate.)

6. When you are ready to bake the turnovers, preheat the oven to 375° F.

7. Bake on the center shelf of the oven until golden, about 15 to 20 minutes. Remove, and cool 4 to 5 minutes. Serve each turnover on a salad plate garnished with watercress sprigs.

Serves 10

A COOK'S REFLECTIONS

The word "timbale" has undergone several changes of meaning in the cooking repertoire. Originally a timbale (from the Arabic *thabal,* meaning "drum") was defined as a small metal receptacle, round in shape and intended to hold a beverage. Later the word was used to describe various types of bowls made of metal, pottery, or china. Then the term came to be applied to the food itself, which was baked in a pie crust shaped by a mold. Today the word most often refers to a custard-like mixture, similar to the basic filling used in quiches, which has been baked in a mold, then unmolded, and is often accompanied by a sauce.

Shrimp and Scallop Timbales

This seafood dish—a beautiful blend of colors, textures, and tastes—takes time to prepare, but it is worth the effort.

Special equipment: Six ½-cup timbale molds, ramekins, or soufflé dishes; food processor

Tomato Watercress Sauce
3 tablespoons unsalted butter
½ cup chopped shallots
1 can (28 ounces) Italian-style tomatoes, drained well and
*   coarsely chopped*
Pinch of sugar
¾ teaspoon dried thyme
½ teaspoon salt
¼ teaspoon freshly ground pepper
1 cup homemade chicken stock (see Index) or good-quality canned
*   broth*
¼ cup heavy or whipping cream
½ cup chopped watercress leaves (no stems)

Timbales
4 ounces uncooked, shelled, deveined shrimp (6 ounces unshelled)
4 ounces bay scallops
1 tablespoon unsalted butter
1½ teaspoons finely chopped garlic
¼ cup finely chopped shallots
½ cup heavy or whipping cream
Grating of fresh nutmeg
½ teaspoon salt
¼ teaspoon freshly ground white pepper
Several dashes of hot pepper sauce
3 large eggs
6 dollops red or black caviar, for garnish (optional)
6 watercress sprigs, for garnish

1. To prepare the sauce, melt the butter in a medium-size skillet over medium heat. Add the shallots and cook, stirring, for 3 to 4 minutes. Don't let the shallots brown. Add the tomatoes and toss well. Add the sugar, thyme, salt, and pepper, and mix. Then add the stock. Simmer, uncovered, until the tomatoes are quite soft and the

mixture resembles a purée, about 20 minutes.

2. Purée the tomato mixture in a food processor, blender, or food mill. Return the sauce to the skillet and add the cream. Cook over high heat until the sauce has reduced and coats the back of a spoon. Taste, and add more salt and pepper if desired. (The sauce may be made a day in advance to this point. Refrigerate, covered, until needed.)

3. To prepare the timbales, preheat the oven to 350° F.

4. Purée the shrimp and scallops in a food processor until you have a paste. Melt the butter in a small skillet and sauté the garlic and shallots 3 to 4 minutes. Add the garlic and shallots to the food processor and process several seconds.

5. Pour the cream through the feed tube while the machine is running. Process until the mixture is very smooth. Add the nutmeg, salt, white pepper, hot pepper sauce, and eggs. Process only a few seconds more, until seasonings and eggs are incorporated.

6. Generously butter the bottom and sides of six ½-cup timbale molds, ramekins, or soufflé dishes. Cut rounds of waxed paper to fit the bottom of the molds. Butter the paper and place it in the molds, butter side up. Fill each mold three-quarters full with the shrimp mixture. Put the molds in an ovenproof baking pan. Fill the pan with enough simmering water to come halfway up the side of the molds. Place the baking pan in the oven, and bake until a knife inserted in the center of a timbale comes out clean, 15 to 20 minutes.

7. While the timbales are baking, reheat the sauce until simmering. Then add the watercress leaves and cook only 1 minute more.

8. Remove the molds from the pan and run a knife around the inside edge; invert the molds and rap them forcefully on a work counter to release the timbales. Remove the waxed paper from the top of each timbale. If the unmolded timbales do not stand straight, slice a thin layer off the bottom so they rest flat.

9. Ladle enough sauce on six warmed salad plates to coat the bottoms generously. Arrange a timbale on each plate in the center of the sauce. Place a dollop of caviar on top of each timbale, and garnish with a sprig of watercress. Serve hot.

Serves 6

A COOK'S REFLECTIONS

Gnocchi can be prepared in several ways. They can be made with a paste of flour, water, butter, and eggs, or with a combination of mashed potatoes, flour, and eggs. These types of gnocchi are usually cut into small cylinder shapes and then poached in simmering water or stock.

Gnocchi with Sun-Dried Tomatoes and Basil

When I was first married and a totally inexperienced cook, my husband and I were invited to dinner by Italian friends, who served us gnocchi. We had never sampled these Italian "dumplings" before, but we both agreed that they were addictive. Over the years I have made gnocchi countless times—this is one of my variations.

Special equipment: 1½- to 2-inch diamond-shaped or round cookie cutter

1 quart milk
1 cup regular or quick-cooking farina (not instant), such as
  Cream of Wheat
1 cup grated imported Parmesan cheese
2 teaspoons salt
2 large egg yolks
7 tablespoons unsalted butter
⅓ cup finely chopped sun-dried tomatoes, packing oil drained
¼ cup chopped fresh basil
8 sprigs basil, for garnish

1. Heat the milk in a heavy saucepan over medium heat until hot but not boiling. Lower the heat and add the farina, pouring it in a thin, slow stream and beating it steadily with a whisk. Continue beating until it forms a thick mass on the whisk. This will take 5 to 10 minutes with regular farina but less time with quick farina.

2. Remove the saucepan from the heat and add ⅔ cup of the Parmesan cheese, the salt, egg yolks, and 2 tablespoons of the butter. Mix rapidly, to avoid coagulating the eggs, until all the ingredients are well blended. Then stir in the sun-dried tomatoes and the chopped basil.

3. Moisten a clean countertop with cold water and spread the farina mixture on it, using a spatula or broad-bladed knife to spread it to an even thickness of about ½ inch. Let the mixture cool completely. (Or spread the mixture on a baking sheet and refrigerate it for 30 minutes.)

4. With a 1½- to 2-inch diamond-shaped cookie cutter or a round cutter of similar size, cut diamonds or rounds out of the farina and

AT THE MARKET

Sun-dried tomatoes have a strong, distinctive taste and are one of my favorite ''new'' ingredients for cooking. An Italian product that has in the last few years begun to appear in our markets, they are made by halving and seeding fresh tomatoes, then drying them under special conditions. These dark red dried tomatoes are marinated, along with herbs, in olive oil for several weeks and then packed in virgin olive oil.

Even a small jar of imported sun-dried tomatoes is fairly expensive, but because their taste is robust, a little goes a long way. They are especially good chopped and added to herbed bread stuffings for meat and poultry. And mushroom caps mounded with a mixture of sautéed chopped sun-dried tomatoes, shallots, parsley, and bread crumbs are superb. These tomatoes sometimes tend to be salty, so you may want to add less salt in recipes where they are included.

Store unused sun-dried tomatoes in the refrigerator in their oil with the jar tightly closed. Before using, let sit at room temperature for 30 minutes to allow the oil to liquify.

place them in a single layer in a generously buttered baking pan. (If you do not have a cutter, you can shape the gnocchi by using a heaping tablespoon of the mixture and shaping it into a ball. Then flatten the ball into a round and place it on the baking pan.)

5. Cut the remaining 5 tablespoons butter into small pieces and dot the gnocchi with the butter. (Gnocchi may be made several hours in advance to this point and covered with plastic wrap and refrigerated.)

6. When you are ready to bake the gnocchi, preheat the oven to 350° F.

7. Place the baking pan in the oven and bake until the gnocchi are lightly browned, 30 to 40 minutes. Remove the pan from the oven. Use a metal spatula to remove the gnocchi. Arrange about 6 gnocchi on each of eight salad plates. Sprinkle each serving with some of the remaining Parmesan cheese, and garnish with a sprig of basil.

Makes 4 dozen or more

MAIN EVENTS

When I teach menu classes at La Belle Pomme, I always explain how important it is to carefully select a meal's entrée, and I offer suggestions for making a wise choice. First, look at the guest list. If it's a large party, a buffet for example, the main course should be one that can be easily cooked for a crowd and that will hold up well on a serving table. If the dinner is a small sit-down affair, sautéing or broiling foods at the last minute can be managed efficiently.

Another consideration is the type of diners you will have at your table. Are they people who prefer simple preparations or do they have sophisticated tastes? Even those without adventurous palates seem to love pasta, so I often serve one of the pasta entrées in this section. On the other hand, I will pull out all the stops for a group of "good eaters," offering them such dishes as the Veal Chops Stuffed with Chèvre and Dill or the Roast Stuffed Filet of Beef.

And, of course, I keep the season in mind—an essential element in preparing a menu.

We usually spend the longest part of any meal enjoying the main course, so time spent carefully selecting the entrée will always be well rewarded.

PASTAS

If in doubt, serve pasta! This has become my credo, whether I'm planning a last-minute family supper or a special-occasion dinner. People seem to love pasta in every way, shape, and form, and why not? It is easy and quick to assemble and lends itself beautifully to dozens of variations. Certainly, the recipes included in this section reflect the versatility of pasta. There's the elegant Epicure's Pasta—linguine lightly coated with a cream sauce, then tossed with a julienne of smoked salmon and fresh snow peas—the hearty Fettuccine with Sausage, Red Peppers, and Mushrooms (my son's favorite), and the unusual Szechuan-Peppered Chicken and Pasta.

Freshly made pasta is always my first choice, but if time is a consideration, there are many fine commercial products available today. They can be substituted in any of these recipes.

AT THE MARKET

Szechuan peppercorns are available in Oriental markets or in the Oriental products section in some grocery stores. Stored in a tightly covered glass jar, they will keep for up to a year.

Szechuan-Peppered Chicken and Pasta

Cleaning my kitchen the day after I had cooked a fairly large Chinese buffet, I found an entire bag of unused Szechuan peppercorns. These peppercorns are unlike any others I know. Mildly hot and slightly sweet at the same time, they have a delicate taste and are a brownish red color. Since I like these peppers so much, I decided to try them in a non-Chinese preparation. In this dish, the chicken is marinated in fresh lemon juice, then rubbed generously with the crushed peppercorns, and finally sautéed quickly in olive oil. Unfettered by ethnic tradition, I serve the chicken over buttered fettuccine noodles mixed with Parmesan cheese.

6 tablespoons fresh lemon juice (about 2 lemons)
8 large boneless, skinless chicken breast halves
3 tablespoons whole Szechuan peppercorns (see "At the Market")
Salt to taste
3 tablespoons olive oil, plus more if needed
1½ tablespoons salt
1¼ pounds fresh fettuccine noodles (see Index), or 1 pound good-
*   quality dry fettuccine*
2 tablespoons unsalted butter, melted
⅓ cup grated imported Parmesan cheese
3 tablespoons chopped fresh parsley, for garnish

1. Place the lemon juice in a medium-size shallow bowl or dish (not aluminum), and add the chicken breasts. Marinate 25 to 30 minutes, turning several times. Drain the chicken breasts and pat them dry with paper towels.

2. Crush the peppercorns coarsely by placing them between two pieces of waxed paper and crushing with a meat pounder or rolling with a rolling pin. Salt each piece of chicken lightly and then press the peppercorns in on both sides.

3. Heat the olive oil over medium-high heat in a skillet large enough to contain the chicken pieces in a single layer. Or use two skillets and divide the oil evenly between them. When the oil is quite hot but not smoking, add the chicken and cook 8 to 9 minutes, turning several times, until the chicken is golden. When the chicken is done it will spring back when touched lightly with a finger and the juices will

GREAT ACCOMPANIMENTS

Fresh sautéed green beans and a seasonal salad tossed in a vinaigrette make nice accompaniments to this chicken. The Apricot Sorbet is a good light dessert to offer.

run clear when the meat is pierced with a knife.

4. While the chicken is sautéing, bring 4 quarts of water to a boil in a large heavy pot over high heat. Add the 1½ tablespoons salt and the fettuccine to the water and stir with a long-handled spoon. Cook until *al dente,* tender but still firm to the bite. Fresh pasta will cook in 2 to 3 minutes, while dried pasta will take longer. Drain the pasta well in a strainer or colander. Place it in a large bowl and toss with the melted butter and Parmesan cheese.

5. To serve, place the pasta on a heated serving dish, arrange the chicken pieces on top, and sprinkle with parsley. Serve immediately.

Serves 4 to 8

Fettuccine with Sausage, Red Peppers, and Mushrooms

On a weekend trip to Washington, D.C., one winter, I ate in a small Italian restaurant called Cantina d'Italia. Everything I sampled was very good, but one particular dish—tri-colored red, white, and green pasta tossed with fried sausage, crushed red peppers, and tomatoes—was outstanding. When I came home, I made a few changes (using all white pasta noodles and replacing the tomatoes with sweet red peppers) and reproduced this dish in my own kitchen. Then I used the recipe in my weekly Columbus food column. Nothing could have pleased me more than when a local fireman called to tell me he had seen the recipe and was planning to make it for his co-workers.

4 tablespoons olive oil
1 pound hot Italian sausages
1 medium onion, halved vertically and cut into ¼-inch slices
3 red bell peppers, cored, seeded, and cut into ¼-inch-wide strips
12 ounces mushrooms, cleaned and thinly sliced through the
*   stems*
2 cups heavy or whipping cream
1½ tablespoons salt
1¼ pounds fresh fettuccine noodles (see Index), or 1 pound good-
*   quality dry fettuccine*
1½ cups grated imported Parmesan cheese
Salt to taste

1. Heat the olive oil in a large heavy skillet over medium-high heat. Remove the casing from the sausages, break the meat into very small pieces, and add to the hot oil. Cook, tossing frequently, until the sausage is lightly browned, 5 to 7 minutes.

2. Add the onion and continue to cook, stirring, until translucent, 3 to 4 minutes. Then lower the heat, add the red peppers and the mushrooms, and cook, stirring, until the peppers and mushrooms are tender, 5 minutes or longer. The sausage should be crispy and the mushrooms browned at this point. Remove from the heat and drain on paper towels.

3. Put the cream in a large heavy saucepan and place over high heat. Cook until the liquid has reduced by half and has thickened, about 10 minutes. Remove from the heat. (Both the sausage mixture and the cream can be prepared several hours in advance to this point. Refrigerate covered until needed.)

GREAT ACCOMPANIMENTS

I always serve this pasta dish, which is very filling, with a basket of Garlic Toasts and a salad of spinach, romaine and Boston lettuce dressed with a vinaigrette. This still leaves a little room for the Espresso Cheesecake, a great finale.

4. When you are ready to prepare the pasta, bring 4 quarts of water to a boil in a large heavy pot over high heat. Add the 1½ tablespoons salt and the fettuccine to the water and stir with a long-handled spoon. Cook until the pasta is *al dente,* tender but still firm to the bite. Fresh pasta will cook in only 2 to 3 minutes, while dried pasta will take longer. Drain the pasta well in a strainer or colander, and then place it in a large bowl.

5. Reheat the sausage mixture, stirring, until hot. Reheat the cream until hot.

6. Toss the pasta with the sausage mixture and the cream. Then add 1 cup of the cheese and toss again. Taste, and add salt if desired.

7. To serve, arrange the pasta on a heated serving platter and sprinkle with the remaining ½ cup cheese. Serve immediately.

Serves 4

A COOK'S REFLECTIONS

Shelling Shrimp: Although we shell literally hundreds of pounds of shrimp every year for classes at La Belle Pomme, we haven't discovered a way to speed the process. We just put our favorite tapes in the tape deck and listen to music while we work!

You can cook shrimp in the shell and then shell and devein them or you can remove the shells and veins before cooking. We do more of the latter at the school. For deveining, we've found that either a small beak-shaped paring knife or a shrimp deveiner, a special tool 4 to 5 inches long with a curved, flat blade, makes easier work of removing the veins.

Fettuccine with Shrimp and Garlic Butter

This is one of my students' favorite dishes. It is simple to prepare (especially for beginning pasta cooks), makes a beautiful presentation, and is absolutely delicious!

Garlic Butter (recipe follows)
1 pound large shrimp in the shell
4 tablespoons (½ stick) unsalted butter
2 tablespoons olive oil
½ cup dry white wine
1½ tablespoons salt
1¼ pounds fresh fettuccine noodles (see Index), or 1 pound good-
*   quality dry fettuccine*
¼ cup heavy or whipping cream
⅔ cup grated imported Parmesan cheese
⅔ cup chopped fresh parsley
Salt and freshly ground pepper to taste

1. When you are ready to prepare the fettuccine and shrimp, bring the Garlic Butter to room temperature.

2. Shell and devein the shrimp.

3. Heat the butter and the olive oil in a medium-size skillet over medium heat. When the butter has melted and the mixture is hot, add the shrimp and cook, stirring, until they turn pink and curl up, 2 to 3 minutes. Add the wine and cook only 2 minutes more. Remove from the heat.

4. Bring 4 quarts of water to a boil in a large heavy pot over high heat. Add the 1½ tablespoons salt and the fettuccine to the water and stir with a long-handled spoon. Cook until the pasta is *al dente,* tender but still firm to the bite. Fresh pasta will cook in only 2 to 3 minutes, while dried pasta will take longer. Drain the pasta well in a strainer or colander and then place it in a large bowl.

5. Gently reheat the shrimp and wine in the skillet, then add to the fettuccine and toss. Stir in the Garlic Butter and mix well until all the butter has melted. Stir in the cream, grated cheese, and half the parsley. Mix well.

6. Taste the pasta, and add salt and pepper as desired.

GREAT ACCOMPANIMENTS

I like to serve this pasta with a romaine salad tossed in a vinaigrette, along with a basket of hot crusty Italian bread. The Red Grape and Green Grape Sorbets make an excellent dessert.

7. To serve, mound the pasta on a large heated serving platter and sprinkle with the remaining parsley. Serve immediately.

Serves 4

GARLIC BUTTER

¾ cup (1½ sticks) unsalted butter, at room temperature
2 teaspoons very finely chopped garlic
3 tablespoons finely chopped shallots
½ cup chopped fresh parsley
⅛ teaspoon salt
Freshly ground pepper to taste

Place all the ingredients in a mixing bowl and mix well to incorporate. Cover and refrigerate. Bring to room temperature before using. (The butter can be made 2 days in advance and kept refrigerated.)

Makes approximately ¾ cup

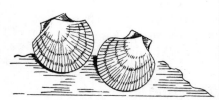

Pasta with Lobster and Scallops

Elegant and sophisticated, this is a pasta to serve on very special occasions. The sauce and the lobsters can be cooked ahead so that there is not much work at the last minute. With both lobster and scallops as ingredients, this is an expensive dish to prepare, but it's so good it's worth it!

1½ tablespoons salt
1¼ pounds fresh linguine or fettuccine noodles (see Index),
    or 1 pound good-quality dry noodles
5 tablespoons unsalted butter
1 pound sea scallops, well rinsed and patted dry
Cooked Lobster (recipe follows)
Tomato Sauce (recipe follows)
2½ cups julienned fresh spinach leaves (cleaned, dried, and
    stemmed)
½ cup grated imported Parmesan cheese

1. Bring 4 quarts of water to a boil in a large heavy pot over high heat. Add the salt and the linguine or fettuccine to the water and stir

A COOK'S REFLECTIONS

To *julienne* means to cut foods into thin, matchstick strips. Most often vegetables, and sometimes cheese or meats, are julienned.

According to Craig Claiborne in his *New York Times Food Encyclopedia*, the word *julienne* most likely originated in the late seventeenth century, and probably derives from a chef named Julien, who invented the technique. However, as Mr. Claiborne so rightly points out, *julienne* is the feminine form of Julien, but, he concludes, no woman, especially in seventeenth-century France, would have been given credit for her invention!

with a long-handled spoon. Cook until the pasta is *al dente,* tender but still firm to the bite. Fresh pasta will cook in only 2 to 3 minutes, while dried pasta will take longer. Drain the pasta well in a strainer or colander, and then place it in a large bowl. Toss with 2 tablespoons of the butter, and cover with foil to keep warm.

2. Melt the remaining 3 tablespoons butter in a large heavy skillet over medium-high heat. When it is hot, add the scallops and sauté, tossing frequently, until the scallops are opaque, about 4 minutes. Add the lobster meat and cook, stirring, until the lobster is heated through, only 2 to 3 minutes. Remove and keep warm.

3. Reheat the Tomato Sauce and add the julienned spinach to it. Cook for 1 minute.

4. Arrange beds of pasta on six warm dinner plates. Ladle the sauce over the pasta. Then use a slotted spoon to arrange the scallops and lobster meat over the sauce. Sprinkle each serving with Parmesan cheese, and serve immediately.

Serves 6

COOKED LOBSTER

Special equipment: Extra-large stockpot or lobster pot; nutcracker; kitchen shears

Salt (see Step 1)
2 live lobsters (1¼ to 1½ pounds each)

1. Bring at least 4 quarts water to a boil in an extra-large stockpot. Add 1 tablespoon salt for each quart of water. When the water returns to a boil, add the lobsters, lower the heat, cover, and cook at a simmer, 10 to 12 minutes. To test for doneness, see "A Cook's Reflections," page 105.

2. Remove the lobsters from the pot and run under cold water to cool. Gently crack the shell with a nutcracker so you don't crush the flesh underneath. Use kitchen shears to cut open the shell of the claws and the tail and remove the meat. (You only need the claw and tail meat for this dish. Any additional meat picked out of the legs or body can be enjoyed separately.) Cut the meat into 1-inch pieces, cover it with plastic wrap, and refrigerate. (The lobsters can be cooked several hours in advance.)

GREAT ACCOMPANIMENTS

Since this is a rich and filling dish, I serve with it just a salad of mixed greens (Boston, Bibb, and leaf lettuce) and sliced mushrooms tossed in a red wine vinaigrette, plus hot buttered French bread. The Frozen Chocolate Marbled Mousse would be a wonderful dessert to offer with this special menu.

TOMATO SAUCE

⅓ cup olive oil
1 cup chopped onions
1 tablespoon chopped garlic
1 large can (35 ounces) Italian-style tomatoes, well drained and
    coarsely chopped
2 tablespoons chopped fresh basil, or 2 teaspoons dried
2 cups heavy or whipping cream
½ teaspoon salt
Freshly ground pepper to taste

1. Heat the olive oil in a medium-size skillet over medium-high heat. Add the onions and garlic and sauté until softened, 4 to 5 minutes. Add the tomatoes and basil and stir well. Lower the heat and cook at a simmer until the tomatoes are mushy, about 30 minutes. Remove from the heat and purée in a food processor, blender, or food mill.

2. Return the puréed sauce to the skillet over low heat. Add the cream, salt, and pepper. (The sauce can be made a day in advance and kept covered and refrigerated.)

Makes about 3½ cups

GREAT ACCOMPANIMENTS

A spinach salad with a light lemon dressing works well with this pasta, as does the Frozen Chocolate Marbled Mousse for dessert.

Fettuccine with Smoked Mozzarella and Zucchini

When I first tasted smoked mozzarella cheese, I was completely won over by its heady and provocative flavor. I immediately began to use it in all manner of dishes—I made savory tarts with it, prepared smoked mozzarella fritters, and even included it in some robust salads. This pasta dish, made with a generous amount of the surprisingly strong cheese, is one of the most interesting inventions I tried.

AT THE MARKET

Smoked mozzarella is sold in cheese shops and in specialty food stores. It is a small round cheese, faintly orange colored, with a soft rind or coating. It doesn't resemble plain, bland mozzarella at all. The smoked variety has an assertive flavor and adds a robust touch to any dish in which it is used.

Pancetta is Italian-style bacon that is salted rather than smoked and comes rolled in a spiral. If unavailable you can substitute a good-quality smoked bacon.

4 small zucchini

8 ounces pancetta (Italian-style bacon) or slab smoked bacon (rind removed)

1 pound smoked mozzarella cheese (rind removed), grated

2 cups heavy or whipping cream

3 tablespoons olive oil, plus more if needed

½ cup pine nuts

1 teaspoon finely chopped garlic

½ cup peeled, seeded, chopped tomatoes

Salt and freshly ground pepper to taste

1½ tablespoons salt

1¼ pounds fresh fettuccine noodles (see Index), or 1 pound good-quality dry fettuccine

2 tablespoons finely chopped fresh parsley, for garnish

1. Cut the zucchini into thin strips 1½ inches long and ¼ inch wide. Set aside.

2. Cut the pancetta or bacon into ¼-inch dice and set aside.

3. Combine the cheese and cream in a large heavy saucepan and place over medium-high heat. Cook, stirring constantly, until the cheese has melted and the mixture is smooth, 4 to 5 minutes. Remove the pan from the heat and set aside.

4. In a medium-size heavy skillet over medium-high heat, sauté, stirring, the pancetta (or bacon) cubes until crisp and lightly browned. Remove and drain on paper towels.

5. Pour all fat from the skillet. Then add the olive oil and place over medium heat. Add the pine nuts. Stir constantly and sauté until golden, only 2 to 3 minutes. Remove the nuts with a slotted spoon and drain on paper towels.

6. If there is not enough oil to make a very thin film on the bottom of the skillet, add some more and heat until hot. Then add the zucchini and cook over medium heat, tossing, until just crisp-tender, about 3 minutes. Add the garlic and the tomatoes and cook only 1 minute more. Return the pine nuts and bacon to the skillet and mix well. Remove the skillet from the heat. Taste, and add salt and pepper as needed.

7. To prepare the pasta, bring 4 quarts of water to a boil in a large heavy pot over high heat. Add the 1½ tablespoons salt and the fettuccine to the water and stir with a long-handled spoon. Cook until the pasta is *al dente,* tender but still firm to the bite. Fresh

pasta will cook in only 2 to 3 minutes, while dried pasta will take longer. Drain the pasta well in a strainer or colander, and then place it in a large bowl.

8. Reheat the cheese sauce, stirring continually. When it is hot, toss the pasta in the bowl with the sauce. Taste, and add salt and pepper if desired.

9. Reheat the zucchini mixture. Divide the pasta evenly among four heated dinner plates. Top each serving with some of the zucchini and pine nut mixture. Sprinkle with parsley. Serve immediately.

Serves 4

The Epicure's Pasta

As the name implies, this is a pasta for those with finely tuned palates. Its success depends on using the best possible ingredients— fine smoked salmon, fresh crisp snow peas, and homemade or good store-bought linguine. The pearly strands of pasta twirled with coral pieces of salmon and bright green pea pods make a beautiful dish.

6 ounces thin-sliced best-quality smoked salmon
1½ tablespoons plus ½ teaspoon salt
1¼ pounds fresh linguine noodles (see Index), or 1 pound good-
*   quality dry linguine*
6 ounces snow peas, trimmed on the diagonal
Cream Sauce (recipe follows)
Salt and white pepper to taste
¼ cup grated imported Parmesan cheese
3 tablespoons chopped fresh chives or parsley, for garnish

1. Cut the smoked salmon into thin strips 1½ inches long and ¼ inch wide. Set aside.

2. When you are ready to prepare the pasta, bring 4 quarts of water to a boil in a large heavy pot over high heat. (Put another pot with 2 quarts of water over high heat for step 3.) Add the 1½ tablespoons salt and the linguine to the water and stir with a long-handled spoon. Cook until the pasta is *al dente,* tender but still firm to the bite. Fresh pasta will cook in only 2 to 3 minutes, while dried pasta will take longer. Drain the pasta well in a strainer or colander, and then place it in a large bowl.

AS A VARIATION

Asparagus (cut into 2-inch diagonal pieces) or broccoli flowerets could be substituted for the snow peas. Parboil either vegetable until bright green and just tender.

Although I serve this seafood pasta as an entrée, it also could be offered as a first course to precede grilled lamb chops or roast chicken. The recipe would easily serve six when used this way.

GREAT ACCOMPANIMENTS

Cucumber and Watercress Salad is particularly good with this pasta, and the Spiced Madeleines, served with fresh strawberries or raspberries, makes an excellent dessert.

3. When the second pot of water comes to a boil, add the ½ teaspoon salt and the snow peas. Boil until the peas are bright green and just tender, 2 to 3 minutes. Remove from the heat, drain, and keep warm.

4. Reheat the Cream Sauce over low heat, stirring. When it is hot, add it to the pasta in the bowl and toss well. Then add the smoked salmon and the snow peas and toss again to mix. Taste, and add salt and white pepper as desired.

5. To serve the pasta, mound it on a heated serving platter. Sprinkle the top with Parmesan cheese and chopped chives. Serve immediately.

Serves 4

CREAM SAUCE

2 tablespoons unsalted butter
2 tablespoons all-purpose flour
2 cups heavy or whipping cream
½ cup grated imported Parmesan cheese
Generous grating of fresh nutmeg
Salt and white pepper to taste

1. Melt the butter in a medium-size heavy saucepan over medium heat. Add the flour and stir constantly for about 2 minutes, being careful not to let the mixture brown.

2. Whisk in the cream, continuing to whisk the mixture until it comes to a boil and thickens, 3 to 4 minutes. Then gradually whisk in the cheese. Remove the pan from the heat and stir in the nutmeg. Taste, and add salt and white pepper as desired. (The sauce can be made several hours in advance. Cover the top of the cooled sauce directly with plastic wrap, and refrigerate. Reheat over low heat, stirring constantly, before using.)

Makes 2 cups

Fettuccine with Prosciutto and Porcini Mushrooms

I have been doing variations of this simple and uncomplicated pasta for more years than I can remember. One of my students described it well, saying, "It is a perfect main course for someone who works all day, comes home tired, and still wants to serve a very good last-minute meal."

2 ounces dried porcini mushrooms
½ pound thinly sliced prosciutto
10 tablespoons (1¼ sticks) unsalted butter
2 cups broccoli flowerets
1½ tablespoons salt
1¼ pounds fresh fettuccine noodles (see Index), or 1 pound good-
*   quality dry fettuccine*
5 large egg yolks
1¾ cups heavy or whipping cream
Generous grating of fresh nutmeg
Salt and freshly ground pepper to taste
½ cup grated imported Parmesan cheese
4 tablespoons chopped fresh parsley, for garnish

1. Place the mushrooms in a small bowl and cover with warm water. Soak 30 minutes and drain. If the mushrooms seem very gritty, rinse them thoroughly to remove all dirt. Dry the mushrooms with paper towels and chop coarsely.

2. Cut the prosciutto into strips 4 inches long and ½ inch wide.

3. Melt 2 tablespoons of the butter in a medium skillet over high heat. When it is hot, add the mushrooms and stir. Sauté 3 to 4 minutes, then remove the skillet from the heat and set aside.

4. Place the broccoli flowerets in a large saucepan with boiling water to cover. Boil the broccoli until it is bright green and crisp-tender, 2 to 3 minutes. Remove from the heat and drain well. Pat the broccoli dry with paper towels, and reserve.

5. To prepare the pasta, bring 4 quarts of water to a boil in a large heavy pot over high heat. Add the 1½ tablespoons salt and the fettuccine to the water and stir with a long-handled spoon. Cook until the pasta is *al dente,* tender but still firm to the bite. Fresh

GREAT ACCOMPANIMENTS

This dish is filling and a meal in itself. A light mixed-greens salad in a lemon vinaigrette would go well with it, and fresh strawberries with a plate of Amaretto Brownies makes a fine dessert.

pasta will cook in only 2 to 3 minutes, while dried pasta will take longer.

6. When you put the pasta water on to boil, start to prepare the sauce: Combine the egg yolks, cream, and nutmeg in a mixing bowl and whisk together until well incorporated. In a large heavy pot, melt 4 tablespoons of the butter over medium heat. When it is hot, add the prosciutto and toss. Sauté for 2 to 3 minutes. Carefully add the cream mixture to the pot. Whisk constantly until the sauce thickens lightly. Watch it carefully and keep stirring so the eggs do not curdle. Lower the heat if necessary.

7. When the sauce is done, add the reserved mushrooms and broccoli to it and stir well, just to heat through. If the pasta is still not done at this point, remove the sauce from the heat. Then reheat it gently, stirring, over *low* heat to rewarm.

8. When the pasta is cooked, drain it well and place it in a large bowl. Add the remaining 4 tablespoons butter and toss until it has melted. Then add the warm sauce and toss again. Taste, and add salt and pepper as needed.

9. To serve, mound the pasta on a large heated serving plate. Sprinkle the top with Parmesan cheese and chopped parsley. Serve immediately.

Serves 4

Lasagne with Spinach, Artichokes, and Lemon

My students are wild about the taste and appearance of this dish. Made with Mornay sauce and assembled by layering fresh spinach leaves, ricotta cheese, and a zesty artichoke, lemon, and prosciutto filling between the noodles, this lasagne is a delicious and different alternative to the usual tomato and sausage variety. It's perfect to serve for large crowds because it can be readied a day in advance and one recipe will feed twelve generously.

A COOK'S REFLECTIONS

The zest of a citrus fruit is the thin, colored outer layer. It contains the oils of the fruit and thus has a very strong flavor. If you grate the fruit to remove the zest, be certain to use a sharp grater and avoid the white pith underneath, which has a bitter taste.

In addition to grating, there are two other ways to obtain zest. You can use a sharp paring knife to remove thin strips of the skin from the fruit and then mince it, or you can use a special tool called a zester to scrape small flecks of the skin from the fruit.

Mornay Sauce

¾ cup (1½ sticks) unsalted butter
¾ cup all-purpose flour
5 cups milk
1 cup grated imported Parmesan cheese
1 teaspoon salt
1 teaspoon white pepper

Lasagne Noodles

2 tablespoons salt
1¼ pounds fresh lasagne noodles (see Index), or 8 ounces good-quality dry lasagne (12 to 15 noodles)

Artichoke Filling

2 packages (9 ounces each) frozen artichoke hearts, thawed
6 ounces thinly sliced prosciutto
¼ cup olive oil
3 cups chopped leeks, white parts only
1 tablespoon finely chopped garlic
5 teaspoons coarsely grated lemon zest
Salt to taste

Cheese and Spinach Filling

6 ounces fresh spinach leaves, trimmed, well rinsed, and patted dry
1 pound ricotta cheese
1 cup grated imported Parmesan cheese
Salt and white pepper to taste
1 pound mozzarella cheese, coarsely grated

1. To prepare the sauce, melt the butter in a large heavy saucepan over medium heat. When it is hot, add the flour and stir steadily until the mixture is smooth, about 2 minutes. Gradually whisk in the milk. Cook, whisking constantly, until the mixture thickens and coats the back of a spoon, 3 to 4 minutes. Then stir in the Parmesan cheese, a little at a time. Add the salt and white pepper. Remove from the heat and reserve.

2. Bring 6 quarts of water to a boil in a large heavy pot over high heat. Add 2 tablespoons salt and the lasagne noodles to the water and stir with a long-handled spoon. Cook until the noodles are *al dente,* tender but still firm to the bite. (Fresh noodles will cook more quickly than the dried variety.) Drain the noodles well in a strainer or colander, and dry on clean kitchen towels. Reserve.

GREAT ACCOMPANIMENTS

*When I taught this dish, I offered
with it a salad of mixed greens with
sliced mushrooms and walnuts,
dressed in a balsamic vinaigrette.
Pink Grapefruit Sorbet with Campari won rave reviews as the ideal
conclusion to this menu!*

3. To prepare the artichoke filling, first dry the defrosted artichoke hearts and cut them into ½-inch-wide strips. Cut the prosciutto into strips 3 inches long and ½ inch wide.

4. Heat the olive oil in a large heavy skillet over medium heat. When the oil is hot, add the leeks and garlic and cook, stirring, about 5 minutes. Do not let them brown. Add the artichoke hearts and prosciutto; cook 2 to 3 minutes more, stirring frequently. Remove from the heat and stir in the lemon zest. Taste the mixture, and add salt as desired. Reserve.

5. Preheat the oven to 350° F.

6. Spread a third of the Mornay sauce in a 4-quart baking pan (14 x 10 inches). Lay a third of the noodles over the sauce. Spread half the spinach leaves over the noodles.

7. Combine the ricotta with the Parmesan cheese in a mixing bowl and stir well. Taste, and season with salt and white pepper as desired. Spread half this cheese mixture over the spinach leaves. Sprinkle with a third of the grated mozzarella.

8. Spread half of the artichoke filling over the cheese layer, and cover with another third of the noodles.

9. For the next layer, spread a third of the sauce over the noodles and cover with the remaining spinach leaves. Spread the remaining ricotta mixture over the spinach, and top with another third of the grated mozzarella. Spread the remaining artichoke filling over the cheese layer.

10. Layer the final third of the lasagne noodles over the artichoke filling. Cover with the remaining sauce, and sprinkle with the rest of the grated mozzarella. (This lasagne can be completely assembled a day in advance. Cover with plastic wrap and refrigerate. Bring to room temperature, remove plastic wrap, and bake as directed.)

11. Bake the lasagne until it is hot and lightly browned, 45 to 50 minutes. Cool 10 to 15 minutes, and then slice and serve.

Serves 12

SEAFOOD

When I moved to Columbus in the early 1970s, there were only a handful of fish markets in that inland Ohio city of over 1 million. By 1985 the scene was quite different: most of our large groceries had a fresh-fish counter, and even small corner food stores stocked such shellfish as oysters and shrimp. And this same change of scene took place in many other parts of the country as well. Since I love to cook seafood, nothing could have pleased me more than this Neptunian transformation! Being able to buy scallops, shrimp, lobster, salmon, sole, or swordfish regularly in our markets has served as inspiration for such special dishes as the Salmon Filets Baked with Lemons, Scallions, and Parsley and the Batter-Fried Sea Scallops with Dill Mayonnaise. Of course, all dishes in this collection should always be made with the freshest fish available.

AT THE MARKET

Students often ask me how to determine whether the shrimp are small, medium, or large. I use the following guidelines for shrimp still in the shell:

Medium: 31 to 40 per pound
Large: 21 to 30 per pound
Extra large: 16 to 20 per pound
Jumbo: 10 to 15 per pound

Garlic Shrimp with Watercress Rice

Without a doubt the most popular seafood in Columbus, Ohio, where I live, is shrimp—no matter how it is prepared. Maybe it's because we are a landlocked town and this shellfish is one of the few fish we see every day in our markets (shipped in from other parts of the country). I have prepared shrimp in countless ways for my classes, and this recipe is one of the easiest and most attractive preparations.

2 pounds large shrimp in the shell
8 tablespoons (1 stick) unsalted butter
4 teaspoons very finely chopped garlic
3 tablespoons chopped fresh chives
2 teaspoons fresh thyme leaves, or ¾ teaspoon dried (not powdered)
1 teaspoon grated lemon zest
Salt to taste
⅛ teaspoon cayenne pepper, or to taste
Watercress Rice (recipe follows)
6 thin lemon slices, for garnish
6 sprigs watercress, for garnish

1. Shell and devein the shrimp. Set them aside.

2. Melt the butter in a large heavy skillet over medium-high heat. When it is hot, add the garlic and cook, stirring, only 30 seconds. Then add the shrimp and cook, stirring, until they turn pink and curl, only 4 to 5 minutes. Add the chives, thyme, and lemon zest. Cook, stirring continually, 1 minute more. Season the shrimp to taste with salt and cayenne pepper (you may want less than ⅛ teaspoon).

3. To serve, warm four dinner plates. Arrange some Watercress Rice in a ring on each plate. Place a serving of the shrimp mixture in the center of the ring. Slit each lemon slice just enough so that you can twist it, then garnish each serving with a twist of lemon and a sprig of watercress.

Serves 4

GREAT ACCOMPANIMENTS

If you make this dish in the summer, serve the Chilled Carrot Soup as a first course; in cooler weather offer the Cream of Asparagus Soup. For dessert, either the Coconut Cream Mousse Pie or the Raspberry Mousse Pie make a wonderful conclusion.

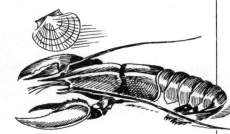

WATERCRESS RICE

6 tablespoons (¾ stick) unsalted butter
2 cups long-grain rice
4 cups homemade chicken stock (see Index) or good-quality canned broth
Salt to taste
1 cup freshly chopped watercress leaves (no stems)

1. Melt the butter in a large heavy saucepan over medium-high heat. Add the rice and toss until all the grains are coated with butter. Add the stock, and salt to taste. Bring the mixture to a simmer, cover, and reduce the heat to low. Cook until all the liquid has been absorbed, 20 to 30 minutes. After the first 20 minutes, check often to see when the liquid has been absorbed. Remove the pan from the heat and keep covered until ready to use. (You may place the saucepan in a 250° F oven to hold for 30 to 45 minutes before serving if needed.)

2. When you are ready to serve the rice, add the watercress leaves and toss well. Serve immediately.

Serves 4

Lobster and Scallops with Braised Leeks and Endive

When Jim Budros, a financial planner by vocation and a superb cook and cooking teacher by avocation, participated in the Columbus March of Dimes Gourmet Gala, he won first prize for this elegant, sophisticated creation. Pierre Franey was one of the judges that night, and he later printed Jim's recipe in the *New York Times Magazine*, praising it as among the finest dishes presented at these events throughout the country.

This dish will require last minute preparation and should then be served immediately. To do this, have everything ready and out on the counter, including all foods and utensils. Then start to cook.

Special equipment: Extra-large kettle or lobster pot

A COOK'S REFLECTIONS

Lobsters: There are two ways to kill a lobster. You can cut through the spinal cord by inserting a sharp knife in the space between the head and the body, or you can plunge the lobster head first in a pot of boiling water. The second method is quicker and less difficult for the squeamish cook, and is the one I recommend for this recipe.

Tom and Peggy Turgeon, teachers at La Belle Pomme, and good friends, spend their summers in Maine and are lobster chefs *par excellence.* They tell me that when they want to cook lobsters, they simply walk down to the coast, fill a bucket with seawater and come home. Most of us aren't lucky enough to have that option, so when boiling lobsters in tap water, add a generous amount of salt to simulate the sea; about 1 tablespoon salt per quart is a good guide. The Turgeons also recommend adding the seaweed in which many live lobsters come packaged to the cooking liquid.

The cooking time for lobsters varies depending on size. Add the lobsters to the pot of boiling water and when the water returns to boiling, start timing. A 1-pound lobster will take 10 to 12 minutes. You should add about 3 minutes for each additional pound. One good way to test for doneness is to remove the lobster from the boiling water and carefully twist one of the thin legs from the body. If the leg pulls off easily and quickly, the lobster should be done.

¾ pound (3 large) Belgian endive
¾ pound (2 to 3) leeks, white parts and tender green stems only
Salt (see Step 3)
2 live lobsters (about 1¼ pounds each)
¾ cup (1½ sticks) unsalted butter
Freshly ground pepper to taste
¼ cup dry white wine
1 pound bay scallops, well rinsed and patted dry
2 tablespoons finely chopped shallots
¼ cup white wine vinegar
½ cup heavy or whipping cream
6 teaspoons black caviar

1. Trim the tough ends from the endive and trim away any brown spots on the leaves. Cut each endive in half crosswise. Then cut each half into very thin (⅛-inch-wide) strips. There should be approximately 4 cups.

2. Trim the ends from the leeks. Cut the leeks, crosswise, tender green stems included, into 2-inch lengths. Cut each length into very thin (⅛-inch-wide) strips. There should be about 4 cups. Place the leeks in a strainer or colander and rinse under lukewarm water to remove all dirt and grit. Pat them dry with a kitchen towel. (Both the endive and leeks can be cut several hours in advance and refrigerated until needed.)

3. Bring at least 4 quarts of water to boil in an extra-large stockpot. Add 1 tablespoon salt for each quart of water. When the water returns to a boil, add the live lobsters, lower the heat, cover, and cook at a simmer 10 to 12 minutes. To test for doneness, see "A Cook's Reflections." Drain, and set the lobsters aside, covered loosely with aluminum foil to keep warm.

4. Melt 4 tablespoons of the butter in a large heavy skillet over medium heat. When it is hot, add the leeks. Cook, stirring, about 10 minutes. Add the endive, stirring to mix well. Taste, and add salt and pepper as desired. Cover the mixture with a lid and cook, stirring occasionally, about 3 minutes. Remove the pan from the heat and keep covered to keep warm.

5. Put the wine in a small skillet over high heat. Bring to a boil, add the scallops, and then immediately take the skillet off the heat. Leave the scallops in the wine only 1 minute and then strain them, reserving the cooking liquid. Wrap the scallops in aluminum foil to keep warm.

GREAT ACCOMPANIMENTS

Since this is a fairly rich dish, you could serve Cucumber and Watercress Salad and hot crusty French bread as complements. The Poached Pears with Blueberry-Cassis Sauce would be an elegant dessert.

6. In a medium-size heavy saucepan, add the scallop cooking liquid, the shallots, and the vinegar. Place the pan over high heat and reduce the liquid, watching carefully, until a syrupy glaze just coats the bottom of the pan. Stir in the cream and salt and pepper to taste, and reduce the cream over high heat by one half.

7. Then gradually, 1 tablespoon at a time, whisk in the remaining 8 tablespoons butter until you have a smooth sauce. Set the sauce aside and cover the saucepan with a lid slightly ajar.

8. Pull apart and crack the lobsters, and remove the meat from the tails and claws. Cut the meat into bite-size portions.

9. To serve, arrange the hot leeks and endive on six warmed dinner plates. Arrange the lobster meat on top of the vegetables, and place the scallops around the lobster meat. Spoon the sauce over the lobster and scallops. Sprinkle each serving with a teaspoon of caviar.

Serves 6

GREAT ACCOMPANIMENTS

Sesame Green Beans and a good old-fashioned cole slaw or Corn on the Cob with Parmesan-Garlic Butter would be good side dishes to offer with the scallops. The Coconut Cream Mousse Pie would make a scrumptious ending.

Batter-Fried Sea Scallops with Dill Mayonnaise

These scallops, moist and succulent and enclosed in a golden feather-light coating, are delectable.

Special equipment: Deep-frying thermometer; 8 wooden or stainless steel 10-inch skewers

¾ cup plus 2 tablespoons all-purpose flour
¼ teaspoon salt
½ cup warm water
½ cup beer
2 tablespoons olive oil
2 large egg whites
1 quart vegetable oil for deep-frying
40 sea scallops (1¾ to 2 pounds), well rinsed and patted dry
8 sprigs fresh dill, for garnish
Dill Mayonnaise (recipe follows)

1. Measure the flour and salt into a bowl, and make a well in the center. Mix the water, beer, and olive oil in a small bowl, and pour about half the mixture into the well. Gently incorporate the flour

AS A VARIATION

*I often serve these scallops as an
hors d'oeuvre for small groups. You
can place a bowl of the mayonnaise
in the center of a serving tray and
arrange small wooden skewers with
a single fried scallop on each in a
starburst pattern around the mayonnaise.*

AT THE MARKET

**Fresh dill is much better than
dried in this recipe and should be
used if available.**

into the liquid with a whisk. Add the rest of the liquid gradually. When the batter is smooth, strain it through a large very-fine-mesh sieve, and let it rest, covered, at room temperature, for 2 to 3 hours.

2. When you are ready to use the batter, beat the egg whites to form soft peaks, and fold them into the batter.

3. Heat the vegetable oil in a 3- to 4-quart saucepan to 350° F.

4. Dip 5 to 6 scallops into the batter and then gently drop them into the oil. Let the scallops cook for 30 to 40 seconds, then turn them continually until they are golden, about 4 minutes. Continue frying the scallops in small batches, allowing the oil to return to 350° F before frying the next batch. Remove them with a slotted spoon.

5. Drain the scallops on paper towels. When all the scallops are cooked, gently skewer 5 scallops onto each skewer. Arrange two skewers of scallops on a dinner plate, and garnish with a sprig of fresh dill and a dollop of Dill Mayonnaise. Serve immediately.

Serves 4

DILL MAYONNAISE

Special equipment: Food processor

*2 large egg yolks, at room temperature
1 large egg, at room temperature
3 tablespoons fresh lemon juice
1 tablespoon Dijon mustard
½ teaspoon salt
1 clove garlic
1 cup corn oil
1 cup olive oil
⅓ cup chopped fresh dill, or 1½ tablespoons dried*

1. Place the egg yolks and the whole egg in the bowl of a food processor. Add the lemon juice, mustard, salt, and the garlic clove.

2. Pulse the machine on and off several times. Then, with the machine running, add the oils slowly in a very thin stream, until all the oil has been added and the mayonnaise has thickened.

3. Add the dill and process several seconds until incorporated. Refrigerate the mayonnaise, covered, until it is well chilled.

Makes 2¼ cups

Gratin of Scallops, Tomatoes, and Basil

Any dish with tomatoes and basil will pique my interest. Add scallops and I know I will like it. This entrée, in which each of these flavors complements the other, has become a favorite (and easy) main course at my house.

Special equipment: Medium-size gratin or baking dish, or 6 individual ramekins or soufflé dishes

1¼ pounds bay scallops, well rinsed and patted dry
¾ cup milk
2 or 3 ripe tomatoes
Salt and freshly ground pepper to taste
¾ cup all-purpose flour, plus more if needed
5 tablespoons unsalted butter, plus more if needed
2 tablespoons olive oil, plus more if needed
1 teaspoon finely chopped garlic
1½ tablespoons finely chopped fresh basil leaves,
    or 1½ teaspoons dried
½ cup heavy or whipping cream
¾ cup grated Gruyère or baby Swiss cheese
Several sprigs fresh basil, for garnish (optional)

1. Preheat the oven to 400° F.

2. Place the scallops in a bowl, add the milk, and soak the scallops for 1 hour.

3. While the scallops are soaking, peel, seed, and coarsely chop the tomatoes. You should have 1½ cups. Set aside.

4. Drain the scallops well on paper towels and then sprinkle them with salt and pepper to taste. Spread the flour on a plate and coat the scallops with flour.

5. Heat 4 tablespoons of the butter and the 2 tablespoons oil in a large heavy skillet over high heat. When the butter is very hot but not smoking, lower the heat slightly and sauté a few of the scallops, tossing gently, until they are golden. This should take only 3 to 4 minutes. Be careful not to overcook the scallops, which will make them tough.

GREAT ACCOMPANIMENTS

*Parmesan Garlic Rolls and a salad
of seasonal greens tossed in a vinaigrette would be good partners for the
scallop gratin. The Grapefruit
Mousse with Berries and Mint is
light and refreshing, and would
make a good conclusion to this
menu.*

6. Remove the scallops with a slotted spoon and drain on paper towels. Continue sautéing until all the scallops are cooked, adding more butter and oil in the same proportions if necessary.

7. Pour any residue out of the skillet, and wipe it clean with paper towels. Melt the remaining tablespoon of butter in the skillet over medium heat. When it is hot, add the chopped tomatoes and garlic. Toss and cook 1 minute. Add the basil and reserved scallops and toss. Taste, and add more salt and pepper as desired.

8. Transfer the mixture to a medium-size gratin or baking pan, or to six small ramekins or soufflé dishes. Pour the cream over the scallops, and sprinkle the top with the cheese.

9. Bake until the cheese has melted and the mixture is bubbling, 10 minutes or longer. Remove the pan from the oven and garnish with fresh basil sprigs.

Serves 4

A COOK'S REFLECTIONS

There are seven varieties of
salmon: six Pacific species and
one Atlantic. The Pacific ones include such familiar names as
Coho, Chinook, King, and Sock-
eye. The Atlantic type is called by
different names: In addition to
fresh Norwegian salmon, there is
smoked Danish salmon, smoked
Irish salmon, and Scotch smoked
salmon. For this recipe I always
try to buy fresh Atlantic salmon,
preferably Norwegian, but Pacific
salmon works well too.

Salmon Filets Baked with Lemons, Scallions, and Parsley

I first tasted this dish at the home of Mike and Shelly Young, good friends and talented cooks. The presentation of the salmon was outstanding and the taste even better. When I asked about the origin of the recipe, Mike told me that he had gotten the directions while talking with an elderly fishmonger in the Pike Place Market in Seattle. The merchant swore to him that this was the easiest and best way to cook fresh salmon. I could not agree more!

Special equipment: Rimless baking sheet; clean tweezers

2 Norwegian salmon filets (1½ pounds each), 1 inch thick
Salt and freshly ground pepper to taste
1 cup finely chopped fresh parsley
½ cup finely chopped scallions (green onions)
3 lemons, thinly sliced
*2 teaspoons very finely julienned lemon zest (see step 4), for
    garnish*
Mustard-Glazed Cucumbers (recipe follows)
Fresh tarragon sprigs, for garnish (optional)

GREAT ACCOMPANIMENTS

As a first course, either the Cream of Fennel Soup or the Cream of Jerusalem Artichoke Soup would be excellent. Wild Rice and Pine Nut Pilaf is an attractive dish to serve with this fish (you can omit the nuts if you like), and the Chocolate Apricot Pecan Torte makes a fine sweet conclusion.

1. Preheat the oven to 450° F.

2. Line a rimless baking sheet with aluminum foil; grease it well with vegetable oil. Generously oil the salmon skin. Place the fish skin side down on the foil. Run your fingers over the flesh sides of the salmon. If you feel any bones, remove them with tweezers. Salt and pepper the fish.

3. Combine the parsley and scallions, and spread the mixture over the salmon. Arrange the lemon slices, slightly overlapping, over the parsley mixture.

4. To make the lemon zest garnish, cut several strips of lemon zest into very fine thread-like strands. Set aside.

5. Place the baking sheet on the center shelf of the oven and bake until the fish is opaque, about 14 minutes. Remove the sheet from the oven, remove the lemon slices, and scrape off the parsley mixture.

6. Cut each salmon filet into three equal pieces and transfer them to a heated platter. Spoon the glazed cucumbers down the center of each serving, and then garnish with lemon zest and tarragon.

Serves 6

MUSTARD-GLAZED CUCUMBERS

4 medium cucumbers
6 tablespoons (¾ stick) unsalted butter
1 cup chopped shallots
1 cup dry white wine
8 teaspoons Dijon mustard
2 tablespoons finely chopped fresh tarragon, or 2 teaspoons dried
Salt and freshly ground pepper to taste

1. Peel the cucumbers, cut them in half lengthwise, and remove the seeds. Cut into small strips, ½ inch long and ¼ inch wide.

2. Cook the cucumbers in a large pot of boiling water until crisp-tender, 1 to 2 minutes. Remove and drain; then rinse under cold water and drain again. Pat dry with a kitchen towel.

3. Melt the butter in a heavy skillet over medium-high heat. Add the shallots and cook, stirring, 2 minutes. Add the wine and mustard and simmer until the mixture has reduced to a glaze, about 5 minutes. (The recipe can be made several hours ahead to this point.

Cover the cucumbers and the sauce, separately, with plastic wrap. Reheat the glaze before finishing the sauce.)

4. To complete the sauce, add the cucumbers and the tarragon to the warm sauce, and stir until the cucumbers are heated through. Season with salt and pepper.

Makes about 2 cups

AS A VARIATION

You can grill the salmon instead of broiling it, if you wish. For grilling, rub the skin side of the salmon generously with vegetable oil. Oil the grill rack generously also. Place the salmon, skin side down, on the grill rack and cook, without turning, until the fish flakes and is opaque. (The cooking time will vary depending on the type of grill and the intensity of the heat.)

Filet of Salmon with Tomato-Cilantro Relish

I especially like this recipe because I can make the relish in advance and then only have to spend a few minutes in the kitchen broiling the salmon to finish the dish.

Special equipment needed: Clean tweezers

2 salmon filets 1 inch thick, (1¼ pounds each)
3 tablespoons fresh lemon juice
1 teaspoon Dijon mustard
½ teaspoon salt
¼ teaspoon coarsely ground pepper
½ cup olive oil
Tomato-Cilantro Relish (recipe follows)
6 sprigs cilantro (fresh coriander), for garnish

1. Place the salmon filets, skin side down, in a shallow non-aluminum baking pan. Run your fingers over the flesh sides of the salmon. If you feel any bones, remove them with tweezers.

2. In a small bowl, combine the lemon juice, mustard, salt, and pepper. Whisk in the olive oil. Pour the mixture over the salmon, and marinate at least 2 hours, turning several times. If the room is cool, you can leave the marinating salmon out. If not, refrigerate it, covered.

3. When you are ready to cook the salmon, preheat the broiler and arrange a rack 5 to 6 inches from the heat.

4. Remove the filets from the marinade and place in a broiler pan flesh side up. Broil until the flesh is opaque and flakes easily when pierced with a knife, 5 to 8 minutes.

GREAT ACCOMPANIMENTS

This salmon is delicious served on a bed of buttered linguine or fettuccine noodles and offered with a seasonal green salad dressed with a vinaigrette. The Peaches and Cream Cheesecake garnished with fresh strawberries makes a good ending to this menu.

5. When the salmon is done, remove it from the oven and cut each filet into three serving pieces. Arrange the pieces on a heated platter, top each with several tablespoons of the relish, and add a sprig of cilantro. Pass the remaining relish separately.

Serves 6

TOMATO-CILANTRO RELISH

6 tablespoons olive oil
1 cup chopped onions
2 tablespoons capers, well drained
4 cups peeled, seeded, finely chopped tomatoes (about 3 large tomatoes; 1¼ pounds)
1 teaspoon salt
½ teaspoon coarsely ground pepper
2 tablespoons grated lemon zest
6 tablespoons chopped cilantro (fresh coriander leaves)

1. Place the oil in a medium-size heavy skillet over medium heat. When it is hot, add the onions and sauté, stirring, 3 to 4 minutes, until the onions are translucent. Add the capers and tomatoes, stir, and cook another 2 to 3 minutes. Add the salt, pepper, and lemon zest and stir well.

2. Remove the mixture from the heat and strain in a fine-mesh sieve to drain off any excess liquid. Transfer the relish to a small bowl.

3. Stir in the cilantro. Taste, and add more salt and pepper if desired. (The relish can be made 1 day in advance. Cool, cover, and refrigerate. Bring to room temperature before using.)

Makes 2 cups

Broiled Fish Filets with Garlic and Shallot Butter

GREAT ACCOMPANIMENTS

Buttered and peppered small red-skin potatoes and Sesame Green Beans are great side dishes with the filets. For dessert try the Walnut Orange Cake with Orange Peel Confetti.

When I first started making this dish several years ago, I always prepared it with striped bass. But recently this fish has become much harder to find in our local markets, so I have tried a variety of other fish filets with wonderful success. The important thing to remember is that the broiling time will depend on the thickness of the filets.

AT THE MARKET

I buy my fish from a very knowledgeable and experienced fish merchant, who always advises me to leave the skin on one side of the filets because there is a small fat layer between the flesh and the skin which helps keep the fish moist during cooking.

Among the thicker fish you could use are striped bass, sea bass, white or black bass. Sole, flounder, pickerel, and skate are flatfish possibilities.

10 tablespoons (1¼ sticks) unsalted butter, at room temperature
2½ tablespoons finely chopped shallots
1½ teaspoons finely chopped garlic
2½ tablespoons chopped fresh parsley
1½ teaspoons grated lemon zest
¼ teaspoon salt
2 pounds fish filets
Juice of 1 lemon
¼ cup dry bread crumbs, plus more if needed
Lemon wedges, for garnish
Parsley sprigs, for garnish

1. Combine the butter, shallots, garlic, parsley, lemon zest, and salt in the bowl of a food processor, and process until the mixture is smooth and softened, about 30 seconds. If you do not have a processor, cream the mixture with a wooden spoon until it is smooth and well blended.

2. Place a sheet of aluminum foil on a broiling pan rack and oil the foil generously. Then arrange the filets on top of the foil. (If you have one large filet from a large fish such as a bass, cut it into four serving portions. If you are using flat, smaller fish you will already have several pieces.) Squeeze the lemon juice over the filets. Then, with a butter spreader or a knife, spread the butter mixture evenly over the surface of each filet. Sprinkle the filets lightly with bread crumbs. (The filets can be prepared several hours in advance to this point. Cover with plastic wrap and refrigerate until needed.)

3. When you are ready to cook, preheat the broiler.

4. Place the pan about 4 to 5 inches from the heat and broil, watching carefully, until the fish is opaque and flakes easily. (The broiling time will depend on the thickness of the filets. Measure the filets at their thickest point and then count on 10 minutes per inch of thickness. If the filets are thinner at the ends, cut down on the time to avoid overcooking the ends.)

5. Serve the filets garnished with lemon wedges and sprigs of parsley.

Serves 4

AT THE MARKET

Fresh dill makes a big difference in this dish. If at all possible, use fresh rather than dried.

Sautéed Dover Sole in Lemon-Dill Batter

The key to the success of this recipe, as in all fish preparations, is to buy the freshest fish available. Then it is simply a matter of coating the filets with the fragrant batter and quickly sautéing them.

1 egg, separated
⅔ cup milk
3 tablespoons fresh lemon juice
¾ cup all-purpose flour
Salt to taste
3 tablespoons chopped fresh dill, or 1 teaspoon dried
Freshly ground pepper to taste
4 fresh filets of Dover sole (6 to 8 ounces each)
Vegetable oil
4 thin lemon slices, for garnish
4 sprigs fresh dill, for garnish

1. To prepare the batter, place the egg yolk, milk, and lemon juice in a medium-size mixing bowl and mix just until incorporated. Sift in half of the flour, and whisk until the mixture is smooth. Sift in the remaining flour, and whisk. Strain the batter through a fine-mesh sieve (to remove any lumps) into another bowl. Add salt to taste and the dill. Let the batter rest, covered with plastic wrap, at room temperature for 30 minutes.

2. When you are ready to use the batter, beat the egg white until soft peaks form, and gently fold it into the batter.

3. Lightly salt and pepper the filets.

4. Pour vegetable oil to a depth of 1 inch in a heavy skillet large enough to contain the filets in a single layer. (If necessary, use two skillets, filling each with 1 inch of oil.) Place the skillet over medium-high heat.

5. When the oil is quite hot but not smoking, dip each filet into the batter, coating well on both sides, and place it in the pan. Cook the filets 2 to 3 minutes per side. Remove and serve immediately, garnished with a slice of lemon and a sprig of dill.

Serves 4

THE RIGHT EQUIPMENT

My favorite pans for sautéing and frying are well-seasoned cast iron black skillets. They work beautifully for this recipe.

GREAT ACCOMPANIMENTS

Buttered and parsleyed new potatoes and the Green Bean and Snow Pea Salad are great accompaniments to the sole. For dessert, either the Frozen Chocolate Marbled Mousse or the Puff Pastry Heart Tarts make an ideal sweet conclusion.

Swordfish with Vegetables in Lemon Cream Sauce

More often than not I grill swordfish, because the fish lends itself so well to that preparation—but in this recipe I sauté it, nap it with a light lemon cream sauce, and then arrange a colorful border of fresh cooked vegetables around the fish. A meal in itself, this dish needs to be accompanied by no more than a seasonal green salad and hot French bread to go with it.

4 small zucchini
6 medium carrots, peeled
1½ tablespoons sugar
1 teaspoon salt
8 small new potatoes (1½ inches in diameter), cleaned but not
*   peeled*
6 tablespoons (¾ stick) unsalted butter
6 pieces of swordfish, 1 inch thick (8 ounces each)
Salt to taste
6 tablespoons finely chopped shallots
2 tablespoons fresh lemon juice
2 cups heavy or whipping cream
Freshly ground pepper to taste
½ tablespoon chopped fresh dill, or ½ teaspoon dried
6 sprigs fresh dill, for garnish (optional)

1. Trim the ends off the zucchini and cut into ¼-inch-thick slices. Place the zucchini in boiling salted water to cover and simmer until they are just crisp-tender, 1 to 2 minutes. Remove, drain, and reserve.

2. Cut the carrots on the diagonal into ¼-inch-thick slices. Combine 6 cups water, the sugar, and 1 teaspoon salt in a saucepan and bring to a boil. Add the carrots and simmer until just tender, 5 to 6 minutes. Remove, drain, and reserve.

3. Place the potatoes in boiling salted water to cover and cook until tender but not mushy, 8 to 10 minutes. Remove and drain. Peel the potatoes and cut them into quarters. Reserve. (All the vegetables can be prepared several hours in advance to this point. Cover and leave at room temperature.)

AT THE MARKET

You will probably need to buy large swordfish slices and cut them into serving portions.

GREAT ACCOMPANIMENTS

Cucumber and Watercress Salad is a good choice to offer with this entrée, and either the Hot Apricot Almond Tart or the Apricot Sorbet served with Chocolate and Almond Crisps makes an excellent dessert.

4. When you are ready to cook the swordfish, melt 4 tablespoons of the butter over high heat in a heavy skillet large enough to hold the fish in a single layer. (If necessary, divide the ingredients between two skillets.) When it is hot but not smoking, add the fish and sauté about 2 minutes per side. Then reduce the heat to low, cover the skillet, and cook until the fish is opaque and flakes easily when touched with a fork, 6 to 8 minutes. (Watch it carefully.) Remove the fish, salt it lightly, and keep warm.

5. Melt the remaining 2 tablespoons butter in the same skillet over medium-high heat. When it is hot, add the shallots and cook, stirring, 2 to 3 minutes. Add the lemon juice and cook 1 minute more. Then stir in the cream and lower the heat. Add the reserved vegetables and cook 4 to 5 minutes to thicken the sauce slightly and reheat the vegetables. Taste, and add salt and pepper as desired. Then sprinkle the mixture with the dill.

6. Arrange a piece of swordfish in the center of each of six warmed dinner plates. Then, using a slotted spoon, make a border of the vegetables around the fish. Ladle the remaining sauce over the swordfish and vegetables. Garnish each serving with a sprig of dill, if desired.

Serves 6

POULTRY

I think I've cooked poultry at my school every way imaginable—sautéed, deep fried, stir-fried, roasted, stewed, braised, broiled, to name a few methods. I've served the birds whole or cut into serving pieces; I've boned breasts and legs for some recipes, and used the wings for special dishes. And I have prepared it in as many ethnic contexts, it seems, as there are nations represented at the U.N. What all this conveys to me is that poultry is the common denominator of the culinary world.

Whatever the choice—chicken, turkey, capon, or duck—poultry is versatile, readily available, inexpensive, and without a doubt a cook's best friend in the kitchen.

Chicken Breasts Stuffed with Fruit and Almonds

This is a wonderful fall dish to serve at a buffet. The chicken breasts can be assembled and the sauce prepared completely in advance. Only a quick sautéing is necessary at the last minute.

Special equipment needed: Wooden toothpicks

Stuffing

½ cup dried apricots
1½ tablespoons currants or dark raisins
1½ tablespoons golden raisins
½ cup homemade chicken stock (see Index) or good-quality
    canned broth, warmed
3 tablespoons unsalted butter
1 cup finely chopped mushrooms
3 tablespoons chopped shallots
1 cup fresh bread crumbs
3 tablespoons slivered, toasted almonds (see Index)
¾ teaspoon chopped fresh sage, or ¼ teaspoon dried (not
    powdered)
¾ teaspoon fresh thyme, or ¼ teaspoon dried (not powdered)
Salt and freshly ground pepper to taste

Chicken Breasts

12 boneless, skinless chicken breast halves (about 3 pounds)
Salt and freshly ground pepper to taste
4 tablespoons (½ stick) unsalted butter
4 tablespoons vegetable oil

Sauce

½ cup water
⅓ cup red currant jelly
½ teaspoon grated orange zest
½ cup fresh orange juice
2 tablespoons brown sugar
1 tablespoon cornstarch
3 tablespoons Madeira
Sage sprigs, for garnish (optional)

1. To prepare the stuffing, dice the apricots into small cubes and place them, along with the currants and golden raisins, in a small mixing bowl. Pour the warm chicken stock over the dried fruit and let it soak until the fruit has softened and swelled, 20 minutes. Drain the fruit, set it aside, and discard the stock.

2. In a medium-size heavy skillet over medium heat, melt the butter and add the mushrooms and shallots. Cook, stirring, over medium-high heat until most of the liquid released by the mushrooms has evaporated, about 5 minutes. Remove the skillet from the heat and add the bread crumbs and toss well. Add the reserved fruit and the almonds, sage, and thyme. Mix well, and add salt and pepper to taste. The mixture should be slightly moist. If you feel it is too dry, add an additional tablespoon of chicken stock or water.

3. To prepare the chicken, place the breasts in the freezer for 20 to 30 minutes to make them firmer. Then place them on a cutting surface, and with a sharp knife held parallel to the work surface, start at the thicker side of the breast and make a lengthwise slit partially through the meat to create a cavity about 2 inches long by 1½ inches deep. Repeat with each breast, being careful not to tear through the flesh. Place 2 tablespoons of stuffing in each pocket and secure the opening with toothpicks. Salt and pepper each breast. (The breasts can be prepared to this point several hours in advance. Cover and refrigerate.)

4. When you are ready to cook the chicken, heat the butter and oil in a large heavy skillet over medium-high heat. When it is hot, add the chicken and cook until golden on all sides, 10 to 12 minutes. Cover the skillet, lower the heat, and cook 5 minutes more. Remove the chicken from the skillet and keep warm. Remove the toothpicks.

5. To prepare the sauce, combine all the ingredients except the Madeira in a medium-size heavy saucepan over medium-high heat. Simmer, stirring constantly, until the mixture thickens slightly and is clear, 4 to 5 minutes. Then add the Madeira. (The sauce can be made several hours in advance. Cover and refrigerate. Reheat, stirring constantly, over low heat.)

6. Serve the stuffed chicken breasts on a platter napped with a little of the sauce. Garnish the platter with sage sprigs. Serve the remaining sauce separately.

Serves 8 to 12

GREAT ACCOMPANIMENTS

I love to serve these stuffed chicken breasts for holiday buffets. The Wild Rice and Pine Nut Pilaf, made without the pine nuts since there are nuts in the poultry stuffing, and the Bourbon Carrots make excellent side dishes. Either Pumpkin Cheesecake or the Chocolate-Glazed Chestnut Rum Cheesecake make a fine finale.

Breasts of Chicken Stuffed with Spinach and Ginger

To "ginger" something means to "enliven or put spirit into" it, and
that is exactly what the ginger does for this dish. These boned
breasts of chicken—stuffed with fresh spinach, chopped fresh ginger,
shallots, and garlic—are sautéed until golden and served with a
smooth, rich cream sauce. Since it can be made several hours in
advance, this is a great dish to use for entertaining.

Special equipment: Wooden toothpicks

Spinach Stuffing

*20 ounces fresh spinach, or 1½ packages (10 ounces each) frozen
    chopped spinach, thawed*
½ pound smoked slab bacon
1 cup finely chopped shallots
4 teaspoons finely chopped garlic
4 teaspoons peeled and finely chopped fresh ginger
Salt and freshly ground pepper to taste

Chicken and Sauce

*8 boneless, skinless whole chicken breasts (7 to 8 ounces each
    after boning)*
Salt and freshly ground pepper to taste
4 tablespoons (½ stick) unsalted butter
4 tablespoons vegetable oil
*2¼ cups homemade chicken stock (see Index) or good-quality
    canned broth, plus ½ cup chicken stock or water, if preparing
    the chicken in advance*
2 teaspoons arrowroot
2 cups crème fraîche (see Index)
2 teaspoons Dijon mustard
16 uncooked whole spinach leaves, for garnish

1. To prepare the stuffing, first trim the spinach, removing the
stems. Rinse it well, dry it, and coarsely chop. If you are using
defrosted frozen spinach, squeeze out as much water as you can. Set
the spinach aside.

2. Cut the rind from the bacon and discard it. Cut the bacon into
¼-inch cubes. Sauté it in a heavy 10-inch skillet over medium heat

until crisp. Remove the bacon with a slotted spoon, and reserve.

3. Pour off all but 3 tablespoons of the bacon fat in the skillet and reheat over medium heat. Add the shallots and cook, stirring, 1 to 2 minutes. Add the garlic and ginger and cook, stirring, 1 to 2 minutes more. Then add the spinach and stir until the spinach is just wilted, 1 to 2 minutes more. Taste, and season as needed. Set aside.

4. To prepare the chicken, lay a chicken breast smooth (skin) side down on a work surface. Remove the two small filets with the white veins (save them for another use, such as a stir-fry dish). Pound the breast to a thickness of ¼ to ⅓ inch. Salt and pepper the breast well. Then spread ¼ cup of the Spinach Stuffing on one half of the breast. Fold the other half over the stuffing and secure with toothpicks. Repeat with the other breasts.

5. Heat the butter and oil over medium-high heat in a heavy skillet large enough to hold the breasts in one layer. If necessary, divide the ingredients between two skillets. When it is hot, add the chicken breasts and brown until golden on both sides, 12 to 15 minutes. Pour off any fat remaining in the skillet. Add 2 cups of the chicken stock and bring to a simmer. Place a lid slightly ajar on the skillet, and simmer for about 10 minutes more. Test for doneness by piercing the chicken with a sharp knife. If the juices run clear, the meat is done.

6. Remove the chicken to a warm platter and keep warm. Reduce the liquid in the skillet over high heat by half. Mix together the arrowroot and the remaining ¼ cup chicken stock until the arrowroot is well dissolved. Reduce the heat under the skillet to low, and whisk in the arrowroot mixture. Cook, stirring constantly, until the sauce begins to thicken, 3 to 4 minutes. Then add the crème fraîche and mustard and cook, stirring for 2 minutes more. Taste, and add salt and pepper as desired. (The chicken and sauce can be made several hours in advance. Keep each covered and refrigerated until needed. When ready to use, reheat the chicken by placing the breasts in a baking dish and sprinkling with the additional ½ cup chicken stock. Drape aluminum foil loosely over the dish and place in a preheated 300° F oven to heat through, 10 minutes or longer. Reheat the sauce over low heat.)

7. To serve, arrange each piece of chicken on two spinach leaves on a serving plate. Ladle sauce over the chicken, and sprinkle it with the reserved bacon cubes. Pass any remaining sauce separately.

Serves 8

AT THE MARKET

If you can't find a whole piece of bacon for the cubes, buy ¼-inch-thick bacon slices and dice them.

GREAT ACCOMPANIMENTS

As a first course, serve the Baked Chèvre with Tomatoes and Garlic Toasts. To go with the chicken, the Oven-Fried Parmesan Potatoes and buttered baby carrots look fine and taste delicious. Lemon Mousse Squares are light and tempting for dessert.

Chicken Breasts Stuffed with Prosciutto and Mozzarella

Fresh *mozzarella di bufala,* the pearly white, creamy, buttery cheese produced in Italy from buffalo milk, is one of the best cheeses for cooking that I have ever used. I first tasted it back in the late 1960s in a New York food store called Manganaro's, where I ate it spread over crusty bread and topped with a thin slice of prosciutto. I loved the taste so much, I thought I had died and gone to heaven! For years afterward, while I lived in Pennsylvania and then in Ohio, I searched for this product to no avail. Then two years ago a new Italian supermarket opened in Columbus, and much to my surprise and delight, there it was—fresh *mozzarella di bufala* resting in a tub of water at the cheese counter. Of course I bought more than I could use and promptly went home and started cooking with it. This is one of the recipes I created during my "mozzarella craze."

Special equipment: Wooden toothpicks

6 large boneless, skinless chicken breast halves (about 1½ pounds total)
6 ounces fresh mozzarella di bufala, *shredded*
Freshly ground pepper to taste
Generous grating of fresh nutmeg
Salt to taste
3 tablespoons chopped fresh basil leaves, or 1 tablespoon dried
2 ounces very thinly sliced prosciutto, cut into small pieces
½ cup all-purpose flour
1¾ cups dry bread crumbs
½ cup milk
1 large egg
Vegetable oil
½ cup peeled, seeded, chopped tomatoes, for garnish
Basil sprigs, for garnish

1. Place the chicken breasts in the freezer for 20 to 30 minutes to make them firmer. Then place them on a cutting surface and with a sharp knife held parallel to the work surface, start at the thicker side of the breast and make a lengthwise slit partially through the meat to create a cavity about 2 inches long by 1½ inches deep. Repeat with each breast, being careful not to tear through the flesh.

GREAT ACCOMPANIMENTS

Fettuccine or linguine tossed with butter and Parmesan cheese, plus the Stir-Fry of Zucchini, Onions, and Sweet Red Peppers, are good served with this chicken dish. Apricot Sorbet served with a garnish of fresh berries makes a light and colorful dessert.

2. Combine the cheese, pepper, nutmeg, a pinch of salt, the basil, and the prosciutto in a bowl and mix well. Place about 2 tablespoons of this mixture in the pocket of each breast. Pat each breast together and secure with toothpicks.

3. After the breasts have been stuffed, salt and pepper them on each side. Then spread the flour on one dinner plate and the bread crumbs on another. Mix the milk and egg together in a small bowl.

4. Dredge each breast in flour, then dip it into the milk and egg mixture, and finally coat it with bread crumbs. (The breasts may be prepared several hours ahead to this point. Cover and refrigerate.)

5. Place enough oil to make a thin layer in the bottom of a medium-size heavy skillet, and place it over medium-high heat. When the oil is hot, add the prepared chicken breasts. Cook until the chicken is golden and crisp on the outside and the juices run clear when it is pierced with a knife, 5 to 6 minutes per side. Remove the chicken from the pan and take out the toothpicks.

6. To serve, arrange the chicken on a heated platter. Garnish each piece with a little of the chopped tomatoes and a sprig of basil.

Serves 4 to 6

AT THE MARKET

Cèpes are dried mushrooms which can be found in specialty food stores and in some Oriental groceries. Other dried mushrooms may be substituted, following the same soaking procedures.

Fricassee of Chicken Breasts with Garlic and Cèpes

One July during a month's stay in Paris, our family rented an apartment rather than stay in a hotel. I was delighted with this arrangement because it gave me an opportunity to go shopping for groceries daily in the French markets. I couldn't wait to fill my little net bags called *filets* with crème fraîche, tiny green beans, Normandy butter, cheeses that I couldn't buy at home, and local wines. During the stay I bought several bags of dried cèpes, large mushrooms common in France, and invented this quick but special dish for one of our evening meals.

Special equipment: Sieve lined with a coffee filter

1 ounce dried cèpes
2 cups very warm water
12 boneless, skinless chicken breast halves (about 3 pounds)
Salt and freshly ground pepper to taste
¾ cup all-purpose flour
3 tablespoons unsalted butter
3 tablespoons vegetable oil
1½ tablespoons finely chopped garlic
½ cup dry red wine
2 cups homemade chicken stock (see Index) or good-quality
*   canned broth*
2 tablespoons chopped fresh chives or parsley

1. Soak the cèpes in the water until they are soft, about 15 minutes. Drain, discard the soaking water, and rinse the cèpes well under running water to remove any grit. Soak them again in 1 cup warm water for 5 minutes. Drain, reserving the water and the cèpes. Strain the soaking water through a sieve lined with a coffee filter, to be sure to remove any grit. If there is still some grit left, strain it a second time, using a clean filter. Reserve the cèpes and water.

2. Sprinkle the breasts all over with salt and pepper. Spread the flour on a dinner plate and dredge the chicken breasts lightly in it. Melt the butter in a large non-stick skillet over medium-high heat. Add the oil, and when it is hot, sauté the breasts until nicely browned on both sides, 4 to 5 minutes per side. Remove the chicken from the skillet and set aside. Reduce the heat under the skillet to low, add the garlic, and cook 1 to 2 minutes. Do not let it brown. Return the chicken to the skillet and add the wine, stock, cèpes, and soaking liquid. Cook the chicken at a simmer 8 to 10 minutes. Remove the chicken and mushrooms to a warm platter, cover with foil, and put in a preheated 250° F oven.

3. Cook the sauce over high heat, stirring frequently, until it has thickened and reduced to 2 cups, 8 to 10 minutes. Taste the sauce, and add salt and pepper as desired. To serve, nap the chicken with the sauce, and sprinkle with chopped chives or parsley.

Serves 6

GREAT ACCOMPANIMENTS

Serve the chicken garnished with small halved and buttered new potatoes plus the Green Bean, Walnut, and Red Onion Salad. Apple Cinnamon Ice Cream is an easy and good dessert.

New Orleans Ragoût of Chicken, Sausages, Tomatoes, and Leeks

Most people visit Bloomingdale's in New York City for shopping, but in the past few years I have discovered that it is also an interesting place for eating. I often go to the store's Tasting Bar located on the lower level, adjacent to the gourmet food area. The menu changes regularly and usually reflects a theme. On one of my visits there was a listing of international dishes, and I tried an American entry called New Orleans Chicken Stew. Similar but not identical to a gumbo, it was superb. When I got back to Ohio, I couldn't wait to prepare my own variation. We ate it twice that week at home, and my husband—who was born in New Orleans and loved this spicy ragoût—insisted it was even better the second time around!

Special equipment: 6 large shallow soup bowls

1 chicken (3 to 3½ pounds), cut into serving pieces (see Step 1)
⅓ cup vegetable oil
1 pound sweet Italian sausages, cut into 1-inch pieces
3 small leeks, white parts only, cleaned and cut into 1-inch pieces
2 teaspoons finely chopped garlic
Salt and freshly ground black pepper to taste
½ teaspoon cayenne pepper
4½ cups homemade chicken stock (see Index) or good-quality canned broth
1 can (28 ounces) Italian-style tomatoes, drained and coarsely chopped
1 green bell pepper, cored, seeded, and cut into 1-inch squares
6 cups cooked rice, kept warm

1. For this recipe use 2 breasts, 2 wings, 2 thighs, and 2 legs. Reserve the rest of the chicken for another use. Pat the pieces dry.

2. Heat the oil in a 4- to 5-quart heavy deep-sided casserole over medium heat. When it is hot, add the chicken and sauté, turning several times, until golden on all sides, about 15 minutes. Remove the chicken to a side dish and reserve. Add the sausage and sauté until browned on all sides, about 10 minutes. Remove and reserve.

3. Pour off all but 2 tablespoons oil in the pan. Add the leeks and garlic and sauté, stirring, 4 to 5 minutes. Return the chicken and

GREAT ACCOMPANIMENTS

This dish really is a meal in itself and needs only a tossed green salad in a mustard vinaigrette and hot crusty French bread to accompany it. A plate of Chestnut Brownies makes an easy and good finish to this menu.

sausage to the pan. Season the chicken generously with salt, black pepper, and cayenne pepper. Add the stock and tomatoes, and bring the mixture to a simmer. Lower the heat and simmer, covered, for about 45 minutes. Add the green pepper and cook, uncovered, another 15 minutes. Remove the chicken, sausage, and vegetables from the pan and set them aside, covered with aluminum foil to keep warm. Place the pan over high heat and reduce the liquid by one third.

4. To serve, use six large shallow soup bowls and mound 1 cup of rice in each. Arrange some chicken, sausage, and vegetables over the rice, and then ladle a generous amount of broth into each bowl. (The broth will not be as thick as a sauce but will have body.) Serve hot.

Serves 6

Cheese Biscuits with Creamed Chicken, Ham, and Apples

Here is wonderfully unpretentious "chicken and biscuits" with a slightly different twist.

10 tablespoons (1¼ sticks) unsalted butter
½ cup all-purpose flour
2 cups milk
2 cups homemade chicken stock (see Index) or good-quality canned broth
½ teaspoon salt, plus more if needed
⅛ teaspoon cayenne pepper, or to taste
Generous grating of fresh nutmeg
4 large egg yolks
3 cups cooked chicken, cut into 1-inch pieces
1½ cups thin strips (1½ inches long and ¼ inch wide) baked ham (about 6 ounces)
2½ cups thin (⅛ inch thick) Granny Smith apple slices (about 2 medium apples)
6 Cheddar Cheese Biscuits (see Index)
1½ tablespoons salt (for cooking the beans)
2 pounds tender green beans, trimmed
2 teaspoons chopped fresh parsley

AS A VARIATION

I replace the chicken with leftover turkey during the holidays. It works equally well.

GREAT ACCOMPANIMENTS

Since this dish is a complete and filling main course in itself, I usually offer only a plate of Chestnut Brownies or Lucy's Nanaimo Bars and a bowl of fresh fruit for dessert.

1. Melt 8 tablespoons of the butter in a large heavy saucepan over medium heat. Add the flour and cook, stirring constantly, for about 2 minutes. Whisk in the milk and stock, whisking constantly until the mixture thickens and comes to a boil. Remove the pan from the heat and add the ½ teaspoon salt, cayenne pepper, and nutmeg.

2. Place the egg yolks in a bowl and whisk to mix well. Then very gradually whisk in ½ cup of the sauce. Slowly whisk the egg yolk mixture into the remaining sauce in the pan. Add the chicken and ham, and set aside.

3. In a medium-size heavy skillet over medium heat, melt the remaining 2 tablespoons butter and sauté the apple slices until just slightly softened and golden. Remove, and add to the sauce.

4. Taste the sauce, and if desired, add more salt and cayenne pepper. (The sauce can be made several hours in advance to this point. Cover the surface of the sauce directly with plastic wrap, and refrigerate until needed.)

5. When you are ready to serve the dish, reheat the biscuits if necessary, and keep them warm.

6. Bring 3 quarts of water to a boil, and add the 1½ tablespoons salt. Simmer the green beans, uncovered, until just tender, about 8 minutes. Drain and keep warm.

7. Reheat the sauce over low to medium heat, stirring constantly (too high a heat could curdle the sauce).

8. To serve, split the biscuits and arrange them in the center of six warmed serving plates. Ladle a generous amount of sauce over the biscuits, and sprinkle parsley over the sauce. Place a small bunch of green beans at either side of the biscuits. Serve hot.

Serves 6

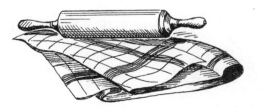

Spicy Indonesian Chicken

On our last trip to Amsterdam my husband, son, and I—after several nights of eating huge *rijstafels*—decided to try instead simple spicy Indonesian chicken in one of our favorite restaurants. A sauté of tender boneless chicken, sweet red peppers, onions, and tomatoes, the dish was outstanding. When I asked the owner for the recipe, he willingly gave me the directions. Three items—lemon grass, Thai sweet sauce, and galanga root—were unfamiliar to me, but much to my surprise, when I returned home I found them in a local Oriental grocery.

2 medium onions
1 small green bell pepper
2 red bell peppers, 1 small and 1 medium
4 tomatoes (about 1¼ pounds)
6 tablespoons peanut or corn oil
4 teaspoons finely chopped garlic
1½ teaspoons dried red pepper flakes
½ cup finely chopped lemon grass (see "At the Market")
2 thin slices dried galanga root (see "At the Market")
4 boneless, skinless chicken breast halves (1 to 1¼ pounds total),
*   cut into 1½-inch pieces*
⅔ cup Thai sweet sauce (see "At the Market")
Salt and freshly ground pepper to taste
4 nice small Boston lettuce leaves, rinsed and dried
6 cups cooked white rice, kept warm
Toasted Coconut Garnish (recipe follows)
Carrot-Cabbage Garnish (recipe follows)

1. Prepare the vegetables and set them aside separately: Peel the onions, cut them in half lengthwise, and cut them into ¼-inch slices. Core and seed the green pepper and the small red pepper; cut them into 1-inch pieces. Core and seed the medium-size red pepper, and cut it into julienne strips. Peel and seed the tomatoes, and cut them into 1-inch pieces; you should have 3 cups.

2. Heat the oil in a large heavy skillet over medium-high heat. When it is hot, add the onions and cook, stirring, over high heat, 2 minutes. Add the garlic, pepper flakes, lemon grass, and galanga slices and cook, stirring, only 1 or 2 minutes more. Add the chicken pieces, a handful at a time, and cook, stirring, until the meat turns

white, losing its uncooked appearance, 8 to 10 minutes. Continue until all the chicken has been added.

3. Add the 1-inch pieces of red and green pepper and cook, stirring, about 3 to 4 minutes. Then add the tomatoes and sweet sauce, and cook over medium heat, stirring, 4 to 5 minutes more. Taste, and add salt and pepper as desired. Remove and discard the galanga slices.

4. To serve, arrange a lettuce leaf on the edge of four dinner plates. Place 4 or 5 julienne strips of red pepper in a fan pattern on the lettuce. Mound 1½ cups of rice in the center of the plate, and spoon a generous serving of the chicken mixture over the rice. Place the coconut and the carrot-cabbage garnishes in serving bowls and serve separately. (The coconut should be sprinkled over the chicken and the carrot and cabbage mixture eaten as a side dish.)

Serves 4

TOASTED COCONUT GARNISH

1 cup unsweetened coconut flakes
1 teaspoon very finely chopped garlic
⅓ cup very finely chopped onion

Heat a skillet until hot and add the coconut flakes. Toss 1 minute, and then add the garlic and onions. Continue to cook, stirring, until the coconut is golden brown, 3 to 4 minutes. Remove from the heat and reserve. (This can be made several hours in advance. Keep covered at room temperature.)

Makes 1¼ cups

CARROT-CABBAGE GARNISH

2 tablespoons sugar
2 tablespoons white vinegar
¼ teaspoon salt
⅓ cup coarsely grated carrots
1 cup grated cabbage

Combine the sugar, vinegar, and salt in a mixing bowl and mix well. Add the carrots and cabbage, and toss to coat well. Reserve. (This can be made several hours in advance; cover and refrigerate.)

Makes 1¼ cups

GREAT ACCOMPANIMENTS

This chicken is really a complete one-course meal. I usually just serve a simple dessert, such as peeled orange sections (membranes and seeds removed) served with sweetened, softly whipped cream.

Chicken with Fresh Peas and Cantaloupe

In the spring and early summer, when fresh tender peas, dark green watercress, and juicy cantaloupe are available, I love to make this colorful dish. Since it can be made and assembled several hours ahead, it is nice to serve during warm weather at a luncheon or for a light evening meal.

2 quarts homemade chicken stock (see Index) or good-quality canned broth
6 boneless, skinless chicken breast halves
3 cups shelled fresh peas (about 2½ pounds in the shell)
½ cup chopped scallions (green onions), with 1 to 2 inches of green stems
Salt and freshly ground pepper to taste
1 ripe cantaloupe, halved and seeds removed
Watercress Mayonnaise (recipe follows)
6 sprigs watercress

1. Place the chicken stock in a large saucepan and bring to a simmer. Add the chicken breasts and simmer, uncovered, until the chicken is tender and cooked through, 10 to 12 minutes. Remove the chicken, reserving the stock, and refrigerate, covered, until cold, at least 1 hour.

2. Bring the chicken stock back to a simmer. Add the peas and scallions and simmer until just tender, about 5 minutes. Drain the vegetables and refrigerate until cold. Taste, and add salt and pepper as desired. (Save stock for another use.)

3. To assemble, cut the cantaloupe into six wedges and remove the peel. Arrange the peas and scallions on a round or oval serving plate. Place the chicken breasts in a spoke pattern on top of the peas. Nap each breast with Watercress Mayonnaise, and garnish with a watercress sprig. Place the cantaloupe wedges in an overlapping border around the perimeter of the dish. Serve cold.

Serves 6

GREAT ACCOMPANIMENTS

A basket of warm Cheddar Cheese and Thyme Brioches would taste good with the chicken. And the Coconut Caramel Flan would make a wonderful conclusion.

WATERCRESS MAYONNAISE

2 large egg yolks, at room temperature
1 large whole egg, at room temperature
1 teaspoon Dijon mustard, at room temperature
4 teaspoons fresh lemon juice, at room temperature
1 teaspoon grated lemon zest
½ teaspoon salt
Freshly ground pepper to taste
½ cup corn oil
½ cup olive oil
⅔ cup watercress leaves, rinsed and dried

1. Place the egg yolks, whole egg, mustard, lemon juice, lemon zest, salt, and pepper in the bowl of a food processor or blender. Process several seconds and then gradually, in a thin stream, pour in both oils with the machine running.

2. Add the watercress, and process just until the leaves are finely minced, 5 to 10 seconds. Remove the mayonnaise to a bowl, cover, and refrigerate. (The mayonnaise can be made 1 to 2 days in advance and kept covered and refrigerated until needed.)

Makes about 1½ cups

GREAT ACCOMPANIMENTS

Either the cold Summer Tomato and Watercress Soup or the hot Cream of Jerusalem Artichoke Soup makes a good beginning to this chicken dish. Serve it with a cold rice salad tossed with diced red and green bell peppers and pine nuts, and for dessert offer a bowl of fresh strawberries served with sweetened whipped cream and Amaretto Brownies.

Chicken and Prosciutto with Herbed Mayonnaise

This is a striking dish: cold chicken breasts are wrapped in thin slices of prosciutto, then napped with herbed mayonnaise and decorated with a lattice of fresh chives. The chicken is served in large romaine lettuce leaves and garnished with black olives. In the summer, I serve this chicken at large buffets. During the cold-weather months, I add a warm first-course soup to the menu and offer this make-ahead entrée at late-night dinners after the theater, the symphony, or the opera.

*3 quarts homemade chicken stock (see Index) or good-quality
    canned broth*
8 chicken breast halves
8 thin slices prosciutto
Herbed Mayonnaise (recipe follows)
Bunch of thin-stemmed chives
8 large romaine lettuce leaves
1 cup good-quality black olives

1. Bring the chicken stock to a simmer in a stockpot or other large deep-sided pot. Add the chicken breasts and cook at a simmer, uncovered, until tender when pierced with a knife, 25 to 30 minutes or longer. Remove the breasts from the stock and allow them to cool. Remove the skin. (The breasts can be poached a day in advance, then covered and refrigerated until needed.)

2. To assemble the chicken, wrap each breast in a slice of prosciutto. Then coat each piece generously on the top side with an even layer of the mayonnaise. For each breast, cut six chive stems so they measure 3 inches long. Place three stems on the diagonal and an inch apart on top of the mayonnaise-coated chicken breast. Place 3 more stems going in the opposite direction, to create a lattice effect. Arrange the lettuce leaves on a serving platter, and put the prepared chicken on the leaves. Garnish the platter with black olives. Refrigerate. (The chicken can be prepared several hours in advance to this point and kept refrigerated.)

Serves 8

HERBED MAYONNAISE

2 large egg yolks, at room temperature
1 large egg, at room temperature
1 tablespoon fresh lemon juice, at room temperature
½ teaspoon Dijon mustard, at room temperature
½ teaspoon salt
Generous pinch of cayenne pepper
1 cup olive oil, at room temperature
½ cup vegetable oil, at room temperature
1 tablespoon chopped fresh chives
1 tablespoon chopped fresh parsley
1 tablespoon chopped fresh tarragon, or ½ teaspoon dried

1. Place the egg yolks, whole egg, lemon juice, mustard, salt, and cayenne pepper in the bowl of a food processor.

2. Process several seconds, and then slowly, with the machine running, add the olive oil and vegetable oil in a very thin stream. When all the oil has been added, the mixture should be thick and smooth. Remove the mayonnaise from the processor bowl and stir in the herbs. If you add herbs to the processor while it is running, you will have green mayonnaise rather than white. (The mayonnaise can be made 1 to 2 days in advance and kept covered and refrigerated until needed.)

Makes about 1½ cups

Roast Capon with Sausage and Sweet Red Pepper Stuffing

When I was growing up in the South, one of my favorite dishes was my mother's cornbread dressing. For years I never knew that any other type of filling existed for poultry! When I began to cook seriously, however, I discovered countless ways to stuff birds. One of my own inventions is this sausage stuffing which I use for capon.

Special equipment: String for trussing capon

1 capon (7 to 8 pounds)
Sausage and Sweet Red Pepper Stuffing (recipe follows)
1½ tablespoons unsalted butter, at room temperature
4½ cups homemade chicken stock (see Index) or good-quality canned broth, plus more if needed
¾ cup heavy or whipping cream
2 tablespoons arrowroot
Fresh thyme or rosemary sprigs, for garnish (optional)

1. Preheat the oven to 375° F.

2. Clean the cavity of the capon removing any loose fat and other clinging particles. Fill the cavity loosely with stuffing; do not pack stuffing in tightly. (Place any extra stuffing in a buttered baking dish and bake in the oven with the capon, sprinkling with ¼ cup stock every 20 minutes to prevent it from drying out. When the sausage is cooked through and the top of the stuffing is lightly browned it is done, about 1 hour).

3. Truss the capon and rub the entire surface with the butter. Place

GREAT ACCOMPANIMENTS

Boiled new potatoes, quartered and lightly buttered, steamed green beans or zucchini, and Hot Apricot Almond Tart are delicious accompaniments to this rich capon dish.

AT THE MARKET

Whenever I cook a capon in my classes, students always ask exactly what this bird is. A capon is a desexed male chicken, 7 to 8 months old and weighing between 4 and 8 pounds. The meat of a capon is quite tender and the breast especially fleshy.

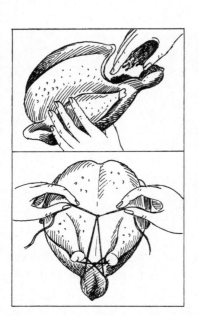

the capon on a rack in a roasting pan, and cook until it is golden brown and the juices run clear when the flesh is pierced with a knife, 1½ to 2 hours. A thermometer inserted in the thigh should register 175° to 180° F. While the bird is roasting, baste every 15 minutes with ¼ cup chicken stock. When it is done, remove the capon from the oven and keep warm.

4. Discard all liquid from the roasting pan, but be careful to leave all brown particles and residue in the bottom of the pan.

5. Add 1½ cups chicken stock to the roasting pan and place over high heat. Using a whisk or spoon, deglaze the pan, scraping all brown particles and residue into the liquid. Cook until the liquid has reduced by one third. Reduce the heat to medium, add the cream, and cook 1 minute more. Then mix the arrowroot with ¼ cup chicken stock, and stir into the sauce. Cook until the sauce has thickened, 2 to 3 minutes.

6. To serve, remove the trussing from the capon and place the bird on a warm serving platter. Garnish with thyme and rosemary sprigs. Place the sauce in a bowl to serve with the chicken.

Serves 8

SAUSAGE AND SWEET RED PEPPER STUFFING

1½ tablespoons unsalted butter
¼ cup finely chopped red bell pepper
6 tablespoons finely chopped onion
1 pound fresh pork sausage meat
4 cups fresh bread crumbs
¾ teaspoon dried thyme
½ teaspoon dried rosemary
½ teaspoon salt
¼ teaspoon freshly ground pepper
1 large egg, lightly beaten

1. Melt the butter in a small heavy skillet over medium heat. When it is hot, add the pepper and onion and sauté, stirring, until just tender, 3 to 4 minutes.

2. In a large mixing bowl, combine the sautéed pepper and onion, the sausage, and the bread crumbs, thyme, rosemary, salt, and pepper. Mix well. Then add the egg and mix well again.

Makes about 6 cups

Roast Turkey with Cornbread-Apricot Dressing

I think there are as many recipes for roasting turkey as there are cooks who prepare this bird for Thanksgiving. I know of no two people who roast a turkey in identical fashion. My favorite way to roast this fowl is to stuff the cavity with fresh whole oranges rather than stuffing. During the roasting process, the flavor of the oranges subtly permeates the turkey. Externally, I baste the bird with butter, stock, and orange juice so that when finished I always have a turkey with skin that is a rich dark mahogany color and meat that is tender and succulent. The Cornbread-Apricot Dressing is baked separately—and is a delicious side dish, as is Shirley's Cranberry Chutney.

Special equipment: String for trussing the turkey

*1 turkey (10 to 12 pounds), fresh if possible, rinsed and dried,
      neck and giblets reserved
¼ cup vegetable oil
¾ cup chopped onions
¾ cup chopped carrots
¾ cup chopped celery
7 cups homemade chicken stock (see Index) or good-quality
      canned broth
½ cup dry red wine
1 teaspoon salt
1 bay leaf
½ teaspoon dried thyme
Salt and freshly ground pepper to taste
1 or 2 oranges
¾ cup (1½ sticks) unsalted butter, at room temperature, plus
      more if needed
Juice of 3 oranges
1½ tablespoons cornstarch
¼ cup cold water
1 bunch watercress, for garnish
2 oranges, thinly sliced, for garnish
Cornbread-Apricot Dressing (recipe follows)
Shirley's Cranberry Chutney (recipe follows)*

THE RIGHT EQUIPMENT

Meat Thermometers: A good meat thermometer is a wise investment for all cooks and is especially useful when determining when poultry is done. My favorite kind is the instant-reading thermometer. They are the most accurate and efficient. You simply insert the thermometer in the center of the fleshiest part of a beef, veal, lamb, or pork roast (avoiding any bones), or in the thigh of a whole chicken, capon, or turkey, and get a reading within seconds.

Standard meat thermometers are placed in the raw meat or poultry and remain for the entire cooking time, to be read whenever needed.

GREAT ACCOMPANIMENTS

In addition to the Cornbread-Apricot Dressing, for Thanksgiving dinner I always serve Brandied Sweet Potato Soufflé, Honey-Glazed Carrots and Parsnips, Shirley's Cranberry Chutney, and for dessert, the Chocolate Walnut Caramel Tart.

1. To prepare the stock, remove the neck and giblets from the turkey. Cut the neck into 2-inch pieces, quarter the heart, and cut the gizzard in half. Cut off and reserve the wing tips. Save the liver for another use or discard it.

2. Heat the oil in a large heavy saucepan over medium heat. When it is hot, add the neck, giblets, and wing tips and brown, stirring continuously, 5 to 6 minutes. Remove the meat with a slotted spoon and set aside.

3. Add the onions, carrots, and celery to the pan and cook over medium heat, continuing to stir, 4 to 5 minutes. Return the browned meat to the saucepan, and add 3 cups of the chicken stock, the wine, 1 teaspoon of the salt, the bay leaf, and the thyme. If the liquids do not cover the giblets, add enough water to cover.

4. Bring the mixture to a simmer and cook, uncovered, until the stock has a good flavor, 2 to 2½ hours. (You may need to add more water as the sauce cooks down.) When the stock is done, remove it from the heat and strain. You should have 2 cups; add water if needed to make that amount. Taste, and add salt and pepper as desired. Set the stock aside. (You may prepare the stock a day in advance and refrigerate it until needed; or you can make it while you are roasting the turkey.)

5. To roast the turkey, preheat the oven to 325° F.

6. Season the cavity of the bird with salt to taste. Then place 1 or 2 oranges (according to the size of the cavity), whole and unpeeled, in the cavity. Truss the bird ("A Cook's Reflections," page 134), and rub 2 tablespoons of the butter over the entire outer surface. Place the turkey on a rack in a roasting pan.

7. Roast the turkey, basting with ¼ cup chicken stock every 20 minutes. After each basting, spread 1 tablespoon of butter on the surface as well. When the turkey has roasted for 2¾ hours, pour two thirds of the orange juice over it. Continue roasting and basting an additional ¾ to 1¼ more hours. The bird will be done when the skin is well browned and the juices run clear when the flesh in the thickest part of the thigh is pierced with a knife. A meat thermometer inserted in the thigh should register 180° to 185° F.

8. Remove the turkey from the oven and let it rest 20 minutes before serving.

9. To make the sauce, spoon off all the fat from the roasting pan but leave any juices and brown particles. Place the pan on a burner over high heat, and add 1 cup of the chicken stock. Deglaze the pan by scraping all the brown pieces into the liquid with a whisk or fork. Cook over high heat, 2 to 3 minutes. Add the reserved turkey stock and cook over high heat, stirring, until the sauce has reduced by about one third, 4 to 5 minutes. Combine the cornstarch and the cold water and stir well to make a paste. Add the remaining orange juice and the cornstarch mixture to the pan and cook until the sauce has thickened slightly, 3 to 4 minutes more. Taste, and season with salt.

10. To serve, place the turkey on a heated platter and garnish with watercress sprigs and a border of sliced oranges. (If you prefer, you can carve the bird in the kitchen, arrange the turkey on a warm serving platter, and then garnish.) Serve the sauce, the Cornbread-Apricot Dressing, and Shirley's Cranberry Chutney separately.

Serves 10 to 12

CORNBREAD-APRICOT DRESSING

This is my variation on traditional cornbread dressing. The apricots are a splendid touch and add extra moistness to this dish.

2 cups homemade chicken stock (see Index) or good-quality
  canned broth
1 cup finely chopped dried apricots
6 tablespoons (¾ stick) unsalted butter
1 cup chopped onions
¾ cup chopped celery
4 to 4½ cups fine fresh cornbread crumbs (see Index)
4 cups fresh bread crumbs
1 teaspoon salt
½ teaspoon freshly ground pepper
1½ teaspoons crumbled dried sage
4 large eggs, lightly beaten

1. Warm ½ cup of the chicken stock and soak the apricots in it until softened, 20 to 30 minutes.

2. Melt the butter in a medium-size skillet over medium heat, and when it is hot, add the onions and celery. Sauté, stirring, until softened, 5 minutes or longer. Set the vegetables aside in the skillet.

3. Combine the cornbread crumbs and bread crumbs in a large mixing bowl, and add the cooked onions, celery, and any melted

A COOK'S REFLECTIONS

This dressing should be very moist, really almost wet, when it goes into the oven. If you want to stuff a bird with it, cut the stock down by a third since the juices from the bird will add moisture to the stuffing. You will need ½ to ¾ cup stuffing per pound of turkey to fill the cavity.

butter in the pan. Add the salt, pepper, and sage and mix well. Add the soaked apricots and any soaking liquid, and mix well. (The dressing can be made a day in advance to this point; cover and refrigerate.)

4. When you are ready to bake the dressing, preheat the oven to 350° F.

5. Add the eggs and the remaining 1½ cups chicken stock to the dressing, and mix well. The dressing should be very wet. Taste, and if desired, add more salt and pepper. Place the dressing in a large buttered baking dish.

6. Bake until a light brown crust forms on top, 35 to 40 minutes.

Serves 10 to 12

SHIRLEY'S CRANBERRY CHUTNEY

Shirley Rubinstein, a talented cooking teacher and a wonderful colleague, shared this recipe with me several years ago. I serve it all through the year with roast turkey, grilled chicken, or baked ham. And during the holiday season, I package this deep red chutney in glass jars, tie them festively with ribbons and holly sprigs, and offer them as gifts to friends.

1 cup water
1 cup granulated sugar
2 cups fresh cranberries
2 tablespoons cider vinegar
½ cup seedless golden raisins
¼ cup slivered almonds
1 tablespoon light brown sugar
¼ teaspoon ground ginger
½ teaspoon finely chopped garlic

1. Combine the water and granulated sugar in a heavy 3-quart saucepan over medium-high heat. Stir to dissolve the sugar, and then bring to a boil without stirring.

2. Add all the remaining ingredients. Boil very slowly, stirring occasionally, until fairly thick, 5 minutes or longer.

3. Allow the chutney to cool, then cover and refrigerate. (The chutney keeps well for 5 to 7 days in the refrigerator.)

Makes about 2 cups

A COOK'S REFLECTIONS

If you increase this recipe, the cooking time for thickening the chutney will need to be increased slightly.

Although this chutney holds up several days under refrigeration, you can also put it into sterilized canning jars, leaving ¼ inch of headspace at the top. Seal and process the jars according to the manufacturer's directions.

AT THE MARKET

Applejack is a brandy made by distilling hard cider (fermented apple juice). The drink has a strong apple flavor, and is widely available throughout the country. Calvados, a French apple brandy made in the region of Normandy, can be used in this recipe, but it is often more difficult to find.

Roast Breast of Turkey with Apple-Currant Stuffing

Turkey breast, a beautiful cut of poultry, is something many cooks have not discovered. It is as tender as veal but costs considerably less, and for the creative cook it has unlimited versatility. For this dish, I have the butcher bone a whole turkey breast, then I butterfly it and fill it with an apple, currant, and apricot bread stuffing. Rolled into a cylinder, the meat is basted with fresh cider and applejack while roasting. When the cooked breast is sliced, a striking spiral pattern is revealed. My students tell me repeatedly that this is a great main course to serve for buffet dinners.

Special equipment: String for tying the roast; meat pounder

7 tablespoons diced dried apricots
3½ tablespoons currants
6 tablespoons (¾ stick) unsalted butter, at room temperature
½ medium onion, chopped
6 tablespoons slivered almonds
2 medium tart green apples, peeled and cut into small dice
2¼ cups dry bread crumbs
½ teaspoon salt, plus more if needed
¼ teaspoon crumbled dried sage
*3 to 4 tablespoons homemade chicken stock (see Index) or good-
    quality canned broth*
*1 fresh whole turkey breast (5 to 5½ pounds), boned and trimmed
    but not skinned*
Salt
3 cups apple cider
½ cup applejack
1½ cups crème fraîche (see Index)
Additional applejack (optional)
Fresh lemon juice (optional)
Fresh sage leaves, for garnish (optional)

1. To prepare the stuffing, soak the apricots and currants in boiling water to cover until plumped and soft, about 15 minutes. Drain.

2. Melt 1 tablespoon of the butter in a medium-size heavy skillet over medium heat. Add the onion and cook until slightly softened, stirring occasionally, about 6 minutes. Drain on paper towels.

3. Melt 1 tablespoon butter in the same skillet over medium heat. Add the almonds and toss until golden brown, 2 to 3 minutes. Drain on paper towels.

4. Melt 2 tablespoons butter in the same skillet over medium heat. Add the apples and cook until slightly softened, tossing occasionally, about 5 minutes. Drain apples on paper towels.

5. Combine the apricots, currants, onion, almonds, apples, bread crumbs, salt, and sage in a large bowl. Blend in 3 tablespoons chicken stock. If the stuffing is too dry, add 1 more tablespoon stock. Adjust the seasoning with salt as desired. Cool completely. (The stuffing can be prepared 1 day ahead; cover and refrigerate.)

6. To butterfly the turkey, lay the meat skin side down in front of you (the shape should resemble a heart). Starting at the center, hold a knife parallel to the meat with the blade facing left, and make a lengthwise cut through the meat on the left side; do not cut to the edge. Open the flap. Turn the meat and repeat on the other side. Spread the meat out flat and cover it with waxed paper. Gently pound it to a thickness of ½ to ¾ inch. Season the meat generously with salt, and spread it with the stuffing, leaving a ½-inch border all around. Starting with the long edge, roll the meat into a 16 x 3-inch cylinder. Tie it at 1- to 2-inch intervals with kitchen twine, and secure the ends with toothpicks. (The meat can be prepared to this point several hours ahead or the day before. Cover with plastic wrap and refrigerate until needed.)

7. When you are ready to cook the roast, preheat the oven to 350° F.

8. Mix the cider and applejack together. Rub the turkey with the remaining 2 tablespoons butter and set it on a rack in a roasting pan. Roast until the skin is brown and the juices run clear when the meat is pierced with a knife, about 1 hour. Baste every 15 minutes with ½ cup of the cider mixture. Remove the turkey from the oven and let it stand 15 minutes.

9. Meanwhile, skim the grease from the liquid in the pan. Pour the remaining pan liquid into a measuring cup and add enough remaining cider mixture to make 1½ cups. Stir this back into the roasting pan over high heat, scraping up the browned bits in the pan. Add the crème fraîche and boil until the sauce thickens. Strain the sauce and season with salt to taste. If the sauce is too sweet, add extra applejack and some lemon juice to taste.

GREAT ACCOMPANIMENTS

The Cream of Butternut Squash and Leek Soup makes a good first course before this entrée. As side dishes, I suggest the Carrot and Belgian Endive Sauté and the Wild Rice and Pine Nut Pilaf. The Cassis Walnut Tart or Cranberry-Walnut Strudels makes a great ending.

10. Remove the twine and toothpicks from the turkey and cut it into ½- to ¾-inch slices. Arrange the slices on a heated platter and garnish with sage leaves. Pass the sauce separately.

Serves 12 to 14

Old-Fashioned Turkey Pot Pies

For many people the best part of Thanksgiving is not the feast served on the fourth Thursday of November, but rather the leftover turkey to be enjoyed on the following days. Certainly that is the case at my house. These turkey pot pies are a post-holiday creation we particularly enjoy. I like them so well I serve them not only on Thanksgiving weekend, but throughout the year as well.

Special equipment: Eight 1-cup ramekins or soufflé dishes, or a 2-quart gratin dish

Pastry Crust
2 cups sifted all-purpose flour
1 teaspoon salt
1 cup (2 sticks) unsalted butter, well chilled, and cut into pieces
1 large egg
1 tablespoon heavy or whipping cream

Filling
2 small zucchini
2 carrots, peeled
10 tablespoons (1¼ sticks) unsalted butter
⅓ cup chopped onion
½ pound mushrooms, cleaned and very thinly sliced
4 tablespoons all-purpose flour
1½ cups homemade chicken or turkey stock (see Index) or good-quality canned broth
1½ cups heavy or whipping cream
¾ cup grated Gruyère cheese
½ teaspoon salt
⅛ teaspoon freshly grated nutmeg
Pinch of cayenne pepper
2½ to 3 cups diced cooked turkey
1 large egg yolk
1½ tablespoons cold water

1. To prepare the crust by hand, place the flour and salt in a bowl and cut in the butter using a pastry blender or two knives, until the mixture resembles oatmeal flakes. Gradually work in the egg and cream. Form the dough into a ball.

For the food processor method, place the flour, salt, butter, egg, and cream in the work bowl. Process, turning off and on rapidly, for 15 seconds. Continue processing until a ball of dough is formed. Wrap the dough in plastic wrap and refrigerate for 30 minutes.

2. Roll the dough out on a well floured surface to form a 16 x 8-inch rectangle. With a short side nearest you, fold the dough into thirds as for a business letter. Lift the dough off the work surface, scrape the surface clean, and reflour. Return the dough to the work surface with a short side nearest you and the open flap on your right, just like a book. Roll out and fold the dough in this way two more times. Cover with plastic wrap and refrigerate 30 minutes or longer.

3. To prepare the filling, quarter the zucchini lengthwise, and then thinly slice. Cut the carrots into ¼-inch dice. You should have about ⅔ cup. Melt 6 tablespoons of the butter in a medium-size skillet over medium heat. Add the onion, zucchini, carrots, and mushrooms and cook, stirring, until all the vegetables are coated with butter, 1 to 2 minutes. Lower the heat, cover the skillet, and cook 4 minutes. Remove the vegetables, drain well, and reserve.

4. Melt the remaining 4 tablespoons butter in a heavy 3-quart saucepan over medium heat. Add the flour and cook, stirring, 1 to 2 minutes. Whisk in the chicken or turkey stock and the cream, stirring constantly until the mixture thickens and comes to a boil. Remove the pan from the heat and gradually stir in the cheese. Add the salt, nutmeg, and cayenne pepper. Add the drained vegetables and the turkey pieces.

5. Divide the mixture among eight individual baking dishes, or place it in a 2-quart gratin pan.

6. On a floured surface, roll out the pastry ⅛ inch thick. If you are using individual ramekins, cut circles 1 inch wider than the diameter of the ramekins. Cover each dish with a circle of dough, and press the overlapping portions against the outside of the dish. Make a ½-inch slit to serve as a vent in the center of each crust. If you are using a gratin dish, cut a piece of dough larger than the dish and prepare in the same manner. If you have any leftover pastry scraps, cut out designs and decorate the pies with these pieces.

GREAT ACCOMPANIMENTS

A tossed green salad in a white wine vinaigrette, and Shirley's Cranberry Chutney on the side, would be good with these pies. Apple Cinnamon Ice Cream with Apple Wedges would be an easy and delicious dessert.

AT THE MARKET

Fresh ducks are the best for this recipe, but if they are unavailable, use frozen ones. Just be sure to allow at least 24 hours or more to thaw the ducks in the refrigerator.

7. Blend the egg yolk with the cold water, and paint this on the tops of the pastry with a pastry brush. Paint the decorations with the egg glaze also. Place the pies in the refrigerator for 30 minutes or longer. (If you plan to freeze the pies, do not glaze them. Cover tightly with plastic wrap and then with foil. To bake, paint the frozen pastry with the egg glaze and bake in a preheated 375° F oven.)

8. To bake the pies, preheat the oven to 375° F.

9. Bake until the pastry is lightly browned, about 25 minutes.

Serves 8

Braised Duck with Apples

Many of my students tell me they are too intimidated to cook duck: "It's hard to carve" or "It's too greasy." With those thoughts in mind, I developed this recipe. The duck is cut into serving pieces (eliminating the need for tableside carving) and sautéed until golden with all excess fat discarded. Then the duck is braised along with flavorful root vegetables in stock and fresh cider.

2 ducks (5 pounds each)
Salt and freshly ground pepper to taste
1 slab (6 ounces) smoked bacon, partially frozen for easier
*   cutting*
6 tablespoons (¾ stick) unsalted butter
2 cups finely chopped onions
1 cup finely chopped turnips
1 cup finely chopped carrots
1 cup finely chopped celery
1 cup finely chopped leeks, white parts only
2 teaspoons finely chopped garlic
4 cups cider, preferably fresh
4 cups homemade chicken stock (see Index) or good-quality
*   canned broth, plus more if making duck in advance*
2 bay leaves, broken in half
½ teaspoon dried thyme
5 sprigs parsley
1½ cups crème fraîche (see Index)
3 tablespoons Calvados or applejack
2 tart red apples

1. Using poultry shears or a sharp knife, remove the backbone section and the wings from each duck. (The wings and backbone will not be needed for this recipe, but they can be used for making poultry stock.) Using a cleaver or a large sharp knife, cut each duck into 2 breasts, 2 legs, and 2 thighs. Cut the breasts halves, which are usually quite large, in half. Salt and pepper the duck pieces. You will have a total of 16 pieces from the two ducks.

2. Cut the rind from the bacon and discard it. Cut the bacon into ¼-inch dice. In a large heavy casserole or skillet over medium-high heat, sauté the bacon cubes until golden. Remove, and drain on paper towels. Pour off all but a thin layer of fat in the skillet. Then sauté the duck pieces, a few at a time, until well browned. When all the pieces are browned, put them back in the skillet and cover with a lid. Cook 5 minutes more. Remove the duck from the skillet and set aside.

3. Pour off and discard all fat in the skillet. Add 4 tablespoons of the butter to the skillet and melt over medium heat. When it is hot, add the onions, turnips, carrots, celery, leeks, and garlic. Sauté, stirring, until softened, 4 to 5 minutes. Return the bacon to the skillet and mix it in with the vegetables. Then add the duck pieces. Add the cider, 4 cups of the stock, the bay leaves, thyme, and parsley. Bring the mixture to a simmer, cover, and cook at a simmer until the duck pieces are tender when pierced with a knife, about 45 minutes.

4. Remove the duck pieces from the skillet, cover them loosely with foil, and keep warm in oven. Strain the sauce, reserving the vegetables and the bacon. Discard the bay leaves and parsley sprigs. Keep the vegetables and bacon warm, covered with foil, in the oven. Pour the strained sauce into a saucepan and skim all fat from the liquid. Cook the sauce over high heat until it has reduced to 2 cups. Then reduce the heat to low, whisk in the crème fraîche, and continue to cook over low heat until it is smooth and thickened, 3 to 4 minutes. Add the Calvados or applejack. Taste, and add salt if desired. Keep the sauce warm over low heat. (The duck and sauce can be prepared 2 to 3 hours in advance to this point. Cool the duck pieces, and then cover and refrigerate. Cover and refrigerate the sauce, as well as the vegetables. When you are ready to use them, place the duck pieces in a shallow baking pan, cover loosely with foil, and reheat in a preheated 300° F oven until heated through. Do not let the duck get dry; sprinkle it with ¼ to ⅓ cup chicken stock if necessary to keep it moist. Reheat the sauce in a saucepan, and reheat the vegetables in a skillet, stirring, until hot.)

GREAT ACCOMPANIMENTS

The Belgian Endive and Spinach Salad, and the Chocolate Walnut Caramel Tart for dessert, are dishes I like to serve with the duck.

5. When you are ready to assemble the dish, core, but do not peel, the apples. Then cut them into ¼-inch-thick slices. Melt the remaining 2 tablespoons butter in a medium-size skillet over medium heat, and sauté the apple slices in it until golden and just slightly softened.

6. To serve, spread the vegetables on a warm serving tray and place the duck pieces on top. Scatter the apple slices over the duck. Coat the duck slices with some of the sauce, and pass the remaining sauce separately.

Serves 8

MEATS

When I lived in Philadelphia, I loved to shop in the Italian market, an old area of town with narrow streets lined with small food shops. I didn't realize it at the time, but these shopping forays were an important part of my training. The butchers taught me the most: only pale-hued milk-fed veal would do; the beef had to be deep red with plenty of marbling; lamb cuts must come from very young animals; and pork had to be carefully trimmed.

Today, my message to students is always the same: The success of the dish depends on the quality of the meat, and a conscientious cook must know how to shop for it. Talk to your butcher. Ask questions when you order; discuss the color, amount of fat, age, anatomy, and of course the grading (choice or prime). It won't take long before you can distinguish between excellent and inferior cuts.

AT THE MARKET

It's not always easy to find a whole filet of beef at the meat counter of the supermarket. More often than not I special order this cut. Filets can be purchased un-trimmed, with the fat left on, or trimmed, with the fat removed. The price per pound is higher for the trimmed version, but this is the way I always buy it.

Whole trimmed filet of beef is a boneless elongated piece of meat with a large, rounded portion on one end that tapers to a thin slighty flattened tail at the other. Many famous cuts of beef come from the entire filet. The larger and thicker end of the filet is called the head of the filet, the next area is the *Chauteaubriand*, followed by the filet section, the *tournedos*, the *filet mignon*, and finally the tail.

Cold Roast Filet of Beef with Two Accompaniments

The technique used in this recipe for roasting filet of beef is foolproof and always yields moist, flavorful meat. There are two different accompaniments that I like to serve with this beef. For one presentation I slice the filet, garnish it festively with red pepper rings and scallions, and offer it with a bowl of delicious Sweet Red Pepper and Zucchini Relish. On other occasions I make a creamy and piquant mousse flavored with horseradish and green peppercorns and serve it unmolded with the filet slices around it. The mousse is the invention of Suzanne Karpus, a talented teacher at La Belle Pomme and a creative caterer.

The meat can be roasted two days ahead, the relish prepared as much as five days, but at least two days, in advance, and the mousse the day before. I have served this filet with one or the other of these accompaniments at countless cocktail buffets with great success.

10 slices bacon
1 filet of beef (3 pounds), trimmea
6 tablespoons vegetable oil
½ cup chopped onions
½ cup chopped carrots
½ cup chopped celery
2 bay leaves
Sweet Red Pepper and Zucchini Relish or Suzanne's Horseradish
*   Mousse (recipes follow)*

Garnishes with the Relish
Curly endive
1 red bell pepper, cut into thin rings
6 scallions (green onions), trimmed, with 2 inches of green stems

Garnishes with the Mousse
Curly endive
Pumpernickel and rye bread, sliced

1. Blanch the bacon in simmering water to cover for 10 minutes. Drain well and set aside.

2. Preheat the oven to 350° F.

3. Pat the beef dry with paper towels. Heat the oil in a large heavy skillet over medium-high heat. When it is hot, add the meat and brown well on all sides. Transfer the meat to a rack in a roasting pan. Combine the chopped onions, carrots, and celery in a bowl and mix well. Pat the vegetables onto the top and sides of the meat. Crumble the bay leaves over the vegetables. Drape the bacon slices over the vegetables so they extend down the sides of the meat.

4. Roast the meat to desired doneness, about 45 minutes for medium rare. A meat thermometer should read 140° to 145° F. Discard the vegetables and bacon, and let the meat cool completely. Cover, and refrigerate until firm. (The roast can be prepared two days ahead.) Cut the meat diagonally into ¼-inch slices.

5. To serve with the relish, set a bowl of relish at one end of a large oval platter. Arrange the meat on the platter, slices overlapping. Cover the edge of the platter with curly endive. Top the endive with pepper rings and scallions.

To serve with the mousse, arrange a border of endive around the mousse, then arrange meat in overlapping slices in a border around the endive. Serve with baskets of sliced pumpernickel and rye bread.

Serves 8

SWEET RED PEPPER AND ZUCCHINI RELISH

½ cup water
¼ teaspoon ground allspice
⅛ teaspoon dried red pepper flakes
1 bay leaf
¼ cup balsamic vinegar
¼ cup olive oil
1 tablespoon minced garlic
1½ cups chopped onions
1½ cups chopped red bell peppers
1½ cups chopped zucchini
1 cup homemade beef stock (see Index) or good-quality canned
*   broth*
Salt and freshly ground pepper to taste

1. Bring the water, allspice, pepper flakes, and bay leaf to a boil in a small non-aluminum saucepan over medium-high heat. Reduce the heat and simmer 5 minutes. Then add the vinegar and simmer 5 minutes more. Discard the bay leaf and set the sauce aside.

2. Heat the oil in a large heavy skillet over medium heat. Add the garlic and onions and stir 4 minutes. Do not let them get brown. Add the red peppers and stir 3 minutes. Add the zucchini and stir 3 minutes. Blend in ¼ cup of the stock and 2 tablespoons of the vinegar mixture. Cook until the liquid has evaporated. Repeat, adding stock and vinegar sauce in the same amounts, three more times. Each time let the liquids cook down until almost evaporated. Season with salt and pepper, and cool to room temperature. Spoon the relish into a glass bowl, cover, and chill at least 2 days. (The relish can be made 5 days ahead; keep covered and refrigerated.)

Makes about 2½ cups

SUZANNE'S HORSERADISH MOUSSE

Special equipment: 4-cup mold or soufflé dish

1 envelope unflavored gelatin
½ cup water
6 ounces prepared horseradish
1 teaspoon Dijon mustard
1 cup heavy or whipping cream
1 cup sour cream
2 tablespoons green peppercorns (packing liquid drained well)
2 tablespoons very finely chopped green scallion (green onion)
  tops

1. Place the gelatin in a small bowl and add the water. Stir, then let stand until the gelatin softens, about 5 minutes.

2. Drain the horseradish thoroughly, and then squeeze it dry in a clean kitchen towel.

3. Stir the mustard and cream together in a medium-size heavy saucepan. Place the pan over medium heat and bring to a simmer. Remove from the heat and whisk in the softened gelatin. Put the sour cream in a mixing bowl, and gradually whisk the cream mixture into it until well incorporated. Stir in the horseradish and green peppercorns.

4. Generously oil a 4-cup mold or soufflé dish. Pour the mousse mixture into the mold, and cover loosely with plastic wrap. Refrigerate 6 hours or until set. (The mousse can be prepared 1 day in advance. Cover and refrigerate until needed.)

5. To unmold, run a sharp knife around the edge of the mold. Invert the mold onto a serving plate and tap the bottom with the handle of

GREAT ACCOMPANIMENTS

For a holiday cocktail buffet, I arrange a table of substantial foods for sampling along with drinks. With this filet, accompanied by either the relish or the mousse, I have served the Smoked Salmon Butter, Cherry Tomatoes Filled with Avocado Mousse, Chinese Roasted Pork Tenderloins with Dipping Sauce, and a platter of interesting cheeses garnished with fresh fruit.

For dessert, a napkin-lined basket filled with Chocolate and Almond Crisps, a plate of Lucy's Nanaimo Bars, and a bowl of Spiced Madeleines are tempting creations that can easily be eaten by hand.

a knife. If the mousse does not drop out, immerse the mold in an inch of warm water and repeat the process. Sprinkle the mousse with the chopped scallion tops.

Makes about 3½ to 4 cups

Roast Stuffed Filet of Beef

My students are wild about filet of beef—not just plain roast tenderloin, but sophisticated preparations to use when entertaining. Stuffed with a colorful filling of sun-dried tomatoes, toasted pine nuts, and parsley, this makes a very elegant presentation.

Special equipment: String for tying the roast; meat pounder

7 tablespoons olive oil
⅔ cup pine nuts
½ cup chopped shallots
4 teaspoons finely chopped garlic
⅔ cup chopped sun-dried tomatoes (packing oil drained)
2 cups fresh bread crumbs
½ cup chopped fresh parsley
Salt and freshly ground pepper to taste
1 large egg, lightly beaten
1 filet of beef (3½ pounds), trimmed
Thin sheets of beef fat to cover the roast

1. Heat 3 tablespoons of the oil in a medium-size heavy skillet over medium heat. When it is hot, add the pine nuts. Toss and stir until golden, 2 to 3 minutes. (Pine nuts brown very quickly, so watch carefully.) Remove the nuts with a slotted spoon and drain them on paper towels. Add the shallots to the pan and cook, stirring, until softened, 2 to 3 minutes. Then add the garlic and sun-dried tomatoes, and cook, stirring, 2 to 3 minutes more.

2. Remove the skillet from the heat and stir in the pine nuts, bread crumbs, and parsley. Season with salt and pepper to taste. Let the mixture cool, and then add the egg and mix well.

3. Place the filet of beef on a work surface, and using a sharp knife, make a slit lengthwise down the center of the meat, cutting about two thirds of the way through the meat. Spread the meat open; then pound each side with a pounder to flatten slightly. Pat the stuffing

AT THE MARKET

Ask the butcher to give you a thin piece of fat to cover the filet while roasting. You may have to use several pieces to completely cover the meat. The fat will baste the meat and keep it moist while cooking.

GREAT ACCOMPANIMENTS

For hors d'oeuvres, I often serve the Mushroom Pâté before this entrée. To go with the beef, the Garlic and Butter–Roasted Potatoes and the Stir-Fry of Zucchini, Onions, and Sweet Red Peppers are excellent complements. The Frozen Chocolate Marbled Mousse served in scooped-out lemon shells makes a great finale.

over the prepared surface of the meat, and bring the two halves back together. Tie the meat at 1½-inch intervals to close.

4. Preheat the oven to 375° F.

5. Heat the remaining 4 tablespoons olive oil in a large heavy skillet over medium-high heat. When it is very hot, add the filet. Brown the meat well on all sides. Salt and pepper the meat, then place it on a rack in a roasting pan. Drape the fat over the roast. Cook until the meat is medium rare and a meat thermometer registers 140° to 145° F, about 45 minutes.

6. Remove the roast from the oven and let it rest 10 minutes. Remove the fat. Cut the meat into 1-inch-thick slices. Remove the strings and arrange overlapping slices on a heated serving platter.

Serves 8 to 10

Corned Beef and Cabbage Pot Pies

I love to serve these for a fireside Sunday night supper during cold weather. The puff pastry bakes to a golden brown, and the corned beef and cabbage filling is rich and creamy.

Special equipment: Six 1-cup ramekins (4 inches in diameter)

8 ounces best-quality cooked corned beef, very thinly sliced
1 small head cabbage (about ¾ pound)
3 tablespoons unsalted butter
3 tablespoons all-purpose flour
1 cup milk
1 cup grated Gruyère cheese
¼ teaspoon freshly grated nutmeg
Generous sprinkling of cayenne pepper
¼ teaspoon dried dill
1½ tablespoons stone-ground mustard
Puff Pastry (recipe follows)
1 large egg
1 teaspoon cold water

1. Cut the corned beef into strips 4 inches long and ½ inch wide.

AT THE MARKET

I have made these pot pies with many kinds of corned beef, but I think the corned beef bought at a good delicatessen always tastes best.

GREAT ACCOMPANIMENTS

These pies are filling, so usually I serve a seasonal green salad in a red wine vinaigrette to go with them. The Lemon Mousse Squares are a fine dessert to offer for this menu.

2. Cut out the tough inner core from the cabbage. (If you have bought a larger head of cabbage, reserve the extra for another use.) Then cut the cabbage into strips ½ inch wide. Cook the cabbage in lightly salted boiling water to cover until tender, 5 to 8 minutes. Remove, drain, and dry the cabbage.

3. Melt the butter in a medium-size heavy saucepan over medium heat. Add the flour and cook, stirring, 2 minutes. Whisk in the milk, and whisk constantly until the mixture is smooth and very thick, 4 to 5 minutes. Add the grated cheese gradually, a handful at a time. Stir in the nutmeg, cayenne pepper, dill, and mustard. Add the corned beef and cabbage and mix well. Taste the mixture, and adjust the seasonings if desired. The filling will be very thick. (The filling may be made several hours in advance to this point. Cool the mixture, cover with plastic wrap, and refrigerate until needed.)

4. To assemble the pies, divide the filling evenly among six individual ramekins. Then cut the prepared puff pastry in half. On a lightly floured surface, roll half the dough out to form a rectangle about 14 x 12 inches and ⅜ inch thick. Cut out three dough circles 6¼ inches in diameter. Carefully set aside the pastry scraps, which will be used later for the garnish.

5. Blend the egg and the cold water, and paint one side of each pastry circle with some of this egg glaze. Then carefully place a pastry round, glazed side down, over one of the ramekins. Firmly press the overlapping pastry against the outside of the ramekin, pushing slightly up at the rim until the pastry adheres. It is important to only push against the sides of the ramekins. If you press down from the top, you might cut the dough on the edge of the ramekin.

6. Press the tines of a fork around the pastry sides to make a decorative pattern. Then, with a small sharp knife, trim the overhanging pastry to make an even border all around the ramekin. You should have a ¾-inch overhang around the edge after trimming.

7. Repeat this process with the remaining pastry rounds. Then roll out the remaining pastry dough, cut out three more rounds, and repeat. Save the scraps from the second batch of pastry as well.

8. When all the pies are covered with pastry, brush the tops and sides with egg glaze. Score the tops, making several diagonal lines to form a grid pattern. Be careful to make just a tracing in the dough and not to cut through it.

9. Using the reserved scraps, cut out twelve leaves or hearts or other decorative shapes, and brush them with egg glaze. Place the pies and the decorative shapes on a baking sheet and refrigerate, loosely covered with aluminum foil, at least 1 hour. (The pies and cutouts can be prepared several hours or 1 day ahead to this point, then kept loosely covered and refrigerated.)

10. When you are ready to bake, preheat the oven to 400° F.

11. Place the baking sheet with the pies and cutout shapes on the center shelf, and bake until golden brown, 20 to 25 minutes. Remove the pan from the oven and top each pie with a leaf or a heart. Place the pies on serving plates. Use the remaining decorative shapes as a garnish for each plate.

Serves 6

PUFF PASTRY

The puff pastry for this recipe gets four instead of six turns. The pastry works better as a topping for the pies without the final two turns. If you plan to freeze the dough, make four depressions in the dough with the ball of your finger as a reminder that only four turns have been made.

Special equipment: Heavy-duty standing mixer

3¼ cups (6½ sticks) unsalted butter
3 cups unbleached all-purpose flour
1 cup cake flour
1½ teaspoons salt
½ cup ice water, plus more if needed

1. Cut each stick of butter into paper-thin slices. Place the slices on a plate and freeze for 15 minutes.

2. Combine the two flours and the salt in the bowl of an electric mixer, preferably one fitted with a flat beater. Place the butter on top.

3. On slow speed, blend the butter and flour together. Mix until the butter still remains in lumps but is coated well with flour. Add just enough ice water to make the mixture form a mass of dough (with butter still in lumps). Add the water gradually, since you may need slightly less than ½ cup. Only if the flour is very dry will you need more.

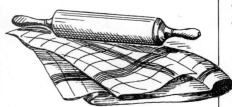

AS A VARIATION

For St. Patrick's Day, I cut out and bake shamrock shapes and garnish the pies with these Irish accents.

4. On a lightly floured surface, roll the dough out to form an 18 x 8-inch rectangle. The lumps of butter will show through the rolled dough. Lightly flour the dough.

5. With the short side of the rectangle nearest you, fold the dough into thirds as for a business letter. Lift the folded dough off the work surface, scrape the surface clean, and reflour. Return the dough to the work surface with a short side nearest you. Roll out and fold the dough in this way three more times for a total of four turns. Cover with plastic wrap and refrigerate 40 minutes. (The dough may be used now, or you can freeze it and then defrost it in the refrigerator for later use.)

Roast Veal with Chestnuts and Shiitake Mushrooms

When I lived in Dijon, my French "mother," a fabulous Burgundian cook, always browned her roast in bacon fat and then cooked it in a mixture of wine and stock. Sautéed mushrooms and pearl onions were a frequent garnish to the meat. For my version, I've included shiitake mushrooms and fresh chestnuts.

1 boneless veal rump roast (4 to 4½ pounds), rolled and tied
3 large cloves garlic, cut into thin slivers
1 slab (8 ounces) smoked bacon, partially frozen for easier cutting
¾ cup finely chopped carrots
¾ cup finely chopped leeks, white parts only
¾ cup finely chopped celery
3 cups homemade beef stock (see Index) or good-quality canned broth
1½ cups dry red wine
1 bay leaf, crumbled
Salt and freshly ground pepper to taste
2 tablespoons cornstarch
3 tablespoons cold water
32 Cooked Fresh Chestnuts (recipe follows), or 32 canned unsweetened chestnuts
Sautéed Shiitake Mushrooms (recipe follows)

1. Preheat the oven to 350° F.

AT THE MARKET

My favorite time of the year for this recipe is the fall, when I can get fresh chestnuts. The fresh nuts are far superior in taste, texture, and aroma to canned ones in this dish.

2. Stud the veal roast all over with the garlic slivers.

3. Cut the rind from the bacon and discard it. Cut the bacon into ¼-inch dice. In a large heavy ovenproof skillet over medium-high heat, sauté the bacon cubes, stirring, until they are golden and fat is rendered, 4 to 5 minutes. Remove the bacon with a slotted spoon, drain on paper towels, and reserve.

4. Pour off and set aside all but 4 tablespoons of the fat in the skillet. Reheat the fat in the skillet over medium heat, and when it is hot, brown the roast well on all sides. Remove the roast and set it aside. Add the chopped carrots, leeks, and celery to the skillet, and sauté until just softened, 4 to 5 minutes. (If necessary, add 1 to 2 tablespoons of the bacon fat to the pan to sauté the vegetables.)

5. Place the veal roast on top of the vegetables. Then mix the stock and wine together and pour ½ cup of this mixture over the roast. Add the crumbled bay leaf, and salt and pepper the roast. Place the skillet in the oven and cook until the meat is tender, 1½ to 2 hours. Baste the meat every 20 to 25 minutes with ½ cup of the wine/stock mixture. The roast is done when it is tender when pierced with a knife and when a meat thermometer registers 150° F. Remove the roast from the skillet, drape it loosely with foil to keep it warm, and let it rest 20 minutes before slicing.

6. While the roast is resting, prepare the sauce: Strain the vegetables and pan juices from the skillet through a large fine-mesh sieve into a medium-size saucepan. Press down on the vegetables to extract all the juices. Skim the fat from this mixture, and then measure 2 cups of this liquid. If you do not have 2 cups, add more wine and stock (1 part wine and 2 parts stock).

7. Place the saucepan over medium heat and bring the liquid to a simmer. Mix the cornstarch with the water to form a paste. Whisk this mixture into the sauce, and continue to whisk until the sauce thickens, about 2 to 3 minutes. Taste, and add salt and pepper as desired. Add the chestnuts, mushrooms, and reserved bacon to the sauce, and cook just to heat through, only 1 to 2 minutes.

8. To serve, slice the veal roast into ½-inch-thick pieces and arrange them in overlapping slices on a warm serving platter. Using a slotted spoon, sprinkle the chestnuts, mushrooms, and bacon over the veal. Ladle some of the sauce over the veal, and pass the remaining sauce separately.

Serves 8

GREAT ACCOMPANIMENTS

*Garlic and Butter–Roasted Potatoes
and either buttered fresh green
beans or glazed carrots are good side
dishes to serve with the veal. The
Grapefruit Mousse makes an excellent ending to this menu.*

COOKED FRESH CHESTNUTS

*32 chestnuts
2 tablespoons unsalted butter
2 cups homemade beef stock (see Index) or good-quality canned
   broth*

1. With a sharp knife, cut an "x" through the skin on one side of
each chestnut. Drop the chestnuts into boiling water and cook for 3
minutes. Drain, cool, and peel off the skin.

2. Preheat the oven to 325° F.

3. Melt the butter in a heavy ovenproof casserole or skillet. When it
is hot, add the chestnuts and toss well for 2 to 3 minutes. Add the
stock and bring it to a simmer. Cover the casserole and put it in the
oven. Bake until the chestnuts are tender when pierced with a knife,
45 to 60 minutes. (The chestnuts can be prepared several hours or 1
day ahead; cool, cover, and refrigerate until needed.)

SAUTEED SHIITAKE MUSHROOMS

*6 to 8 ounces fresh shiitake mushrooms
2 tablespoons unsalted butter
2 tablespoons oil*

1. Remove and discard the stems from the mushrooms, and slice the
mushrooms into ½-inch strips. (See note.)

2. Heat the butter and oil in a large heavy skillet over high heat.
When it is hot, add the mushrooms and sauté, stirring constantly, for
2 to 3 minutes. Remove, and drain on paper towels. (The mushrooms
can be prepared several hours in advance and kept loosely covered at
room temperature.)

Makes about 1 cup

Note: If you can't find fresh shiitake mushrooms, you can use 2
ounces dried. Soak them in boiling water to cover until softened,
about 30 minutes. Drain, pat dry, and slice. Then sauté as described.

Roast Stuffed Veal with Red Wine and Shallot Butter

I spent many weeks perfecting this recipe, and my colleagues and fellow teachers, Jim Budros and Rich Terapak, both of whom helped test and retest this dish, contributed many hours as well. The result is a real star. Filled with thin slices of prosciutto and a parsley-lemon stuffing, the veal is rolled, tied, and roasted. When sliced, the meat reveals a beautiful pattern of the white veal, pink prosciutto, and green filling. Rounds of Red Wine and Shallot Butter top the roast.

Special equipment: String for tying the meat

4 cups loosely packed fresh bread crumbs
4 cups loosely packed chopped fresh parsley
8 garlic cloves, minced
4 scallions (green onions), white parts and 2 inches of green
    stems, minced
2 large eggs, beaten
3 tablespoons snipped fresh chives
2 teaspoons grated lemon zest
1 rack of veal (7 to 8 pounds), boned and trimmed, ribs reserved
    and separated
Freshly ground pepper to taste
24 thin slices prosciutto
3 tablespoons unsalted butter, at room temperature
1 cup dry white wine
1 cup homemade chicken stock (see Index) or good-quality canned
    broth
Red Wine and Shallot Butter (recipe follows)

1. To make the stuffing, combine the bread crumbs, parsley, garlic, scallions, eggs, chives, and lemon zest in a large bowl. Set aside.

2. Cut off the top fatty layer of the meat (flank portion) and discard. Trim all fat from the roast.

3. Using a sharp knife, cut away and reserve the long cylindrical piece of meat (rib eye) along the long side of the roast. Trim off any remaining fat. Arrange the larger piece of meat on a work surface, boned side up. Sprinkle it with pepper.

4. Layer half of the prosciutto slices, overlapping, on top of the

AT THE MARKET

You will most likely need to special-order this cut of veal. Ask for a 7- to 8-pound rack of veal, and have the butcher remove the backbone and then separate and reserve the ribs. The butcher should remove the shoulder blade and all sinew and cartilage from the meat. The prepared meat should weigh about 4 pounds.

GREAT ACCOMPANIMENTS

Braised Fennel, Carrots, and Snow Peas and a salad of seasonal greens in vinaigrette make festive garnishes to the veal. The Coconut Caramel Flan is a perfect dessert.

meat. Spread the reserved stuffing evenly over the prosciutto layer. Top with the remaining prosciutto.

5. Place the rib eye section along one long edge of the roast, and roll the roast up jelly roll fashion. Tie the roll with string at 1-inch intervals, and rub the surface with the butter. (The veal can be prepared up to 6 hours ahead; keep covered and refrigerated.)

6. When you are ready to roast the veal, preheat the oven to 375° F.

7. Set the veal on a rack in a large roasting pan. Place the rib bones around the edge of the pan. Pour the wine and stock over the roast. Cook, basting the roast with pan juices every 20 minutes, until the meat is tender and a thermometer inserted in the thickest part registers 150° F, about 1 hour and 20 minutes.

8. Remove the roast from the oven and let it stand 20 minutes. Remove the string, and cut the meat into ½- to ¾-inch slices. Arrange the slices on a warm platter and top with the slices of Red Wine and Shallot Butter. Discard the veal bones.

Serves 6

RED WINE AND SHALLOT BUTTER

13 tablespoons unsalted butter, at room temperature
6 tablespoons chopped shallots
1 teaspoon minced garlic
½ cup dry red wine
⅛ teaspoon salt, or to taste

1. Melt 1 tablespoon of the butter in a medium-size heavy skillet over medium-high heat. Add the shallots and stir until soft, 2 to 3 minutes. Add the garlic and stir 1 minute. Add the wine and let it boil until all the liquid evaporates, stirring frequently, about 5 minutes. Cool completely.

2. Using a rubber spatula, work the shallot mixture and the salt into the remaining butter. Shape the butter into a 1½-inch-diameter log. Wrap it in foil and refrigerate until firm. (The butter can be prepared 2 days ahead. Keep covered and refrigerated.)

3. Cut the butter into ¼-inch-thick rounds. Let them stand at room temperature 10 to 15 minutes before serving.

Makes one 6-ounce log

Veal Ragoût with Red Peppers and Olives

One of the questions my students most frequently ask is "Can I make it in advance?" This wonderful veal stew not only can be made ahead but actually improves in flavor when prepared the day before.

3 pounds veal stew meat (see step 1)
5 tablespoons olive oil, plus more if needed
½ cup chopped onion
½ cup chopped carrots
4 tablespoons all-purpose flour
1 teaspoon dried thyme
½ teaspoon dried basil
1 bay leaf, broken in half
3 sprigs parsley
2 cloves garlic, crushed
½ teaspoon plus 1½ tablespoons salt
Freshly ground pepper to taste
1 can (28 ounces) Italian-style tomatoes, well drained
4 cups homemade chicken stock (see Index) or good-quality canned broth
1 cup dry white wine
1 large red bell pepper, stemmed, seeded, and cut diagonally into 1-inch squares
1¼ pounds fresh fettuccine noodles (see Index), or 1 pound good-quality dry fettuccine
4 tablespoons (½ stick) unsalted butter
½ cup pitted black olives, drained
Parsley Lemon Garnish (recipe follows)

1. Meat cut from the veal shoulder works well in stews. Cut the meat into 1½-inch chunks, trimming away all the fat and gristle (or ask the butcher to do this). Pat the veal dry.

2. In a large, heavy, flameproof 4- to 5-quart casserole with a lid, heat 5 tablespoons olive oil over medium-high heat. Add the veal, and brown it in the hot oil a few pieces at a time. Remove the browned meat to drain on paper towels, and continue until all the meat is browned. (It may be necessary to add more oil during the browning process.)

GREAT ACCOMPANIMENTS

A crisp tossed green salad, Parmesan Garlic Rolls, and Espresso Cheesecake complete the menu for this meal.

3. When all the meat has been browned, put the onions and carrots in the casserole, add more oil if necessary, and cook, stirring, 4 to 5 minutes. Return the veal to the casserole, sprinkle with the flour, and toss while cooking for 2 to 3 minutes. Remove the casserole from the heat, and add the thyme, basil, bay leaf, parsley, garlic, ½ teaspoon salt, a generous grinding of pepper, tomatoes, stock, and wine. Return the casserole to medium heat and bring to a simmer, stirring. Cover, and cook at a simmer over low heat for 1 hour.

4. Remove the lid, and cook 20 to 25 minutes more. Then add the pieces of red pepper, and cook another 10 to 15 minutes.

5. Strain the meat and vegetables, reserving the liquid, and remove the parsley sprigs and bay leaf. Return the liquid to the casserole and skim off any fat. Over high heat, reduce the liquid by one third, or until thickened. This will take 10 to 15 minutes.

6. While the liquid is reducing, bring 4 quarts of water to a boil in a large pot over high heat. Add the 1½ tablespoons salt and the fettuccine to the water, and stir with a long-handled spoon. Cook until *al dente,* or just firm to the bite. (Fresh pasta will cook in 2 to 3 minutes; dried pasta will take longer.) Drain the pasta well, toss it with the butter, and keep warm.

7. Return the meat and vegetables to the casserole, add the olives, and reheat 4 to 5 minutes. (The ragoût, but not the pasta, may be made 1 to 2 days in advance to this point. Cover and refrigerate. Reheat over low heat, and cook the pasta, before serving.)

8. When you are ready to serve the ragoût, arrange it on a large deep platter, and sprinkle with the Parsley Lemon Garnish. Serve surrounded with fettuccine noodles.

Serves 6

PARSLEY LEMON GARNISH

½ cup chopped fresh parsley
2 teaspoons finely chopped garlic
2 teaspoons finely chopped lemon zest
¼ cup chopped scallions (green onions)

Mix all the ingredients together in a mixing bowl. (The garnish can be prepared several hours in advance; cover and refrigerate.)

Makes about ¾ cup

Cold Roast Veal with Tomato-Sage Relish

A beautiful presentation, this roast of veal studded with slivers of black olives reveals a striking black-and-white pattern when sliced. The colorful relish made with summer tomatoes, fresh sage, and onions is a perfect complement to the meat. Best of all, this entire dish can be prepared a day ahead, making it an ideal main course to serve for a special summertime dinner.

1 boned veal rump roast (3¾ pounds)
½ cup pitted and slivered Niçoise olives
3 cloves garlic, slivered
¼ cup olive oil
Salt and freshly ground pepper to taste
1½ cups homemade chicken stock (see Index) or good-quality
  canned broth
1½ cups dry white wine
1 lemon, cut in half
Tomato-Sage Relish (recipe follows)

1. Preheat the oven to 325° F.

2. If the roast has been tied, untie it. Using a sharp knife, stud the entire surface of the meat with the olive slivers. Then stud the meat with the garlic slivers. (When the meat is untied, the roast will open up slightly. Stud the inside as much as possible with olive and garlic slivers too.) Retie the roast and pat it dry.

3. Heat the olive oil in a large heavy skillet over medium-high heat. Add the roast and brown well on all sides. Remove the roast, salt and pepper it well, and place it on a rack in a roasting pan. (Do not clean the skillet in which roast was browned. It will be used when you make the Tomato-Sage Relish.)

4. Place the roast in the oven. Combine the chicken stock and white wine, and baste the meat every 20 minutes with ½ cup of this mixture. If the basting mixture evaporates too quickly on the bottom of the roasting pan, pour in more of the mixture. After the roast has cooked 30 minutes, squeeze the juice of one lemon half over it. After the roast has cooked 1 hour, squeeze the juice of the remaining lemon half over it. The roast will take 1½ to 2 hours to cook. The temperature should be 150° F when done.

AT THE MARKET

Small black Niçoise olives are usually packed in olive oil. I think they are the most flavorful and nicest to use with this roast, but other Mediterranean-style olives can be substituted.

GREAT ACCOMPANIMENTS

The Summer Pesto Tart makes an excellent first course. Accompany the veal with the Zucchini, Yellow Squash, and Romaine Salad, and end with the Red Grape and Green Grape Sorbets.

5. Remove the roast from the pan and reserve ¼ cup pan juices for the relish. Cool the roast to room temperature. Cover and refrigerate until cold, 1 to 2 hours, or longer. (The roast can be prepared 1 day ahead.) While the roast is cooling, prepare the Tomato-Sage Relish.

6. To serve the roast, slice it when cold into ¼-inch-thick slices. (Try not to make the slices thicker, because the thin slices look nicer and work better with the amount of relish for each serving.) Place the relish in a bowl in the center of a serving platter, and arrange the veal, overlapping, around the relish.

Serves 8

TOMATO-SAGE RELISH

Olive oil
1½ cups chopped onions
3 teaspoons finely chopped garlic
2½ cups peeled, seeded, chopped ripe tomatoes, well drained
Reserved ¼ cup basting juices
¼ teaspoon salt
¾ teaspoon freshly ground white pepper
1 teaspoon chopped fresh sage leaves
Sage sprigs, for garnish

1. Using the skillet in which the roast was browned, add enough oil to make 3 tablespoons. Heat the oil over medium heat. When it is hot, add the onions and garlic. Cook, stirring, 2 to 3 minutes. The onions will turn brown.

2. Squeeze the chopped, drained tomatoes gently in a clean kitchen towel to extract as much liquid as possible, and then add them to the skillet. Toss well, and add the reserved basting liquid, salt, and white pepper. Stir gently, and cook only 3 to 4 minutes.

3. Remove the skillet from the heat and set it aside to cool. Drain the mixture in a colander if it is runny. Add the chopped sage. Taste, and add more salt and pepper if desired. (The relish can be made 1 day in advance. Cover and refrigerate. Bring relish to room temperature before serving.) To serve, place the relish in a bowl, and garnish with sprigs of sage.

Makes about 2 cups

Veal Chops Stuffed with Chèvre and Dill

This is one of my favorite veal dishes. The chops, stuffed with chèvre and fresh dill, are breaded and sautéed until golden and crisp. When guests cut into them, they are always surprised and delighted to find this delicious filling.

Special equipment: Wooden toothpicks

6 veal rib chops, trimmed (see step 1)
8 ounces chèvre, preferably Montrachet
2 tablespoons minced fresh dill, or 2 teaspoons dried
1½ teaspoons grated lemon zest
½ teaspoon coarsely ground pepper
1 cup milk
1 large egg, beaten
1⅓ cups dry bread crumbs
¾ cup all-purpose flour
Salt and freshly ground pepper to taste
Vegetable oil
6 thin slices lemon, for garnish
6 sprigs dill, for garnish

1. Ask your butcher to cut the chops ¾ inch thick, with 2- to 3-inch bones and all the meat to one side of the bone.

2. Freeze the chops until firm but not solid, to facilitate cutting, about 30 minutes. Place a chop on a work surface. Holding a knife parallel to the surface, cut a deep, wide pocket in the center of the chop. Repeat with the remaining chops.

3. Mix the chèvre, minced dill, lemon zest, and pepper in a bowl. Spread 2 tablespoons of this mixture in the pocket of each chop. Secure with toothpicks. (The chops can be prepared 6 hours ahead. Cover and refrigerate.)

4. Mix the milk and egg together in a small bowl. Spread the bread crumbs on one plate and the flour on another. Season the chops with salt and pepper. Dip each chop in the flour and shake off any excess. Then dip it in the milk mixture, and finally in the bread crumbs; shake off any excess.

AT THE MARKET

Veal chops can be cut from the shoulder, the veal rib rack, or the loin. For this recipe, ask your butcher to cut the first four chops from a veal rib rack to make up your order. These are the nicest and best chops for stuffing. If the fifth through the eighth chops are used, make certain they are trimmed well so all the meat is on one side of the bone. The chops should be about ¾ to 1 inch thick.

GREAT ACCOMPANIMENTS

The Shrimp and Scallop Timbales are a fine first course to precede the veal. Braised Fennel, Carrots, and Snow Peas and the Wild Rice and Pine Nut Pilaf, made without the pine nuts, are elegant dishes to serve with the chops. For dessert, the Cassis Walnut Tart makes a splendid finish.

5. Heat a ⅛-inch-deep layer of oil in two large heavy skillets over medium heat. When it is hot, add the chops and cook until they are crisp on the outside and just pink in the center, 4 to 5 minutes per side. (To check for doneness, make a very small cut with a paring knife and check color. This small slit won't spoil the appearance of the chop.)

6. Remove the toothpicks, and arrange the chops in pairs on a heated platter, crossing the bones. Top each serving with a lemon slice and a dill sprig.

Serves 6

Alsatian Stuffed Veal Chops with Cabbage

I love the earthy quality of this hearty dish. The chops, stuffed with a mixture of bacon and mushrooms, are sautéed until golden and served on a bed of cabbage cooked with garlic. A mustard cream sauce, flavored with Gruyère cheese and cayenne pepper, adds a delicious flavor to the veal.

Special equipment: Wooden toothpicks

6 veal rib chops (see step 1 and "At the Market," page 163)
3 thick slices bacon
6 tablespoons (¾ stick) unsalted butter
3 tablespoons finely chopped shallots
6 ounces mushrooms, cleaned and finely chopped
Salt and freshly ground black pepper to taste
1 medium-size head cabbage (about 1¼ pounds)
1 teaspoon salt
2 cloves garlic, crushed
1½ cups heavy or whipping cream
½ cup grated Gruyère cheese
1 tablespoon stone-ground mustard
⅛ teaspoon cayenne pepper
½ cup milk
1 large egg, lightly beaten
⅔ cup all-purpose flour
¾ cup dry bread crumbs, plus more if needed
4 tablespoons vegetable oil

1. Ask your butcher to cut the rib chops 1 inch thick, with 2- to 3-inch bones and all the meat to one side of the bone. Trim the chops of all excess fat, and partially freeze them for easier cutting, about 30 minutes.

2. Fry the bacon in a medium-size heavy skillet over medium-high heat. When it is crisp, remove the bacon and drain on paper towels. Discard the grease in the skillet. Add 2 tablespoons of the butter to the skillet and melt over medium-high heat. Add the shallots and mushrooms and cook, stirring, until all the liquid in the pan has evaporated, 4 to 5 minutes. Crumble the bacon and mix it with the mushrooms and shallots. Taste, and add salt and pepper as desired. Remove from the heat.

3. Place a chop on a work surface. Holding a knife parallel to the surface, cut a deep, wide pocket in the center of the chop. Repeat with the remaining chops. Stuff each pocket with some of the mushroom filling. Secure with toothpicks. Salt and pepper each chop. (The chops can be prepared 6 hours ahead to this point. Cover and refrigerate. Bring to room temperature before sautéing.)

4. Thirty minutes before you are ready to cook the veal, prepare the cabbage: Core the cabbage and cut it into ½-inch-wide strips. Bring 2 quarts of water to a boil in a large heavy saucepan. Add 1 teaspoon salt, the garlic, and the cabbage, and cook at a simmer until the cabbage is tender, about 10 minutes. Remove and drain. Discard the garlic, and add salt and pepper to taste. Keep warm.

5. While the cabbage is cooking, prepare the sauce: Place the cream in a large heavy saucepan over medium-high heat, and reduce to 1 cup, about 5 minutes. Then slowly stir in the cheese. When it has melted, stir in the mustard and cayenne pepper. Taste, and adjust the seasonings if desired. Keep warm.

6. Mix the milk and egg together in a shallow bowl. Spread the flour on one plate and the bread crumbs on another. Dredge the chops in the flour, and shake off any excess. Then dip the chops in the milk mixture, and finally in the bread crumbs; shake off any excess. Divide the remaining 4 tablespoons butter and the vegetable oil between two large heavy skillets. Place the skillets over medium-high heat, and when the butter and oil are hot, add the chops and sauté until golden and crisp on the outside and just pink in the center, 4 to 5 minutes per side. (To check for doneness, make a small cut with a paring knife and check the color. It won't spoil the appearance of the chop.) Remove, and pull out the toothpicks.

GREAT ACCOMPANIMENTS

Serve the Garlic and Butter–Roasted Potatoes and a seasonal green salad in a vinaigrette with these chops. The Wine and Ginger-Marinated Hot Fruit, served with Spiced Madeleines, is a perfect ending for this menu.

7. To serve, arrange a bed of cabbage on an ovenproof gratin pan or platter. Place the chops on top, and cover with the reserved sauce. Place under a preheated broiler to brown lightly, 1 to 2 minutes. Serve hot.

Serves 6

Roast Lamb with a Pepper Coating

A good friend, who is an editor of a food magazine, described this dish well: "So easy, so sophisticated, so delicious."

½ cup olive oil
½ cup dry red wine
½ cup soy sauce
2 large cloves garlic, crushed
2 bay leaves, halved
1 leg of lamb (6 pounds), trimmed of all but a thin coating of fat
2½ tablespoons black peppercorns, coarsely crushed
1 tablespoon unsalted butter, at room temperature
Bay leaves or watercress sprigs, for garnish

1. Combine the oil, wine, soy sauce, garlic, and bay leaves in a large non-aluminum baking dish. Stir well. Add the lamb, and turn to coat it well. Refrigerate 24 hours, covered, turning occasionally.

2. Bring the lamb to room temperature.

3. Preheat the oven to 450° F.

4. Remove the lamb from the marinade and pat it dry with paper towels. Combine the peppercorns and butter in a small bowl and rub the mixture over the entire surface of the lamb.

5. Place the lamb on a rack in a roasting pan and roast 15 minutes. Reduce the temperature to 350° F and continue roasting until a thermometer inserted in the thickest part of the meat registers 140° F for medium rare, 45 to 60 minutes. Remove the roast from the oven and let it stand 20 minutes before carving.

6. To serve, arrange the lamb on bay leaves or garnish with watercress.

Serves 8

AT THE MARKET

When buying a leg of lamb, ask for one with the shank bone attached. This gives the finished roast a more attractive appearance.

GREAT ACCOMPANIMENTS

The Smoked Mozzarella Fritters are perfect as an hors d'oeuvre; the Stir-Fry of Zucchini, Yellow Squash, and Cherry Tomatoes and the Potatoes Baked with Cream, Wine, and Sage make wonderful complements to the roast; and the Poached Pears are a colorful and elegant ending to a meal featuring this lamb entrée.

Marinated Racks of Lamb with Tomato-Mustard Sauce

I like nothing better than racks of lamb for a special dinner party. They make an impressive presentation and are easy to prepare. For this dish I marinate and then broil the lamb, and serve it with a piquant sauce. The sauce can be made in advance and the meat must be marinated ahead, so the only last-minute work is the quick roasting of the lamb.

2 racks of lamb (see step 1)
2 cups red wine
½ cup olive oil
3 cloves garlic, crushed
2 bay leaves, broken in half
Pinch of dried thyme
¼ teaspoon freshly ground pepper
2 tablespoons chopped fresh parsley
Salt and freshly ground pepper to taste
Tomato-Mustard Sauce (recipe follows)

1. Ask the butcher to remove the back (chine) bone and the shoulder blade from each rack of lamb. Then ask to have all excess fat from both sides of the racks trimmed away. (There are several thick layers of fat along the exterior rib cage area of each rack that should be removed.) Have the sinew in the loin area removed also. Finally, for an attractive appearance, have the butcher cut away 2 inches of fat around the rib bones so that 2 inches of the bones are exposed. Each rack should contain 8 ribs and weigh 2½ pounds after trimming.

2. Combine the wine, olive oil, garlic, bay leaves, thyme, pepper, and parsley in a large non-aluminum bowl or dish. Stir well, then add the lamb and marinate it 6 hours or overnight (covered, in the refrigerator). Turn several times during the marinating process.

3. Remove the lamb from the marinade and pat it dry with paper towels. Salt and pepper it well.

4. Preheat the oven to 450° F.

5. Place the lamb on racks in roasting pans, with the bones of the ribs pointing upward. Roast until a meat thermometer registers

GREAT ACCOMPANIMENTS

The Sauté of Jerusalem Artichokes, Sweet Red Peppers, and Zucchini and the Baked New Potatoes with Lemon-Thyme Butter are great companions for the lamb. For dessert, the Cassis Walnut Tart makes for a special conclusion.

140° F for medium rare, 25 to 30 minutes. If desired, make a small incision in the middle of one of the racks to check for doneness. Let the meat rest for 10 minutes before carving.

6. To serve, place the racks on a serving tray with the ribs of one rack crossed with ribs of the other. Slice between the ribs to get single-chop servings. Serve the chops with a generous serving of Tomato-Mustard Sauce.

Serves 6 to 8

TOMATO-MUSTARD SAUCE

2 tablespoons olive oil
6 tablespoons chopped shallots
1 tablespoon chopped garlic
1 can (28 ounces) Italian-style tomatoes, drained well and
*   coarsely chopped*
1 cup homemade chicken stock (see Index) or good-quality canned
*   broth, plus more if needed*
Salt to taste
¼ teaspoon freshly ground pepper
¾ teaspoon sugar
1 tablespoon stone-ground mustard
2 teaspoons Dijon mustard
3 tablespoons chopped fresh parsley

1. Heat the olive oil in a medium-size skillet over medium heat. Add the shallots and cook, stirring, 2 to 3 minutes. Add the garlic and cook 1 minute more. Add the tomatoes and 1 cup chicken stock, and cook over medium heat, stirring occasionally, until the tomatoes and shallots are soft and mushy, about 15 minutes. Remove the mixture and purée it in a food processor, food mill, or blender.

2. Place the puréed mixture in a medium-size saucepan and add the salt, pepper, and sugar. Stir in both mustards and place over medium heat. Stir constantly until heated through, 1 to 2 minutes. If the sauce is too thick, thin with additional chicken stock. (The sauce can be made 1 day in advance to this point, then kept covered and refrigerated. Reheat before using.) Stir in the parsley.

Makes 1½ to 2 cups

Lamb Chops with Spinach and Chèvre

I remember the first sampling I had of chèvre. I was a young college student making my first crossing to Europe, aboard the ocean liner *Le France*. At dinner each evening after the salad course, a waiter would bring to the table a huge tray laden with cheeses in varying shapes and sizes. It was during one of these tastings that I became familiar with this biting and pungent cheese. I took an instant liking to goat cheese and have been a fan ever since. Now, many years after that experience, I buy this cheese not only for eating along with French bread, but for cooking as well. In this recipe, marinated broiled lamb chops are served on a bed of creamed spinach seasoned with crumbled chèvre.

6 tablespoons fresh lemon juice
3 cloves garlic, crushed
2 teaspoons black peppercorns, coarsely crushed
¾ teaspoon salt
1 cup plus 2 tablespoons olive oil
12 rib lamb chops, cut 1 inch thick and trimmed of excess fat
1½ pounds fresh spinach, rinsed and trimmed
6 tablespoons (¾ stick) unsalted butter
6 tablespoons chopped shallots
9 ounces chèvre, softened and crumbled
3 tablespoons heavy or whipping cream
Salt and freshly ground pepper to taste
4½ tablespoons chopped fresh parsley, for garnish
1½ teaspoons grated lemon zest, for garnish
12 strips lemon zest, 1½ inches long and ¼ inch wide, for garnish

1. To prepare the marinade, combine the lemon juice, garlic, 1½ teaspoons of the peppercorns, the salt, and the olive oil in a shallow non-aluminum pan. Mix well, then add the lamb chops. Turn them to coat well, and marinate 6 hours or overnight, covered, in the refrigerator. Turn the meat several times while marinating.

2. Cook the spinach in boiling salted water to cover until just wilted, about 2 minutes. Drain, and squeeze the spinach dry in a clean kitchen towel. Chop coarsely.

AT THE MARKET
These chops look best if all meat and fat are trimmed from the lower part of the rib bones.

GREAT ACCOMPANIMENTS

The Early Autumn Soufflés make a colorful first course to serve before the lamb. The Garlic and Butter–Roasted Potatoes go well with it, and for dessert, the Red Grape and Green Grape Sorbets and a basket of Spiced Madeleines make a wonderful and refreshing finale.

AS A VARIATION

These chops are also delicious grilled. Cook them 4 to 5 minutes per side over a hot fire. The chops are best when just pink inside. Check while grilling so that you do not overcook them.

3. Melt the butter in a medium-size heavy skillet over medium heat. Add the shallots and cook until softened, 2 to 3 minutes. Add the spinach and cook until hot, 1 to 2 minutes. Stir in the cheese and the cream, and continue to cook until the cheese has melted and the mixture resembles creamed spinach. Taste, and add salt and pepper as desired. Reserve and keep warm.

4. Prepare the garnish: combine the parsley, grated lemon zest, and remaining ½ teaspoon crushed peppercorns in a small bowl. Mix well and set aside.

5. Preheat the broiler, and arrange the rack 4 to 5 inches from the heat.

6. Remove the lamb chops from the marinade and place them on a rack in a broiling pan. Broil 4 to 5 minutes per side. Check for doneness by making a small slit with a knife in the center of a chop. The meat should be just pink.

7. To serve, mound some of the spinach mixture on four warm dinner plates. Place three lamb chops on top of the spinach, crisscrossing the bones. Sprinkle some of the parsley mixture over the chops, and place a strip of lemon on top of each chop.

Serves 4

Lime-Marinated Lamb Chops with Tomato Chutney

While I was testing the recipes for this book, I invited friends for small dinners to help sample the fare and offer candid opinions and suggestions. This lamb chop preparation, the creation of my good friend and colleague Jim Budros, is one of the dishes that drew the most praise and approval.

¼ cup fresh lime juice
½ cup olive oil
2 cloves garlic, crushed
¼ teaspoon cayenne pepper
2½ teaspoons Hungarian paprika
¾ teaspoon salt
12 rib lamb chops, cut 1 inch thick and trimmed of excess fat
Tomato Chutney (recipe follows)

1. Place the lime juice, olive oil, garlic, cayenne pepper, paprika, and salt in a mixing bowl and stir well. Arrange the lamb chops in a shallow non-aluminum pan, and pour the marinade over the lamb. Cover and marinate the lamb in the refrigerator, turning several times, 4 to 5 hours.

2. When you are ready to cook the lamb, preheat the broiler and arrange a rack 4 to 5 inches from the heat.

3. Remove the chops from the marinade, and broil until just pink inside, 4 to 5 minutes per side. Remove and keep warm.

4. Gently heat the Tomato Chutney in a skillet or saucepan.

5. Serve the lamb chops garnished with a little of the chutney. Pass extra chutney in a separate bowl.

Serves 4

TOMATO CHUTNEY

2 cups peeled, seeded, coarsely chopped ripe tomatoes
1½ cups peeled, cubed (in ½-inch dice) Granny Smith apples
1 clove garlic, finely chopped
½ cup coarsely chopped red bell pepper
⅓ cup loosely packed dark brown sugar
⅓ cup cider vinegar
¼ teaspoon cayenne pepper
1 teaspoon chopped crystallized ginger

1. Combine all the ingredients in a heavy 3- to 4-quart saucepan over medium-high heat. Mix the ingredients well and bring the mixture to a boil. Then lower the heat to a simmer and cook, uncovered, until the tomatoes and apples are softened and the liquid has reduced to the consistency of a light glaze, 1 to 1½ hours. The cooking time can vary depending on the juiciness of the fruit and vegetables. (The chutney will keep, covered and refrigerated, for 4 to 5 days; or you can seal it in sterilized canning jars.)

2. Serve the chutney at room temperature or warmed, as desired.

Makes about 2 cups

AS A VARIATION

If you should have any leftovers, this makes a good sandwich. I cut pita breads in half, spread some stone-ground mustard inside the pockets, and fill them with the pork and a few sprigs of watercress.

Sautéed Filet of Pork Waldo

Waldo Shank was at one time the vice president of food operations at Lazarus Department Stores. He was the only executive I knew whose office shelves were lined with cookbooks rather than retail publications. Waldo loved food, and it was the center of every conversation with him. One day he gave me this recipe for his favorite way to cook sliced pork tenderloin. The meat, coated with bread crumbs and grated Gruyère cheese and then fried until crisp and golden, is delicious. Waldo moved away several years ago, but I am always reminded of him when I make this innovative dish.

Special equipment: Meat pounder

2 pork tenderloins (10 to 12 ounces each)
Salt and freshly ground pepper to taste
1⅓ cups Italian-style seasoned bread crumbs
1 pound Gruyère cheese, grated
2 large eggs
½ cup milk
Vegetable oil
Thin lemon slices, for garnish
Watercress sprigs, for garnish

1. Cut the pork tenderloins on the diagonal into ½-inch-thick slices. You should get 16 to 18 slices. Pound each piece until it is ¼ inch thick. Salt and pepper each slice well.

2. Place the bread crumbs and the grated cheese in the bowl of a food processor. Process, turning on and off, until the cheese is finely mixed with the bread crumbs.

3. Place the eggs and milk in a bowl and beat just until the eggs are incorporated into the milk. Place the bread crumb mixture on a dinner plate. Dip each slice of pork into the egg mixture and then coat on both sides with the bread crumbs. Let the prepared slices rest for 15 minutes before cooking.

4. Pour enough vegetable oil to reach ¼-inch depth in each of two skillets. Place the skillets over medium-high heat, and when the oil is quite hot but not smoking, add enough pork to fit comfortably in the skillets.

5. Cook 4 to 5 minutes per side. If the meat appears to be browning

GREAT ACCOMPANIMENTS

Since these sautéed pork slices are so quick and easy to prepare, I usually make simple side dishes to go with them. Fresh cooked green beans tossed in melted butter and seasoned with dill, plus buttered new potatoes, taste good with the pork. Vanilla ice cream topped with Hazelnut Hot Fudge Sauce is an easy and tempting dessert.

too quickly, lower the heat. The pork should be crisp and golden on both sides. Remove, cover loosely with foil, and keep warm in a preheated 200° F oven while you continue until all the pork has been sautéed. Arrange the pork on a warm platter, and garnish with lemon slices and watercress sprigs.

Serves 6

Crown Roast of Pork with Mustard-Herb Butter

This crown roast really does make a spectacular presentation. It is studded with thin slivers of garlic and then basted with a combination of Dijon mustard, herbs, and sesame oil. After the pork has cooked to a rich mahogany brown, it is served with a piquant sauce made by combining crème fraîche with some of the mustard glaze.

Special equipment: Soufflé dish or ramekin with the same diameter as the opening in the center of the roast

Mustard Herb Butter

¾ cup (1½ sticks) unsalted butter, at room temperature
6 tablespoons Dijon mustard
1¼ teaspoons crushed dried rosemary
1¼ teaspoons crumbled dried thyme
Scant ½ teaspoon salt
Freshly ground pepper to taste
3 tablespoons Oriental sesame oil

Crown Roast

1 crown roast of pork with 16 ribs (about 7 pounds, see "At the Market,"page 174)
4 large cloves garlic, slivered
⅓ cup crème fraîche (see Index)
½ cup homemade chicken stock (see Index) or good-quality canned broth
Thyme sprigs, for garnish
Rosemary sprigs, for garnish

1. Prepare the Mustard Herb Butter: Using an electric mixer, cream the butter. Beat in the mustard. Then mix in the rosemary, thyme,

---

A COOK'S REFLECTIONS

I have served this crown roast both at formal sit-down meals and at buffet dinners with equal success. The meat always makes a striking presentation. I always use a very sharp knife first to remove the string tying the racks together, then to cut the roast into individual chops.

THE RIGHT EQUIPMENT

I used to degrease pan juices or sauces by removing the fat with a spoon, a job that often took 5 minutes or more. Now I use a plastic degreasing cup. There are several available styles, but the one I like best has a small opening on the bottom of the cup covered by a lever. To use, you simply pour the pan juices into the cup; the juices will sink to the bottom while the fat floats on the top. When you pull the lever to uncover the opening, all the juices will flow out. What is left in the cup is fat. This whole process takes only a few seconds.

AT THE MARKET

I never see crown roasts of pork in our markets, so I always need to special-order one. I ask the butcher to tie together two racks of pork with eight ribs each to form a crown. I also ask him to trim away the fat between the rib bones so that the bones are exposed, giving the roast a more attractive appearance.

GREAT ACCOMPANIMENTS

The Cream of Apple, Carrot, and Caraway Soup is an excellent first course to offer before the pork. The Barley with Leeks and Celery is beautiful served inside the center of the roast, and the Belgian Endive and Spinach Salad makes a fine side dish. The Chocolate Apricot Pecan Torte is a fabulous dessert to end this meal.

salt, and a generous amount of pepper. Blend in the sesame oil. Divide the butter between two bowls. Cover and refrigerate one bowl while preparing the roast. Keep the other at room temperature.

2. Preheat the oven to 350° F.

3. Make small slits all over the roast and insert the garlic into the slits. Stand the roast on a rack in a roasting pan. Brush one third of the room-temperature Mustard Herb Butter over the meat. Cover the bone tips with foil.

4. Place a soufflé dish or ramekin in the center of the roast to hold the shape. Roast the pork 17 minutes per pound, about 2 hours for a 7-pound roast, brushing with more Mustard Herb Butter every 30 minutes. A meat thermometer should register 170° F when the roast is done.

5. Transfer the roast to a heated platter. Cover it loosely with a foil tent, and let it stand 20 minutes before carving.

6. Meanwhile, beat the chilled Mustard Herb Butter with an electric mixer until smooth and creamy. Mix in the crème fraîche until just incorporated.

7. Degrease the pan juices. Then add the stock to the roasting pan and bring to a boil, scraping up any browned bits. Transfer the sauce to a serving bowl.

8. Remove the soufflé dish or ramekin from the center of the roast and discard the foil and string. Garnish with the sprigs of herbs. Top each serving with pan juices and Mustard Herb Butter.

Serves 8

Roast Loin of Pork Braised in Cider

I like to make this roast pork in the fall, when the first bottles of fresh cider appear at roadside stands. The roast is browned well and then cooked with cider plus seasonings of garlic, thyme, and bay leaf. Served with a sauce made from the cider, cream, and mustard, this is a robust entrée that I serve for both family and company meals.

AT THE MARKET

Although fresh cider is my preference for this dish, you can also use apple juice.

A COOK'S REFLECTIONS

Larding is a French technique. The noun *lard* in French means pork fat and the verb *larder* means to insert strips of pork fat into meat. In earlier times, meat was much tougher and contained less fat, so larding was a way to keep it moist during cooking. With better meats available today, larding is something cooks do much less frequently. Because pork roasts tend to dry out during roasting, I sometimes use the technique for this meat.

Traditionally larding is done with a special tool, a *lardoire* or larding needle. Long strips of fat are placed in the hollow shaft of this needle and inserted into the meat. I know only a handful of cooks who own this piece of equipment, so I tell my students to lard their pork roasts by making incisions with a sharp knife and inserting slivers of ham in the slits. Not only does the larding help to baste and moisten the roast, it also produces an attractive design. When sliced, the roast reveals a pattern of rose-hued dots of ham against white pork.

GREAT ACCOMPANIMENTS

As an hors d'oeuvre, offer the Mushroom Pâté before the pork. The Bourbon Carrots or the Carrot and Belgian Endive Sauté and buttered fresh green beans are good complements to the roast. For dessert, the Apricot, Pear, and Almond Strudels are an excellent choice.

¼ pound lean baked or boiled ham
1 boneless loin of pork (3 pounds)
4 tablespoons vegetable oil
Salt and freshly ground pepper to taste
3 cups fresh apple cider, plus more if needed
2 bay leaves
Pinch of dried thyme
4 sprigs parsley
1 large clove garlic, crushed
1 cup heavy or whipping cream
2 teaspoons Dijon mustard
1 bunch watercress, for garnish

1. Preheat the oven to 375° F.

2. Cut the ham into strips 1½ inches long and ¼ inch thick.

3. Pat the pork loin dry with paper towels. Using a small sharp paring knife, make incisions in the pork and insert the ham strips. (This technique, called larding, will keep the pork moist while it cooks.)

4. Heat the oil in a large heavy casserole over medium-high heat. When it is hot, brown the pork loin on all sides, turning as necessary.

5. Remove the casserole from the heat and take out the meat. Drain off the oil and return the roast to the pan. Salt and pepper the meat. Pour 3 cups of cider around the meat; add the bay leaves, thyme, parsley, and garlic to the pan. Bring to a simmer on top of the stove. Cover, and place in the oven.

6. Cook for 45 minutes, then turn the roast over and reduce the temperature to 350° F. Cook for another 45 minutes. The roast is done when a meat thermometer registers 170° F. Remove the roast from the pan and place it on a warm platter. Cover with aluminum foil to keep warm.

7. Strain the cooking liquid into a large measuring cup. Skim off any fat. There should be 3 cups liquid. Add extra cider to make this amount if necessary. Pour the liquid back into the original pan. Cook over high heat on top of the stove until the liquid has reduced by half, about 5 minutes or longer. Combine ⅓ cup of the hot sauce with the cream, whisking well. Then whisk the cream mixture into the remaining sauce. Reduce this sauce over high heat by half, 5 to 10 minutes. Remove it from the heat and stir in the mustard.

8. Slice the roast and arrange it on a heated serving platter. Nap the pork with some of the sauce, and garnish with watercress. Pass the remaining sauce separately.

Serves 6

Suzanne's English Farmhouse Tart

The idea for this delicious puff pastry tart came from Suzanne Karpus and Sharon Reiss, teachers at La Belle Pomme and catering partners. Enclosed in flaky pastry, the filling is composed of sautéed sausage, onions, walnuts, and cheese. This tart, which can be prepared completely ahead and frozen, is a wonderful robust entrée to serve for a fall or winter meal.

Special equipment: Jelly roll pan or baking sheet with rim

4 tablespoons (½ stick) unsalted butter
3½ cups halved and very thinly sliced onions
½ pound mild pork sausage meat
½ teaspoon dried thyme
¼ teaspoon dried rosemary
⅛ teaspoon cayenne pepper
¼ teaspoon freshly ground black pepper
¼ teaspoon salt
1 tablespoon Dijon mustard
½ pound English Farmhouse Cheddar cheese, grated
½ cup chopped walnuts
Quick Puff Pastry (see Index), or 1¾ pounds good-quality
*   commercial puff pastry*
1 large egg
1 tablespoon cold water

1. To prepare the filling, melt the butter in a large heavy skillet over medium-high heat. Add the onions and cook, stirring frequently, until lightly browned, 8 to 10 minutes.

2. Add the sausage to the skillet and cook, breaking it into very small pieces with a wooden spoon. Cook the mixture until the sausage is well browned. The onions will continue to cook and caramelize, becoming a darker brown. Remove the skillet from the

AT THE MARKET

English Farmhouse Cheddar Cheese is made at farmhouses, not in factories, in Somerset, England. Made in a long cylinder shape, it is usually wrapped in cheesecloth and has a sweet, nutty, assertive taste. Specialty food shops and cheese shops are the best places to find this distinctive cheese. A good-quality sharp Cheddar can be substituted.

GREAT ACCOMPANIMENTS

Fresh green beans sautéed in butter and a salad of seasonal greens and sliced tart red apples in a vinaigrette are good offerings to serve with this entrée. A plate of Chestnut Brownies makes a simple but delectable ending to this meal.

heat and carefully drain off all excess fat.

3. Return the skillet to medium heat and stir in the thyme, rosemary, cayenne pepper, black pepper, salt, and mustard. Cook, stirring, 2 to 3 minutes more. Remove the skillet from the heat and allow the mixture to cool to room temperature. Then stir in the cheese and walnuts, mixing well. Set the filling aside.

4. Divide the puff pastry in half and keep one half refrigerated. Roll out the other half to ¼-inch thickness, and then trim to a 9-inch square. Reserve the trimmings. Place the dough on an ungreased jelly roll pan or rimmed baking sheet. Place the filling in the center of the square and spread it out to within 1 inch of the edge. The filling should be slightly mounded in the center. Brush the exposed borders with cold water.

5. Roll the remaining pastry out to ¼-inch thickness and trim to a 9½-inch square. Center this sheet of pastry on top of the square spread with the filling. Press the edges together to seal, and then crimp them with a fork. Trim the edges to make a neat square. Score the top of the tart lightly with a sharp knife (do not cut through the pastry) to make a lattice design. Cut four slits, 1½ inches long, in a starburst pattern in the center of the square, completely through the crust, to allow steam to escape during baking.

6. Roll out the reserved scraps of dough and cut out eight leaves, four small and four large. Mix the egg and 1 tablespoon cold water together, and then brush the tart with this glaze. Arrange one large and one small leaf slightly overlapping at each corner. Brush them with glaze.

7. Refrigerate the tart 30 minutes or longer, uncovered. (The tart can be made a day in advance; cover with plastic wrap and then aluminum foil and keep refrigerated. The tart can also be frozen; bring to refrigerator temperature before baking. If you are making the tart ahead, attach the leaves with water before refrigerating. Glaze the tart before baking it.)

8. To bake, preheat the oven to 425° F.

9. Bake the tart until golden brown, 35 to 40 minutes. Remove it from the oven and carefully lift it to a serving dish with two spatulas. Cool 10 to 15 minutes, then slice into nine squares.

Serves 6

Pork Chops Baked with Chestnuts and Mushrooms

My husband, who is not usually an enthusiastic fan of pork chops, loves the hearty flavor of this dish. I like it because the chops are so tender they can be eaten with a fork alone.

16 to 18 fresh chestnuts or unsweetened canned chestnuts
9 tablespoons corn oil
3 cups sliced onions (about 3 medium onions)
¼ teaspoon sugar
Salt and freshly ground pepper to taste
6 center-cut pork chops, cut ¾ inch thick and well trimmed
½ cup all-purpose flour
2½ cups homemade beef stock (see Index) or good-quality canned broth, plus more if needed
6 ounces medium-size mushrooms with stems, cleaned and quartered

1. Preheat the oven to 350° F.

2. If you are using fresh chestnuts in the shell, bring 2 quarts of water to a boil. With a small knife make an "x" on one side of each chestnut, and drop the chestnuts into boiling water for 3 to 4 minutes. Drain, and when cool enough to handle, peel off the shells with a small sharp knife. Peel away the inner skin as well. Slice the chestnuts in half lengthwise, and reserve. If you are using prepared chestnuts, drain well and reserve.

3. Heat 5 tablespoons of the oil in an 11- to 12-inch ovenproof skillet. When the oil is hot, add the onion slices and cook slowly over medium heat, stirring. When the onions start to brown, sprinkle them with the sugar. Cook, stirring frequently, until well browned, 10 to 15 minutes. Remove the onions and drain them on paper towels. Pour any remaining oil from the skillet and clean it out with paper towels.

4. Heat the remaining 4 tablespoons oil in the same pan. Salt and pepper each chop and then dredge it in flour. Add the pork chops to the pan in a single layer and brown well, cooking the chops 5 to 8 minutes per side. If necessary, add more oil.

5. After the chops are browned, pour off any remaining oil. Then

THE RIGHT EQUIPMENT

Even though I have lots of special pots and pans in my kitchen, I like to use an old-fashioned cast iron skillet for this dish. The pork chops brown beautifully in this type of pan, and the conduction is excellent.

GREAT ACCOMPANIMENTS

The Barley with Leeks and Celery tastes wonderful with these pork chops. You might also like to add the Bourbon Carrots for color. The Cassis Walnut Tart makes a fine conclusion.

add the stock and sprinkle the chestnuts, onions, and mushrooms over the meat. Bring the liquid to a simmer, and cover the skillet with a sheet of aluminum foil and then with a lid. Place the skillet in the oven and bake until the meat is very tender when pierced with a knife, about 45 minutes. If no liquid is left at the end of the cooking time, add ½ to 1 cup extra stock to the pan with the meat and heat on top of the stove until warm. (This dish may be prepared completely in advance and reheated, covered, in a 350° F oven for 15 to 20 minutes. It may be necessary to use extra stock when reheating.)

6. Serve the pork chops on a heated serving platter, garnished with the chestnuts, onions, and mushrooms and napped with some pan juices.

Serves 6

FROM THE GRILL

If I had to pick the most popular class at La Belle Pomme, it would be the annual barbecue course. I've lost track of how many times Jim Budros has offered this standing-room-only session. However, I do know that students are so enthusiastic about learning how to grill foods that they begin calling in December to get the June dates for this yearly event.

Certainly, American cooks are by far the most adventurous and innovative grill cooks. We grill everything today—not only chicken, ribs, and steaks, but Cornish hens, turkey, filets of salmon, tuna, and swordfish as well as legs of lamb and roasts of veal. All fish, fowl, and meats are fit for pit or spit! We cook with gas, or over charcoal, or over exotic woods. There seems to be no end to our imagination when it comes to grilling.

Creole Barbecued Shrimp

My husband has a favorite menu which he requests every July for his birthday. A good Southerner, he likes to begin his fête with mint juleps, the only part of the meal he prepares himself. The main course is always Creole Barbecued Shrimp, served with fresh buttered green beans and caraway potato salad, and crème caramel for dessert. His favorite part of this special menu is the entrée—garlic and butter-marinated shrimp smoked over hickory chips and served with a dipping sauce. Our guests always have fun shelling their own shrimp—which are grilled in their shells—and dipping them in the flavorful sauce.

Special equipment: Eight 2-inch hickory chunks, soaked in water 15 minutes and then drained

18 scallions (green onions)
1 cup (2 sticks) unsalted butter
12 cloves garlic, chopped
1¾ cups dry white wine
2 tablespoons plus 1 teaspoon fresh lemon juice
Freshly ground pepper to taste
36 large shrimp in the shell, legs removed
1 cup chopped fresh parsley
Hot pepper sauce to taste
Salt to taste
Lemon wedges
2 tablespoons minced fresh parsley, for garnish
2 tablespoons minced scallions (green onions), for garnish
2 tablespoons chopped fresh chives, for garnish

1. Chop the scallions, including 2 inches of the green stems. Melt the butter in a heavy Dutch oven or deep casserole (not aluminum) over medium-low heat. Add the scallions and garlic and cook, stirring, 3 minutes. Add the wine and simmer 15 minutes.

2. Remove the pan from the heat and stir in the lemon juice and a generous amount of pepper. Set aside to cool to room temperature.

3. Using a paring knife, cut the shrimp down the back and devein, but do not peel. Toss the shrimp and the 1 cup of parsley in the scallion mixture. Refrigerate, covered, 6 hours or overnight, turning occasionally.

GREAT ACCOMPANIMENTS

If you want to try my husband's fa-vorite menu, you can serve the Loui-siana Mint Juleps, Red Potato Salad with Caraway, and Coconut Cara-mel Flan.

4. Prepare a charcoal grill. When the coals are hot, add the hickory chunks and heat them until the wood smokes, about 15 minutes.

5. Meanwhile, remove the shrimp from the marinade. Heat the marinade in a medium-size heavy saucepan. Strain, and return it to the pan. Cook over medium-high heat until reduced by half, 5 to 10 minutes. Add the hot pepper sauce and salt to taste. Cover the sauce and keep it warm.

6. Place the shrimp on the grill and cook until they curl up and turn pink, 5 to 6 minutes. Turn once during the grilling time. Do not overcook, or the shrimp will become tough and the shells will be hard to remove.

7. Mound the shrimp on a warm serving platter. Garnish with lemon wedges. Pour the sauce into individual ramekins or a serving bowl. Sprinkle the minced parsley, scallions, and chives over the sauce. Serve the shrimp and dipping sauce immediately.

Serves 6

Grilled Salmon Steaks Wrapped in Peppered Bacon

Peppered bacon is available in most of the local groceries where I live. I have found that fresh fish or chicken wrapped with strips of this bacon and then grilled is very flavorful. For the following recipe, I wrap salmon steaks with thin slices of the bacon and then cook them over a charcoal fire.

Special equipment: Wooden toothpicks

6 salmon steaks, 1½ inches thick, skinned
6 thin peppered bacon strips (see "At the Market")
Vegetable oil
6 tablespoons (¾ stick) unsalted butter, melted
2½ tablespoons fresh lemon juice
6 lemon wedges

1. Cut around the bone at the top of the salmon steaks and remove it. Trim 1 inch off the tail ends of the salmon steaks. Wrap each salmon steak with bacon, securing with a toothpick. (The steaks can be prepared 6 hours ahead; cover and refrigerate.)

AT THE MARKET

Peppered bacon is bacon with a generous coating of pepper on the rind. If it is unavailable, substi-tute regular bacon sprinkled with crushed black pepper.

GREAT ACCOMPANIMENTS

The Summer Tomato and Watercress Soup makes a good first course to precede the fish. Along with the salmon offer the Baked New Potatoes with Lemon-Thyme Butter and fresh blanched snow peas seasoned with dill. The Blueberry Strudels with Blueberry Cassis Sauce are an excellent finale.

AS A VARIATION

Other fish can be substituted for the trout. For example, salmon steaks are delicious served with the Minted Hollandaise. You can also grill whole filet of salmon this way. Just make certain the grill and the fish are coated generously with oil.

2. Prepare a charcoal grill. Generously coat the rack with oil.

3. Combine the butter and lemon juice in a small bowl. Brush one side of the salmon with the butter, and when the coals are hot, arrange the salmon on the grill, buttered side down. Cook 5 minutes.

4. Brush the top of the salmon steaks with the butter mixture. Turn the salmon over and cook until just opaque, about 5 minutes. Remove the salmon from the grill and discard the toothpicks. Brush the salmon with the remaining butter and arrange the steaks on a heated platter. Garnish with lemon wedges and serve immediately.

Serves 6

Grilled Trout with Minted Hollandaise

One day several summers ago, one of my students, just returned from trout fishing in northern Ohio, called to ask if I might like some of the catch. I quickly replied yes, my mouth watering at the thought of such fresh fish. Since it was midsummer and my garden was filled with herbs, I decided to grill the fish and then serve them with a minted hollandaise. The fresh fish takes on a wonderful flavor when grilled and tastes superb with the hollandaise made with chopped fresh mint leaves.

Vegetable oil
6 fresh rainbow trout (about ¾ pound each), cleaned, either
*   whole or with heads removed*
Minted Hollandaise (recipe follows)
6 lemon wedges, for garnish
6 mint sprigs, for garnish

1. Prepare a charcoal grill and oil the rack generously with vegetable oil. Brush each fish on all sides with oil, and when the coals are hot, place the fish on the rack. (If your grill has a lid, put the lid on and make certain all vents, top and bottom, are open.) Cook the fish, without turning, until the flesh is opaque and white and flakes easily when pierced with a knife, 12 to 15 minutes. The time will vary depending on the type of grill and the intensity of the heat.

2. Use a large metal spatula to transfer the fish from the grill to a warm serving plate. If the skin on the underside of the fish sticks to the grill, do not worry. Serve the fish with the good side up.

3. Nap each trout with 2 tablespoons of the Minted Hollandaise, and garnish with lemon wedges and mint sprigs. Pass the remaining hollandaise separately.

Serves 6

MINTED HOLLANDAISE

1 cup (2 sticks) unsalted butter
¼ cup finely chopped shallots
6 large egg yolks, at room temperature
¼ cup fresh lemon juice
½ teaspoon salt
Generous sprinkling of cayenne pepper
6 tablespoons chopped fresh mint leaves

1. Melt 1 tablespoon of the butter in a small skillet over medium heat, and add the shallots. Sauté, stirring, until the shallots are softened, 2 to 3 minutes. Remove the shallots from the pan and allow to cool.

2. Melt the remaining butter in a saucepan over low heat until bubbling, and keep hot. Do not allow it to burn.

3. To make the sauce in a food processor, place the egg yolks, lemon juice, salt, and cayenne pepper in the processor bowl. With the machine running, pour the hot butter in a very fine stream through the feed tube. When all the butter has been added, the sauce should be thick and smooth. Remove the sauce to a serving bowl and stir in the shallots. Keep the sauce warm by placing the bowl in a pan of hot (not boiling) water for up to 45 minutes.

To prepare the sauce in a double boiler, put the egg yolks, lemon juice, salt, cayenne pepper, and shallots in the top of the double boiler. Fill a large bowl halfway with ice water. Place the double boiler top over simmering water. Stir the mixture with a whisk, and very slowly, 1 tablespoon at a time, whisk in the melted butter. The sauce should be smooth and thick after all the butter has been added. If at any time the yolks seem to be thickening too quickly and look as if they might curdle, plunge the top of the double boiler into the bowl of ice water to lower the temperature of the sauce. When the mixture has cooled, replace the top of the double boiler over the bottom and continue to add the remaining melted butter. (The sauce

GREAT ACCOMPANIMENTS

Buttered halved new potatoes and fresh asparagus are good side dishes to the trout. Either the Deep-Dish Nectarine Pie or the Blueberry Strudels make a fine conclusion.

can be prepared in advance to this point and kept warm as in the food processor method.)

4. Mix in the mint just before serving.

Makes approximately 1½ cups

Grilled Lemon Chicken with Chile Hollandaise

My family likes spicy dishes, and this grilled chicken served with a hollandaise seasoned with chiles and cilantro is an entrée they look forward to every summer.

3½ pounds chicken pieces, trimmed of excess fat
½ cup fresh lemon juice
4 teaspoons grated lemon zest
2½ teaspoons coarsely ground pepper
2 teaspoons Dijon mustard
¾ teaspoon salt
1 cup olive oil
3 cloves garlic, crushed
Vegetable oil
Lemon leaves, for garnish
Chile Hollandaise (recipe follows)

1. Place the chicken in a large non-aluminum bowl or baking dish. Blend the lemon juice, lemon zest, pepper, mustard, and salt in a medium-size bowl. Slowly whisk in the oil in a thin stream. Then mix in the garlic. Pour this marinade over the chicken, turning to coat. Cover, and refrigerate overnight.

2. Prepare a charcoal grill and oil the rack generously. Remove the chicken from the marinade, and when the coals are hot, arrange the pieces on the rack. Grill until the chicken is crisp and the juices run clear when the flesh is pierced with a knife, about 10 minutes per side. To serve, arrange lemon leaves on a serving platter and place the chicken on top. Ladle some Chile Hollandaise over the chicken, and pass the remaining sauce separately.

Serves 4 generously

GREAT ACCOMPANIMENTS

The Chilled Tomato Soup with Avo-cado Cream Garnish is a wonderful first course to precede the chicken. As side dishes offer the Monterey Jack Corn Cakes and a green salad with julienned strips of sweet red peppers. The Red Grape and Green Grape Sorbets make a light and cool finale.

CHILE HOLLANDAISE

8 tablespoons (1 stick) unsalted butter
3 large egg yolks, at room temperature
4½ teaspoons fresh lemon juice
2½ tablespoons minced cilantro (fresh coriander leaves)
1 or 2 serrano or cayenne chiles, seeded and minced (see Index
    for "Hot Pepper Warning")
Salt to taste

Special equipment: Rubber gloves

1. Melt the butter in a saucepan over low heat until bubbly, and keep hot. Do not allow it to burn.

2. To prepare the sauce in a food processor, place the egg yolks and lemon juice in the processor bowl. With the machine running, pour the hot butter in a very fine stream through the feed tube. When all the butter has been incorporated, the sauce should be thick and smooth. Remove the sauce to a serving bowl, and mix in the cilantro and chiles. Taste, and add salt as desired. Keep the sauce warm by placing the bowl in a pan of hot (not boiling) water for up to 45 minutes.

To prepare the sauce in a double boiler, place the egg yolks and lemon juice in the double boiler top. Fill a large bowl halfway with ice water. Place the double boiler top over simmering water. Stir the mixture with a whisk and very slowly, a tablespoon at a time, whisk in the melted butter. The sauce should be smooth and thick after all the butter has been added. If at any time the yolks seem to be thickening too quickly and look as if they might curdle, plunge the top of the double boiler into the bowl of ice water to lower the temperature of the sauce. When the mixture has cooled, replace the top of the double boiler over the bottom and continue to add the remaining melted butter. Transfer the sauce to a serving bowl and mix in the cilantro and chiles. Taste, and add salt as desired. Keep the sauce warm as in the food processor method.

Makes about ¾ cup

Chicken Marinated in Lime and Honey

Since I work in a large department store that has several interesting specialty food shops, I am always looking to see what new items are on the shelves. Several years ago, when the store had a big event featuring British products, a fabulous herb and spice shop called Culpepper's was installed (the original store is in London). I was fascinated with all the unusual merchandise and as part of my purchases bought a bottle of their West Indian lime juice. I wasn't sure how I would use it, but after a little reflection created this easy and uncomplicated preparation.

Salt and freshly ground pepper to taste
8 large chicken breast halves, with bone and skin
¾ cup fresh lime juice
½ cup honey
½ cup vegetable oil
2 teaspoons chopped garlic
4 teaspoons peeled and finely chopped fresh ginger
8 large sprigs watercress, for garnish
8 thin slices lime, for garnish
Rice with Sweet Red Peppers and Pine Nuts (recipe follows)

1. Salt and pepper the chicken pieces generously. Combine the lime juice, honey, vegetable oil, garlic, and ginger in a shallow non-aluminum dish. Add the chicken and marinate, covered and refrigerated, at least 6 hours or, better, overnight.

2. Prepare a charcoal grill. Remove the chicken breasts from the marinade and discard the marinade. When the coals are hot, place the chicken on the grill and cook, turning several times, until the skin is slightly charred and the juices run clear when the flesh is pierced with a knife, about 15 minutes. The time will vary depending on the type of grill and the intensity of the heat. Watch carefully.

3. Remove the chicken from the grill, and serve each piece garnished with a sprig of watercress and topped with a slice of lime. Serve the rice with the chicken.

Serves 8

AS A VARIATION

If you wish, you can broil the chicken. Preheat the broiler and place the chicken breasts on a broiler pan about 4 inches from the heat. Broil until the skin is just charred and the juices run clear when the flesh is pierced with a knife, 7 to 9 minutes per side.

GREAT ACCOMPANIMENTS

A cucumber salad and the Left Bank Coconut Sorbet, garnished with fresh strawberries, are good served with this chicken.

RICE WITH SWEET RED PEPPERS AND PINE NUTS

1 teaspoon salt
2 cups long-grain rice
2 tablespoons vegetable oil
½ cup pine nuts
½ cup finely chopped red bell pepper

1. Bring 4 cups of water to a boil and add the salt. Add the rice and bring to a simmer. Cover, and lower the heat. Cook until all liquid has been absorbed and the rice is fluffy, about 15 minutes.

2. Heat the vegetable oil in a small skillet over medium-high heat. When it is hot, add the pine nuts and sauté until golden, 2 to 3 minutes. (Watch carefully since pine nuts burn easily.) Drain, and set aside.

3. Add the red pepper and pine nuts to the rice and toss well. Taste, and add more salt if needed.

Serves 8

THE RIGHT EQUIPMENT

Although I always do my turkey in a domed Weber grill, my students have used gas grills successfully. They place the moistened hickory chips over the coals and close the grill. However, the cooking time is often less because of the higher heat. If you use a gas grill, monitor the turkey carefully to ensure that you do not overcook it.

Hickory-Smoked Turkey

Quite a few years ago, I attended a victory celebration in the South for an uncle who had been elected to public office. What I remember best about the party is not how many votes my uncle received or whom he defeated, but rather the wonderful food that accompanied the festivities! One dish in particular, a whole smoked turkey, its crispy skin a rich mahogany color and its meat moist and thoroughly permeated with a mellow smoky flavor, was outstanding. This is the way I like best to smoke my own turkeys.

Special equipment: Barbecue grill with a domed lid; 8 to 10 hickory chips, 2 to 3 inches in diameter, plus more if needed; 1 small (1-quart size) fireproof pot or pan

1 turkey (10 to 12 pounds), cleaned and wiped dry
1 bunch watercress, for garnish
Watercress Mayonnaise (see Index; optional)

AS A VARIATION

If you do not wish to do a whole turkey, you can smoke turkey breasts in the same manner. Three turkey breasts, weighing about 2 pounds each, can be smoked together and will be done in about 2 hours. They will not need a second fire.

1. Remove the rack from the grill. Fill the fireproof pan three-quarters full of water, and place the pan in the center of the bottom

GREAT ACCOMPANIMENTS

I usually serve smoked turkey for summer buffets. The Green Bean and Snow Pea Salad and the Souf-fléd Corn with Pancetta and Onions, plus a plate of sliced summer tomatoes sprinkled with fresh mint, make colorful and delicious dishes to serve with the turkey. Either the Deep-Dish Nectarine Pie or the Old-Fashioned Peach Custard Pie makes a special dessert.

part of the grill. Mound a generous amount of charcoal briquets around the pan. Light the fire, and wait until the briquets are thoroughly gray. Soak the hickory chips in water for 5 to 10 minutes, and then place them on top of the gray embers. Put the grill rack back, and place the turkey on the center of the rack.

2. Make certain all bottom vents of the grill are open. Place the lid on, with all its vents open. Cook the turkey for about 3 hours. Check periodically, moving the turkey around slightly to ensure even browning. Replace the water in the pan if necessary. (The water will keep the turkey from drying out while smoking.) Usually the fire will go out after 3 to 3½ hours. Depending on your grill, the bird should be cooked at this point. The turkey is done when the juices run clear if a knife is inserted into the flesh, and when the skin is a very dark brown color.

3. If the bird needs more cooking, light a second fire, using new charcoal and wood chips, and refilling the pan of water. Cook another hour or more, checking the turkey every 20 minutes until it is done, since it will cook more quickly at this point. When it is done, remove the turkey and let it cool. Refrigerate until ready to serve.

4. To serve, either arrange the whole turkey on a serving plate and garnish with watercress, or slice the turkey and arrange it in an attractive pattern on a platter, garnished with watercress. If desired, serve with a bowl of Watercress Mayonnaise (see Index).

Serves 12 to 14

Mustard-Glazed Cornish Hens

I remember clearly how this dish was invented. I was asked by my husband to give a small dinner party for some of his university colleagues with only two days' notice. After agreeing to my spouse's request, I realized I had practically no free time to cook the meal, so I decided to make a very simple main course and accompaniments, plus a salad, and to offer cheese and fruit for dessert. In a local market I found beautiful fresh Cornish hens, which I coated with a mustard and soy glaze. I baked the birds until tender and then finished them on the grill. The result was wonderful!

GREAT ACCOMPANIMENTS

Serve with oven-roasted potatoes and the Belgian Endive and Spinach Salad with Lemon Garlic Vinaigrette. Then offer a plate of cheese and pears for dessert.

3 fresh Cornish hens (1 to 1½ pounds each)
3 tablespoons Dijon mustard
6 tablespoons stone-ground mustard
3 tablespoons soy sauce
6 dashes hot pepper sauce
Freshly ground pepper to taste
1 bunch watercress, for garnish

1. Split the hens in half lengthwise. With poultry shears or kitchen scissors, cut away and discard the backbones.

2. Combine the two mustards, soy sauce, and hot pepper sauce in a mixing bowl and mix well with a whisk.

3. Arrange the split Cornish hens, skin side down, on a flat rack set on a roasting pan. Sprinkle each half with pepper. Then brush the hens generously with the mustard mixture. Turn the hens over and pepper the other side, then brush generously with mustard glaze. You will use about 1 tablespoon glaze per side for each bird. If you have any glaze left over, save it and baste the birds with it while they are baking.

4. Refrigerate the Cornish hens 2½ hours or longer; remove them from the refrigerator 30 minutes before baking.

5. Preheat the oven to 375° F.

6. Bake the hens until the juices run clear when the flesh is pierced with a knife, 30 to 35 minutes. Turn the hens once or twice while baking.

7. Meanwhile, prepare a charcoal grill. Remove the birds from the oven and when the coals are hot, grill them until the skin is crisp and golden, 5 to 8 minutes per side. (If you prefer not to finish the birds by grilling, you can broil them 4 to 5 inches from the heat, 5 to 6 minutes per side.) Watch carefully so they do not burn.

8. To serve, place the watercress in the center of a serving tray, and arrange the Cornish hens in a spoke pattern around it.

Serves 6

GREAT ACCOMPANIMENTS

The Chilled Tomato Soup with Avocado Cream Garnish is a good first course to offer. The French-Fried Sweet Potatoes accompany the steaks beautifully. For dessert, the Deep-Dish Nectarine Pie is a fine conclusion.

Grilled Sirloin Steaks with Banana Chile Pepper Butter

Ifirst tasted this dish at Rigsby's, one of Columbus's best and most interesting restaurants. Kent Rigsby, the owner and creative force behind the establishment, never fails to surprise me with his delicious culinary innovations.

Special equipment: Metal skewers

3 sweet red onions
1 prime-quality boneless sirloin steak (about 2 pounds), about
*   1½ inches thick*
Vegetable oil
Salt and freshly ground pepper to taste
Banana Chile Pepper Butter (recipe follows)

1. Prepare a charcoal grill. Peel the onions, quarter them lengthwise, and push the pieces onto metal skewers. Brush the meat and the skewered onion quarters generously with vegetable oil, and when the coals are hot place them on the grill rack. Cook the meat, turning several times, until done as desired—for medium rare, about 15 minutes. Cook the onions, turning several times, until they are softened but still crisp, and slightly charred. Remove them and keep warm if they finish cooking before the steak. The cooking time for the steak and onions will depend upon the type of grill and the intensity of the heat.

2. When the meat is done, remove it from the grill and place it on a warm serving platter. Remove the onions from the skewers and arrange them around the meat.

3. Salt and pepper the steak, and cut it into serving portions. Garnish each portion with a generous dollop of the Banana Chile Pepper Butter.

Serves 4

AT THE MARKET

Banana chile peppers are pale yellow, slender, and 4 to 5 inches long. They are available in many groceries today. These peppers are hot, so to prepare them for chopping, wear rubber gloves (see Index for "Hot Pepper Warning"): Cut off the stem ends and slice the peppers lengthwise, then hold the halves under cold running water and scrape out the seeds. Dry the peppers and chop them finely. You will need 1 to 2 peppers to make the 2 tablespoons for this recipe.

BANANA CHILE PEPPER BUTTER

Special equipment: Food processor; rubber gloves

½ cup (1 stick) unsalted butter, cut into small pieces
Scant ½ teaspoon salt
2 tablespoons finely chopped banana chile peppers (see "At the Market")
2 teaspoons fresh lemon juice
1 tablespoon chopped fresh parsley

Place all the ingredients in the bowl of a food processor. Process several seconds until well blended. The mixture should be smooth and fluffy. Remove the butter to a small serving bowl and leave it at room temperature if you will be using it within 3 to 4 hours. (If you wish to make the butter a day ahead, cover and refrigerate it, but bring it to room temperature before using.)

AT THE MARKET

Vidalia onions, named after the town of Vidalia in southeastern Georgia where these onions are grown, are available for only a brief period in May and June. Although they do not store as well as other varieties, keeping them in a cool place will prolong their shelf life.

If Vidalia onions are unavailable, standard yellow cooking onions can be substituted.

Grilled Sirloin Steak with Vidalia Onion Rings

I had never heard of Vidalia onions until several years ago, when a friend from Alabama returned from a trip to the South and shared some with me. At first I couldn't understand her excitement about what looked to me to be an ordinary bag of large white onions. However, once I used these Georgia-grown onions, I could appreciate why my friend was making such a fuss. Milder and sweeter than ordinary cooking onions but not as crunchy as standard varieties, they have become a favorite ingredient for me. This recipe is one of the best ways I know to use these unique onions.

GREAT ACCOMPANIMENTS

Whenever I make these steaks and onion rings, I serve a simple green salad tossed in a light dressing, and hot buttered French bread. For dessert, I like to make either the Old-Fashioned Peach Custard Pie or the Coconut Cream Mousse Pie.

6 tablespoons cider vinegar
2 tablespoons brown sugar
½ cup soy sauce
6 tablespoons Oriental sesame oil
2 sirloin steaks (1½ pounds each), about 1 inch thick
Batter-Dipped Vidalia Onion Rings (recipe follows)
Chopped fresh parsley, for garnish
Rosemary sprigs, for garnish

A COOK'S REFLECTIONS

Grilling: Everyone I know seems to love the taste of grilled food with its slightly charred exterior and its smoky taste. When teaching grilled dishes in my classes, I offer students the following information:

• There are a variety of grills available today—charcoal grills, gas grills, and indoor gas and electric grills. All of them will get the job done, but each works a little differently. Some, for example, cook faster than others, so it's important that you are familiar with the way your grill works. My favorite is the Weber Kettle Grill. Its domed lid and excellent venting system make it very efficient.

• When preparing any grill for cooking, always make certain it is clean. If you are cooking foods like fish that tend to stick to the rack, then oil the rack generously with vegetable oil before adding the food.

• Use charcoal or one of the flavorful woods like hickory or mesquite for your fire. I often use a combination. I prepare a charcoal fire, then scatter chunks of wood (that I have soaked in water for 15 minutes) over the briquets.

• The degree of doneness of grilled foods is one of choice. I think beef and lamb taste best just pink inside. Poultry is done when the juices run clear when the meatiest part is pierced with a knife. Whole fish or fish filets like salmon or trout are ready when the flesh is opaque and flakes easily. Grilled vegetables should retain a degree of crispness.

1. Combine the vinegar, brown sugar, soy sauce, and sesame oil in a large shallow non-aluminum dish. Add the steaks, turn to coat well, cover, and marinate 6 hours or overnight. Turn occasionally while marinating.

2. Prepare a charcoal grill. When the coals are hot, remove the steaks from the marinade. Pat lightly; the steaks should remain lightly coated with oil.

3. Place the steaks on the grill and cook about 5 minutes per side for medium-rare. The time will vary depending on the type of grill and the intensity of the heat. To serve, place the steaks on a serving platter and garnish with a border of onion rings. Sprinkle the steaks with chopped parsley and rosemary sprigs.

Serves 6

BATTER-DIPPED VIDALIA ONION RINGS

Special equipment: Deep-frying thermometer

4½ cups milk
½ cup beer
¼ cup vegetable oil
2 large eggs, separated
1 teaspoon salt
Freshly ground pepper to taste
1¼ cups all-purpose flour
1 tablespoon finely chopped fresh rosemary, or 1 teaspoon dried
2 tablespoons finely chopped fresh parsley
3 large Vidalia onions (about 1¼ pounds), sliced and separated into rings
Vegetable oil for deep-frying

1. About 2 hours before you plan to serve the onion rings, place ½ cup of the milk, the beer, vegetable oil, egg yolks, salt, and pepper in a large bowl and stir well with a whisk. Sift in the flour, and stir to incorporate well. Add the rosemary and parsley and stir. Cover the batter with plastic wrap, and refrigerate 1½ hours. Then remove the batter from the refrigerator and let it sit at room temperature for 30 minutes.

2. While the batter is resting, place the onion rings in a shallow bowl and cover with the remaining 4 cups milk. Soak the onions in the milk for 30 minutes.

3. When you are ready to fry the rings, beat the egg whites until soft peaks form, and fold them into the batter. Pour vegetable oil into a wok until it is about one-third full, or into a large heavy saucepan until it is half full. Heat the oil to 375° F. Dip onion rings into the batter a few at a time, and using a fork or tongs, lift the rings out individually, shaking off any excess batter. Drop the rings into the hot oil and fry 3 to 4 minutes, turning once, until golden. Drain on paper towels placed on a baking sheet. Keep the rings warm in a 200° F oven for 3 to 4 minutes until the steaks are cooked.

Skewers of Beef Tenderloin with Summer Vegetables and Scallion Sesame Rice

I love to use this dish for informal summer entertaining. Bite-size morsels of tenderloin are marinated in an aromatic mixture of soy sauce, vinegar, and sesame oil, then skewered and cooked over a hot grill. Colorful skewers of zucchini, yellow squash, and sweet red peppers make a great garnish and are grilled along with the meat. The easy Scallion Sesame Rice is light and delicious and completes this main course.

Special equipment: Metal skewers

1½ pounds beef tenderloin
½ cup soy sauce
½ cup Oriental sesame oil
3 tablespoons red wine vinegar
¾ teaspoon dry mustard
2 teaspoons finely chopped garlic
2 small zucchini
2 small yellow squash
2 red bell peppers
Scallion Sesame Rice (recipe follows)

1. Trim all fat off the tenderloin, and cut it into 1½-inch cubes.

2. Combine the soy sauce, sesame oil, vinegar, mustard, and garlic

AT THE MARKET

I always buy the thick, dark Oriental sesame oil made from toasted sesame seeds. This oil is much more aromatic than the pale yellow version, and is more desirable for this dish.

GREAT ACCOMPANIMENTS

Serve the Mushroom Pâté as an appetizer before this main course. For dessert, the Peaches and Cream Cheesecake makes a special conclusion.

in a shallow non-aluminum pan. Add the meat and marinate at room temperature, covered, turning several times, for 1 hour or longer.

3. While the beef is marinating, prepare a charcoal grill.

4. To prepare the vegetables, rinse the zucchini and yellow squash. Trim the ends and cut them into ½-inch rounds. Parboil 2 minutes in lightly salted boiling water to cover. Drain, and pat dry.

5. Rinse and dry the peppers. Core and seed them, and cut them into 1-inch squares.

6. Arrange the vegetables on skewers, alternating the red pepper pieces, yellow squash, and zucchini. Remove the beef from the marinade (reserve the marinade), and put the meat on skewers.

7. When the coals are hot, place the skewers of beef on the grill. Add the skewers of vegetables, and baste both generously with the marinade. Cook the beef and vegetables about 4 to 5 minutes, and then turn. Continue cooking, turning as needed and basting, until they have reached the desired point of doneness, about 5 minutes more. The beef is best cooked until it is medium rare—just pink inside. The vegetables should be very lightly charred. Cooking time will vary depending on the type of grill and the intensity of the fire.

8. When the meat and vegetables are cooked, remove them from the skewers and arrange them on a bed of Scallion Sesame Rice. Serve immediately.

Serves 4

SCALLION SESAME RICE

2 teaspoons salt
10 scallions (green onions)
1½ cups raw long-grain white rice
6 tablespoons toasted sesame seeds (see Index)
2 to 4 tablespoons chopped fresh chives

1. To prepare the scallions, bring 2 quarts water and 1 teaspoon of the salt to a boil in a large pot. Rinse and trim the scallions, leaving 2 inches of the green stems. Cut the scallions diagonally into ¾-inch pieces and add them to the water. Blanch about 1 minute, until the color is set, and then remove with a slotted spoon. Rinse under cold water and dry. Reserve.

2. Add the rice and the remaining teaspoon of salt to the boiling water and cook, uncovered, until tender, 12 minutes or longer. Drain the rice.

3. Toss the scallions, the sesame seeds, and the chives with the rice. Taste, and add salt if needed.

Serves 4

AT THE MARKET

Shiitake mushrooms are sometimes called Black Forest, Doubloon, or Golden Oak. They are golden to deep brown in color and range in size from 1 to several inches. The stems are tough and not good for eating, but the caps are tender and have a slightly smoky flavor. They taste best after they have been sautéed.

If fresh shiitake mushrooms are unavailable, 4 ounces of dried shiitake mushrooms can be substituted. Soak in hot water to cover for 30 minutes. Drain, and squeeze out excess moisture. Discard the hard cores and stems.

Grilled Flank Steak with Shiitake Mushrooms

When I demonstrated these grilled flank steaks with sautéed shiitake mushrooms in my cooking classes, I was concerned that my students would not want to spend $10 a pound for the mushrooms to make this dish at home. I should not have worried! Everyone, and especially the men in that course, loved this entrée and assured me that the delicious taste of the mushrooms paired with the grilled steak was worth the extra cost. If fresh shiitake mushrooms are unavailable, you can used dried ones instead.

2 flank steaks (1¼ to 1½ pounds each), all fat removed
½ cup soy sauce
½ cup Oriental sesame oil
3 tablespoons red wine vinegar
Freshly ground pepper to taste
2 cloves garlic, crushed
1 pound fresh shiitake mushrooms, stems removed
4 tablespoons (½ stick) unsalted butter
4 tablespoons vegetable oil
2 cups homemade unsalted beef stock (see Index) or good-quality canned broth, plus more as needed
4 teaspoons Dijon mustard
4 teaspoons stone-ground mustard
½ cup heavy or whipping cream
Salt to taste

1. Place the steaks in a non-aluminum pan. Whisk the soy sauce, sesame oil, vinegar, and a generous amount of pepper in a medium bowl. Mix in the garlic. Pour this marinade over the steaks, turning to coat all sides. Cover the pan tightly and refrigerate 24 hours, turning the steaks occasionally.

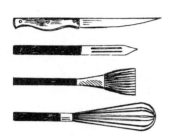

GREAT ACCOMPANIMENTS

Smoked Mozzarella Fritters are a wonderful appetizer to precede the steaks. The Sauté of Jerusalem Artichokes, Zucchini, and Sweet Red Peppers is a good combination of vegetables to serve with this entrée. The Frozen Chocolate Marbled Mousse makes a wonderful conclusion.

2. To prepare the sauce, reserve six mushrooms that are 2 inches in diameter for the garnish. Cut the remaining mushrooms into ½-inch-wide strips. Heat 3 tablespoons of the butter with 3 tablespoons of the oil in a large heavy skillet over medium-high heat. Add the mushroom slices and stir 3 minutes. Mix in 1 cup of the stock and both mustards. Increase the heat to high, and boil until reduced by half, about 5 minutes. Add the remaining 1 cup stock, ¼ cup at a time, boiling until the sauce is reduced by half after each addition. Stir in the cream, and boil until the sauce coats a spoon, about 3 minutes. Season with salt and pepper. (The sauce can be prepared 1 day ahead. Chill sauce and reserved mushrooms separately.)

3. Prepare a charcoal grill. When the coals are hot, remove the steaks from the marinade and arrange them on the grill rack. Cook about 4 minutes per side for medium rare. The cooking time will vary depending on the type of grill and the intensity of the heat. (Steaks can also be cooked in the broiler. Preheat broiler and broil steaks 4 to 5 inches from heat, 4 to 5 minutes per side for medium rare.) Transfer the steaks to a platter and let them rest 5 minutes.

4. Reheat the sauce over low heat, stirring occasionally.

5. Heat the remaining 1 tablespoon butter with the remaining 1 tablespoon oil in a small heavy skillet over high heat. Add the reserved mushroom caps and cook until heated through, about 2 minutes per side. Drain the mushroom caps on paper towels.

6. Cut the steaks diagonally across the grain into ⅜-inch slices. Arrange in a circular pattern on a heated platter. Thin the sauce with extra stock if desired, and ladle half of the sauce onto the center of the platter. Arrange the mushroom caps in pairs around the edge of the platter. Serve immediately, passing the remaining sauce separately.

Serves 6

ASIDES

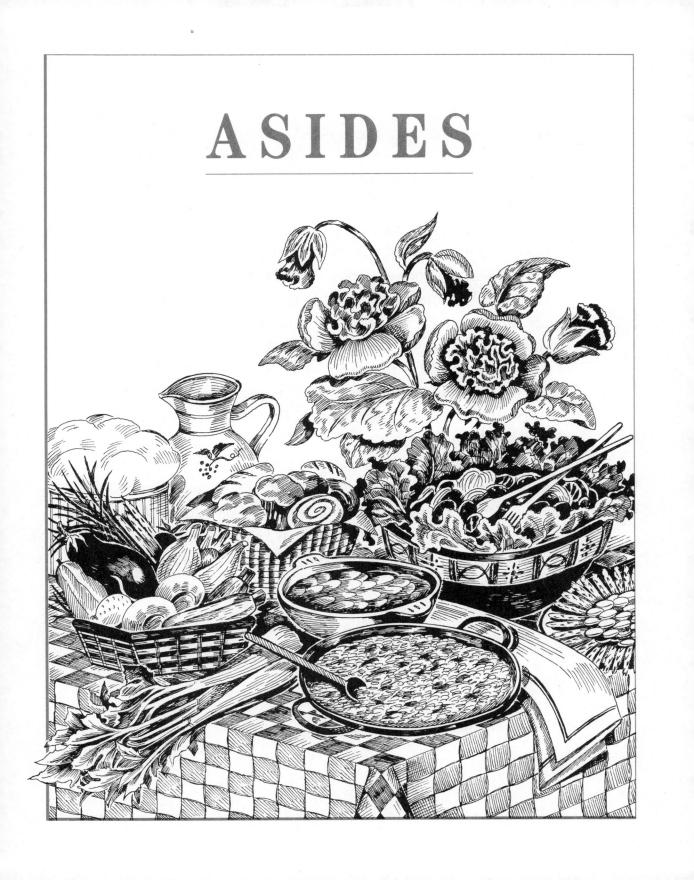

While I was working on this cookbook, one of the assistants at the school told me that she hoped I would include a large selection of side dishes. She explained that too often she spends all her energy deciding on the main course and doesn't pay enough attention to the accompaniments. For her, and others as well, the vegetable, potato, or salad choices are merely afterthoughts.

My colleague's concerns were valid, because the accompaniments are an important part of any meal. Companion dishes to the entrée should always be chosen to complement that dish. For example, if you plan a complex dish—a boned stuffed leg of lamb or sautéed steaks with a rich sauce—then the accompanying foods should be simple and uncomplicated. On the other hand, for plain but perfectly roasted chicken or broiled fish, you could offer more sophisticated side dishes.

This section is laden with ideas for varied accompaniments. There are vegetable sautés and gratins and a selection of potato and rice dishes. There are salads for every season and breads for all occasions. Whatever you decide upon as an accompaniment, just make certain it works well as part of the complete meal.

SALADS

Every spring I give a salads class, and it is always filled within a few days of its announcement. I prepare salads that can serve as side dishes and others that might be main courses. I offer tossed as well as composed combinations, and I serve some preparations cool and others warm.

This chapter includes favorite dishes from these classes, grouping the recipes by season. In the spring, try the colorful Asparagus, Scallops, and Pine Nut Salad for a luncheon; in summertime, serve the Paella Salad as a main course. The make-ahead Pasta Salad with Lemon, Thyme, and Prosciutto is a fine accompaniment for an autumn dinner, and the Winter Salad of Cabbage, Ham, and Gruyère is a welcome sight when the days are short and cold.

SPRING SALADS

Asparagus, Scallop, and Pine Nut Salad

On more than one occasion I have been asked to describe what I would choose for a favorite meal. My response is always the same: a dinner that includes at least one preparation with scallops! There are, in my opinion, no accolades too great for this small, succulent shellfish. In this salad, scallops are "cooked" in a marinade of fresh lemon juice and then tossed with asparagus and scallions in olive oil. Served with a garnish of toasted pine nuts, this is one of the most attractive and delicious scallop dishes in my repertoire. I like to serve it as a first course for special spring menus.

1 pound bay or sea scallops, rinsed and dried
Juice of 4 lemons
1½ pounds medium asparagus
4 tablespoons olive oil
4 tablespoons finely chopped scallions (green onions)
Salt and freshly ground pepper to taste
⅓ cup toasted pine nuts (see Index)
Thin lemon wedges

1. If you are using large sea scallops, slice them against the grain into ½-inch medallions. Leave bay scallops as they are. Put the scallops and the lemon juice in a non-aluminum bowl to marinate. This is all the "cooking" the scallops will need. Refrigerate, covered, at least 2 hours or as long as overnight.

2. To prepare the asparagus, cut off the tough woody end of the stalk. Using a vegetable peeler, peel the asparagus from just below the tip. Cut a piece 3 inches long off the top of each asparagus. Cut the remaining stalk into ½-inch pieces. Put the spears and pieces in boiling salted water to cover, and cook at a simmer until they are just tender when pierced with a knife, 3 to 5 minutes. Place the asparagus in a colander or large sieve and rinse under cold running water to refresh. Drain the asparagus, and dry them. Then cover and refrigerate. (The asparagus can be prepared several hours ahead to this point.)

AT THE MARKET

Bay scallops that are ¾ to 1 inch in diameter are my first choice for this salad. Very small bay scallops (less than ½ inch wide) do not work as well. Larger sea scallops can be used, but should be sliced into smaller portions as noted in the recipe.

Medium-size asparagus spears work better here than the very thin stalks.

AS A VARIATION

Sometimes I serve this salad on a single large serving plate, with the asparagus spears in a spoke pattern and the scallop mixture mounded on top. For individual servings you can also arrange a bed of asparagus spears (points facing outward) on scallop shells and mound the scallops over the spears. However you serve this salad, the pearly white of the shellfish and the rich green of the asparagus make a striking color combination.

3. Forty-five minutes before serving, pour off all the liquid from the bowl with the scallops. Add the olive oil, scallions, and asparagus pieces and spears to the bowl, and toss well. Taste, and add salt and pepper as desired.

4. When you are ready to serve the salad, arrange the asparagus spears in a spoke pattern on four salad plates. Place a mound of scallop mixture on top of the spears, and sprinkle each serving with some toasted pine nuts. Garnish with lemon wedges.

Serves 4

Scallop, Tomato, and Bacon Salad with Chèvre Dressing

This is a chic salad, perfect to begin a sophisticated dinner party. The warm chèvre dressing flavored with sherry wine vinegar, shallots, and bacon is absolutely delicious served over the sautéed scallops, tomatoes, and spinach.

6 small ripe tomatoes
4 ounces spinach leaves, rinsed and dried
1 slab (4 ounces) smoked bacon, partially frozen for easier cutting
4 tablespoons sherry wine vinegar
¼ cup finely chopped shallots
1 cup heavy or whipping cream
4 ounces chèvre, broken into pieces
Salt and freshly ground pepper to taste
6 tablespoons olive oil, plus more if needed
2 pounds sea scallops, rinsed and dried

1. Core the tomatoes, and cut each one into eight wedges. Set them aside.

2. Cut the spinach into strips 3 inches long and ½ inch wide. Set them aside.

3. Cut the rind from the bacon and discard it. Cut the bacon into ¼-inch dice. Fry the bacon cubes until crisp in a medium-size heavy skillet over medium-high heat. Remove the bacon with a slotted spoon, drain on paper towels, and reserve.

4. Discard all the fat in the skillet. Put the skillet back over medium heat, and add the vinegar and shallots. Cook, stirring, 2 to 3 minutes. Then pour in the cream and stir well. Finally add the cheese, and stir well until it has melted and the dressing is smooth. Taste the dressing, and season with salt and pepper as desired. (The dressing can be made several hours ahead and kept covered and refrigerated. Reheat over low heat, stirring constantly, when needed.)

5. When you are ready to serve the salad, heat 4 tablespoons of the oil in a large heavy skillet over medium-high heat. When it is hot, add the scallops and sauté, tossing and turning, until they are opaque, 3 to 4 minutes. Remove the scallops with a slotted spoon and place them in a ovenproof baking dish. Keep warm in a 200° F oven.

6. Discard all the oil and any scallop liquid that has collected in the skillet. Add the remaining 2 tablespoons oil, and heat over medium-high heat. When it is hot, add the tomato wedges and sauté them, stirring gently, until just heated through and coated lightly with oil, 2 to 3 minutes. If necessary, add more oil to the pan. Season the tomatoes generously with salt and pepper and add them to the scallops in the oven.

7. To serve, arrange a border of tomato wedges on six salad plates. Place some of the julienned spinach inside the tomato border, then arrange the scallops over the spinach. Ladle a generous amount of the warm chèvre dressing over the scallops, and sprinkle the reserved bacon cubes on top. Serve the salad immediately. Pass any extra dressing separately, in a warmed bowl.

Serves 6

Smoked Salmon, Mushroom, and Watercress Salad

What I like best about this dish is the contrasting colors—the bright coral hue of the fish, the pearly beige of the mushrooms, and the dark crisp green of the watercress leaves. Tossed lightly in a balsamic vinaigrette, the ingredients make a striking composition of epicurean tastes. This works well as a first course on a brunch menu.

AT THE MARKET

Use best-quality thinly sliced smoked salmon, such as Petrossian, in this salad for the best results.

6 ounces thinly sliced best-quality smoked salmon
1 pound mushrooms
¾ cup Balsamic Vinaigrette (recipe follows)
2 cups watercress leaves

1. Cut the smoked salmon into strips 1½ inches long and ¼ inch wide. Set aside.

2. Rinse and dry the mushrooms, and quarter them through the stems.

3. Place half the Balsamic Vinaigrette in a large non-aluminum bowl and whisk well. Add the mushrooms, toss well, and set aside to marinate 30 minutes.

4. When you are ready to serve the salad, add the smoked salmon pieces and the watercress leaves to the mushroom mixture, and toss well. Add enough remaining dressing to coat the ingredients lightly. Be careful not to saturate the salad; reserve any remaining dressing for another use. To serve, arrange the salad on six individual salad plates.

Serves 6

BALSAMIC VINAIGRETTE

3 tablespoons balsamic vinegar
½ teaspoon salt
Scant ½ teaspoon Dijon mustard
½ cup plus 1 tablespoon olive oil

Whisk the vinegar, salt, and mustard in a bowl. Gradually whisk in the olive oil, pouring it in in a thin stream. (The dressing can be made several hours in advance and kept at room temperature. Whisk well before using.)

Makes ¾ cup

Green Bean and Snow Pea Salad

This salad of fresh green beans, snow peas, and mushrooms in a zesty mustard dressing holds well and is wonderful to serve as part of a buffet dinner. The lettuce and radicchio leaves can be cleaned, the beans and peas blanched, the mushrooms quartered, and the dressing prepared early in the day. Only a quick final assembly is necessary just before serving time.

4 teaspoons salt
1½ pounds green beans, ends trimmed on the diagonal
¾ pound snow peas, ends trimmed on the diagonal and strings removed
½ pound mushrooms
¾ cup Mustard Vinaigrette (recipe follows)
Salt and freshly ground pepper to taste
6 large Boston lettuce leaves, rinsed and dried
6 large radicchio leaves, rinsed and dried
1½ tablespoons chopped chives or chopped parsley, for garnish

1. Bring 4 quarts of water to a boil in a large pot. Add the salt and the green beans. Cook the beans, uncovered, until just tender, 4 to 5 minutes. Then add the snow peas and cook 1 minute more. Drain the beans and peas in a colander, then rinse them under cold running water to stop the cooking process. Drain, pat dry, and reserve.

2. Thinly slice the mushrooms through the stem. (The beans, peas, and mushrooms can be prepared several hours ahead to this point. Cover and refrigerate. Bring to room temperature 30 minutes before using.)

3. When you are ready to finish the salad, place the Mustard Vinaigrette in a large non-aluminum bowl and whisk it well. Add the beans, snow peas, and mushrooms and toss well. Marinate, uncovered, 15 minutes. Taste, and add salt and pepper if needed.

4. To serve, arrange alternating Boston lettuce and radicchio leaves in a border on a serving platter. Arrange the vegetables on top, and sprinkle with chives or parsley.

Serves 8

A COOK'S REFLECTIONS

I love planning and preparing the side dishes in a meal. I always consider three points when making my selections: color, texture, and taste.

In many cases it's the vegetable or salad that adds the needed burst of color to a plate. Grilled lamb chops, for example, look much more attractive if surrounded by a colorful sauté of zucchini, yellow squash, and cherry tomatoes.

The texture is equally significant. If you serve tender poached chicken breasts napped with a velvety smooth sauce, then a wild rice pilaf or other dish that offers a contrasting texture would be appropriate.

Naturally, the tastes should work well together. If your entrée is a spicy peppered soup, a cool, light salad, including some sliced cucumbers, would be the right counterpoint.

GREAT ACCOMPANIMENTS

For a nice buffet dinner I like to serve the Szechuan-Peppered Chicken Breasts on fettuccine noodles along with this salad and a basket of hot buttered French bread. The Blueberry Strudels make an excellent ending for this menu.

AS A VARIATION

Once when I made this salad I was able to get quail eggs from a friend who raises quail on her farm. If you have access to these small distinctive eggs, you could use them instead. They will take less time to hard-cook than chicken's eggs, only about 8 to 10 minutes.

MUSTARD VINAIGRETTE

3 tablespoons red wine vinegar
½ teaspoon salt
2 tablespoons Dijon mustard
½ cup plus 1 tablespoon olive oil
3 tablespoons chopped shallots
Freshly ground pepper to taste

Place the vinegar, salt, and mustard in a mixing bowl and whisk well. Gradually whisk in the olive oil, pouring it in a thin stream. Add the shallots and pepper. (The dressing can be made several hours in advance and kept at room temperature. Whisk well before using.)

Makes about ¾ cup

Asparagus and Potato Salad

I created this composed salad for Easter one year. It was a big success and one I have repeated for other meals many times since.

1¼ pounds medium asparagus
¾ pound small red-skinned new potatoes
6 large eggs
6 ounces prosciutto, sliced ¼ inch thick
1 tablespoon vegetable oil
½ cup finely chopped shallots
4 teaspoons Dijon mustard
1 tablespoon red wine vinegar
1 cup homemade chicken stock (see Index) or good-quality canned broth
Salt and freshly ground pepper to taste
12 Bibb or Boston lettuce leaves
¼ cup chopped fresh chives, for garnish
2 tablespoons chopped fresh mint leaves, for garnish

1. Cut off and discard the tough ends of the asparagus stalks. Peel the stalks with a vegetable peeler, beginning just below the tips. Cut off the tips, then cut the spears into 2-inch diagonal pieces. Put the tips and spear pieces in boiling salted water to cover, and cook until just tender, 3 to 4 minutes. Drain, rinse under cold running water, and pat dry.

A COOK'S REFLECTIONS

When hard-cooking eggs, there
are several points to remember.
Always start the eggs in cold
water and then bring it to a boil.
Reduce the heat to low and simmer 15 minutes. Plunge the eggs
into cold water to chill before
shelling. It is even easier to shell
the egg under water.

2. Cook the unpeeled potatoes in boiling salted water to cover until
tender, 12 to 15 minutes. Peel the potatoes, and cut each into eight
wedges.

3. Hard-cook the eggs. Shell the eggs and quarter them lengthwise.
(The asparagus, potatoes, and eggs can be prepared several hours in
advance. Keep covered and refrigerated, then bring to room temperature before finishing the salad.)

4. When you are ready to serve the salad, cut the prosciutto into
¼-inch cubes. Heat the vegetable oil in a large heavy skillet over
medium-high heat. When the oil is hot, add the prosciutto cubes and
sauté, stirring, until crisp, 3 to 4 minutes. Pour off all but 1
tablespoon fat from the pan. Add the shallots and cook, stirring, 2 to
3 minutes. Add the mustard and vinegar to the pan, and mix well.
Add the stock, and simmer until the dressing has reduced by one
third.

5. Place the asparagus and potatoes in a non-aluminum mixing
bowl, and toss with three quarters of the warm dressing. Taste the
salad, and season with salt and pepper as desired.

6. Arrange two lettuce leaves on each salad plate. Using a slotted
spoon, mound the salad on the leaves. Arrange the egg wedges in a
border around each salad, and pour a little of the remaining dressing
over each serving. Garnish with chopped chives and mint.

Serves 6

Cucumber and Watercress Salad

A light and refreshing salad, this is a dish I include in my menus all
the time. It is particularly good as an accompaniment to fish entrées.

3 cucumbers
4 large bunches watercress
½ cup Light Tarragon Vinaigrette (recipe follows)
Salt and freshly ground pepper to taste
12 Bibb or Boston lettuce leaves

1. Peel the cucumbers and halve them lengthwise. Use a spoon to
scrape out all the seeds. Cut each half into ¼-inch-thick crescents.

2. Rinse and pat dry the bunches of watercress. Then remove

GREAT ACCOMPANIMENTS

I like to serve this salad with The Epicure's Pasta, with Broiled Fish Filets with Garlic and Shallot Butter, and with Sautéed Dover Sole in Lemon-Dill Batter.

enough leaves to make 3 cups. You can use the stems for making soup or for another use. (Both the cucumbers and watercress leaves can be prepared 2 to 3 hours ahead. Place the cucumbers in a bowl, cover, and refrigerate. Place the watercress leaves in a bowl, and cover with a folded moistened kitchen towel and then with plastic wrap.)

3. When you are ready to serve the salad, place the dressing in a non-aluminum bowl and whisk it well. Add the cucumbers and watercress leaves and toss well. Taste, and add more salt and pepper if needed. To serve, arrange two lettuce leaves on each salad plate. Mound the salad on top of the lettuce leaves.

Serves 6

LIGHT TARRAGON VINAIGRETTE

2 tablespoons tarragon vinegar
1 teaspoon Dijon mustard
½ teaspoon salt
Freshly ground pepper to taste
6 tablespoons olive oil

Place the vinegar, mustard, salt, and a generous grating of pepper in a non-aluminum mixing bowl and whisk well. Gradually whisk in the olive oil, pouring it in in a thin stream. (The dressing can be made several hours in advance and kept at room temperature. Whisk well before serving.)

Makes approximately ½ cup

SUMMER SALADS

Smoked Turkey Salad on Cantaloupe Slices

The smoked turkey makes this salad special. Cut into julienne strips, the turkey is combined with strips of Gruyère cheese, grapes, toasted almonds, chopped celery, and scallions and tossed with fresh Tarragon Mayonnaise. Served well chilled and mounded on slices of cantaloupe, it tastes delicious as a light main course for lunch or dinner.

About 1 pound smoked turkey
¼ pound Gruyère cheese
2 cups seedless green or red grapes, halved
¾ cup finely diced celery
1 cup toasted almond slivers (see Index)
4 tablespoons chopped scallions (green onions)
2 cups Tarragon Mayonnaise (recipe follows)
Salt and freshly ground pepper to taste
2 ripe cantaloupes
8 sprigs fresh tarragon, for garnish

1. Cut the turkey and the cheese into strips 2 inches long and ¼ inch wide. Combine them with the grapes, celery, almonds, and scallions in a large mixing bowl. Toss well, then add the mayonnaise and stir to mix thoroughly. Taste, and add salt and pepper as needed. Refrigerate the salad, covered, until well chilled, 2 to 3 hours. (The salad can be prepared several hours in advance and kept covered and refrigerated.)

2. To serve the salad, cut the cantaloupes into quarters and remove all the seeds. Mound each cantaloupe quarter with a generous amount of the salad, and garnish with a sprig of tarragon.

Serves 8

AS A VARIATION

Sometimes I use this turkey salad for sandwiches. I often halve pita breads, butter the insides, warm them in the oven, and then fill them with the salad.

TARRAGON MAYONNAISE

3 large egg yolks, at room temperature
½ teaspoon salt
Generous pinch of white pepper
Generous pinch of cayenne pepper
2 tablespoons plus 1 teaspoon fresh lemon juice
1 teaspoon Dijon mustard
¾ cup corn or vegetable oil
¾ cup olive oil
1½ tablespoons chopped fresh tarragon

1. Have all ingredients at room temperature.

2. To make the mayonnaise by hand, rinse a mixing bowl with hot water and dry it. Place the egg yolks in the bowl and add the salt, white pepper, cayenne pepper, lemon juice, and mustard. Mix until incorporated. Very slowly, using medium speed on an electric mixer or whisking by hand, add the two oils only a drop or two at a time. After about ½ cup oil has been added in this manner, start adding the oil in a very thin stream until all the oil has been incorporated. It is important to add the oil slowly; otherwise the mixture may separate or curdle.

To make the mayonnaise in a food processor, place the egg yolks, salt, white and cayenne peppers, lemon juice, and mustard in the work bowl, and with the machine on, gradually add the oils in a very fine stream.

3. When all the oil has been added, the mayonnaise should be smooth and thick. Stir in the tarragon. (The mayonnaise can be made 1 to 2 days in advance; cover and refrigerate.)

Makes about 2 cups

AS A VARIATION

You can vary the seafood in this salad to your own taste. I sometimes use cooked lobster meat and cooked scallops along with the shrimp. No matter how I serve it, my guests always take second helpings.

Paella Salad

This is one of the most popular salads I have ever taught in my classes. Students are wild about the taste and the look of this special dish. It is a beautiful make-ahead entrée to serve on hot summer evenings, when temperatures in Ohio regularly soar to the nineties.

1¼ cups olive oil
2 cups raw long-grain rice
5 cups homemade chicken stock (see Index) or good-quality canned broth
2 generous pinches saffron
1½ teaspoons salt
⅓ cup red wine vinegar
1½ pounds large shrimp, cooked and shelled with tails left on, and deveined
½ cup julienne slivers red bell pepper
½ cup julienne slivers green bell pepper
1 cup green peas, cooked and drained
½ cup quartered black olives
¼ cup chopped fresh parsley
¼ cup chopped fresh chives
8 to 10 large Boston lettuce leaves, rinsed and dried

1. In a large heavy casserole with a lid, heat ¼ cup of the oil over medium-high heat. When the oil is hot, add the rice and cook, stirring, until it is opaque, 2 to 3 minutes. Add the stock, saffron, and ½ teaspoon of the salt. Stir well to dissolve the saffron, and bring the mixture to a simmer. Lower the heat and cook, covered, until all liquid has been absorbed, about 20 minutes. When the rice is cooked, remove the lid and let it cool to room temperature.

2. To assemble the salad, place the vinegar and the remaining 1 teaspoon salt in a large non-aluminum mixing bowl. Whisk in the remaining 1 cup olive oil. Add the shrimp, red and green peppers, peas, and olives. Let marinate 10 minutes. Then add the rice, parsley, and chives, and mix well.

3. To serve, arrange a border of lettuce leaves on a large serving platter and mound the salad in the center. Serve at room temperature or slightly chilled.

Serves 6

GREAT ACCOMPANIMENTS

When I serve this dish as an entrée, I usually offer a soup, such as the Chilled Carrot Soup with Coriander, as a first course. A basket of hot crusty French bread to go with the soup and the salad, plus the Chocolate Walnut Caramel Tart for dessert, completes the menu.

Summer Vegetable Salad with Bacon Dressing

I can't resist beautiful produce when it starts to appear in our markets in the summer, and all too often I buy everything in sight and then am confronted with devising a way to use it when I return home. This salad made with quintessential summer bounty—corn, zucchini, and tomatoes—is one I invented after a buying spree one August day.

2 medium zucchini
6 scallions (green onions)
2 ears sweet fresh yellow corn
2 medium tomatoes
6 ounces thinly sliced bacon
2 tablespoons red wine vinegar
½ teaspoon salt
2 tablespoons olive oil
2 tablespoons chopped fresh parsley
2 tablespoons chopped fresh chives
Salt and freshly ground black pepper to taste
Cayenne pepper to taste
Red lettuce leaves, rinsed and dried

1. Trim the ends off the zucchini and cut into ½-inch dice. Set aside.

2. Chop the scallions, including 1½ inches of the green stems. You should have at least ½ cup. Set them aside.

3. Cook the corn in a large pot of lightly salted boiling water until tender, 4 to 10 minutes depending on the age of the corn (older corn takes longer). Drain the corn in a colander, rinse the ears under cold running water, and pat dry. Scrape the kernels from each ear. You should have about 1 cup. Set aside.

4. In another pot of boiling water to cover, cook the zucchini just to blanch, 1 to 2 minutes. Remove the zucchini with a slotted spoon and rinse under cold running water. Pat dry with a kitchen towel and set aside.

5. Using the same pot in which the zucchini were cooked, plunge the tomatoes into boiling water for 10 to 12 seconds. Remove them

GREAT ACCOMPANIMENTS

This is a colorful and very flavorful salad that goes well with grilled chicken, steaks, or barbecued ribs.

with a slotted spoon and rinse under cold running water. Using a paring knife or your fingers, peel the skin from the tomatoes, and remove the core. Cut the tomatoes in half horizontally, and squeeze the seeds and juice into a bowl. Discard the juice and seeds and then coarsely chop the tomato pulp. Place the chopped tomatoes in a large sieve or colander to drain. (The vegetables can be prepared several hours in advance; cover and refrigerate. Bring to room temperature 30 minutes before assembling the salad.)

6. In a large heavy skillet, fry the bacon until crisp. Remove, and drain on paper towels. Add the scallions to the skillet and cook only about 2 minutes. Remove them with a slotted spoon and drain on paper towels. Reserve 2 tablespoons bacon fat for the salad dressing.

7. Combine the vinegar and salt in a large non-aluminum mixing bowl. Whisk in the olive oil and reserved bacon fat. Add the corn and zucchini. Crumble the bacon and add it, and toss well. Then add the parsley, chives, scallions, and tomatoes, and toss gently. Taste, and add salt, black pepper, and cayenne pepper as desired.

8. To serve, arrange the lettuce leaves on a platter. Using a slotted spoon, arrange the salad on the leaves. (Or place a large leaf of lettuce on individual salad plates and arrange the salad on top). Serve immediately.

Serves 6

Red Potato Salad with Caraway

Made with red-skinned potatoes, scallions, and green peppers all tossed in a sour cream dressing seasoned with caraway seeds, this is my favorite potato salad. It is easy and uncomplicated to assemble, and tastes even more flavorful if prepared a day ahead.

3 pounds small red-skinned new potatoes, scrubbed but not
*   peeled*
¼ cup tarragon vinegar
2 to 3 tablespoons sugar
¼ teaspoon paprika
Salt and freshly ground pepper to taste
⅓ cup chopped green bell pepper
¼ cup chopped scallions (green onions)
1 teaspoon caraway seeds, crushed
¼ teaspoon celery seeds
½ cup sour cream
½ cup mayonnaise
Large Boston lettuce leaves
3 tablespoons snipped fresh chives

1. Cook the potatoes in a large pot of boiling water until just tender when pierced with a knife, 10 to 12 minutes. Drain and pat dry. Allow the potatoes to cool slightly, then cut them into ¼-inch-thick slices.

2. Combine the vinegar, 2 tablespoons sugar, paprika, salt, and a generous amount of pepper in a large bowl and whisk well. Mix in the warm potatoes and set aside to marinate for 45 minutes.

3. Gently mix the green pepper, scallions, caraway seeds, and celery seeds with the potatoes. Combine the sour cream and mayonnaise, and mix into the salad. Adjust the seasoning, adding the remaining 1 tablespoon sugar if desired. Cover, and refrigerate until well chilled, at least 2½ hours. (The salad can be prepared 1 day ahead; keep covered and refrigerated.)

4. Let the salad stand at room temperature for 30 minutes before serving. Line a large shallow bowl or platter with lettuce leaves. Add the salad, and sprinkle with chives.

Serves 6

GREAT ACCOMPANIMENTS

This potato salad is delicious with Creole Barbecued Shrimp or Grilled Salmon Steaks Wrapped in Peppered Bacon.

GREAT ACCOMPANIMENTS

I like to arrange these salad baskets on tables outdoors during warm weather as a first course. The Roast Lamb with a Pepper Coating and the Stir-Fry of Zucchini, Onions, and Sweet Red Peppers, followed by fresh strawberries with crème fraîche for dessert, make an excellent menu to follow the salad.

AS A VARIATION

You can use whatever ingredients you like for these baskets. Just choose a good variety of fresh seasonal produce.

Provençal Salad Baskets

I can't remember a more enjoyable evening than the one I spent with a group of friends at La Ferme St. Michel, a French country restaurant located high in the hills above Nice on one of the mountain roads called corniches. Long trestle tables were covered with bright cotton cloths, and in the center of each was a large rustic basket filled with crisp romaine lettuce, red cabbage leaves, red and green peppers, bunches of radishes, fennel bulbs, plum tomatoes, and clusters of carrots. Guests were given plates and cutlery, including sharp knives, and were invited to compose their own salads. A bowl of Niçoise olives and another containing a vinaigrette were also on the table, along with a basket of country French bread. Everyone loved all the food served in this restaurant, but the salad baskets were the star attraction. When I returned home I re-created my own version of this Provençal specialty.

Special equipment: Medium-size wicker basket

3 heads salad greens (romaine, Boston, leaf lettuce, or a combination), rinsed and dried
3 small heads radicchio, or several red cabbage leaves, separated, rinsed, and dried
1 bunch radishes, preferably with stems and leaves, rinsed and dried
4 carrots, peeled
3 fennel bulbs, green stems removed
6 scallions (green onions), rinsed, with 4 inches of green stems
6 small tomatoes
1 cup finely chopped black olives, preferably Niçoise
1 cup Vinaigrette (recipe follows)

Arrange the lettuce greens, the radicchio or red cabbage leaves, and the vegetables attractively grouped in a basket. Serve with a bowl of black olives and a bowl of Vinaigrette.

Serves 6

4 tablespoons red wine vinegar
¾ teaspoon salt
1 teaspoon Dijon mustard
¾ cup olive oil

Combine the vinegar, salt, and mustard in a mixing bowl and mix well. Gradually whisk in the olive oil, pouring it in in a thin stream. (The dressing can be made several hours in advance and kept at room temperature.)

Makes 1 cup

Tomatoes Stuffed with Summer Potato Salad

I prepared this potato salad served in scooped-out tomato halves for a picnic class one summer. Students told me they liked the taste and appearance of the dish, but best of all they were delighted that everything could be done completely in advance.

2 pounds small red-skinned new potatoes, scrubbed but not
   peeled
1 tablespoon plus ¼ teaspoon salt
1 slab (8 ounces) smoked bacon, partially frozen for easier
   cutting
2 large egg yolks
2½ tablespoons red wine vinegar
½ teaspoon Dijon mustard
Freshly ground pepper to taste
¼ cup olive oil
¼ cup vegetable oil
¼ cup chopped fresh chives
5 large tomatoes

1. Bring 2½ quarts of water to a boil. Add the potatoes and 1 tablespoon of the salt, and boil until just tender, 12 to 15 minutes. Allow the potatoes to cool, then cut them in half and cut each half into ¼-inch-thick slices.

2. Cut the rind from the bacon and discard it. Cut the bacon into

AT THE MARKET

For this salad, potatoes 1½ to 2 inches in diameter are the ideal size.

GREAT ACCOMPANIMENTS

Serve this salad with fried chicken and Sesame Green Beans. The Peaches and Cream Cheesecake makes an excellent dessert.

¼-inch dice. In a medium skillet over medium-high heat, fry the bacon cubes until crisp. Drain on paper towels, and reserve.

3. Place the egg yolks in a large mixing bowl with the vinegar, mustard, remaining ¼ teaspoon salt, and pepper. Whisk until well mixed, and then gradually whisk in the two oils, pouring them in in a thin stream. The dressing will look like a very thin mayonnaise.

4. Add the potatoes, bacon, and chives, and toss well. Taste, and season as desired with salt and pepper.

5. Cut the tomatoes in half and scoop out the pulp, leaving a shell. Mound potato salad into the tomato halves, cover, and refrigerate until chilled, 2 hours. (The salad can be prepared to this point several hours ahead.)

Serves 10

AUTUMN SALADS

Wild Rice and Shrimp Salad

This is a wonderful salad that works equally well as a first course, a main course, or as part of a salads buffet. However you serve it, chilled dry white wine and hot buttered French bread are great accompaniments.

1 tablespoon plus 2 teaspoons salt
1½ cups raw wild rice
1 cup raw long-grain white rice
6 tablespoons red wine vinegar
1 cup plus 2 tablespoons olive oil
2½ cups thinly sliced mushrooms, including stems
1 cup finely chopped green bell peppers
1 cup chopped scallions (green onions)
1½ pounds large shrimp, cooked, shelled, and deveined
¼ cup finely chopped fresh parsley
¼ cup finely chopped fresh chives
Boston or Bibb lettuce leaves, rinsed and dried

1. Bring 3 quarts of water to a boil in a large saucepan. Add 1 tablespoon of the salt and the wild rice, and cook, uncovered, 8 to 10 minutes. Remove from the heat and drain.

2. Bring 4½ cups water to a boil in a large heavy saucepan, and add 1 teaspoon of the salt, the drained wild rice, and the white rice. Cover the saucepan tightly, and cook over low heat until all liquid has been absorbed and the grains are fluffy, 25 to 30 minutes.

3. While the rice is cooking, prepare the vinaigrette: Combine the vinegar and the remaining 1 teaspoon salt in a large mixing bowl. Gradually whisk in the olive oil, pouring it in in a thin stream.

4. Add the mushrooms, green peppers, scallions, and shrimp to the vinaigrette. Toss well.

5. While the rice is still hot, add it to the shrimp mixture. Toss well. Check the seasonings, and add more salt if needed. (The salad may be made several hours in advance; cover and refrigerate.)

6. Bring the salad to room temperature before serving. When you are ready to serve it, add the chopped parsley and chives. Arrange the salad on a bed of lettuce leaves on a serving platter. Or if you prefer, arrange lettuce leaves on six individual salad plates and mound salad on each.

Serves 6

Warm Tomato Slices with Herbed Chèvre

This is a colorful and delicious salad to begin a fall dinner. The tomatoes topped with rounds of herbed chèvre, then sprinkled with bread crumbs and toasted pine nuts, are broiled quickly and served on a bed of Bibb lettuce.

4 ripe tomatoes (1½ pounds total)
6 ounces chèvre (without an ash coating)
2 tablespoons finely chopped fresh chives
2 tablespoons finely chopped fresh parsley
Freshly ground pepper to taste
¼ cup toasted pine nuts (see Index)
¼ cup dry bread crumbs
2 tablespoons olive oil
12 Bibb or Boston lettuce leaves, rinsed and dried

A COOK'S REFLECTIONS

The only lettuce I remember seeing in the refrigerator when I was growing up was iceberg, and that was always used on sandwiches at our house. My mother was not a salad maker; occasionally she would slice tomatoes and pour a little dressing over them, but that was the extent of her interest. It was not until I spent a year in France as a student that I discovered the satisfaction of a simple, well-prepared salad. That year I had some type of salad at almost every meal, and to this day a dinner does not seem complete without one.

1. With a sharp slicing or serrated knife, cut the bottom and top off each tomato. Reserve these slices for another use. Core the tomatoes and cut each into ½-inch-thick slices. You will need a total of 8 slices. Save any extra tomato for another use.

2. In a mixing bowl, combine the chèvre, chives, and parsley. Mix well with a wooden spoon until the herbs are well incorporated into the cheese. Divide the cheese mixture into eight equal portions. Then, using the palm of your hand, flatten each portion into a circle slightly smaller than the diameter of the tomato slices.

3. Line a baking sheet with aluminum foil, and place the tomato slices on it, several inches apart. Pepper each slice lightly. Place a round of herbed cheese on top of each tomato slice. Spread some of the pine nuts on top of the cheese, and sprinkle with some of the bread crumbs. Drizzle each slice with a little olive oil. (The tomatoes can be prepared several hours ahead; cover and refrigerate. Thirty minutes before cooking, bring to room temperature.)

4. Preheat the broiler and place a rack 4 inches from the heat.

5. Broil the tomatoes until the cheese is hot and melted, 2 to 3 minutes. Watch constantly—the time varies with the type of broiler. Using a spatula, carefully lift each tomato onto a heated serving platter. Arrange the lettuce leaves in an attractive border around the platter. (Or you can use four individual salad plates. Arrange three lettuce leaves on each, and place two tomato slices on the leaves.) Serve immediately.

Serves 4

Green Bean, Walnut, and Red Onion Salad

In Columbus, where I live, people are "football crazy." Every Saturday afternoon at Ohio State home games, fans gather all over the sprawling campus and enjoy tailgating. My students tell me that this robust salad, which can be completely assembled in advance, is an ideal dish to serve at these informal alfresco gatherings.

AT THE MARKET

Walnut oil, which is made from pressed walnuts, has a strong, heady flavor. It is most often used as a salad oil—rarely for sautéing or frying. Since it is expensive and does not keep well, I always recommend that my students buy it in small quantities and use it as promptly as possible once a bottle or can is opened.

2½ pounds green beans
2 tablespoons salt
1¼ cups Walnut Vinaigrette (recipe follows)
1⅓ cups walnut halves
2 cups halved and thinly sliced red onions
Salt and freshly ground pepper to taste
Boston, Bibb, or romaine lettuce leaves
2 tablespoons chopped fresh parsley

1. Trim the green beans and cut them diagonally into 2-inch pieces. Bring 4 quarts of water to a boil, and add the salt and the beans. Cook, uncovered, until the beans are bright green and just crisp-tender, about 8 minutes. Drain the beans in a colander and rinse them under cold running water. Pat dry. (The beans can be prepared several hours ahead or overnight. Wrap in a clean kitchen towel and then in a plastic bag, and refrigerate.)

2. When you are ready to serve the salad, place the Walnut Vinaigrette in a large non-aluminum bowl. Add the beans, walnuts, and red onion slices, and toss well. Let the mixture marinate 15 to 20 minutes. Taste, and season as desired with salt and pepper.

3. To serve, line a large shallow bowl with lettuce leaves, or place the leaves in an attractive border if using a plate. Mound the salad in the bowl, and sprinkle with parsley. (The salad can be assembled 1 hour in advance and kept covered at room temperature.)

Serves 6 to 8

WALNUT VINAIGRETTE

6 tablespoons red wine vinegar
1 teaspoon Dijon mustard
¾ teaspoon salt
¾ cup plus 2 tablespoons walnut oil

Combine the vinegar, mustard, and salt in a non-aluminum mixing bowl. Gradually whisk in the walnut oil, pouring it in in a thin stream. (The dressing can be made several hours in advance and kept at room temperature. Whisk well before using.)

Makes about 1¼ cups

Zucchini, Yellow Squash, and Romaine Salad

Many of my friends (unlike me) are skilled gardeners and find themselves with far too much produce on their hands at season's end. In the early fall they often bring me baskets laden with homegrown squash, corn, tomatoes, and more. Two items I always receive in abundance are zucchini and yellow squash. This salad, a combination of julienned zucchini, yellow squash, and romaine lettuce in a rosemary-flavored dressing, is one I love to make when these good friends share their harvest with me.

1½ pounds small zucchini
1½ pounds small yellow crookneck squash
¾ cup Rosemary Vinaigrette (recipe follows)
1 large head romaine lettuce
Salt and freshly ground pepper to taste

1. Cut the zucchini and the yellow squash into thin strips 2 inches long and ¼ inch wide. Drop them into a large pot of boiling water until just crisp-tender, about 1½ minutes. Drain the squash in a colander and then rinse under cold running water. Pat dry. (The vegetables can be prepared 6 hours ahead. Wrap them in a kitchen towel, then in plastic wrap, and refrigerate until needed.)

2. When you are ready to assemble the salad, place half the Rosemary Vinaigrette in a large non-aluminum mixing bowl. Add the zucchini and yellow squash, and toss well. Marinate for 10 minutes.

3. While the vegetables are marinating, remove six to eight outer leaves from the head of romaine lettuce. Rinse and pat them dry, and set aside. Rinse the remaining leaves, and then cut out the tough center stems. Cut the leaves into strips 2 inches long and ½ inch wide. Add the romaine strips to the squash. Add enough of the remaining vinaigrette to coat well. Toss well, and then season the salad to taste with salt and pepper.

4. To serve, line a large attractive salad bowl with the reserved romaine leaves. Mound the salad in the center.

Serves 8

AT THE MARKET

Fresh rosemary is really preferable in this salad dressing. It is more assertive than the dried herb.

ROSEMARY VINAIGRETTE

2 tablespoons plus ¾ teaspoon balsamic vinegar
1½ teaspoons Dijon mustard
¾ teaspoon salt
½ cup plus 1½ tablespoons olive oil
1 teaspoon finely chopped fresh rosemary leaves, or ⅓ teaspoon dried

Combine the vinegar, mustard, and salt in a non-aluminum mixing bowl. Gradually whisk in olive oil, pouring it in in a thin stream. Stir in the rosemary. (The dressing can be made several hours in advance and kept at room temperature.)

Makes ¾ cup

Pasta Salad with Lemon, Thyme, and Prosciutto

This recipe came to me in a roundabout way. A fellow cooking teacher in New Jersey sent me a copy, explaining that she had gotten it as a handout at a culinary demonstration held at a large department store in Philadelphia. In tracing the origins of the dish, I finally discovered that this was the invention of chef Kamol Phutlek of Alouette Restaurant in Philadelphia. When I called the restaurant to tell them how much I liked this exquisite light salad, they were delighted, and generously offered to let me include it here.

8 ounces thin-sliced prosciutto
1 tablespoon salt
1¼ pounds fresh capellini noodles (see Index), or 1 pound good-quality dried noodles
¼ cup olive oil
2 teaspoons grated lemon zest
3 tablespoons fresh thyme leaves
2 tablespoons chopped fresh parsley
1½ tablespoons fresh lemon juice
1 teaspoon finely chopped garlic
Dash of Tabasco
Salt and freshly ground pepper to taste
Several sprigs fresh thyme, for garnish (optional)

GREAT ACCOMPANIMENTS

This pasta salad makes a very good side dish to grilled or roast chicken.

1. Cut the prosciutto into thin strips 2 inches long and ¼ inch wide. Reserve.

2. Bring 4 quarts of water to a boil in a large heavy pot. Add 1 tablespoon salt and the noodles, and stir with a long-handled spoon. Cook until the pasta is *al dente,* tender but still firm to the bite. This pasta, whether fresh or dried, will cook quickly because it is so thin, 2 to 3 minutes for fresh; 5 to 6 for packaged. Drain the pasta well in a strainer and then rinse under cold running water. Drain again, and place in a large bowl. Toss the pasta with the olive oil to prevent sticking.

3. Combine the prosciutto with the lemon zest, thyme, parsley, lemon juice, garlic, and Tabasco. Mix thoroughly with the pasta. Check the seasoning, and add salt and pepper as desired. To serve, arrange the salad in a large shallow bowl or platter. If you are using the thyme sprigs, place a bouquet of them in the center. (This salad can be made several hours ahead, covered, and refrigerated. Bring to room temperature before serving.)

Serves 8

WINTER SALADS

Winter Salad of Cabbage, Ham, and Gruyère

Of all the salads I have ever taught, this is the most popular. Students always love the interesting combination of flavors in this wonderful, hearty dish.

1½ heads cabbage
¾ pound thinly sliced baked ham
¾ pound Gruyère cheese
2 to 2¼ cups Roquefort Vinaigrette (recipe follows)
6 tablespoons chopped fresh parsley
Salt and freshly ground pepper to taste
Boston, Bibb, or romaine lettuce leaves
1 or 2 black truffles, cut into thin slivers (optional)

1. Core the cabbage and cut the leaves into thin strips 2 inches long and ¼ inch wide. You should have 8 cups.

2. Cut the ham and the cheese into thin strips 2 inches long and ¼ inch wide.

3. Place the Roquefort Vinaigrette in a large non-aluminum bowl and whisk well. Add the cabbage, ham, and cheese strips, and toss to coat thoroughly. Add 4 tablespoons of the parsley and mix well. Taste, and season with salt and pepper if needed. (The salad can be made to this point 4 to 5 hours in advance. Cover and refrigerate.)

4. To serve the salad, arrange a border of lettuce leaves on a large serving platter. Mound the salad on the plate. Sprinkle it with the remaining 2 tablespoons parsley, and if desired with slivered black truffles.

Serves 8 to 10

ROQUEFORT VINAIGRETTE

½ cup red wine vinegar
1 tablespoon stone-ground mustard
1 large clove garlic, finely minced
1½ cups olive oil
⅓ cup Roquefort cheese, crumbled and softened

To prepare the dressing by hand, place the vinegar, mustard, and garlic in a large non-aluminum bowl and mix well. Whisk in the olive oil gradually, pouring it in in a thin stream. Then add the crumbled Roquefort and mash until smooth and well incorporated.

To prepare the dressing in a food processor, place the vinegar, mustard, garlic, and Roquefort in the bowl of a food processor. Process until smooth, 30 seconds, and then gradually, with the machine on, pour the oil in a thin stream through the feed tube. Process until the oil is well blended.

The sauce can be made a day in advance and refrigerated. Whisk well and bring to room temperature before using.

Makes 2 to 2¼ cups

Belgian Endive and Spinach Salad

I serve salad almost every night at my house, and this is one of my favorites. An attractive combination of subtle shades of green, it is crisp and light in flavor and works well as an accompaniment to many main courses.

10 ounces spinach leaves
4 to 5 medium heads Belgian endive
1 head Boston lettuce
¾ cup Lemon Garlic Vinaigrette (recipe follows)
Salt and freshly ground pepper to taste

1. Rinse and dry all the greens. Remove the stems from the spinach and tear the leaves into bite-size pieces. Reserve eighteen endive leaves, and cut the rest into 1-inch slices. Tear the Boston lettuce into bite-size pieces. You should have 2 cups of each.

2. Place the greens in a large non-aluminum mixing bowl, and toss to mix well. Pour half the vinaigrette over the greens and mix well. Then gradually add enough remaining vinaigrette to coat the greens lightly. Taste, and add salt and pepper if desired.

3. To serve the salad, arrange three whole endive leaves in a starburst pattern on each plate. Mound the salad on the plates, and serve immediately.

Serves 6

LEMON GARLIC VINAIGRETTE

3 tablespoons fresh lemon juice
1 clove garlic, very finely chopped
½ teaspoon salt
¼ teaspoon coarsely ground pepper
⅓ cup chopped scallions (green onions), including 2 inches of
*   green stems*
½ cup plus 1 tablespoon olive oil

Combine the lemon juice, garlic, salt, pepper, and scallions in a non-aluminum mixing bowl and mix well. Gradually whisk in the olive

AS A VARIATION

Sometimes I sprinkle each salad serving with a few toasted pine nuts and a little sautéed diced prosciutto.

oil, pouring it in in a thin stream. (The dressing can be made several hours in advance and kept at room temperature.)

Makes about ¾ cup

Winter Potato Salad with Green Beans and Walnuts

This is one of the few potato salads I serve in cold weather. Instead of offering this dish well chilled, as I do for summer potato salads, I serve it at room temperature. It is a perfect accompaniment to sautéed or grilled sausages or chicken.

1½ pounds small red-skinned new potatoes, scrubbed but
*   unpeeled*
½ pound fresh green beans
1½ tablespoons salt
½ cup walnut pieces
¼ cup finely chopped shallots
¼ cup plus 1 tablespoon chopped fresh parsley
1¾ cups Thin Mayonnaise (recipe follows)
Salt and freshly ground pepper to taste
12 leaves Boston or leaf lettuce, rinsed and dried

1. Cook the potatoes in boiling water to cover until tender when pierced with a fork, about 15 minutes. Cooking time will vary, depending on the size of the potatoes. Drain, and allow the potatoes to cool to room temperature. Reserve.

2. Trim the ends from the green beans and cut the beans into 2½-inch pieces. Drop the beans and the salt into 3 quarts boiling water. Cook, uncovered, until the beans are just tender and are bright green, about 8 minutes. Drain the beans in a colander and rinse them under cold running water. Pat dry. (Both the potatoes and the beans can be cooked several hours ahead. Cover and refrigerate. Bring to room temperature before using.)

3. Cut the cooled potatoes into ½-inch rounds and place in a mixing bowl. Add the green beans, walnuts, shallots, and ¼ cup of the parsley. Add half the mayonnaise and gently toss to mix well. Continue to add mayonnaise, a little at a time, until all ingredients are well coated. Taste, and add salt and pepper as desired.

AT THE MARKET

Potatoes 1½ to 2 inches in diameter are just the right size for this salad.

GREAT ACCOMPANIMENTS

I like to serve this salad with the Grilled Mustard-Glazed Cornish Hens or with grilled or sautéed bratwurst sausages.

4. Place the lettuce leaves on a serving platter and top with potato salad. Sprinkle the salad with the remaining 1 tablespoon parsley, and serve immediately at room temperature.

Serves 6

THIN MAYONNAISE

This mayonnaise will be thinner than usual because a large amount of vinegar is included. It will be slightly thicker than heavy cream and will coat the back of a spoon.

4 large egg yolks, at room temperature
1 teaspoon Dijon mustard
½ teaspoon salt
Freshly ground pepper to taste
⅓ cup red wine vinegar
½ cup plus 2 tablespoons olive oil
½ cup vegetable oil

1. Have all the ingredients at room temperature.

2. To prepare the mayonnaise by hand, place the egg yolks, mustard, salt, and pepper in a mixing bowl and stir with a whisk until well blended. Then whisk in the vinegar until it is thoroughly combined with the egg mixture. Very slowly, drop by drop, start to whisk in the oil. Make sure all oil has been absorbed before adding the next amount. After ½ cup has been added, add the remaining oil in a thin stream, whisking all the time.

To prepare the mayonnaise in a food processor, place the egg yolks, mustard, salt, pepper, and vinegar in the bowl. With the machine running, slowly add the oil through the feed tube in a very thin stream.

When all the oil has been added, the mayonnaise will be smooth and somewhat thickened.

Makes 1¾ cups

Triple White Salad

The idea for this salad came from two creative teachers and caterers, Suzanne Karpus and Sharon Reiss, who prepared it for one of their classes. I kept the principal ingredients—cucumbers, Jerusalem artichokes, and white radishes—and added some horseradish to the sherry vinaigrette and included watercress as a garnish. It's a light and attractive salad which I like to serve during the winter.

4 large cucumbers
2 pounds Jerusalem artichokes (see Index)
1 or 2 bunches white icicle radishes, rinsed, leaves and roots
*   trimmed*
¾ cup Horseradish Sherry Vinaigrette (recipe follows)
1 bunch fresh watercress
Freshly ground pepper to taste

1 Peel the cucumbers and halve them lengthwise. Scrape out the seeds, and then cut each half into ⅛-inch-thick crescents. You should have 4 cups sliced cucumbers. Place the cucumbers in a colander, salt them well, and allow them to sit for 30 minutes. Then rinse thoroughly under cold running water. Pat dry, place in a bowl, and cover with ice cubes to recrisp. Set aside.

2. Peel the Jerusalem artichokes and cut them into ⅛-inch-thick slices. You should have 3 cups. Cook in lightly salted boiling water to cover until just tender, only about 2 minutes. Drain well and pat dry.

3. Cut the radishes into ⅛-inch diagonal slices. You should have 1½ cups.

4. Remove the ice cubes from the cucumbers and drain. Pat the cucumbers dry. Combine the cucumbers, Jerusalem artichokes, and radishes in a non-aluminum mixing bowl and toss well. Pour in the dressing, toss well, and let marinate for 30 to 45 minutes.

5. When you are ready to serve the salad, chop enough watercress leaves to make 1 tablespoon. Arrange a bed of watercress sprigs on a serving platter. Taste the salad, and add more salt if needed. Use a slotted spoon to drain any excess dressing, and mound the salad on the watercress. Sprinkle the tablespoon of chopped watercress over the salad. Then grate some pepper over the salad.

Serves 6

GREAT ACCOMPANIMENTS

This salad holds up well for a long time, so it is good for a buffet. I often serve it as a side dish to either grilled chicken or the Roast Lamb with a Pepper Coating.

HORSERADISH SHERRY VINAIGRETTE

3 tablespoons sherry vinegar
½ teaspoon Dijon mustard
½ teaspoon salt
Freshly ground pepper to taste
2 tablespoons prepared horseradish
½ cup plus 1 tablespoon olive oil

Place the vinegar, mustard, salt, pepper, and horseradish in a non-aluminum mixing bowl. Mix well. Then gradually whisk in the olive oil, pouring it in in a thin stream. (The dressing can be made several hours ahead and kept at room temperature. Whisk well before using.)

Makes approximately ¾ cup

Warm Seafood Salad Da Giacomo

I have wonderful memories of enjoying this seafood salad with good friends at a restaurant called Da Giacomo's in Genoa, Italy. It was recommended by the owner of the establishment as one of the best offerings on the menu, and he was right! Waiters arrived at our table with a cart and with great fanfare began to toss shellfish and vegetables together in a copper chafing dish. Then, with their arms held high above the pan, they squeezed lemon juice and poured olive oil into the mixture and stirred again. Their creation was superb and one I wasted no time in duplicating when I returned home to the States.

2 ribs celery
¾ red bell pepper, cored and seeded
¾ green bell pepper, cored and seeded
2 large heads radicchio
7 tablespoons olive oil
¾ pound large shrimp, shelled and deveined
¾ pound sea scallops, rinsed and dried
Salt and freshly ground pepper to taste
3 tablespoons fresh lemon juice

1. Trim the celery and cut the ribs into very thin slices, ¼ inch wide (you should have ¾ cup). Cut the peppers into very thin slices, 2

AS A VARIATION

You can vary the shellfish in this dish to your own taste. For example, you could include cooked lobster along with the shrimp and scallops. You will only need to sauté cooked lobster to heat it through.

inches long and ¼ inch wide (you should have ½ cup of each). Reserve twelve radicchio leaves for garnish and cut the rest into very thin pieces, 2 inches long and ¼ inch wide (you should have ½ cup).

2. Heat 2 tablespoons of the oil in a wok or a heavy 11- or 12-inch skillet over high heat. When it is hot, add the shrimp and sauté, stirring, until they turn pink and curl, 3 to 4 minutes. Remove the shrimp with a slotted spoon and set them aside, loosely covered with foil to keep warm.

3. Discard the liquid in the pan, and add 2 more tablespoons oil. When the oil is hot, sauté the scallops until they are opaque, 3 to 4 minutes. Remove them with a slotted spoon, cover loosely with foil, and reserve.

4. Discard the liquid in the pan, and add 1½ tablespoons additional oil. When it is hot, add the celery and cook, stirring, 2 minutes. Then add the red and green peppers and stir-fry 2 minutes more. Return the shrimp and scallops to the pan, and toss until all are hot.

5. Using a slotted spoon, transfer the mixture to a heated shallow serving bowl. Taste, and season as desired with salt and pepper. Add the lemon juice to the mixture and stir well; then add the remaining 1½ tablespoons olive oil. Toss in the julienned radicchio. Tuck the radicchio leaves around the edge of the bowl to form a border. Serve immediately on heated plates.

Serves 4 (2 as an entrée)

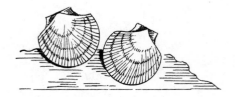

VEGETABLES

In my cooking classes, I always offer students two guidelines when preparing vegetables: first, to use the freshest and best produce they can find, buying seasonal items as often as possible, and second, not to be afraid to use these products imaginatively. I especially love to mix and match vegetables of a variety of colors and textures, as the multi-hued sautés and gratins in this section will attest. Sometimes I add a single ingredient to give a dish a new twist—for example, sprinkling bourbon over sautéed carrots or tossing toasted sesame seeds over cooked green beans. And I think one can do more than simply bake, boil, or fry potatoes. All the selections are interesting departures from what one usually thinks of doing with that common tuber.

VEGETABLE SAUTES

Carrot and Belgian Endive Sauté

This is a colorful sauté that I often serve with roast fowl or veal. You can cook the carrots ahead and then need only simmer the endive and quickly sauté the vegetables to finish.

1 pound baby carrots
2 cups homemade chicken stock (see Index) or good-quality
*   canned broth*
1½ tablespoons sugar
¾ teaspoon salt
18 ounces (4 to 5 small heads) Belgian endive
1 tablespoon fresh lemon juice
Generous pinch of sugar
2 tablespoons unsalted butter
Freshly ground pepper to taste
Freshly grated nutmeg to taste
1 tablespoon chopped fresh chives, for garnish

1. Peel and trim the carrots; cut them in half lengthwise. Bring 2 cups water, the stock, sugar, and ½ teaspoon of the salt to a boil in a large saucepan. Add the carrots, reduce the heat, and simmer until tender, about 15 minutes. Drain, reserving the liquid. Pat the carrots dry. (The carrots can be prepared a day ahead. Cool completely, cover, and refrigerate.)

2. Rinse the endive. Reserve ten to twelve leaves, and cut the rest into ½-inch slices. Combine the sliced endive and lemon juice in a large skillet. Sprinkle with ¼ teaspoon salt and the pinch of sugar. Add the reserved carrot cooking liquid, and bring to a boil over medium heat. Reduce the heat, cover partially, and simmer until the endive is tender, about 10 minutes. Drain well, and pat dry.

3. Melt the butter in a large heavy skillet over medium heat. Add the carrots and endive, and toss until heated through. Taste, and season generously with pepper and nutmeg, and more salt if desired. Remove the skillet from the heat.

4. Arrange the reserved endive leaves in a border, with ends pointing outward, on a serving dish, then mound the vegetables in the center. Sprinkle with chives.

Serves 6

Stir-Fry of Zucchini, Yellow Squash, and Cherry Tomatoes

I love to serve this vegetable stir-fry with lamb or chicken dishes. Both squashes can be sliced and steamed in advance, and the final stir-frying, which can be done in either a wok or a large skillet, takes only five minutes to complete.

Special equipment: Vegetable steamer

4 medium zucchini, ends trimmed
4 small yellow squash, ends trimmed
⅓ cup olive oil
1 cup cherry tomatoes, stems removed
4½ teaspoons minced fresh basil, or 1½ teaspoons crumbled
*   dried*
Salt and freshly ground pepper to taste

1. Using a small sharp knife, peel ½-inch-wide lengthwise strips of skin from the zucchini and yellow squash to create a striped appearance. Cut the zucchini and yellow squash into ¾-inch-thick rounds. Cook in a vegetable steamer over boiling water until crisp-tender, about 4 minutes. Rinse under cold water, drain, and pat dry. (The zucchini and yellow squash can be prepared 1 day ahead. Wrap them in a kitchen towel, then in plastic wrap, and refrigerate.)

2. When you are ready to serve the vegetables, heat the oil in a wok or a large heavy skillet over medium-high heat. Add the zucchini and yellow squash, and stir until heated through, about 4 minutes. Add the tomatoes and basil, and toss 1 minute. Season with salt and pepper, and serve.

Serves 6 to 8

GREAT ACCOMPANIMENTS

This vegetable stir-fry is good with the Roast Lamb with a Pepper Coating, the Lamb Chops with Spinach and Chèvre, or the Grilled Mustard-Glazed Cornish Hens.

GREAT ACCOMPANIMENTS

This is good with the Roast Stuffed Veal with Red Wine and Shallot Butter, the Sautéed Veal Scallops with Watercress Mustard Sauce, or the Chicken Breasts Stuffed with Prosciutto and Mozzarella.

Braised Fennel, Carrots, and Snow Peas

It was only a few years ago, when fennel started to appear regularly in Columbus markets, that I became familiar with this Italian vegetable. I like the slightly anise flavor and the crunchy texture of this pale green bulb. In this dish, sliced fennel and carrots are sautéed in butter and then braised until tender in chicken stock. Just before serving, blanched snow peas are added. This is a particularly good accompaniment to veal or chicken main courses.

3 fennel bulbs, tough outer layer discarded, trimmed
4 medium carrots (8 ounces total), peeled and trimmed
¼ pound snow peas, stringed and halved
4 tablespoons (½ stick) unsalted butter
½ to ¾ cup homemade chicken stock (see Index) or good-quality canned broth
Salt and freshly ground pepper to taste

1. Halve the fennel lengthwise and discard the tough inner core. Cut the bulbs crosswise into ¼-inch-thick slices. Cut the carrots diagonally into ¼-inch-thick slices.

2. Blanch the snow peas in a large pot of boiling salted water until just tender, about 2 minutes. Drain the snow peas in a colander and rinse them under cold running water. Pat dry. (The vegetables can be prepared 1 day ahead. Wrap them in kitchen towels, keeping the fennel and carrots together and the snow peas separate, put them in a plastic bag, and refrigerate.)

3. Melt the butter in a large heavy skillet over medium-high heat. Add the fennel and carrots, and stir until coated with butter. Add ½ cup stock and bring to a simmer. Reduce the heat to low. Cover, and cook until the vegetables are tender, stirring occasionally, 10 to 12 minutes. Add an extra ¼ cup stock if all liquid evaporates before the vegetables are cooked.

4. Uncover and boil to evaporate the liquid, if necessary. Add the snow peas and stir until they are heated through, about 1 minute. Season with salt and pepper, and serve immediately.

Serves 6

GREAT ACCOMPANIMENTS

*I like to serve this colorful sauté
with the Grilled Flank Steak with
Shiitake Mushrooms or the Lamb
Chops with Spinach and Chèvre. On
occasion I have also offered these
vegetables as a garnish to the Grilled
Mustard-Glazed Cornish Hens.*

Sauté of Jerusalem Artichokes, Sweet Red Peppers, and Zucchini

One of my favorite combinations of sautéed vegetables, this is a dish that I use often to accompany steaks or lamb chops. The Jerusalem artichokes, with their slightly smoky taste, add an unusual and delicious flavor to the sauté.

1¼ pounds small zucchini, ends trimmed
1 pound Jerusalem artichokes
2 tablespoons unsalted butter
2 tablespoons olive oil
2 red bell peppers, cut into 1-inch pieces
1 teaspoon dried thyme, crumbled
Salt to taste

1. Cut the zucchini diagonally into ¼-inch-thick slices. Peel the Jerusalem artichokes, and cut them into ¼-inch-thick rounds.

2. Cook the zucchini in boiling salted water to cover until just crisp-tender, about 2 minutes. Using a slotted spoon, transfer the zucchini to a colander. Add the Jerusalem artichokes to the cooking water and boil until just tender, about 2 minutes. Drain in another colander. Pat the vegetables dry. (The zucchini and Jerusalem artichokes can be prepared several hours ahead; cover and refrigerate.)

3. Heat the butter with the oil in a large heavy skillet over medium-high heat. Add the red peppers and cook until almost crisp-tender, stirring frequently, about 3 minutes. Add the Jerusalem artichokes and stir 2 minutes. Add the zucchini and stir until heated through, about 2 minutes. Stir in the thyme, and add salt to taste. Serve the vegetables in a shallow bowl.

Serves 6

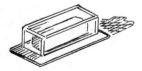

Sauté of Asparagus, Carrots, and Snow Peas with Prosciutto

On a trip to Madrid, I had a chance to dine in the elegant restaurant Zalacain. My dinner partner, a Spanish friend, suggested that for a first course I order vegetables cooked with Spanish country ham. The dish was superb, and when I returned home I created this version—a combination of sautéed asparagus, carrots, and snow peas flavored with diced prosciutto and garnished with chopped watercress leaves. I use this sauté as a vegetable accompaniment, but it could be a beginning course as well.

1 pound slim asparagus
2 teaspoons salt
8 ounces carrots
1 tablespoon sugar
½ pound snow peas, ends trimmed on the diagonal, strings
*   removed*
5 tablespoons unsalted butter
4 ounces prosciutto, cut into ¼-inch dice
Salt and freshly ground pepper to taste
¼ cup chopped watercress leaves, for garnish

1. Cut or break off and discard the tough ends of the asparagus spears. Then, using a vegetable peeler, peel the asparagus starting just below the tip. Cut the tip from each stalk, and cut the stalks on the diagonal into ½-inch pieces. Bring 1½ quarts of water to a boil. Add 1 teaspoon of the salt and the asparagus, and cook until just tender, 3 to 4 minutes. Drain the asparagus in a colander and rinse under cold running water. Pat dry and set aside.

2. Peel the carrots, and cut them on a sharp diagonal into ⅜-inch-thick slices. Bring 1 quart water to a boil. Add the sugar and ½ teaspoon of the salt. Add the carrots, and cook until just tender, 10 to 12 minutes. Drain the carrots in a colander and rinse under cold running water. Pat dry and set aside.

3. Drop the snow peas and the remaining ½ teaspoon salt into 1 quart of boiling water and cook 2 to 3 minutes. Drain in a colander and rinse under cold running water. Pat dry and set aside. (All the vegetables can be prepared several hours in advance to this point and refrigerated, covered separately, until needed.)

GREAT ACCOMPANIMENTS

The Marinated Roast Racks of Lamb with Tomato-Mustard Sauce and the Grilled Mustard-Glazed Cornish Hens are both good served with this vegetable sauté.

4. When you are ready to serve the vegetables, melt the butter in a heavy 11- to 12-inch skillet over medium-high heat. When it is hot, add the prosciutto and stir well. Then add the carrots and cook 3 to 4 minutes, stirring to coat well with butter. Add the asparagus and snow peas, and stir until heated through, 3 to 4 minutes. Taste the vegetables, and season as desired with salt and pepper. Sprinkle with chopped watercress, and serve.

Serves 6

Honey-Glazed Carrots, Parsnips, and Currants

A hearty dish to accompany roast fowl or pork, this is easy and quick to assemble for a fall or winter menu.

8 ounces carrots, peeled
1 teaspoon salt, plus more if needed
1 tablespoon sugar
8 ounces parsnips, peeled
2 tablespoons currants
2 tablespoons unsalted butter
2 tablespoons stone-ground mustard
2 tablespoons honey

1. Soak the currants in hot water to cover until softened and plump, 10 to 15 minutes. Drain and pat dry. (The carrots, parsnips, and currants can be prepared a day ahead. Cover and store each separately in the refrigerator.)

2. Cut the carrots into strips 2 inches long and ¼ inch wide. Bring 2 quarts of water to a boil, and add ½ teaspoon of the salt and the sugar. Add the carrots and cook until just tender, about 6 minutes. Drain and pat dry.

3. Cut the parsnips into strips 2 inches long and ¼ inch wide. Bring 2 quarts of water to a boil, and add the remaining ½ teaspoon salt. Add the parsnips and cook until just tender, 2 to 3 minutes. Drain and pat dry.

4. When you are ready to serve the vegetables, melt the butter in a large skillet over medium-high heat. Stir in the mustard, then add

AT THE MARKET

Many of my students tell me they are unfamiliar with parsnips. This root vegetable, which resembles a carrot in shape, is pale beige in color and has a crisp texture. They are available in the market in late autumn and winter; choose small to medium parsnips since the larger ones tend to be woody and tough.

GREAT ACCOMPANIMENTS

These glazed carrots and parsnips are delicious with Pork Chops Baked with Chestnuts and Mushrooms or with the Roast Loin of Pork Braised in Cider.

GREAT ACCOMPANIMENTS

I particularly like to serve this vegetable sauté with Chicken Breasts Stuffed with Prosciutto and Mozzarella; Lamb Chops with Spinach and Chèvre; Roast Lamb with a Pepper Coating; and Grilled Flank Steak with Shiitake Mushrooms.

the honey and stir well. Add the carrots and parsnips and toss until heated through, about 4 minutes. Add the currants and toss 1 minute more. Taste, and add salt as desired.

Serves 4

Stir-Fry of Zucchini, Onions, and Sweet Red Peppers

A favorite dish of many of my students, this is a beautiful and interesting accompaniment to serve with beef, chicken, or lamb.

1 large onion
2 red bell peppers
4 small zucchini (about 2 pounds), ends trimmed
⅓ cup olive oil
1 teaspoon dried thyme
Salt and freshly ground pepper to taste
¼ cup grated imported Parmesan cheese

1. Cut the onion in half lengthwise. Then cut each half into ¼-inch-thick slices.

2. Core the peppers, cut them in half lengthwise, and remove the seeds and membranes. Then cut the peppers into strips 3 inches long and ¼ inch wide.

3. Cut the zucchini in half lengthwise, then into strips 3 inches long and ¼ inch wide. Blanch the zucchini in boiling salted water to cover, only 1 to 2 minutes. Drain the zucchini in a colander and rinse under cold running water. Pat dry. (All the vegetables can be prepared several hours in advance; cover separately and refrigerate.)

4. To sauté the vegetables, heat the oil in a wok or a large heavy skillet over medium-high heat. When it is hot, add the onions and cook, stirring, 2 to 3 minutes. Add the red peppers and sauté until softened, 3 to 4 minutes. Then add the zucchini and toss just until heated through, 2 to 3 minutes. Add the thyme and stir well. Taste, and season with salt and pepper. Place in a serving dish and sprinkle with Parmesan cheese.

Serves 6

VEGETABLE GRATINS

Gratin of Eggplant and Spinach with Two Cheeses

A wonderful make-ahead dish, this is a recipe that I use both as a main course and as a side dish. Composed of layers of sautéed eggplant topped with uncooked spinach leaves, a light tomato sauce, and a combination of mozzarella and ricotta cheeses, the gratin is excellent to offer as a simple entrée along with a salad and hot buttered Italian bread. It works equally well as an accompaniment to roast lamb or chicken.

1 eggplant (1¾ pounds)
Salt
¾ cup milk
1 large egg
2½ cups cornmeal
Vegetable oil
Tomato Sauce (recipe follows)
5 ounces fresh spinach leaves, trimmed, rinsed, and patted dry
1 pound ricotta cheese, preferably freshly made
8 ounces paper-thin slices mozzarella cheese

1. Peel the eggplant and cut it into ¼-inch-thick slices. Place the eggplant slices on a baking sheet and sprinkle well with salt. Let stand 30 minutes. This will extract the water and any bitterness from the eggplant. Place the eggplant in a colander and rinse it under cold running water. Pat the eggplant slices dry.

2. Whisk the milk and egg together in a mixing bowl. Spread the cornmeal on a dinner plate. Dip each slice of eggplant in the egg/milk mixture, and then dredge in cornmeal.

3. Heat enough vegetable oil over medium to coat the bottom of an 11- to 12-inch skillet. If you have two skillets, use both to save time. When the oil is hot, place enough slices in the skillet to make a single layer. Cook until golden, 2 to 3 minutes per side. Remove and drain on paper towels. Cook the remaining eggplant slices in the same way.

AT THE MARKET

Fresh ricotta cheese is available only at Italian markets and some at specialty groceries. It is more perishable than commercially packaged ricotta and should be used within one to two days. If fresh ricotta is unavailable, a good commercial brand will work fine.

GREAT ACCOMPANIMENTS

This gratin is nice plain broiled lamb chops. I usually add a seasonal green salad tossed in a garlic vinaigrette and end the meal with the Espresso Cheesecake.

4. To assemble, spread a thin layer of Tomato Sauce in a 13 x 9-inch baking dish. Place one third of the eggplant slices in a single layer over the Tomato Sauce. Spread a small amount of the Tomato Sauce over the eggplant. Then put one third of the spinach leaves over the eggplant. Crumble one third of the ricotta over the spinach leaves. Lightly salt. Then place one third of the mozzarella slices over the spinach and ricotta. Continue in this manner, making layers of sauce, eggplant, sauce, spinach, ricotta, salt, and mozzarella. (The gratin can be prepared several hours or 1 day ahead to this point. Cover with plastic wrap and refrigerate.)

5. To bake, preheat the oven to 350° F.

6. Bake until the mixture is piping hot and bubbling, 30 to 35 minutes. Remove from the oven and let cool 5 to 10 minutes. Cut into portions and serve.

Serves 8 (6 as an entrée)

TOMATO SAUCE

¼ cup olive oil
1½ cups finely chopped onions
1½ teaspoons finely chopped garlic
2 cans (28 ounces each) Italian-style tomatoes, drained well
1½ teaspoons dried basil
1 teaspoon salt
Pinch of sugar

1. Heat the oil in a heavy 11- to 12-inch skillet over medium-high heat. When it is hot, add the onions and cook, stirring, 3 to 4 minutes. Add the garlic and cook 1 minute more, stirring. Add the tomatoes, basil, salt, and sugar. Stir well, and bring the mixture to a simmer. Lower the heat and cook, uncovered, until the tomatoes and onions are very tender, about 25 minutes.

2. Purée the mixture in a food processor, blender, or food mill. Taste, and add more salt if needed. Reserve. (The sauce can be made a day ahead; cover and refrigerate until needed.)

Makes 2½ to 3 cups

AS A VARIATION

When asparagus is not available, you can substitute other cooked vegetables, such as broccoli or cauliflower (cut into small flowerets and parboiled).

A COOK'S REFLECTIONS

When adding the lemon juice to the reduced cream in this recipe, whisk it in gently. The small amount of lemon juice will not cause the cream to curdle.

GREAT ACCOMPANIMENTS

When I serve this dish as a light entrée, I usually offer the Cucumber and Watercress Salad plus a basket of hot French bread. The Raspberry Mousse Pie with a Brownie Fudge Crust is a fine dessert to complete the menu.

*   As a vegetable side dish, these asparagus are excellent served with plain broiled lamb chops garnished with fresh mint, or with Grilled Mustard-Glazed Cornish Hens.*

Gratin of Asparagus in Lemon Cream Sauce

I have served this easy-to-make gratin as a first course, a light entrée, and a vegetable accompaniment, all with equal success. The dish can be assembled several hours in advance and needs only to be baked before serving.

1½ pounds fresh asparagus
Salt to taste
1½ cups heavy or whipping cream
Juice of ½ lemon
3 ounces thin slices baked ham
3 ounces thin slices Gruyère cheese

1. Cut the ham and Gruyère into strips 3 inches long and ¼ inch wide.

2. Cut or break off and discard the tough end of each asparagus spear. Then, using a vegetable peeler, peel the asparagus starting just below the tip. Fill a large heavy skillet two-thirds full with water, and bring it to a simmer over medium heat. Lightly salt the water, and add the asparagus. Cook until just tender, 3 to 4 minutes. The time will vary according to the size of the asparagus. Drain and pat dry.

3. Place the cream in a large heavy saucepan and cook over high heat until it has reduced by half, about 5 minutes or longer. Remove from the heat and stir in the lemon juice.

4. Generously butter a medium-size ovenproof baking dish (one that can go from the oven to the table). Arrange the cooked asparagus neatly in the dish. Salt lightly. Place the strips of ham and cheese on top of the asparagus, then pour the cream mixture over. (The gratin can be prepared several hours in advance to this point. Cover with plastic wrap and refrigerate.)

5. When you are ready to bake the asparagus, preheat the oven to 350° F.

6. Bake the gratin until the sauce is bubbling, about 10 minutes. Place it under the broiler for 1 minute, or until the top browns lightly.

Serves 6 (4 as an entrée)

AT THE MARKET

Cheshire cheese is English in origin and rich with a special piquancy. There are several varieties available, but for cooking, I use the orange-colored one. It is usually available in specialty cheese shops, but if you can't locate it, a medium to sharp good-quality Cheddar can be substituted.

Gratin of Hearty Vegetables in Cheshire Cheese Sauce

Robust and hearty, this is a perfect gratin to offer with simple sautéed pork chops, roast chicken, or baked ham. The dish, a combination of cooked yellow and green squash, roasted red peppers, and sautéed onions, all napped with a spirited sauce made with Cheshire cheese, has a wonderful flavor and can be completely assembled several hours in advance.

3 medium-size yellow squash (about 1 pound total)
1 zucchini (about ⅓ pound)
1 large onion
Salt
2 small red bell peppers
4½ tablespoons unsalted butter
Cheshire Cheese Sauce (recipe follows)
3 tablespoons dry bread crumbs
½ cup grated Cheshire cheese

1. Cut the yellow squash, zucchini, and onion into ¼-inch slices.

2. Place the yellow squash and zucchini slices in a colander over a bowl, and salt generously. Let stand to remove water from the vegetables, about 30 minutes. Rinse the squash under cold running water and pat dry.

3. Roast the red peppers: Place the peppers on a long fork, or use tongs, and hold them directly over a gas flame. Turn and rotate the peppers until they are charred on all surfaces.

If you have an electric stove, preheat the broiler, place the peppers on a baking sheet, and broil 4 to 5 inches from the heating element. Broil while turning the peppers every 1 to 2 minutes until all surfaces are charred.

After the peppers are charred, wrap them while still hot in moistened paper towels. Place them in a plastic bag and tie with a clasp. Let the peppers stay in the bag until cooled, 15 minutes or longer. Then scrape off the charred skin with a sharp paring knife. Remove the seeds and membranes, and cut the peppers into thin ¼-inch strips. Set aside.

4. Melt 2 tablespoons of the butter in a medium-size skillet over medium-high heat. When it is hot, add the yellow squash and zucchini and cook, tossing, about 5 minutes. The squash and zucchini should be just tender, not mushy, and lightly browned. Remove, drain on paper towels, and set aside.

5. Melt another 2 tablespoons butter in a medium-size skillet over medium-high heat. When it is hot, add the onion slices and cook until they are tender but not browned, about 5 minutes. Remove, drain on paper towels, and set aside.

6. Butter a medium-size gratin or baking dish with the remaining ½ tablespoon butter. Add the cooked squash, zucchini, onions, and peppers. Toss with the Cheshire Cheese Sauce, and mix well. Sprinkle with the bread crumbs and grated Cheshire cheese. (The gratin can be prepared several hours in advance. Cover with plastic wrap and refrigerate until needed.)

7. When you are ready to bake the vegetables, preheat the oven to 375° F.

8. Bake until the sauce is bubbling and the gratin is golden on top, 35 to 40 minutes.

Serves 6

GREAT ACCOMPANIMENTS

This makes a good dish to serve with the Grilled Mustard-Glazed Cornish Hens or with plain roast chicken or grilled steaks.

CHESHIRE CHEESE SAUCE

3 tablespoons unsalted butter, plus additional if preparing ahead
3 tablespoons all-purpose flour
1½ cups milk
1½ cups grated Cheshire cheese
¾ teaspoon salt
Pinch of cayenne pepper

Melt the butter in a medium-size saucepan over medium-high heat. When it has melted, add the flour and stir constantly for 2 minutes. Reduce the heat to medium and whisk in the milk. Cook, whisking, until the sauce becomes thick and smooth, 3 to 4 minutes. Gradually stir in the cheese, and then add the salt and cayenne pepper. (The sauce can be prepared several hours or 1 day ahead. Dot with additional butter to prevent a skin from forming, and cover and refrigerate. Reheat to thin before using.)

Makes 1½ to 2 cups

AT THE MARKET

Pancetta is an unsmoked Italian bacon that is salted and spiced and rolled into a cylinder. It has a particularly pleasing taste that works well in this dish. It is usually available at groceries that sell Italian products. A piece of smoked bacon can be substituted if pancetta is not available.

Souffléed Corn with Pancetta and Onions

I particularly like to serve this soufflé in the summer, when wonderful fresh ears of Ohio-grown corn are everywhere—in our groceries, at roadside stands, and at farmers' markets. The base of the soufflé can be prepared early in the day, so that all that is necessary at the last minute is to beat and add the egg whites and then bake the soufflé.

6 ounces pancetta, cut into ¼-inch dice
Vegetable oil, if needed
1 cup chopped leeks, white parts only
2 cups fresh corn kernels (from 4 or 5 large ears) or frozen corn,
   thawed
2 tablespoons unsalted butter
2 tablespoons all-purpose flour
1 cup milk
1½ cups grated sharp Cheddar cheese
½ teaspoon plus a pinch of salt
½ teaspoon freshly ground pepper
8 to 10 drops Tabasco
3 large egg yolks
5 large egg whites

1. Fry the pancetta cubes in a 10-inch skillet over medium heat until they are golden and crisp and grease has been rendered, 4 to 5 minutes. Remove the pancetta with a slotted spoon and drain on paper towels. Pour out all but 3 tablespoons fat from the pan. If you do not have enough fat, add vegetable oil to make 3 tablespoons.

2. Heat the fat over medium-high heat and add the leeks. Sauté until softened, 3 to 4 minutes. Add the corn, toss well, and cook for about 5 minutes. Remove with a slotted spoon and place in a mixing bowl. Add the pancetta and toss. Set aside.

3. Melt the butter in a medium-size heavy saucepan over medium heat. Add the flour and cook, stirring, for about 2 minutes. Whisk in the milk, whisking continuously until thickened, 3 to 4 minutes. Lower the heat and gradually stir in 1 cup of the cheese, 2 to 3 tablespoons at a time. Make sure each addition of cheese has melted before the next is added. Taste the sauce, and season with ½

GREAT ACCOMPANIMENTS

This tastes delicious with barbecued ribs or chicken, or with the Grilled Sirloin Steaks with Banana Chile Pepper Butter.

teaspoon salt, the pepper, and the hot pepper sauce. Add the egg yolks and incorporate well. Add the corn and pancetta mixture, and stir well. (The soufflé base can be made several hours ahead; keep covered and refrigerated. Bring to room temperature before folding in the egg whites.)

4. When you are ready to bake the soufflé, preheat the oven to 375° F.

5. Beat the egg whites with a pinch of salt until firm but not stiff. Gently fold the whites into the corn mixture. Butter a 13 x 9-inch baking dish and pour in the soufflé mixture. Sprinkle the remaining grated cheese over the top.

6. Bake until the top is lightly browned and the soufflé is puffed, 20 to 25 minutes.

Serves 6

Gratin of Zucchini and Tomatoes

I like the color, the taste, and the texture of this dish. Zucchini, onions, tomatoes, and both Gruyère and Parmesan cheeses blend beautifully when baked together in this gratin. The recipe can be halved to serve four, or doubled or tripled to serve a larger number with no problems.

2½ pounds (5 to 6 medium) zucchini, ends trimmed
¼ cup olive oil
1½ cups chopped onions
1 large clove garlic, finely chopped
3 medium-size tomatoes, firm but ripe
Salt and freshly ground pepper to taste
1½ cups grated Gruyère cheese
½ cup dry bread crumbs
½ cup grated imported Parmesan cheese
2 tablespoons unsalted butter

GREAT ACCOMPANIMENTS

I like to serve this gratin with the Szechuan-Peppered Chicken Breasts, Grilled Salmon Steaks Wrapped in Peppered Bacon, or broiled or grilled lamb chops or steaks.

1. Cut the zucchini into slices ⅛ inch thick. Drop them into 4 quarts of boiling salted water, and cook until softened, 2 to 3 minutes. Remove with a slotted spoon, drain on paper towels, and set aside.

2. Heat the olive oil in a heavy skillet over medium-high heat, and add the onions and garlic. Cook, stirring constantly, about 3 minutes. Remove with a slotted spoon, drain on paper towels, and set aside.

3. Core the tomatoes and cut them into slices ¼ inch thick.

4. Butter a medium-size ovenproof dish. Place one third of the zucchini in the dish, and sprinkle with salt and pepper. Spread one third of the onion mixture on top, then place one third of the sliced tomatoes on top of the onions. Sprinkle with one third of the Gruyère. Continue in the same manner, making two more layers. Combine the bread crumbs and Parmesan cheese, and sprinkle on top. Dot with the butter. (The dish can be prepared several hours ahead. Cover with plastic wrap and refrigerate.)

5. When you are ready to bake the gratin, preheat the oven to 350° F.

6. Bake until the gratin is heated all the way through and the cheese has melted on top, 20 to 30 minutes.

Serves 8

Baked Zucchini with Chèvre and Onions

This is an interesting and delicious way to prepare zucchini— layered with onions and covered with a flavorful cheese sauce. The gratin tastes particularly good with lamb and grilled chicken dishes.

2 pounds (about 5 medium) zucchini
1 large onion
3 tablespoons unsalted butter
Salt and freshly ground pepper to taste
8 ounces chèvre, at room temperature
½ cup heavy or whipping cream, plus more if needed
¼ cup grated imported Parmesan cheese
¼ cup dry bread crumbs

1. Cut the zucchini on the diagonal into ¼-inch-thick slices. Halve the onion lengthwise, and cut it into ¼-inch-thick slices.

2. Cook the zucchini in lightly salted boiling water to cover until just tender, 2 minutes. Drain well and pat dry.

GREAT ACCOMPANIMENTS

I often serve this gratin with the Marinated Racks of Lamb with Tomato-Mustard Sauce, the Lime-Marinated Lamb Chops with Tomato Chutney, the Grilled Salmon Steaks Wrapped in Peppered Bacon, and grilled chicken or steaks.

3. Melt the butter in a medium-size heavy skillet over medium heat. When it is hot, add the onion slices. Sauté, stirring, until they are softened and translucent, 3 to 4 minutes. Remove from the heat.

4. Butter a 13 x 9-inch baking dish. Arrange one third of the zucchini in a layer in the dish. Salt and pepper the zucchini well. Then spread half of the cooked onions over the zucchini. Make another layer of zucchini and onions, seasoning the zucchini with salt and pepper. Finally make a third layer of zucchini, and salt and pepper this layer.

5. Break the chèvre into small pieces and put them in the top of a small double boiler. Add the cream and place over simmering water. Cook, stirring, until the mixture is smooth and thick, 3 to 4 minutes. If the mixture seems too thick to pour easily, add 2 to 4 tablespoons additional cream to thin the sauce. Then pour the cheese mixture over the zucchini and onions in the baking dish. Combine the Parmesan and the bread crumbs, and sprinkle them over the gratin. (The dish can be prepared several hours in advance; cover and refrigerate. Bring it to room temperature before baking.)

6. When you are ready to bake the gratin, preheat the oven to 350° F.

7. Bake until the gratin is hot and the top is golden, 35 to 40 minutes.

Serves 8

VEGETABLES A TO Z

Asparagus with Chive Butter

In the spring, when tender fresh bunches of asparagus appear in our markets, I especially enjoy cooking them this way. A simple and quickly made dish, this is a good accompaniment to broiled lamb chops, roast chicken, or sautéed veal scallops.

GREAT ACCOMPANIMENTS

These asparagus would be a good accompaniment to the Marinated Racks of Lamb with Tomato-Mustard Sauce or the Roast Lamb with a Pepper Coating.

8 tablespoons (1 stick) unsalted butter
2 tablespoons finely chopped shallots
1 teaspoon grated lemon zest
1 tablespoon fresh lemon juice
½ teaspoon salt
2 tablespoons chopped fresh chives
2 teaspoons chopped fresh mint leaves
2½ pounds medium fresh asparagus
Salt and freshly ground pepper to taste
3 thin slices lemon, for garnish

1. Prepare the Chive Butter: Melt 1 tablespoon of the butter in a medium-size heavy saucepan over medium heat. Add the shallots and sauté, stirring, until they are transparent and softened, 2 to 3 minutes. Add the remaining butter and continue stirring until it has melted. Remove from the heat and stir in the lemon zest, lemon juice, and salt. (The butter can be made several hours ahead to this point and kept uncovered at room temperature.) When you are ready to serve, reheat the butter if necessary, and stir in the chives and mint.

2. To prepare the asparagus, cut or break off and discard the tough, woody ends of the stalks. Then, using a vegetable peeler, trim the skin from each stalk starting just below the tip.

3. In a large, deep saucepan or skillet, bring enough water to cover the asparagus to a boil. Lightly salt the water, and add the asparagus. Cook at a simmer until just tender, 3 to 5 minutes. Remove the asparagus and drain well.

4. Transfer the asparagus to a shallow serving bowl and toss with the hot Chive Butter. Taste, and add salt and pepper as desired. Serve the asparagus garnished with lemon slices.

Serves 8

A COOK'S REFLECTIONS

Mint. Mint is one of those herbs that even untalented gardeners like me can grow with great success. It begins to appear in early spring and lasts well into early fall. Mint is so hardy that it will take over a garden plot if not trimmed back regularly.

There are two varieties of mint used in cooking—bright green, peppery, dark-stemmed peppermint and paler green, fragrant spearmint. Either works well, but my favorite is the peppermint.

GREAT ACCOMPANIMENTS

I like to serve Bourbon Carrots with pork dishes, especially Sautéed Filet of Pork Waldo, Pork Chops Baked with Chestnuts and Mushrooms, and Roast Loin of Pork Braised in Cider. I often include these carrots at Thanksgiving dinner, too, along with the Roast Turkey with Cornbread-Apricot Stuffing.

Bourbon Carrots

I have been making Bourbon Carrots ever since I first started cooking, more than twenty years ago. My aunt, a talented southern cook, sent me the recipe when I was first married. It was an easy and fast dish to prepare—perfect for a beginning cook. Through all these years, I have never grown tired of carrots prepared this way and continue to include this special dish in many of my menus.

1½ pounds carrots, peeled
1 tablespoon granulated sugar
3½ tablespoons unsalted butter
½ teaspoon salt, plus more if needed
Freshly ground pepper to taste
2 tablespoons dark brown sugar
2 tablespoons bourbon
1½ tablespoons chopped fresh parsley, for garnish

1. Cut the carrots on the diagonal into ¼-inch-thick slices.

2. In a heavy saucepan, combine the carrots, granulated sugar, 1½ tablespoons of the butter, and ½ teaspoon salt. Add 1½ cups water and bring to a boil. Reduce the heat to a simmer, and cover. Cook until the carrots are tender when pierced with a knife, 10 to 15 minutes. Drain the carrots, taste, and add more salt if needed. Add the pepper.

3. Melt the remaining 2 tablespoons butter with the brown sugar in a heavy skillet over medium-high heat. When the sugar has dissolved, add the carrots, and sauté until they are well coated and heated through. Add the bourbon, and cook 2 to 3 minutes. (Carrots may be cooked several hours before serving time and kept covered at room temperature. Carefully reheat over medium heat.)

4. Garnish with the parsley, and serve.

Serves 6

AT THE MARKET

Most cooks agree that the fresher the corn the better the taste. So if you can, buy just-picked corn from a roadside stand or directly from a farmer and bring it home to cook right away; it will be in its prime. Once corn is picked, the sugar starts to turn to starch, and the corn loses some of its sweetness and tenderness.

AS A VARIATION

Leftover Parmesan-Garlic Butter can be used in several ways. It's delicious tossed with boiled new potatoes or spread on slices of French bread and baked until hot in a 350° F oven, 10 to 12 minutes.

Corn on the Cob with Parmesan-Garlic Butter

In the summer, when sweet fresh corn proliferates, this is how I love to serve it. The delicious Parmesan-Garlic Butter can be made well in advance, so all that needs to be done before serving is to boil the ears of corn.

8 tablespoons (1 stick) unsalted butter, at room temperature
¼ cup grated imported Parmesan cheese
3 tablespoons finely chopped fresh parsley
¼ teaspoon salt
1 teaspoon very finely chopped garlic
8 to 10 ears fresh sweet corn

1. Combine all the ingredients except the corn in a medium-size mixing bowl, and stir well with a wooden spoon. Mold the butter mixture in a small ramekin or crock, and smooth the top with a knife or spatula. Score the top of the butter with a knife to make a grid pattern. Cover with plastic wrap and refrigerate. (The butter can be made 1 to 2 days in advance and kept covered in the refrigerator.)

2. Let the butter sit at room temperature to soften slightly before using, 30 minutes or longer.

3. Bring water to a boil in a large stockpot or deep-sided pan. Shuck the corn while waiting for the water to boil, then drop in the ears and cook until tender when pierced with a knife, 4 to 10 minutes, depending on the freshness of the corn. Fresh corn will cook more quickly. When ready, drain well in a colander.

4. Serve the butter with the corn. Rub each ear generously with the butter.

Serves 4 or 5

Monterey Jack Corn Cakes

My teenage son, Michael, is predictable when it comes to eating habits. He has a hearty appetite for such fare as pizza, hamburgers, French fries, and ice cream, but is often reluctant to try new dishes. But once he tasted these fried corn cakes, he quickly acknowledged that he was crazy about them. In fact, his enthusiasm was so great he even asked if I would show him how to make them! The cakes, prepared from a simple batter, are fried until golden and served garnished with chives. Michael and I always cook them together now.

1 cup all-purpose flour
1 teaspoon baking powder
1 teaspoon salt
⅔ cup milk
1 large egg
1 tablespoon vegetable oil
1 cup (3 ears) fresh corn kernels
½ cup grated Monterey Jack cheese
⅓ cup minced shallots
2 tablespoons minced fresh parsley
2 to 3 dashes of hot pepper sauce
Generous pinch of cayenne pepper
Freshly ground black pepper to taste
4 slices bacon
Chopped fresh chives, for garnish

1. Sift the flour, baking powder, and salt into a large bowl. Whisk the milk, egg, and oil together in another bowl. Make a well in the dry ingredients, and add the liquid ingredients. Combine with a whisk or fork just until a batter forms. Stir in the corn, cheese, shallots, parsley, hot pepper sauce, cayenne pepper, and black pepper. Let the batter stand 30 minutes.

2. Meanwhile, fry the bacon in a heavy skillet over medium heat until crisp. Transfer the bacon to drain on paper towels, reserving the fat in the skillet. Allow the bacon to cool, then chop it finely. Stir the chopped bacon into the batter.

3. Pour off and reserve all but a thin coating of fat from the skillet. Heat the skillet over medium-high heat. Add the batter by heaping tablespoons in batches (do not crowd). Flatten each cake slightly

GREAT ACCOMPANIMENTS

These corn cakes are a wonderful complement to Grilled Lemon Chicken with Chile Hollandaise or Grilled Sirloin Steaks with Banana Chile Pepper Butter.

with the back of a spoon. Cook the corn cakes until golden brown and cooked through, about 2 minutes per side. Add more bacon fat as necessary. Place each batch of cooked corn cakes on a platter, cover loosely with foil, and keep warm in a 250° F oven until all the corn cakes are finished. To serve, sprinkle with the chives.

Serves 6

Sesame Green Beans

Nothing could be simpler or easier to prepare than this vegetable dish—green beans sautéed with minced garlic in aromatic sesame oil, tossed with toasted sesame seeds and seasoned with lemon juice. They make an excellent accompaniment to grilled entrées.

2 tablespoons salt
2½ pounds fresh green beans, ends trimmed
4 to 6 tablespoons Oriental sesame oil
5 teaspoons finely chopped garlic
2½ tablespoons fresh lemon juice
Salt and freshly ground pepper to taste
¼ cup toasted sesame seeds (see Index)

1. Bring 5 quarts of water to a boil and add the salt. Add the beans and cook, uncovered, until they are tender, 8 to 10 minutes. The time will vary slightly, depending on the size and texture of the beans; taste a bean to check for doneness. Drain the beans in a colander and rinse them under cold running water. Pat dry. (Beans may be prepared several hours in advance to this point. Wrap them in a kitchen towel and then plastic wrap and refrigerate.)

2. Heat 4 tablespoons of the sesame oil in an 11- to 12-inch skillet over medium-high heat. When the oil is hot, add the garlic and cook, tossing, about 30 seconds. (If the oil is too hot and the garlic starts to brown, remove the pan from the heat for a minute or more.) Add the beans, a large handful at a time, to the skillet. Toss and stir constantly until all beans have been added and are hot and coated lightly with sesame oil, 3 to 4 minutes. Pour in additional sesame oil if needed. Pour the lemon juice over the beans, and stir well. Taste the beans, and season generously with salt and pepper. Sprinkle the sesame seeds over the beans and toss well. Serve hot.

Serves 6

GREAT ACCOMPANIMENTS

Sesame Green Beans are a flavorful vegetable to serve with Creole Barbecued Shrimp or Grilled Sirloin Steaks with Banana Chile Pepper Butter.

AT THE MARKET
When Vidalia onions are not in
season, other sweet white onions
can be used. Cook them the same
way as the Vidalias.

Vidalia Onions Stuffed with Pecans and Gruyère

Every year, during the brief period from late May through June, Vidalia onions appear on the shelves in our grocery stores in Columbus. I eagerly await the arrival of these sweet white onions, and the minute I see them I buy a 10-pound bag. Knowing of my enthusiasm for this ingredient, one of my students brought me a list of recipes published by the First National Bank and Trust Company in Vidalia, Georgia. This is my variation of a recipe I found in that pamphlet.

*6 large Vidalia onions, 2½ to 3 inches in diameter (about 8
      ounces each)*
7 tablespoons unsalted butter
⅓ cup chopped shallots
1 teaspoon finely minced garlic
¾ cup toasted and finely chopped pecan halves (see Index)
1½ cups fresh bread crumbs
1½ cups grated Gruyère cheese
Salt and freshly ground pepper to taste
¾ teaspoon dried rosemary, crushed well
*½ cup homemade chicken stock (see Index) or good-quality
      canned broth*
½ cup dry white wine
4 tablespoons (½ stick) unsalted butter, melted

1. Prepare each onion by cutting off the ends. Then peel off the skin and the filmy membrane layer underneath. Cook the onions in boiling water to cover just until softened, 10 minutes. Remove and drain. With a sharp paring knife, cut out a cone-shaped core from the top of each onion. Then, using a grapefruit knife or a pointed teaspoon, scoop out the inside of each onion so that you have an onion shell with bottom and sides about ¼ to ⅓ inch thick.

2. Melt the 7 tablespoons butter in a large heavy skillet over medium heat. Add the chopped shallots and sauté, stirring, 2 to 3 minutes. Add the garlic and pecans and stir 2 minutes more. Toss in the bread crumbs and cheese, and stir until the cheese has almost melted, about 2 more minutes. Remove the mixture from the heat, and add salt, pepper, and the crushed rosemary. Stir to mix. Fill each

GREAT ACCOMPANIMENTS

My favorite entrée to serve with these stuffed onions is good grilled beef steaks rubbed generously with coarsely ground black pepper.

onion with stuffing, mounding the stuffing only slightly on top of the onions. (Onions may be prepared several hours in advance to this point. Cover loosely with plastic wrap and refrigerate.)

3. When you are ready to bake the onions, preheat the oven to 350° F.

4. Combine the chicken stock and the wine. Place the onions in a single layer in a medium-size baking pan. Brush the sides and tops of the onions generously with the melted butter. Bake the onions, uncovered, 1 to 1¼ hours, basting every 15 minutes with ¼ cup of the stock/wine mixture. The onions are done when they can be pierced with a sharp knife and are tender but still hold their shape.

Serves 6

AT THE MARKET

If fresh peas are unavailable, two 10-ounce packages of frozen peas can be substituted. Thaw, then cook them with the scallions in the stock for approximately 3 minutes. Continue with the recipe.

Peas with Rosemary and Pine Nuts

I developed this dish as part of a spring brunch menu one year, but I have used it as a vegetable accompaniment at dinner parties as well. A tempting combination of fresh peas tossed with sautéed pine nuts and a hint of rosemary, this makes a colorful garnish to veal, lamb, or chicken.

2 scallions (green onions)
½ cup homemade chicken stock (see Index) or good-quality canned broth
½ teaspoon sugar
3½ cups shelled green peas (about 3 pounds in the shell)
3 tablespoons unsalted butter
¾ cup pine nuts
1 tablespoon chopped fresh rosemary leaves, or 1 teaspoon coarsely crushed dried
Salt and freshly ground pepper to taste
6 large Boston lettuce leaves, rinsed and dried

1. Trim the scallions, leaving 2 inches of green stem. Cut them into ½-inch pieces.

2. Place the chicken stock in a medium-size heavy saucepan over medium heat. Add the sugar and the scallions, and bring the stock to

GREAT ACCOMPANIMENTS

These peas are a good vegetable to serve with Roast Stuffed Veal with Red Wine and Shallot Butter, Grilled Trout with Minted Hollandaise, or simple broiled lamb chops or roast chicken.

AT THE MARKET

For the best flavor, choose turnips that are no larger than tennis balls. They should be firm, with smooth skin (some are white, some have purple shadings) and no blemishes.

a simmer. Add the peas, and cook until just tender, 5 to 8 minutes. Drain. (The pea mixture may be prepared ahead. Cool by spreading the drained vegetables on a clean kitchen towel. When completely cool, store them covered, in the refrigerator.)

3. When you are ready to serve the peas, melt the butter in a large heavy skillet over medium heat. When it is hot, add the pine nuts and cook, stirring constantly, until golden, 2 to 3 minutes. Stir in the rosemary and cook 1 minute more. Add the peas and cook, stirring, until hot, only 2 to 3 minutes. Season to taste with salt and pepper. Arrange a serving of peas on each lettuce leaf.

Serves 6

Turnips Stuffed with Fresh Peas

Turnips are one of those neglected vegetables that people pass over at the grocery, mainly, I think, for lack of information or inspiration as to what to do with them. This is a very interesting and elegant way to prepare this flavorful root vegetable: Cooked turnips are hollowed out and filled with peas and diced turnips, bound in a creamy cheese sauce, and then baked.

6 turnips, 2½ to 3½ inches in diameter, as equal in size as
*   possible*
1 cup cooked peas (fresh or frozen)
4 tablespoons (½ stick) unsalted butter
2 tablespoons all-purpose flour
1½ cups half-and-half
Salt and freshly ground pepper to taste
Freshly grated nutmeg to taste
½ cup grated Gruyère cheese
2 tablespoons dry bread crumbs

1. Preheat the oven to 350° F.

2. Peel the turnips and cook them in boiling salted water to cover until tender when pierced with a knife, 20 to 25 minutes.

3. Drain the turnips, and cut a ½-inch slice off the top of each one. If necessary, cut a small slice off the bottom of each turnip so it will stand easily. Set the slices aside. Scoop out the inside of each turnip, leaving a shell about ½ inch thick. Reserve the portion removed.

GREAT ACCOMPANIMENTS

I like to serve these stuffed turnips as a garnish around roast chicken, duck, or turkey.

4. Dice the reserved turnip slices and the scooped-out flesh, and combine with the cooked peas. Set aside.

5. Prepare the sauce: Melt 2 tablespoons of the butter in a medium-size saucepan over medium heat. Add the flour and cook, stirring constantly, 2 minutes. Add the half-and-half and cook, stirring, until the sauce thickens, 3 to 4 minutes. Add salt and pepper to taste and a grating of fresh nutmeg. Stir in the cheese, and remove the sauce from the heat.

6. Combine two thirds of the sauce with the peas and diced turnips. Stuff the hollowed-out turnips with this mixture, mounding it slightly. Place the turnips in a buttered ovenproof baking dish.

7. Nap the turnips with the remaining sauce. Sprinkle the bread crumbs on top, and dot with the remaining 2 tablespoons butter. (The vegetables may be prepared 5 to 6 hours in advance to this point; keep covered and refrigerated. Bring them to room temperature before baking.)

8. Bake the turnips until bubbling and lightly browned, 10 to 20 minutes.

Serves 6

Zucchini Anna

A creative cook will always find new ways with old themes. That certainly is what I had in mind when I made Zucchini Anna instead of the well-known Potatoes Anna. It took many attempts before the recipe worked, but the results are unusual and truly delicious.

*4 small (1½ to 2 pounds) zucchini, each 5 to 6 inches long and
      1½ inches in diameter*
2 tablespoons unsalted butter
1½ cups paper-thin onion slices
3 large eggs
1 cup heavy or whipping cream
1 teaspoon salt
⅛ teaspoon freshly grated nutmeg
Pinch of cayenne pepper
2 cups grated Gruyère cheese
Salt and freshly ground black pepper to taste

GREAT ACCOMPANIMENTS

I like to serve Zucchini Anna with the Stuffed Roast Filet of Beef Stuffed or with roast chicken.

1. Preheat the oven to 350° F.

2. Butter a 9-inch round baking dish or cake pan generously, and line the bottom with a circle of waxed paper. Butter the paper.

3. Trim the ends off each zucchini and cut them into ⅛-inch-thick rounds. (If you want to use a food processor, use the 3 mm slicing disk.) Set aside.

4. Melt the butter in a medium-size heavy skillet over medium heat. When it is hot, add the onions and sauté until softened, 2 to 3 minutes. Remove, and drain on paper towels.

5. In a medium-size bowl, combine the eggs, cream, salt, nutmeg, cayenne pepper, and all but ⅓ cup of the Gruyère cheese. Whisk until all ingredients are well blended. Set aside.

6. To assemble, arrange one third of the zucchini slices in the prepared pan in an overlapping circular pattern. Spread them with one half of the sautéed onions. Salt and pepper lightly. Pour one third of the cream mixture over this layer. Arrange another third of the zucchini slices over this and top with the remaining onions. Salt and pepper lightly. Pour another third of the cream mixture over this. Arrange a final layer of zucchini slices, and salt and pepper lightly. Pour the remaining third of the cream mixture over this layer.

7. Bake the zucchini until the mixture is completely set, 45 to 50 minutes. (Check it after 30 minutes. Sometimes the dish will cook more quickly; it depends on the water content of the zucchini.) Remove the pan from the oven and allow it to cool for 5 to 10 minutes.

8. Preheat the broiler.

9. Carefully invert the pan onto a round ovenproof platter. Remove the pan and the circle of waxed paper, and sprinkle the reserved ⅓ cup cheese over the top of the unmolded zucchini. If any liquid collects in the serving dish, blot it up with paper towels.

10. Carefully place the unmolded Zucchini Anna under the broiler, 4 to 5 inches from the heat, and broil until the cheese has melted and browned lightly. Remove, and serve by cutting into wedges.

Serves 8

POTATOES

AT THE MARKET

If you are buying potatoes with a certain recipe in mind, it is important to know whether to pick up ones that have a mealy texture or ones that are waxy. Mealy varieties, such as flat, elongated baking potatoes, are good not only for baking but also for dishes calling for mashed or fried potatoes. Waxy varieties, such as new potatoes, hold their shape when cooked and are excellent in boiled dishes or sliced in salads.

GREAT ACCOMPANIMENTS

I have served this potato dish with the Roast Filet of Beef with Sweet Red Pepper and Zucchini Relish, with Lamb Chops with Spinach and Chèvre, and with Roast Lamb with a Pepper Coating. For a very easy menu, I sometimes grill Italian sausages or bratwurst to offer with this potato gratin.

AS A VARIATION

For an entirely different taste, replace the sage with dried tarragon. Prepared this way, the potatoes make a good accompaniment for roast chicken or baked salmon.

Potatoes Baked with Cream, Wine, and Sage

This is the type of dish I like to serve on cold, wintry Ohio nights. It is a rustic gratin composed of layers of sliced potatoes topped with sage and Gruyère cheese and baked in a mixture of white wine and cream. The finished dish has a rich golden crust.

3 pounds baking potatoes
Salt and freshly ground pepper to taste
2 to 2½ teaspoons crumbled dried sage
1½ cups (about 6 ounces) grated Gruyère cheese
1 cup heavy or whipping cream
1 cup dry white wine

1. Preheat the oven to 400° F.

2. Butter a 14 x 9-inch oval ovenproof gratin dish or a baking dish of similar size.

3. Peel the potatoes and cut them into ¼-inch-thick slices. Arrange one third of the potatoes in overlapping slices in the dish. Generously salt and pepper the potatoes, and sprinkle them with one third of the dried sage and one third of the cheese. Continue in this manner, making two more layers of potatoes, seasonings, and cheese.

4. Combine the cream and wine in a bowl and whisk together. Pour this over the layered potatoes. Bake the gratin until the potatoes are tender when pierced with a knife and the top is golden and crusty, 45 to 50 minutes.

Serves 6

Garlic and Butter–Roasted Potatoes

What I like best about this flavorful dish is that it is made with only three simple ingredients—potatoes, butter, and garlic—all of which I almost always have on hand in my kitchen. Uncomplicated to prepare, the potatoes are sliced and then tossed with slivers of garlic in melted butter and finally baked in the oven until golden.

2 pounds small baking potatoes
4 very large cloves garlic
8 tablespoons (1 stick) unsalted butter
Salt and freshly ground pepper to taste

1. Preheat the oven to 375° F.

2. Peel the potatoes and cut them into ¼-inch-thick slices. Pat the slices dry with a clean kitchen towel.

3. Slice the garlic cloves lengthwise into very thin slivers.

4. Melt the butter in a large heavy ovenproof skillet over high heat, but do not let it brown. Add the potato slices, toss until well coated with butter, and cook 4 to 5 minutes. Add the garlic slivers, toss again, and cook, stirring, 2 to 3 minutes more. Salt and pepper the potatoes generously.

5. Place the skillet on the center shelf of the oven and bake until golden and tender when pierced with a knife, 35 to 45 minutes or longer. Stir the potatoes several times while they are baking, so they brown well on all sides.

Serves 6

Oven-Fried Parmesan Potatoes

"Good" and "easy" are the words my students use to describe these potatoes. They are prepared simply by tossing potato wedges in melted butter, sprinkling them generously with very finely grated (powdery) Parmesan cheese and black pepper, and then baking them quickly until they are crisp and golden.

GREAT ACCOMPANIMENTS

Breasts of Chicken Stuffed with Spinach and Fresh Ginger, Grilled Flank Steak with Shiitake Mushrooms, and the Mustard-Glazed Cornish Hens are all good entrées to serve with these potatoes.

6 large baking potatoes (about 2½ pounds total)
8 tablespoons (1 stick) unsalted butter
Salt to taste
1 cup very finely grated imported Parmesan cheese
1 teaspoon coarsely ground pepper

1. Preheat the oven to 400° F.

2. Peel the potatoes and cut them lengthwise into ½-inch-wide wedges.

3. Melt the butter in a heavy ovenproof skillet, preferably cast iron, and add the potatoes and toss until they are coated with butter. Salt the potatoes generously.

4. Place the skillet on the center shelf of the oven and bake, stirring several times, 20 minutes.

5. Remove the skillet from the oven, but leave the oven on. Mix the Parmesan cheese and the black pepper together in a mixing bowl. Sprinkle the cheese mixture over the potatoes and toss well. Return the skillet to the oven and bake until the potatoes are crisp and golden, 15 to 20 minutes. Watch the potatoes carefully during the second baking to make certain they do not burn.

Serves 6

Baked New Potatoes with Lemon-Thyme Butter

Lemon and thyme are wonderfully paired seasonings for this dish. The small red-skinned potatoes absorb these flavors while baking to a light golden brown.

3 pounds small red-skinned new potatoes, about 2 inches in diameter, scrubbed but not peeled
Salt and freshly ground pepper to taste
¾ cup (1½ sticks) unsalted butter
½ cup plus 1 tablespoon fresh lemon juice
1½ teaspoons grated lemon zest
1½ teaspoons crushed dried thyme

1. Preheat the oven to 375° F.

GREAT ACCOMPANIMENTS

These potatoes are good to serve with the Chicken Breasts Stuffed with Prosciutto and Mozzarella, Sautéed Filet of Pork Waldo, or Grilled Salmon Steaks Wrapped in Peppered Bacon.

2. Quarter the potatoes and arrange them in a baking dish large enough to hold them in a single layer. Salt and pepper the potatoes generously.

3. Combine the butter, lemon juice, and lemon zest in a saucepan, and heat until the butter has melted. Pour the butter mixture over the potatoes. Sprinkle the thyme over the potatoes.

4. Place the dish in the oven and bake until the potatoes are tender and lightly browned, 30 to 45 minutes. Remove from the oven and serve.

Serves 6

Potato, Bleu Cheese, and Chive Tart

A beautiful and unusual potato preparation, this tart was created by my friend Jim Budros, a talented cook.

Special equipment: 9-inch tart pan with removable bottom

Pastry Crust

1½ cups all-purpose flour
¼ teaspoon salt
8 tablespoons (1 stick) unsalted butter, chilled and cut into small
*   pieces*
3 to 4 tablespoons ice water

Filling

3 medium baking potatoes (about 1¼ pounds)
1 cup heavy or whipping cream
1 large whole egg
2 large egg yolks
2 ounces best-quality bleu cheese, crumbled
4 tablespoons chopped fresh chives
1 teaspoon Dijon mustard

1. To prepare the pastry by hand, combine the flour and salt in a bowl. Cut in the butter, using a pastry blender or two knives, until the mixture resembles oatmeal flakes. Gradually add the water, mixing just until the dough holds together. Transfer the dough to a

AS A VARIATION

If fresh chives are not available, you can use parsley or finely chopped green scallion stems.

GREAT ACCOMPANIMENTS

I have served this tart as a first course and as a main course. When it is used as an entrée, I offer a seasonal green salad tossed in vinaigrette as a side dish and a bowl of strawberries and the Amaretto Brownies for dessert. Using it as an accompaniment, I like to serve the tart with roast beef or grilled steaks.

lightly floured surface. Using the heel of your hand, smear the dough, ¼ cup at a time, into a 6-inch-long strip. Gather the dough together and repeat two more times. Gather the dough into a ball; flatten it to form a disk. Wrap with plastic wrap and refrigerate at least 1 hour or overnight.

The pastry dough can also be made in a food processor: Place the dry ingredients in the processor bowl, and add the butter. Process until the mixture resembles oatmeal flakes. With machine still running, add the water through the feed tube until a ball of dough forms. Wrap the dough and refrigerate as in the hand method.

The dough can be made 1 day in advance, or it can be frozen.

2. Preheat the oven to 400° F.

3. Roll the dough out on a lightly floured surface to form a round ⅛ inch thick. Transfer it to a 9-inch tart pan. Trim, and crimp the edges. Line the crust with parchment or foil, and fill it with pie weights or dried beans. Bake until the crust is set, about 10 minutes. Remove the paper and weights, and continue baking until the crust is brown, about 5 minutes. Remove the tart shell from the oven. (The tart shell can be prepared several hours in advance. Cover loosely and let sit at room temperature.)

4. Preheat the oven to 375° F.

5. To prepare the filling, bring 3 quarts lightly salted water to a boil. Peel the potatoes and cut them into ¼-inch-thick rounds. Boil until just tender, not mushy, about 6 minutes. Remove, drain, and pat dry.

6. In a small heavy saucepan, combine the cream, egg, egg yolks, and bleu cheese. Stir well with a whisk. Place the saucepan over medium heat, and, whisking constantly, cook until the cheese has melted and the mixture is smooth, 4 minutes or longer. Remove from the heat, and stir in 3 tablespoons of the chives.

7. To assemble, brush the bottom of the tart shell with the Dijon mustard. Arrange the cooked potato slices in the tart shell in neat overlapping circular patterns. Pour the cream mixture over the potatoes.

8. Bake the tart until the custard is set in the center and the top is lightly browned, 25 to 30 minutes. Sprinkle with the remaining 1 tablespoon chopped chives. Serve hot.

Serves 8

AT THE MARKET

Botanically, sweet potatoes and yams are completely different. However, according to many knowledgeable sources, true yams are not grown in the United States. What are labeled ''yams'' in our markets are in fact a variety of sweet potato. The type of sweet potato that has a copper-colored skin, deep orange flesh, and is moist and sweet is the variety sold as ''yams.'' The other type, which has tan skin and pale yellow, almost golden flesh, and is drier than the first variety, is sold as ''sweet potatoes.'' Either one works well in this dish. The bright orange ''yams'' will produce a dish with a more vibrant color, a slightly sweet taste, and a moister texture. However, both varieties will produce a splendid soufflé.

Brandied Sweet Potato Soufflé

When I was first married I received several cookbooks as wedding gifts, and I eagerly read each with the enthusiasm of a young bride. One book, *The Times Picayune Creole Cookbook,* was of special interest to me since I had attended college in New Orleans. Written for cooks more advanced than I, however, the directions were terse and assumed that the reader was well versed in culinary techniques. Over the years, my book took on the appearance of a textbook, with marginal notes and comments covering the pages as I made my own interpretations of the recipes. This delicious sweet potato soufflé is my variation on a recipe from that special cookery book.

3 pounds sweet potatoes
1 cup firmly packed brown sugar
8 tablespoons (1 stick) unsalted butter, at room temperature
1 package (8 ounces) cream cheese, at room temperature
6 large eggs, separated
¼ teaspoon freshly grated nutmeg
¼ teaspoon ground allspice
¼ teaspoon ground cinnamon
1 cup heavy or whipping cream
¼ cup brandy
Salt to taste
Confectioners' sugar, for garnish

1. Preheat the oven to 375° F.

2. Scrub the sweet potatoes and bake in the oven until tender when pierced with a knife, about 1 hour (or you may boil the potatoes until tender). Cool, peel, and purée the potatoes in a food processor or food mill.

3. Transfer the puréed potatoes to a mixing bowl, and add the brown sugar, butter, cream cheese, egg yolks, spices, cream, and brandy. Mix well. Taste, and add salt as desired. (The soufflé base can be made several hours in advance; keep covered and refrigerated. Bring it to room temperature before baking.)

4. When you are ready to bake the soufflé, preheat the oven to 375° F.

5. Beat the egg whites until stiff, and fold them into the potato mixture.

GREAT ACCOMPANIMENTS

My favorite time of the year to serve this soufflé is at Thanksgiving. I always offer it along with the Roast Turkey with Cornbread-Apricot Dressing.

6. Pour the mixture into a buttered 13 x 9-inch baking pan or an oval gratin dish of similar size. Bake until hot and slightly puffed, 35 to 40 minutes. Remove from the oven and let cool 5 minutes. Sprinkle with confectioners' sugar. (You do not need to serve this soufflé immediately, as you would a regular soufflé. The egg whites make it light and airy and give it the texture of a soufflé, but do not cause it to rise above the rim of the baking dish.)

Serves 8 to 10

French-Fried Sweet Potatoes

I first tasted these crisp fried morsels at Rigsby's Restaurant in Columbus, Ohio. Chef Kent Rigsby, one of the most imaginative cooks I know, used them as a garnish for grilled sirloin steak topped with Banana Chile Pepper Butter. These sweet potatoes are simple to prepare and should be served immediately, while they are still piping hot, for the best flavor!

2 pounds sweet potatoes (5 medium)
Vegetable oil
Salt to taste

1. Peel the potatoes and cut them lengthwise into ¼-inch-thick slices; cut the slices into strips ½ inch wide.

2. Using a large heavy skillet, add enough oil to come ½ inch up the sides of pan. Place the skillet over medium-high heat, and when the oil is quite hot (375° F on a thermometer), add enough potatoes to fit comfortably in one layer. Sauté until crisp and golden, turning and tossing, about 5 minutes. Drain the potatoes on paper towels, and keep them warm by covering them loosely with aluminum foil or putting them on a baking sheet in a 250° F oven. Continue until all the potatoes have been fried. Salt the potatoes, and serve.

Serves 6

AT THE MARKET

Make certain you use sweet potatoes, not yams, in this recipe (see At the Market, facing page.)

GRAINS & STUFFINGS

My mother loved rice, and when I was growing up, she would serve it at least twice a week at the family table. Her enthusiasm for this grain must have rubbed off, for I love rice too and am constantly thinking of new ways to cook and serve it. I have learned that the plain white boiled rice of my childhood was only one of many options. I like making dishes with wild rice, brown rice, and other similar grains, such as barley, and have included some of these specialties in this chapter.

Stuffings (or dressings) were another favorite food of my youth. Each of the choices here is baked separately rather than inside the fowl or meat. Prepared this way, they are easier to serve and make attractive side dishes.

RICE & BARLEY DISHES

Wild Rice and Pine Nut Pilaf

This wild rice pilaf is a dish I prepared as part of a menu for the governor of Ohio, Richard Celeste, and his wife, Dagmar. With it, I served baked filet of salmon. The dish can be doubled or tripled easily and holds well after cooking.

1 cup raw wild rice
8 tablespoons (1 stick) unsalted butter
¼ cup finely minced carrots
¼ cup finely minced shallots
1 cup raw long-grain white rice
2½ cups homemade chicken stock (see Index) or good-quality
*   canned broth*
1 bay leaf, broken in half
½ teaspoon dried thyme
½ teaspoon salt, plus more if needed
Freshly ground pepper to taste
1 cup toasted pine nuts (see Index)

1. Cook the wild rice in boiling water to cover for 8 to 10 minutes, and drain well.

2. Melt the butter in a large heavy casserole over medium heat. Add the carrots and shallots and sauté, stirring constantly, 4 to 5 minutes. Add the wild rice and the white rice, and stir until the grains are coated with butter. (The dish can be prepared several hours ahead to this point. Cover and keep in the refrigerator.)

3. When you are ready to bake the pilaf, preheat the oven to 350° F.

4. Add the stock, bay leaf, thyme, ½ teaspoon salt, and a few grindings of pepper to the casserole. Bring the mixture to a simmer on top of the stove, then cover it tightly and transfer it to the oven.

5. Bake the pilaf until all liquid has been absorbed and the rice is tender, 35 to 40 minutes. Check for seasoning and add more salt and pepper if needed. Stir in the pine nuts, and serve.

Serves 6

A COOK'S REFLECTIONS

The word "pilaf," or "pilau" or "pilaw," indicates a method for preparing rice that originated in the Middle East. Rice cooked in this manner is lightly coated in some type of fat, such as butter or oil, and then cooked in a liquid. Often seasonings and other ingredients like shellfish, chicken livers, or nuts are added to these preparations.

GREAT ACCOMPANIMENTS

I especially like to serve this rice with the Salmon Filets Baked with Lemons, Scallions, and Parsley.

AT THE MARKET

You can buy saffron powdered or in long, thin threads, but however you purchase this deep yellow-orange seasoning, you will find it has a strong, pungent taste. The adage, ''less is more,'' certainly applies to saffron. A small amount imparts an assertive flavor, and when this spice is dissolved in water or a light liquid like chicken stock, it adds a yellow hue.

Saffron is considered the most expensive spice in the world. The high cost is due to the enormous amount of labor needed to produce it. Saffron is produced from the dried stigmas of certain crocus plants. Each plant produces three stigmas, and thousands are needed to make only 1 ounce of this dried spice.

GREAT ACCOMPANIMENTS

This is one of my favorite dishes to serve with either grilled lamb chops or skewers of grilled lamb, beef, or shrimp. The Cucumber and Watercress Salad would taste good with a grilled entrée and this pilaf.

Saffron Rice with Almonds and Golden Raisins

This golden-hued pilaf is easy to assemble and a favorite recipe of my students. It can be baked in advance and then held in a warm oven for half an hour.

1 cup (2 sticks) unsalted butter
¾ cup slivered blanched almonds
1¼ cups chopped celery
1¼ cups chopped onions
2 cups raw long-grain white rice
2¾ cups homemade chicken stock (see Index) or good-quality canned broth
2½ teaspoons salt
¼ teaspoon freshly ground pepper
Generous pinch of saffron
⅓ cup golden raisins

1. Preheat the oven to 350° F.

2. Melt 2 tablespoons of the butter in a medium-size skillet over medium heat. When it is hot, sauté the almonds until browned, about 3 minutes. Watch carefully, as they burn easily. Remove, and drain on paper towels.

3. In a heavy casserole, melt the remaining butter and sauté the celery and onions until lightly coated with the butter, 4 to 5 minutes. Add the rice, and cook, stirring constantly, 1 minute more. Add the chicken stock, salt, pepper, and saffron. Then stir in the raisins and almonds.

4. Cover the casserole, and bake until all liquid is absorbed, 50 minutes to 1 hour. (This dish can be prepared and held, covered, in a 250° F oven for 30 to 40 minutes.)

Serves 8

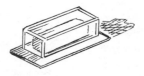

Rice. My students are often curious about the different types of rice that are available in the market. These are the most common grains:

• *Short-, medium-, or long-grain white rice:* These are the most popular and common varieties. White rice is milled so that the bran layer (which is rich in vitamins) is removed. However, almost all varieties are then enriched by a process that coats the grains with successive layers of vitamins. Because of this nutrient coating, these grains should not be rinsed before using.

When cooked, short- and medium-grain white rice tend to be stickier than long-grain rice because of their starch make up and are best used in rice puddings or custards, or rice dishes to be unmolded. Long-grain rice is fluffier when cooked, so it is best used as a side dish or in salads.

• *Brown rice:* This is rice that has been hulled but still retains the bran layer. It is harder than most white varieties and is easier to use if it is soaked or parboiled first. It takes longer to cook than white rice and has a firmer texture and slightly nutty taste. It is somewhat more nutritious than enriched white rice.

• *Wild rice:* Wild rice is indigenous to the United States and is not a true rice but rather the seed of an aquatic grass. These dark, long, slender grains with their crisp texture are expensive, but revered by epicureans. Wild rice benefits from parboiling before being used in a recipe.

Brown Rice with Parmesan Cheese

This is a wonderful and uncomplicated way to prepare brown rice.

2 cups raw brown rice
8 tablespoons (1 stick) unsalted butter
4 cups homemade chicken stock (see Index) or good-quality canned broth
¾ teaspoon salt
½ cup grated imported Parmesan cheese
⅓ cup chopped fresh parsley

1. Bring 2 quarts of water to a boil in a large saucepan. Add the brown rice, boil 5 minutes, and then drain well. (This will help soften the hard outer layer of the brown rice.)

2. In a heavy large saucepan set over medium heat, melt the butter. Then add the parboiled rice and stir well until all the grains are coated well with butter.

3. Add the chicken stock and salt, and stir. Bring the mixture to a simmer and cook, covered, at a simmer until all the liquid has been absorbed, 25 to 30 minutes.

4. Remove the pan from the heat and stir in the cheese, a little at a time, until it is all added. Stir in the parsley, and serve.

Serves 6 to 8

Barley with Leeks and Celery

In my cooking classes I have been surprised to discover that barley is unknown to many cooks. I love the texture and nutty taste of this grain and feel that it can be used very imaginatively in the kitchen. In this recipe, leeks, celery, and barley are sautéed in butter and tossed with seasonings of thyme, bay leaves, and black pepper. The barley and vegetables are then baked with beef stock and red wine. A generous addition of chopped herbs makes this dish a handsome and delicious alternative to more familiar side dishes.

6 tablespoons (¾ stick) unsalted butter
1½ cups chopped leeks (white parts only)
1 cup thinly sliced celery
2 cups raw pearl barley (about 1 pound)
2 bay leaves, broken in half
1 teaspoon crumbled dried thyme
1 teaspoon salt
Freshly ground pepper to taste
3½ cups homemade beef stock (see Index) or good-quality canned broth
½ cup dry red wine
½ cup minced fresh parsley
¼ cup snipped fresh chives

1. Preheat the oven to 350° F.

2. Melt the butter in a heavy flameproof casserole over medium-low heat. Add the leeks and celery and cook until soft, stirring occasionally, about 6 minutes. Add the barley and stir 3 minutes. Add the bay leaves, thyme, salt, and a generous amount of pepper. Mix in the stock and wine, and bring to a boil. Cover tightly and transfer to the oven. Bake until all liquid is absorbed, 35 to 40 minutes.

3. Remove the casserole from the oven and stir in the parsley and chives. Serve immediately.

Serves 8

SPECIAL STUFFINGS

Wild Rice, Sausage, and Fennel Stuffing

I like to bake this stuffing separately. My students and my family are all crazy about this hearty and robust dish. It can be prepared completely in advance and kept warm in a low oven for half an hour.

A COOK'S REFLECTIONS

I always parboil wild rice, as in step 1, before I use it in any recipe. This softens the hard rice grains but still leaves them crisp to the bite.

1½ cups raw wild rice
1 pound good-quality pork sausage
2 to 3 fennel bulbs
3 carrots, peeled
10 tablespoons (1¼ sticks) unsalted butter
1 cup chopped onions
1 cup raw Uncle Ben's Converted long-grain white rice
1 teaspoon dried thyme
1 teaspoon dried tarragon
1 teaspoon salt
1 cup dry white wine
2 cups homemade beef stock (see Index) or good-quality canned broth

1. Bring 2 quarts of water to a boil in a large heavy saucepan. Add the wild rice and cook 10 minutes. Drain the rice well, and reserve.

2. Crumble the pork sausage into small pieces in a large heavy skillet. Cook over medium heat, stirring, until the sausage is well browned, 6 to 8 minutes. Drain on paper towels and reserve.

3. Cut the tough bases and the green tops from the fennel bulbs. Slice the bulbs in half lengthwise, and remove the tough center core from each half. Then cut the halves into ¼-inch-thick lengthwise slices. You need enough sliced fennel to make 1 cup. Reserve.

4. Cut the carrots into thin strips 1½ inches long and ¼ inch thick. You will need 1 cup. Reserve.

5. Melt the butter in a large 4- to 5-quart deep-sided pot over medium heat. When it is hot, add the fennel and carrots, and sauté, stirring, 3 to 4 minutes. Add the onions and cook, stirring, another 3 minutes.

6. Add the wild rice and the white rice to the pot. Stir well to coat all the grains with butter, 3 to 4 minutes. Add the sausage, thyme, tarragon, and salt, and stir. Then add the wine and stock.

7. Bring the mixture to a simmer and then lower the heat. Cover, and cook until all liquid has been absorbed, about 40 minutes. Stir the rice several times during the cooking process to prevent sticking. The rice should be tender but still retain a little crispness. Taste, and add more salt if desired.

Serves 8

GREAT ACCOMPANIMENTS

I like to serve this wild rice with the Roast Turkey (without the Cornbread-Apricot Stuffing).

GREAT ACCOMPANIMENTS

This is a good dish to offer with the Roast Turkey, omitting the Cornbread-Apricot Dressing, or with the Roast Loin of Pork Braised in Cider.

AS A VARIATION

If wild mushrooms—cèpes and morels, for example—are available, you can use them in this recipe. Any of these varieties would impart a special flavor to the rice and would be a nice touch. If fresh wild mushrooms are unavailable, you could use 1½ to 2 ounces dried wild mushrooms. Soak them in hot water to reconstitute, and rinse under cold water to remove all dirt and grit.

Wild Rice and Currant Stuffing

This is another stuffing that I bake in a dish rather than in the cavity of a bird. It is great with roast poultry, game, or pork.

1½ cups raw wild rice
¾ cup (1½ sticks) unsalted butter
¼ cup finely chopped celery
¼ finely chopped carrots
¼ cup finely chopped onions
½ pound mushrooms, cleaned and thinly sliced through the stems
¾ cup raw long-grain white rice
3⅓ cups homemade beef stock (see Index) or good-quality canned broth
1½ teaspoons salt
½ teaspoon dried thyme
1 bay leaf
1 cup currants
⅔ cup toasted sliced almonds (see Index)

1. Preheat the oven to 350° F.

2. Bring 3 quarts of water to a boil, add the wild rice, and cook, uncovered, for 10 minutes. Drain well.

3. Melt the butter in a large heavy casserole over medium heat. Add the celery, carrots, onions, and mushrooms, and cook, stirring, until tender, 5 to 6 minutes. Then add the drained wild rice and the white rice. Toss to coat all ingredients with the butter.

4. Add 3 cups of the beef stock, the salt, thyme, and bay leaf to the mixture. Bring to a simmer on top of the stove, then cover with a lid and transfer to the oven. Bake approximately 40 minutes.

5. While the rice and vegetables are baking, heat the remaining ⅓ cup beef stock. Remove it from the heat, and add the currants. Soak the currants in the stock for 20 minutes.

6. Remove the casserole from the oven, and stir in the currants and the almonds. Toss well, and check the seasoning. Return the casserole to the oven and cook until all liquid has been absorbed, another 10 minutes.

Serves 8 to 10

A COOK'S REFLECTIONS

Madeira is a blended wine fortified with cane spirit. Unlike sherry and port, two other fortified wines, Madeira undergoes a gradual heating process to aid in its maturation. There are four well-known types of Madeira:

- Sercial—the lightest and driest variety
- Verdelho—a dark, sweet version
- Boal—a delicate, sweet version
- Malmsey—a dark, sweet, fruity, and very fragrant variety

The Madeira I like best for cooking is Sercial.

AT THE MARKET

Kielbasa is the sausage I like best for this dish, but you could substitute other firm cooked sausage according to your taste.

GREAT ACCOMPANIMENTS

This stuffing is a good accompaniment to the Roast Loin of Pork Braised in Cider or to roast chicken, turkey, or other fowl.

Sausage and Apple Stuffing

This stuffing is almost a meal in itself. Bake it in a separate dish or inside a bird.

1½ pounds kielbasa or other cooked sausage, skin removed
8 tablespoons (1 stick) unsalted butter
½ cup chopped onions
⅓ cup Madeira
2 teaspoons dried thyme
1 bay leaf, crumbled
4 tablespoons chopped fresh parsley
3½ cups (about 4) peeled, cored, and diced tart apples
1 cup chopped walnuts
4 cups fresh bread crumbs
Salt and freshly ground pepper to taste
2 large eggs, beaten lightly

1. Cut the kielbasa into ¼-inch dice. You should have about 4 cups. Melt the butter in a large heavy skillet over medium heat. When it is hot, add the onions and sauté until softened, 3 to 4 minutes. Then add the kielbasa and cook, stirring, for 2 minutes more. Add the Madeira and cook, stirring, until the liquid has evaporated. Remove the skillet from the heat. Add the thyme, crumbled bay leaf, parsley, apples, and walnuts, and stir well. If the skillet is large enough, add the bread crumbs and mix well. Otherwise transfer the cooked mixture to a large bowl and then stir in the bread crumbs. Season the mixture with salt and pepper to taste. (The stuffing can be made several hours ahead or overnight. Cover and refrigerate.)

2. When you are ready to bake the stuffing, preheat the oven to 325° F.

3. Add the beaten eggs to the stuffing, and mix well.

4. Butter a large shallow 13 x 9-inch baking dish and spread the dressing evenly in it. Bake, uncovered, 1 hour to 1 hour and 15 minutes. Stir the stuffing every 15 to 20 minutes while it is baking to ensure that it cooks through and is not soggy. When it is done, there should be a rich brown crust on top and the dressing should be moist but not wet. Serve hot.

Serves 8 to 10

THE BREAD BASKET

I used only one criterion for choosing the breads in this chapter: these are recipes for breads that cannot be purchased in a bakery. There are no basic loaves of white, rye, or pumpernickel here. Instead, there is a quartet of special muffins—each different and distinctive—and two flaky cheese biscuits, one made with Roquefort, the other with Cheddar, as well as a pair of savory herbed rolls. Among the other offerings are a delicious white bread flavored with cider, brioches baked with Cheddar cheese and thyme, and a whole wheat bread seasoned with apple butter and pecans.

MUFFINS & BISCUITS

Lemon Date Pecan Muffins

These muffins are dense and moist, laden with generous amounts of chopped pecans and dates and seasoned with a lively hint of lemon. I serve them hot from the oven for a special midafternoon treat with tea or coffee.

½ cup firmly packed light brown sugar
6 tablespoons (¾ stick) unsalted butter
5 tablespoons fresh lemon juice
¼ cup honey
½ cup sour cream
1 large egg
1 tablespoon grated lemon zest
1¾ cups all-purpose flour
1½ teaspoons baking powder
¾ teaspoon salt
½ teaspoon baking soda
1 cup chopped dates
⅔ cup coarsely chopped pecans
¼ cup hot water

1. Preheat the oven to 400° F.

2. Generously butter fourteen muffin cups. Combine the brown sugar, butter, lemon juice, and honey in a medium-size heavy saucepan over medium heat. Stir constantly until the mixture is hot. Set aside to cool slightly.

3. Whisk the sour cream, egg, and lemon zest together in a medium-size mixing bowl. Whisk in the warm brown sugar mixture.

4. Combine the flour, baking powder, salt, and baking soda in another mixing bowl. Add this to the liquid ingredients and stir until just blended. Add the dates, pecans, and hot water, and mix 10 seconds; the mixture will be lumpy. Fill the prepared muffin cups two-thirds full with batter.

5. Bake on the center shelf of the oven until the muffins are puffed and golden brown, about 20 minutes. Serve hot or warm. (The muffins are best served hot from the oven. However, they can be baked, covered, and kept at room temperature; reheat, wrapped in foil, in a preheated 350° F oven for 5 to 10 minutes. To freeze the muffins, wrap them tightly in foil; reheat, straight from the freezer and still wrapped in foil, in a preheated 350° F oven for 15 to 20 minutes or longer.)

Makes 14 muffins

Pumpkin Walnut Muffins

Pumpkin adds a delicious flavor to these muffins. Golden and rich, these spiced nut breads are wonderful to serve on a crisp fall day.

2 cups sifted all-purpose flour
1 cup firmly packed dark brown sugar
2 teaspoons baking powder
1 teaspoon baking soda
1 teaspoon salt
¼ teaspoon ground allspice
¼ teaspoon freshly grated nutmeg
1 teaspoon ground cinnamon
8 tablespoons (1 stick) unsalted butter, melted and slightly cooled
2 large eggs, lightly beaten
¾ cup buttermilk
1½ cups canned unsweetened pumpkin
1 Granny Smith apple, peeled, cored, and coarsely grated
1 cup chopped walnuts
1 tablespoon finely chopped crystallized ginger

1. Preheat the oven to 375° F.

2. Generously butter eighteen muffin cups.

3. In a mixing bowl combine the sifted flour, brown sugar, baking powder, baking soda, salt, allspice, nutmeg, and cinnamon. Mix well to combine.

4. In another bowl whisk together the melted butter, eggs, buttermilk, and pumpkin. Add this to the dry ingredients. Add the apple, walnuts, and crystallized ginger. Mix the batter just to blend. Fill the muffin cups two-thirds full with batter.

5. Bake on the center shelf of the oven until the muffins are puffed

and golden and a toothpick inserted in the center comes out clean, 20 to 25 minutes. Allow the muffins to rest 10 minutes before serving, then serve hot. (The muffins are best served hot from the oven. However, they can be baked, covered, and kept at room temperature; reheat the muffins, wrapped in foil, in a preheated 350° F oven for 5 to 10 minutes. To freeze the muffins, wrap them tightly in foil; reheat, straight from the freezer and still wrapped in foil, in a preheated 350° F oven for 15 to 20 minutes or longer.)

Makes 18 muffins

Brandied Applesauce Raisin Muffins

The idea for these muffins came from a very old recipe of my grandmother's for applesauce raisin cake. After making only a few changes I found that the cake batter worked beautifully when used for muffins, These confections, which have become a favorite of many of my students, can be made in advance and reheated.

1 cup raisins
⅓ cup brandy
8 tablespoons (1 stick) unsalted butter
1 cup sugar
1 cup sweetened applesauce
1 large egg, lightly beaten
2 cups all-purpose flour
1 teaspoon baking soda
½ teaspoon salt
½ teaspoon freshly grated nutmeg
½ teaspoon ground cinnamon
1 cup coarsely chopped walnuts
1 large apple (Granny Smith or Winesap), unpeeled, coarsely grated

1. Generously butter eighteen muffin cups.

2. Place the raisins in a small bowl. Heat the brandy until hot but not boiling and pour it over the raisins. Let the raisins soak in the brandy 15 to 20 minutes. (If you wish, you can soak them overnight for a stronger taste.)

3. Preheat the oven to 400° F.

4. Place the butter and sugar in a small saucepan over medium heat. Stir until the butter has melted and the sugar has dissolved. Remove from the heat and stir in the applesauce. Then stir in the egg, and set aside.

5. Combine the flour, baking soda, salt, nutmeg, and cinnamon in a bowl and mix well. Whisk the dry ingredients into the butter mixture, and stir just until blended. Add the raisins plus any soaking liquid, the walnuts, and the grated apple. Mix only a few seconds; the mixture will be lumpy.

6. Fill the muffin cups two-thirds full with batter, and place them on the center shelf of the oven. Bake until golden and firm, 20 minutes. Remove the muffins from the oven and unmold. Serve hot, with butter or softened cream cheese. (The muffins are best served hot from the oven. However, they can be baked, covered, and kept at room temperature; reheat, wrapped in foil, in a preheated 350° F oven for 5 to 10 minutes. To freeze the muffins, wrap them tightly in foil; reheat, straight from the freezer and still wrapped in foil, in a preheated 350° F oven for 15 to 20 minutes or longer.)

Makes 18 muffins

Southern Cornbread

Here is my family's favorite cornbread. Both my mother and my grandmother always used this recipe to make this traditional Southern specialty. This bread is quick and easy to assemble, and is best served hot from the oven. It does not taste as good when made ahead and reheated.

Special equipment: Heavy 9-inch ovenproof black cast iron or other skillet

2 large eggs
¾ cup buttermilk
¼ teaspoon baking soda
¾ teaspoon baking powder
¾ teaspoon salt
1 cup cornmeal (white or yellow)
4 teaspoons vegetable oil

AS A VARIATION

*If you are making crumbs for a
dressing, cool the cornbread. Then
crumble it to the desired consistency
in a food processor. You will have 4
to 4½ cups.*

THE RIGHT EQUIPMENT

I am a big fan of nonstick muffin
tins because I find them easier to
use than the traditional variety.
The baked muffins pop right out
with no trouble at all. If you don't
have nonstick tins, be sure to
grease your molds very generously.

   There are two easy-to-find
muffin tin sizes available. The
standard-size tin has cups approximately 3 inches wide. The mini-
pan cups are about 2 inches in
diameter.

1. Preheat the oven to 450° F.

2. In a mixing bowl, lightly mix the eggs and buttermilk. Add the
baking soda, baking powder, and salt, and mix well. Add the
cornmeal and stir well.

3. Heat the oil in a heavy 9-inch skillet. When it is very hot, stir the
oil into the batter. Then pour the batter into the heated skillet, and
put it in the oven. Bake until the bread is firm to the touch, 15 to 20
minutes. Invert the pan over a plate and let the bread drop easily
onto it. Cut into wedges and serve.

Makes one 9-inch-round cornbread

Chile Cheese Corn Muffins

M y friend Kathy Fleegler, a creative cooking teacher and caterer
from Cleveland, sent me the directions for these corn muffins. I
replaced the Cheddar in the original version with spicier jalapeño
pepper cheese but left everything else the same. These are wonderful
served with bowls of hot chili, or with grilled chicken or barbecued
ribs.

2 cups yellow cornmeal
½ cup all-purpose flour
1 tablespoon baking powder
1 tablespoon sugar
1 teaspoon baking soda
1 teaspoon salt
Scant ⅛ teaspoon cayenne pepper
2 large eggs
2 cups milk
2 tablespoons unsalted butter, melted
2 tablespoons finely chopped onion
1½ cups grated Monterey Jack cheese with jalapeño peppers
    (about 6 ounces)
1½ cups corn kernels (fresh, or thawed and well-drained frozen)
1 can (4 ounces) mild chile peppers, rinsed, seeded, and finely
    chopped
⅓ cup finely chopped red bell pepper

1. Generously butter eighteen muffin cups.

GREAT ACCOMPANIMENTS

These muffins are especially good with the Tomato Soup with Avocado Cream served hot, or with Grilled Lemon Chicken with Chile Hollandaise.

2. Preheat the oven to 375° F.

3. In a mixing bowl stir together the cornmeal, flour, baking powder, sugar, baking soda, salt, and cayenne pepper.

4. In another bowl, beat together the eggs, milk, and melted butter. Stir this into the dry ingredients and mix just until the batter is blended; it will not be completely smooth. Fold in the onions, cheese, corn, chile peppers, and red pepper. Do not overmix. Fill the muffin cups two-thirds full with batter.

5. Place the muffin tins on the center shelf of the oven and bake until the muffins are firm to the touch and a toothpick inserted into the center comes out clean, 25 to 30 minutes. Serve hot. (The muffins are best served hot from the oven. However, they can be baked, covered, and kept at room temperature; reheat, wrapped in foil, in a preheated 350° F oven, 5 to 10 minutes. To freeze the muffins, wrap them tightly in foil; reheat, straight from the freezer and still wrapped in foil, in a preheated 350° F oven for 15 to 20 minutes or longer.)

Makes 18 muffins

GREAT ACCOMPANIMENTS

For special weekend breakfasts, I like to serve a bowl of fresh fruit followed by creamy scrambled eggs, broiled tomato slices, and a basket of these flavorful biscuits.

Roquefort and Bacon Biscuits

Flavored with Roquefort and pieces of crispy fried bacon, these biscuits are certainly beyond ordinary. They are especially good to serve at lunch or for a hearty dinner.

Special equipment: 2-inch round cookie cutter

2 cups sifted all-purpose flour
1 tablespoon baking powder
1 tablespoon sugar
½ teaspoon salt
3 tablespoons unsalted butter, chilled and cut into small pieces
3 tablespoons solid vegetable shortening, chilled and cut into small pieces
5 tablespoons crumbled Roquefort cheese
½ cup (about 5 slices) crumbled fried bacon
¾ cup milk
1 large egg yolk

1. Preheat the oven to 425° F.

2. Place the flour, baking powder, sugar, and salt in a mixing bowl. Cut in the butter and shortening pieces, using a pastry blender or two knives, until the mixture resembles oatmeal flakes.

3. Then stir in the cheese and bacon, and mix well. Make a well in the center of the ingredients, and add ½ cup of the milk and the egg yolk. Stir well, combining the milk with the flour mixture. Continue to stir in enough of the remaining milk to make a soft, pliable dough. (You may not need to add all the milk.) Gather the dough into a round ball, place it on a lightly floured work surface, and knead it gently about ten times.

4. Roll the dough out so it is ½ inch thick. Cut out biscuits with a 2-inch cookie cutter. Reroll the scraps and continue to cut out biscuits until all the dough is used.

5. Place the biscuits 1 inch apart on an ungreased baking sheet, and place the sheet on the center shelf of the oven. Bake until golden, 10 to 12 minutes. Serve warm. (The biscuits are best served hot from the oven, but they can be baked, wrapped in aluminum foil, and then reheated in a preheated 350° F oven for 5 to 10 minutes.)

Makes about 18 biscuits

Cheddar Cheese Biscuits

These biscuits have a distinctive Cheddar taste. They are golden and crisp outside, with soft centers, and are best served piping hot from the oven.

Special equipment: 2-inch round cookie cutter

2 cups sifted all-purpose flour
1 tablespoon baking powder
½ teaspoon salt
3 tablespoons unsalted butter, chilled and cut into small pieces
3 tablespoons solid vegetable shortening, chilled and cut into small pieces
⅓ cup grated Cheddar cheese
¾ cup milk
1 large egg yolk

1. Preheat the oven to 450° F.

GREAT ACCOMPANIMENTS

*These biscuits are particularly good
to serve at a brunch buffet. I often
fill them with country ham and a
little chutney.*

2. Place the flour, baking powder, and salt in a mixing bowl. Cut in the butter and shortening, using a pastry blender or two knives, until the mixture resembles oatmeal flakes. Then stir in the cheese. Make a well in the center, and pour in the milk and egg yolk. Stir until all the flour is blended and the dough leaves the sides of the bowl. The dough will be very moist. (This can also be done in a food processor.)

3. Transfer the dough to a lightly floured surface and knead it about ten times. Roll the dough out so it is ¾ inch thick, and cut out biscuits with a 2-inch cookie cutter. Reroll the scraps and continue to cut out biscuits until all the dough is used.

4. Place the biscuits 1 inch apart on an ungreased baking sheet, and bake on the center shelf for 12 minutes. (The biscuits are best served hot from the oven, but they can be baked in advance, wrapped in aluminum foil, and then reheated in a preheated 350° F oven for 5 to 10 minutes.)

Makes 12 to 14 biscuits

HEARTY LOAVES & ROLLS

Roger's "Sourdough" Bread

My good friend Roger Mandle, who is the director of the Toledo Museum of Art, is one of the busiest people I know, and yet he finds time to bake bread regularly. His plump white bread made with cider is a firm loaf with a slight sourdough taste, perfect for sandwiches.

Special equipment needed: Two 9 x 5 x 2-inch loaf pans

2 envelopes active dry yeast
½ cup warm milk (105° to 115° F)
1 cup milk
*1 cup fresh cider without preservatives (just slightly turned if
    possible)*
2 tablespoons brown sugar
2 teaspoons salt
2 tablespoons unsalted butter, melted
1 tablespoon vegetable oil
6 cups unbleached all-purpose flour, plus more if needed

1. In a large mixing bowl, dissolve the yeast in the warm milk and let stand until foamy, 3 to 4 minutes.

2. Combine the 1 cup milk, the cider, brown sugar, salt, melted butter, and oil in another bowl, and stir lightly to mix well. Make certain the brown sugar and salt are dissolved. Add this mixture to the yeast mixture, and stir just to incorporate. Gradually add 6 cups flour to the mixture, and form into a ball of dough. If the dough is sticky to the touch, work in ¼ to ½ cup additional flour, until the dough is no longer sticky.

3. Knead the dough on a lightly floured surface until it is soft and pliable, about 10 minutes. Place it in a large greased mixing bowl, turn to coat it well, and cover the bowl with a kitchen towel. Let the dough rise in a warm draft-free area until doubled in volume, about 1¼ hours.

4. When the dough has risen, remove it from the bowl and punch it down. Divide the dough in half, shape each into a loaf, and place them in greased 9 x 5 x 2-inch loaf pans.

5. Position a rack in the center of the oven and preheat the oven to 425° F.

6. Bake for 15 minutes, then reduce the heat to 325° F and bake until the crust is very firm and dark brown, another 20 to 25 minutes. Tap the loaves with your finger; if the bread produces a hollow sound, it is done. Remove the loaves from the pans and cool on a rack. (This bread freezes well. Wrap the cooled loaves tightly in foil and then in a plastic bag.)

Makes 2 loaves

GREAT ACCOMPANIMENTS

For a hearty supper I like to serve bowls of the Cold Weather Beef and Lentil Soup along with piping-hot slices of this cheese bread.

Smoked Cheddar and Hot Pepper Bread

There are many recipes for cheese breads, but this one, which is made with smoked Cheddar plus a spirited seasoning of red pepper flakes, is unusual. It took me several weeks of testing to get the flavors well balanced, but I love the final results.

Special equipment: Two 9 x 5 x 2-inch loaf pans, or two 2-quart soufflé dishes 8 inches in diameter; heavy-duty electric mixer

5½ to 6 cups flour
1 tablespoon active dry yeast
2 tablespoons sugar
2 teaspoons salt
¼ teaspoon red pepper flakes
2¼ cups warm water (120° to 125° F)
2½ cups shredded smoked Cheddar cheese, including dark outer
*   coating*

1. Grease two bread pans or soufflé dishes generously with butter and set aside.

2. Place 3 cups of the flour, the yeast, sugar, salt, and red pepper flakes in the bowl of a heavy-duty electric mixer. Mix on slow speed while gradually adding the water. When all the water has been incorporated, beat the dough for 3 minutes more. With the machine running, add the cheese, a handful at a time. When all the cheese has been incorporated, add the remaining flour, ½ cup at a time, until the dough clings to the beaters and cleans the sides of the bowl. (You may not need to add the entire amount of remaining flour; the quantity needed will depend on the dryness of the flour. Generally about 5½ cups total flour per recipe is sufficient.)

3. Remove the dough from the mixing bowl and knead it on a lightly floured surface until it is smooth and elastic, 5 to 6 minutes.

4. Place the dough in a large greased mixing bowl, turn to coat it well, and cover the bowl with plastic wrap. Place the dough in a warm draft-free area to rise until doubled in volume, 1½ hours.

5. When the dough has risen, remove it from the bowl and punch it down. Divide the dough in half, form it into two loaf shapes or two rounds, and put them into the bread pans or soufflé dishes. Cover the pans loosely with plastic wrap, place in a warm area, and let the dough rise again until it reaches just slightly above the edges of the pans, 45 to 60 minutes.

6. Position a rack in the center of the oven and preheat to 375° F.

7. Bake until the crust is nicely browned and firm on top and the bread sounds hollow when tapped with your finger, 45 to 50 minutes. (Check after 30 minutes, and if the crust is browning too quickly, drape aluminum foil loosely over the top.)

8. When the bread is done, remove the pans from the oven, invert the loaves onto a wire rack, and cool 10 to 15 minutes before slicing.

A COOK'S REFLECTIONS

Wheat flour. Wheat flour is the type most commonly used for breads. It is milled from wheat kernels. When whole kernels are milled, the result is whole wheat flour. However, if the kernels are ground very fine, then three products—white flour, bran, and germ can all be sifted out.

Flour is milled from both hard and soft wheat, and commercial flours are made from either or from a combination of the two. Some of the most familiar are:

• All-purpose flour: This is flour produced from both soft and hard wheat. It comes bleached or un-bleached (slightly more nutritional than bleached), and either can be used in any recipe that simply calls for flour.

• Bread flour: Not always as read-ily available as all-purpose, this flour has a high gluten or protein content. Gluten controls the elas-ticity of dough, and the higher the gluten content, the better the flour is for breadmaking.

• Cake flour: This is very finely ground bleached flour, with an al-most silky texture. If it is unavail-able, you can approximate its texture—for every cup of cake flour needed, measure 2 table-spoons of cornstarch into a 1-cup measuring cup, then fill the cup with sifted all-purpose flour. Blend the two together.

• Whole wheat flour: This dark flour, made from whole wheat kernels, gives a coarser texture to bread. It is sometimes referred to as graham flour.

(This bread freezes well. Wrap the cooled loaves tightly in foil and then in a plastic bag. Since it is best hot, defrost it, and reheat wrapped in foil in a 350° F oven for 10 to 15 minutes.)

Makes 2 loaves

Pecan Raisin Whole Wheat Bread

As the primary recipe tester, June McCarthy was an invaluable assistant during the preparation of this book. One of her special talents is breadmaking, and while working on the bread chapter, she invented this delicious pecan raisin whole wheat loaf.

Special equipment: 9 x 5 x 2-inch loaf pan; instant-reading thermometer; heavy-duty electric mixer

½ cup apple juice
½ cup raisins
½ cup apple butter
½ cup buttermilk
2 tablespoons unsalted butter, cut into small pieces
1 cup whole wheat flour
2 cups bread flour or unbleached all-purpose flour
1 envelope active dry yeast
1 teaspoon salt
2 teaspoons sugar
1 teaspoon baking powder
½ cup pecans, toasted and coarsely chopped (see Index)
¼ cup water
½ teaspoon cornstarch

1. Grease a 9 x 5 x 2-inch loaf pan generously with butter, and set aside.

2. Place ¼ cup of the apple juice in a small saucepan over high heat and bring to a boil. Remove it from the heat and add the raisins. Soak the raisins until they are softened and plump, about 15 min-utes. Remove the raisins with a slotted spoon, reserving the soaking liquid.

3. In a medium saucepan, combine the remaining ¼ cup apple juice, the apple butter, buttermilk, and butter. Place over medium

THE RIGHT EQUIPMENT

A good thermometer can be a cook's best friend, especially when making bread. When preparing bread dough, the temperature of the liquid to be combined with the yeast is very important. Water that is under 80° F will delay the growth of the yeast, and water at 140° F will kill it. The dry yeasts available today are excellent and reliable products if the correct temperatures are maintained. When dry yeast is added directly to the warm liquid, the temperature of the liquid should be between 105° and 115° F. However, when the dry yeast is combined with flour before the warm liquid is added, the temperature of the liquid should be higher (120° to 130° F). Because the temperature of the liquid is so important, I recommend you buy a good thermometer, especially if you are just learning to bake bread. I like the instant-reading thermometers (the same ones used for meats and poultry). Once you become familiar with the feel of the water temperatures needed, you'll be able to judge the temperature by simply touching the liquid.

heat, and when the mixture reaches 130° F on a thermometer, remove it from the heat. Add the raisin soaking liquid.

4. In the bowl of a heavy-duty electric mixer, combine the whole wheat flour, 1 cup of the bread or all-purpose flour, the yeast, salt, sugar, and baking powder. With the mixer on very slow speed, mix to blend the dry ingredients. Then, with the mixer still running, pour in the warm liquid mixture. When all the liquid has been added, turn the mixer to high speed and beat for 2 minutes.

5. Reduce the speed to low again, and add ½ cup of the bread or all-purpose flour. Beat just to incorporate. Then, with the machine still on low speed, add the reserved raisins, the chopped pecans, and ¼ cup more bread or all-purpose flour. Continue to beat the mixture until the dough begins to form a solid mass and leaves the sides of the bowl, 1 to 2 minutes.

6. Remove the dough from the mixer. Sprinkle a work surface with 2 tablespoons of the remaining bread or all-purpose flour. Start to knead the dough, incorporating the flour on the work surface. Continue to knead until the dough is soft and pliable, 3 to 5 minutes. If the dough seems too sticky, knead in an additional 1 to 2 tablespoons flour. Knead until the dough is smooth, soft, and elastic, 2 to 3 minutes.

7. Place the dough in a large, lightly greased mixing bowl, turn to coat it well, and cover the bowl tightly with plastic wrap. Set the bowl in a warm draft-free area and let the dough rise until doubled in volume, 1½ to 2 hours.

8. When the dough has risen, place it on a lightly floured work surface. Shape the dough into an oval, pressing carefully and firmly with your hands to release any air pockets. Fold the oval in half, and with your fingers pinch the seam together. Place the dough, seam side down, in a 9 x 5 x 2-inch loaf pan. Press down gently so the dough is spread evenly over the bottom of the pan. Cover the pan loosely with plastic wrap, and place in a warm draft-free area. Let the dough rise until doubled in volume, 1 to 1½ hours.

9. Position a rack in the center of the oven and preheat the oven to 375° F.

10. Bake until the crust is dark and the bread sounds hollow when tapped with your fingers, about 40 minutes. (Check the bread after 25 to 30 minutes; if the crust is getting dark too quickly, cover the bread loosely with aluminum foil.)

11. Remove the pan from the oven, but leave the oven on. Combine the water and cornstarch in a small saucepan over high heat, bring to a boil, and cook, stirring, for 1 minute. Then brush the top of the bread with this glaze.

12. Return the bread to the oven, and bake an additional 5 minutes. Then remove the pan and invert the bread onto a cooling rack. Cool the bread to room temperature. This bread is best eaten within a day. (This bread freezes well. Wrap the cooled bread tightly in foil and then in a plastic bag.)

Makes 1 loaf

Anise Sweet Bread

One day a colleague, David D'Alessandris, brought me a loaf of his mother's homemade anise bread. He was anxious for me to try it because the recipe for this Italian specialty had been handed down through several generations of his family and was a particular favorite. The bread was superb! A beautiful braided loaf with a dark glazed crust, it was sweet but not cloyingly so, and perfectly flavored with anise.

Special equipment: Two 9 x 5 x 2-inch loaf pans

1½ cups sugar
10 tablespoons (1¼ sticks) unsalted butter, cut into small pieces
1 cup evaporated milk
1½ teaspoons salt
1 cup golden raisins
2 envelopes active dry yeast
Pinch of sugar
6 tablespoons warm water (105° to 115° F)
6½ to 7½ cups unbleached all-purpose flour
5 large eggs
4 teaspoons anise extract
¾ teaspoon grated lemon zest

1. Combine the sugar, butter, milk, and salt in a medium-size heavy saucepan over low heat. Stir until the butter has melted and the sugar has dissolved. Cool the mixture until warm (105° to 115° F).

2. Place the raisins in a small bowl and cover with boiling water. Let

A COOK'S REFLECTIONS

This festive bread is perfect to serve at holiday breakfasts or brunches. Since the bread holds up well, it also makes a thoughtful Christmas gift to offer friends.

soak 5 minutes; then drain, and pat dry.

3. Sprinkle the yeast and pinch of sugar over the warm water in a small bowl; stir to dissolve. Let stand until foamy, about 5 minutes.

4. Place 6½ cups flour in a large bowl and make a well in the center. Beat 4 of the eggs together to blend. Put the milk mixture, yeast mixture, eggs, anise, and lemon zest in the well. Mix into the flour with a wooden spoon until a loose dough forms. Then knead the dough on a lightly floured surface until it is smooth and elastic, adding more flour if it is sticky, about 10 minutes. Knead in the raisins.

5. Grease a large bowl and put the dough in it, turning it to coat the entire surface. Cover the bowl with a kitchen towel. Let the dough rise in a warm draft-free area until doubled in volume, about 2 hours.

6. Generously butter two 9 x 5 x 2-inch loaf pans. Punch the dough down and divide it in half. Divide one half into three pieces, and roll each piece into a 12-inch-long rope. Braid the ropes together, tuck the ends under, and fit them into a prepared pan. Repeat with the other half of the dough. Cover the pans with kitchen towels and let the dough rise in a warm draft-free area until almost doubled in volume, about 1¼ hours.

7. Position a rack in the lower third of the oven and preheat the oven to 375° F.

8. Beat the remaining egg, and brush it over the loaves. Bake until the loaves pull away from the sides of the pans, 40 to 45 minutes. If the loaves are browning too quickly, cover them loosely with foil. When they are done, immediately invert the loaves onto a rack. Serve hot or warm. (This bread freezes well. Wrap it tightly in foil and then in a plastic bag.)

Makes 2 loaves

GREAT ACCOMPANIMENTS

These rolls are delicious served with hearty entrées like the Fettuccine with Sausage, Red Peppers, and Mushrooms, or the Veal Ragoût with Red Peppers and Olives.

Parmesan Garlic Rolls

My culinary assistant, Sue Peterson, gave me the recipe for these terrific rolls, which can be made from start to finish in a little more than two hours. Seasoned subtly with garlic, the rolls are brushed with olive oil, then sprinkled with cheese and baked until golden

AS A VARIATION

The cheese and herb topping can be varied easily in this recipe. For example, sometimes I use plain vegetable oil in place of olive oil and sprinkle finely grated Gruyère and thyme on the rolls for an interesting combination, and on other occasions I use grated white Cheddar and dill. Both variations are as delicious as the original.

brown and slightly crisp on top and soft inside. They are best served piping hot.

1 cup warm water (110° F)
1 teaspoon garlic salt
2 tablespoons olive oil
1 teaspoon sugar
1 teaspoon active dry yeast
3 cups unbleached all-purpose flour
¼ cup grated good-quality imported Parmesan cheese
1½ teaspoons lightly crushed dried rosemary

1. In a large bowl, combine the water, garlic salt, 1 tablespoon of the olive oil, the sugar, and yeast. Stir until the yeast dissolves. Gradually beat in the flour to form a moderately firm dough. Then knead the dough on a lightly floured surface until it is smooth and elastic, 8 to 10 minutes. (You can also knead the dough in a heavy-duty electric mixer fitted with a dough hook.) Place the dough in a lightly greased bowl, turn to coat it well, and cover with a kitchen towel. Let it rise in a warm place until doubled in volume, 1½ to 2 hours.

2. Punch the dough down and knead it briefly. Then divide the dough into eight equal pieces. Shape each piece into a slightly domed 3-inch round. Place the shaped dough 2 to 3 inches apart on an ungreased baking sheet. Place the remaining 1 tablespoon olive oil in a small bowl, and brush the top of each roll lightly with the oil. Sprinkle each round with Parmesan cheese and a little rosemary. Let the rolls rise in a warm spot, until doubled in size, 35 to 45 minutes.

3. Preheat the oven to 400° F.

4. Bake the rolls 15 to 20 minutes, until golden. Serve hot, with butter.

Makes 8 large rolls

Rosemary Savory Rolls

What I like best about these herbed rolls is that the dough can be prepared several days in advance and kept refrigerated. Then all I have to do is to shape the dough into rounds and let it have a final rising before baking.

A COOK'S REFLECTIONS

I like to make these special rolls
for large buffets, and in particular
for holiday gatherings, since the
dough can be assembled in advance.

THE RIGHT EQUIPMENT

By baking these rolls in muffin
pans, you get very attractive
rounds of uniform shape.

Special equipment: Heavy-duty electric mixer

1 cup water
12 tablespoons (1½ sticks) unsalted butter, melted
1 teaspoon dried savory
¾ teaspoon dried rosemary
3½ to 4 cups unbleached all-purpose flour
¼ to ⅓ cup sugar
1 tablespoon active dry yeast
1 teaspoon salt
1 large whole egg
1 large egg white
1 tablespoon cold water

1. Bring the 1 cup of water to a boil. Remove it from the heat, and
stir in ⅓ cup (5⅓ tablespoons) of the melted butter. Let the mixture
cool to 130° to 135° F.

2. Crush the savory and rosemary either in a mortar with a pestle or
between two sheets of waxed paper with a meat pounder or other
heavy object. Set the herbs aside.

3. Combine 1 cup of the flour, sugar to taste, the yeast, and salt in
the large bowl of a heavy-duty mixer. Add the water mixture and
beat until a slowly dissolving ribbon forms when the beaters are
lifted, about 2 minutes. Add another ½ cup flour, the whole egg, and
the herbs. Beat until the batter thickens, about 1 minute. Beat in 2
cups of the flour, 1 cup at a time. Cover the bowl with a towel and let
the dough stand for 10 minutes.

4. Turn the dough out onto a lightly floured surface. Wipe the bowl
clean; grease it well. Knead the dough until smooth and elastic,
about 10 minutes. Add up to ½ cup more flour if necessary to prevent
sticking. Transfer the dough to the bowl, turning it to coat the entire
surface. Cover with plastic wrap and refrigerate 2 hours. (The dough
can be prepared up to 4 days ahead.)

5. Brush twenty muffin cups generously with some of the remaining
melted butter. Cut the dough into twenty pieces. Roll each piece into
a round. Dip the rounds into the remaining melted butter, and place
in the muffin cups. Cover with a kitchen towel and let stand in a
warm draft-free area until doubled in volume, 1 to 1½ hours.

6. Position a rack in the center of the oven and preheat the oven to
400° F.

7. Blend the egg white with the cold water, and brush the mixture over the rolls. Bake until golden brown, about 12 minutes. (If the rolls brown too quickly, cover loosely with foil.) Serve immediately.

Makes 20 rolls

Cheddar Cheese and Thyme Brioches

This is my variation on a French classic. I simply added sharp Cheddar cheese and thyme to traditional brioche dough. The sum, however, is greater than its parts in this recipe—these brioches, baked to a rich golden brown, have a wonderful aroma and a taste that seems much more complex than the ingredients would indicate.

Special equipment: Twenty-four 3½-inch brioche molds or two 12-cup muffin pans (preferably nonstick); heavy-duty electric mixer

8 tablespoons (1 stick) unsalted butter, at room temperature
⅓ cup sugar
1 teaspoon salt
¾ cup hot water (120° to 130° F)
3½ to 4 cups all-purpose flour
3 large whole eggs, at room temperature
2 large egg yolks, at room temperature
¼ cup nonfat powdered milk
1 tablespoon crumbled dried thyme
1 envelope active dry yeast
½ pound sharp Cheddar cheese, grated (about 2 cups)
1 tablespoon milk

1. Using a heavy-duty electric mixer, cream the butter with the sugar and salt. Add the hot water. Mix in 1½ cups of the flour, the eggs, 1 of the egg yolks, the powdered milk, thyme, and yeast. Beat 2 minutes. Add another 2 cups of the flour and beat 2 minutes. Mix in more flour if necessary to form a soft, slightly sticky dough. Cover the bowl with plastic wrap. Let the dough rise in a warm draft-free area until it has more than doubled in volume, about 2 hours.

2. Stir the dough down with a wooden spoon. Beat it with the electric mixer for 1 minute. Then add the cheese, and beat until well

THE RIGHT EQUIPMENT

Brioche molds are round, with fluted sides that slant outward slightly. The molds form a nice ridged pattern on the sides of the brioches when they are baked, but muffin pans will work just as well.

GREAT ACCOMPANIMENTS

I love serving these brioches at a brunch where the menu also includes Grilled Salmon Steaks Wrapped in Peppered Bacon, poached eggs, and sautéed cherry tomatoes.

incorporated. Cover the bowl with plastic wrap and refrigerate 4 hours or overnight.

3. Butter twenty brioche molds or muffin cups.

4. Remove the dough from the refrigerator. Break off golf-ball-size pieces. Roll each piece into a small ball. Press down, and with the side of your hand positioned near one end of the flattened dough, roll the dough back and forth three or four times, until it forms a little ball on one end and a larger ball on the other connected by a small neck. Lift the dough by the small end and lower the larger end into the brioche mold or muffin cup. Then, force the small ball of dough into the larger piece, fingertips pushing to the bottom of the tin. (This technique will help form the traditional "knot" which is baked on top of brioches.) Repeat with the remaining dough.

5. Tent plastic wrap or waxed paper over the brioches, using inverted beverage glasses to keep the wrap away from the dough. Let the dough rise in a warm draft-free area until doubled, about 1½ hours.

6. Preheat the oven to 400° F.

7. Blend the remaining egg yolk with the milk, and brush this over the brioches. Bake until golden brown, 10 to 12 minutes. Invert onto racks to cool. (The brioches can be prepared 1 day ahead. Cool completely, wrap in foil, and refrigerate. Reheat, wrapped in foil, in a preheated 350° F oven about 5 minutes.) Serve hot or warm.

Makes 20 brioches

GRAND FINALES

Looking at the recipe files I have created during the past decade, I am not surprised that the dessert section is larger than the others. Desserts are my specialty, and therefore, my favorite part of any dinner to prepare. A sweet morsel at the end of a meal is good not only for the palate, but for the soul as well. Few can resist this temptation; even those on diets seem to find room for dessert. During cooking classes, I frequently see weight-conscious individuals carefully take bird's-size portions of food until they reach dessert; then they will eat even the richest creation with abandon, and shamelessly request seconds!

There are all manner of tempting confections in this chapter: glorious cakes for important occasions; mouth-watering pies, tarts, and strudels; light, icy-cold sorbets perfect to end a heavy meal; little pick-up sweets such as brownies, cookies, and bars; a collection of tempting frozen and chilled desserts; and fresh fruit creations for all seasons. Many of these can be prepared completely or partially in advance, so you can escape the kitchen to be with guests. Some, such as the Caramel Rum Pecan Sauce to serve with ice cream, are quick and easy to assemble, while others—the Chocolate Ribbon Cake, for instance—will take a good deal more time to prepare. (But the time spent is always recompensed by the look of delight on the faces of guests!)

Shakespeare described best the way I feel about dessert: "The end crowns all."

CAKES

Cakes of all kinds—chic European-style tortes, double- and triple-layer cakes with rich, smooth icings, slender and sleek roulades with creamy centers, feather-light angel food cakes, and the quintessential American cheesecake—are desserts I love to teach at La Belle Pomme. The selections in this chapter are my students' ten all-time favorites. Each makes a striking presentation, whether it's the stately Walnut Orange Cake simple garnished with walnut halves and candied orange peel, or the elegant Chocolate Apricot Pecan Torte topped with a bouquet of apricot roses and chocolate leaves. Best of all, as my students always remind me, each can be made completely in advance.

SPECIAL CAKES

Chocolate Ribbon Cake

After this cake appeared on a December cover of *Bon Appétit* magazine, I received phone calls from people all over the country telling me they had made it! It is truly a show-stopper cake, made with three dense nut layers, spread with a chocolate buttercream, and then glazed with a dark chocolate coating. The white and dark chocolate ribbons that garnish the cake are made with a pasta machine. It takes several hours to make this dessert from start to finish, but the cake can be completely prepared (ribbons et al.) in stages and frozen weeks before it is to be served. This is for a very important celebration or occasion!

Special equipment: Three straight-sided 9-inch round cake pans; heavy-duty electric mixer

Cake
1½ cups (3 sticks) unsalted butter, at room temperature
2 cups sugar
8 large eggs, separated, at room temperature
10 ounces semisweet chocolate, melted
1½ cups finely chopped pecans
2 teaspoons vanilla extract
1 teaspoon ground cinnamon
1 teaspoon ground cloves
1 teaspoon freshly grated nutmeg
1⅓ cups all-purpose flour, sifted
Pinch of salt
Pinch of cream of tartar

Buttercream
¾ cup sugar
½ cup light corn syrup
4 jumbo egg yolks
1½ cups (3 sticks) unsalted butter, cut into small pieces, at room temperature
6 ounces semisweet chocolate, melted and cooled
¼ cup dark rum

Glaze

12 ounces semisweet chocolate, broken into small pieces
¾ cup (1½ sticks) unsalted butter, cut into small pieces
2 tablespoons honey
¾ teaspoon instant coffee powder

Garnish

White and Dark Chocolate Ribbons (recipe follows)

1. Position a rack in the center of the oven, and preheat the oven to 350° F.

2. Prepare the cake: Butter and flour three 9-inch round cake pans. Line the bottom of each with waxed paper; butter and flour the paper.

3. Cream the butter in the large bowl of a heavy-duty electric mixer. Gradually beat in the sugar until smooth. Beat in the egg yolks, one at a time. Blend in the melted chocolate. Slowly mix in the pecans, vanilla, and spices. Gently fold in the flour in four batches (the batter will be very thick and dense).

4. Using an electric mixer, beat the egg whites with the salt and cream of tartar until medium peaks form. Gently fold one fourth of the whites into the batter to lighten it; then fold in the remaining whites. Divide the batter among the prepared cake pans, spreading it evenly.

5. Bake the cake layers until a toothpick inserted in the center comes out clean, 35 to 40 minutes. Run a knife around the edge of each cake. Let them stand 10 minutes, then invert the cakes onto racks. Cool to room temperature. (The cake layers can be prepared 2 weeks ahead. Wrap them tightly in plastic wrap, then aluminum foil, and freeze. Bring to refrigerator temperature before using. It will take about 24 hours to thaw in the refrigerator.)

6. Prepare the buttercream: Stir the sugar and corn syrup in a medium-size heavy saucepan over medium heat until the mixture boils. Cook 1 minute, and remove from the heat.

7. Beat the egg yolks with an electric mixer on medium speed until they are pale and thick. Gradually beat in the hot sugar syrup, and continue beating until the mixture is completely cool, about 5 minutes.

8. Beat in the butter one piece at a time, incorporating each piece completely before adding the next. Blend in the chocolate, then the rum. (The buttercream can be made 2 days ahead; cover with plastic wrap and refrigerate. Let stand at room temperature to soften before spreading, 30 minutes to 1 hour.)

9. Set aside ½ cup of the buttercream. Set one cake layer, flat side up, on a rack. Spread it with half of the remaining buttercream. Top with the second cake layer (flat side up), and spread it with the remaining buttercream. Top with the third cake layer (flat side up). Use the reserved ½ cup of buttercream to fill in the "seams" where the layers meet. Wrap the cake loosely in foil and freeze until the buttercream is firm, about 2 hours.

10. Prepare the glaze: Stir the chocolate, butter, honey, and coffee powder together in the top of a double boiler over gently simmering water. Cook until the mixture is smooth and shiny, 4 to 5 minutes. Remove the pan from the heat, and stir until the glaze is thickened, about 5 minutes; do not allow it to set.

11. Pour three quarters of the glaze over the top of the cake. Carefully and quickly tilt the cake back and forth so the glaze coats the sides. Smooth the sides with a spatula, adding some of the remaining glaze where necessary. Refrigerate the cake until the glaze is set, 2 hours or longer. (The cake can be glazed 1 to 2 days in advance. Cover it with plastic wrap and aluminum foil after the glaze is set. The cake can also be frozen; bring to refrigerator temperature before using. It will take about 24 hours to thaw in the refrigerator.) Decorate the cake with the ribbons.

Serves 12 to 14

WHITE AND DARK CHOCOLATE RIBBONS

Special equipment: Pasta machine; rimless baking sheet

7 ounces white chocolate, broken into pieces
½ cup light corn syrup
7 ounces semisweet chocolate, broken into pieces

1. Melt the white chocolate in the top of a double boiler over gently simmering water; stir until smooth. Stir in ¼ cup of the syrup. Pour the mixture onto a rimmed baking sheet and refrigerate until firm, 30 to 40 minutes.

2. Transfer the white chocolate to a work surface and knead it until it is pliable, 3 to 4 minutes. Shape it into a ball, wrap in plastic

AT THE MARKET

White chocolate can be temperamental to work with. I have found Nestlé Ice Caps to be a commercial brand that works well.

wrap, and let it stand at room temperature for 1 hour.

3. Repeat with the semisweet chocolate.

4. Cut the white chocolate into four pieces. Flatten one piece into a rectangle. Turn a pasta machine to its widest setting, and run the chocolate through three times, folding into thirds before each run.

5. Adjust the machine to the next narrower setting. Run the chocolate through the machine without folding. If the chocolate is more than $^1/_{16}$ inch thick, run it through the next narrower setting. Lay that piece on a rimless baking sheet. Repeat the flattening, folding, and rolling with the remaining pieces.

6. Repeat with the semisweet chocolate.

7. Cut four 8 x 1-inch strips from the white chocolate and four 8 x ½-inch strips from the semisweet chocolate. Center the dark chocolate strips on the white chocolate strips to form four ribbons. Run one ribbon from the base of the cake to the center. Arrange the remaining three ribbons equidistant from each other in the same fashion.

8. Cut ten 6½ x 1-inch strips from the white chocolate and ten 6½ x ½-inch strips from the semisweet chocolate. Center the dark chocolate strips on the white chocolate strips to form ten ribbons.

9. Cut the ends off two ribbons on the diagonal. Starting at the center, drape the ribbons over the top and sides of the cake to form "trailers." Fold the remaining eight ribbons in half, layered side out. Cut the ends into V shapes. Arrange the ribbon halves with the V shapes at the center of the cake to form a bow.

10. Cut one 3 x 1-inch strip of white chocolate and one 3 x ½-inch strip of semisweet chocolate. Center the dark chocolate strip on the white chocolate strip. Fold in the ends and pinch to resemble a knot, and place it in the center of the bow. Transfer the cake to a platter. (The ribbons can be prepared 1 day ahead and refrigerated. The cake with the ribbons can also be wrapped in plastic wrap and then with foil and frozen several weeks. Thaw the cake in the refrigerator for 24 hours, then bring it to room temperature before serving.)

Chocolate Apricot Pecan Torte

This is another special cake that graced a cover of *Bon Appétit* magazine.

Special equipment: 8½-inch springform pan

Cake
⅓ cup cognac
1¼ cups (about 6 ounces) dried apricots, cut into ¼-inch pieces
⅔ cup plus 3 tablespoons dry bread crumbs
¾ cup (1½ sticks) unsalted butter, at room temperature
1 cup sugar
5 large eggs, at room temperature
6 ounces semisweet chocolate, melted and cooled
1½ teaspoons vanilla extract
1½ cups coarsely chopped pecans
1 tablespoon all-purpose flour

Icing
½ cup unsweetened cocoa powder
½ cup sugar
½ cup heavy or whipping cream
4 tablespoons (½ stick) unsalted butter, cut into small pieces

Glaze
2 tablespoons cognac, or as needed
½ cup apricot jam
½ cup pecan halves (optional)

Garnish
Apricot Roses (recipe follows)
Chocolate Leaves (recipe follows)

1. Prepare the cake layer: Heat the cognac in a medium-size saucepan over medium heat until just hot. Remove it from the heat and mix in the apricots. Let the apricots soak for 15 minutes, then strain them, reserving any soaking liquid for the glaze.

2. Position a rack in the center of the oven and preheat the oven to 375° F. Butter an 8½-inch springform pan and dust it with 3 tablespoons of the bread crumbs.

3. Using an electric mixer on medium speed, cream the butter until it is light and fluffy. Gradually beat in the sugar. Beat in the eggs one

A COOK'S REFLECTIONS

I have lost track of how many of these cakes I have made. Once for a demonstration, my staff and I prepared eight of them in one week! The following schedule makes it easy to prepare one or more of these tortes: Bake the cake layer the first day; ice and glaze the cake the next day. Then prepare the roses and leaves the following day. The cake holds up beautifully in the refrigerator, fully decorated, for 1 to 2 days.

at a time. The mixture may look curdled. Add the chocolate and vanilla. Mix in the remaining ⅔ cup bread crumbs. Combine the pecans and flour in a small bowl and blend into the batter. Fold in the apricots.

4. Spoon the batter into the prepared pan, and bake until a toothpick inserted in the center comes out clean, about 50 minutes. Cool the cake in the pan on a rack.

5. Run a knife around the cake, and invert it onto a platter.

6. Prepare the icing: Stir all the ingredients together in the top of a double boiler placed over simmering water, and cook until the mixture is shiny and smooth, about 5 minutes. Cool the icing, stirring occasionally, for 5 minutes.

7. Slide sheets of waxed paper under the edges of the cake. Pour the icing over the cake, carefully and quickly tilting the cake to cover it evenly. Using a thin flat spatula, spread the icing over the top and sides of the cake. Refrigerate until the icing is firm, 1 hour.

8. Prepare the apricot glaze: Add enough cognac to the soaking liquid reserved from the apricots to measure 2 tablespoons. Combine it with the jam in a small heavy saucepan. Stir over medium-low heat until liquified, 1 to 2 minutes. Strain the mixture through a fine-mesh sieve into a small bowl. Cool until tepid, about 5 minutes.

9. When the icing is firm, pour the glaze over the top of the cake. Using a thin metal spatula, spread it out evenly (do not let any drip down the sides). Arrange the pecans around the edge of the cake, ends touching. Discard the waxed paper, and refrigerate the cake until the glaze is set.

10. Arrange the Apricot Roses in the center of the torte. Place a large Chocolate Leaf between the flowers, and place a smaller leaf between the large leaves. (The cake can be prepared 1 to 2 days ahead and kept very loosely covered with aluminum foil in the refrigerator.) Let stand at room temperature 1 hour before serving.

Serves 12

APRICOT ROSES

12 moist dried apricots (see Index)

1. Roll each apricot out, sticky side down, between two sheets of waxed paper to a thickness of ¹/₁₆ inch.

2. Roll one apricot up tightly, sticky side in, to form the tight center bud of a rose. Wrap another apricot around the bud, sticky side in, pressing gently to adhere. Repeat with two more apricots, overlapping half of each previous one. Gently bend the top of the outer three apricots outward to form petals.

3. Push a toothpick horizontally through the base of the rose. Cut off any apricot below the toothpick to form a flat base. Repeat with the remaining apricots.

4. Place the roses on a plate and freeze for 30 minutes. (The apricot roses can be prepared 3 days ahead. Cover tightly and refrigerate.) Discard the toothpicks before arranging the roses on the cake.

Makes 3 roses

CHOCOLATE LEAVES

3 ounces semisweet chocolate, melted
3 large lemon or camellia leaves with stems
3 medium lemon or camellia leaves with stems

1. Spread melted chocolate over the veined side of each leaf reaching almost, but not quite, to the edges of each leaf. Place them on a flat plate, chocolate side up.

2. Freeze the leaves until just firm, about 10 minutes. Starting at the stem end, gently peel the leaf away from the chocolate, refreezing it briefly if the chocolate leaf is too soft to peel easily. (The chocolate leaves can be prepared 1 week ahead; wrap tightly and refrigerate.)

Makes 6 leaves

AT THE MARKET

Lemon and camellia leaves can be bought from a florist. Check with your local shop; if they aren't stocked, they can be ordered.

Tea Cake with Lemon Custard Icing and Fresh Berries

This is a glorious cake—light, delicate, and flavored generously with lemon. The sponge-type cake is baked in a tube pan, then split into layers and coated with a creamy lemon custard icing. I like to serve this dessert garlanded with fresh berries and garnished with lemon balm leaves.

A COOK'S REFLECTIONS

Lemon balm is a vigorous herb that resembles mint and has a strong lemon taste and aroma. A perennial, it is as easy to grow as mint, and it is great as a garnish for this lemon cake or to use in lemonade or iced tea.

Special equipment: 10-inch tube pan

Cake

9 large egg whites, at room temperature
1 teaspoon cream of tartar
⅛ teaspoon salt
5 large egg yolks, at room temperature
1½ cups sugar
1 cup cake flour, sifted 5 times
2½ teaspoons grated lemon zest

Custard Icing

1 envelope unflavored gelatin
½ cup fresh lemon juice
3½ cups heavy or whipping cream
5 large egg yolks, at room temperature
¾ cup sugar
2 teaspoons grated lemon zest

Garnish

Fresh lemon balm or lemon leaves (optional)
3 cups fresh berries (blueberries, raspberries, and strawberries)

1. Position a rack in the center of the oven and preheat the oven to 200° F.

2. Prepare the cake: Grease and flour a 10-inch tube pan.

3. Using an electric mixer, beat the egg whites until frothy. Add the cream of tartar and salt, and beat until the whites are stiff but not dry.

4. In another bowl beat the yolks until they are pale yellow and thick. Gradually add the sugar, and beat until the mixture is pale yellow and a slowly dissolving ribbon forms when the beaters are lifted.

5. Gently fold half the whites into the yolks, then gently fold in the flour. Fold in the remaining whites and the lemon zest. Pour the batter into the prepared pan, and bake 15 minutes.

6. Increase the heat to 225° F and bake another 15 minutes. Increase the heat to 250° F and bake another 15 minutes. Increase the heat to 275° F and bake another 15 minutes. Finally, increase the heat to 300° F and bake until the cake is springy to the touch, about 15 minutes. Cool the cake in the pan.

7. Remove the cake from the pan and carefully cut it into three even layers, using a serrated knife. Set the layers aside.

8. Prepare the custard icing: Sprinkle the gelatin over the lemon juice in a small bowl. Heat 1½ cups of the cream in the top of a double boiler placed over simmering water until just warm, 3 to 4 minutes.

9. Using an electric mixer, beat the egg yolks in a medium-size bowl until they are pale yellow. Gradually beat in the sugar, then blend in the warm cream. Return the mixture to the top of the double boiler. Stir over medium-high heat until the custard thickens and coats a spoon, about 10 minutes.

10. Mix in the softened gelatin and the lemon zest, and stir until the gelatin has dissolved. Refrigerate until chilled but not set. Whip the remaining 2 cups of cream until it forms soft peaks, and fold it into the chilled custard.

11. Assemble the cake, spreading each layer with a generous amount of custard. Spread the remaining custard in a swirling pattern over the top and sides of the cake. (The cake can be prepared 1 day ahead. Tent foil loosely over the cake so that you don't disturb the icing, and refrigerate.)

12. To serve, line a platter with lemon balm or lemon leaves. Carefully transfer the cake to the platter, using two spatulas as an aid. Spoon the berries onto the center of the cake and over the leaves. Let the cake stand at room temperature for 30 minutes before serving.

Serves 10

Chocolate Roulade with Walnut Rum Filling and Hot Fudge Sauce

Kathy Fleegler, a talented cooking teacher and caterer from Cleveland, Ohio, is a petite, energetic woman and a confessed chocoholic. She has created countless chocolate confections, but this roulade is one of her easiest and best!

A COOK'S REFLECTIONS

I especially like to serve this dessert for large buffets, since the recipe can be increased easily and both the roulade and the sauce can be assembled in advance. I usually slice the cake and arrange the pieces, overlapping, on a platter with a garnish of lemon leaves. For the Christmas holidays, I use holly sprigs instead of lemon leaves.

Special equipment: 15½ x 10½-inch jelly roll pan

Roulade

7 large eggs, separated
¾ cup granulated sugar
¼ cup unsweetened cocoa powder
1 teaspoon instant coffee powder
1 teaspoon vanilla extract
Pinch of salt
Confectioners' sugar

Filling

2 large egg yolks
2 tablespoons granulated sugar
½ tablespoon all-purpose flour
½ tablespoon cornstarch
6 tablespoons heavy or whipping cream
6 tablespoons milk
1½ tablespoons dark rum
8 tablespoons (1 stick) unsalted butter, at room temperature
6 tablespoons confectioners' sugar
1 cup walnuts, finely chopped
Confectioners' sugar, for garnish
Hot Fudge Sauce (recipe follows)

1. Prepare the roulade: Butter a 15½ x 10½-inch jelly roll pan. Line the bottom and sides with one long piece of aluminum foil. Butter and flour the foil. Set aside.

2. Preheat the oven to 375° F.

3. Place the egg yolks in a large mixing bowl, and with an electric mixer on medium speed, beat until pale yellow, about 2 minutes. Add half of the sugar and continue to beat until very thick, 2 minutes or longer. Reduce the speed to low and add the cocoa powder, instant coffee, and vanilla. Beat until just smooth, and set aside.

4. In another large mixing bowl, combine the egg whites and pinch of salt, and beat on high speed until they begin to form soft peaks. Reduce the speed to medium, gradually add the remaining sugar, and beat until the whites are just firm but not stiff.

5. Fold a quarter of the egg whites into the cocoa mixture to lighten the mixture. Then reverse the procedure, folding the entire lightened cocoa mixture into the remaining whites.

6. Transfer the batter to the prepared pan and spread it evenly with

a spatula. Bake the roulade until the top springs back when lightly touched, 20 to 30 minutes.

7. While the cake is baking, lay a clean kitchen towel on a large flat surface and dust it heavily with confectioners' sugar.

8. When the cake is done, remove the pan from the oven and immediately invert the cake onto the prepared towel. Carefully peel off the foil, and roll up the cake and towel together, starting from a long side. Cool completely.

9. While the roulade is cooling, prepare the filling: Combine the egg yolks, sugar, flour, and cornstarch in a medium-size saucepan. Whisk in the cream, milk, and rum. Place the saucepan over medium heat and whisk constantly until the mixture bubbles and has thickened, 2 to 3 minutes. Pour this mixture into a bowl and cover the surface of the mixture directly with plastic wrap. Let it cool completely.

10. Beat the butter and confectioners' sugar in a mixing bowl until light and fluffy. Fold in the walnuts, and then fold in the cooled egg yolk mixture. Cover and refrigerate the mixture until it is chilled but not too firm to spread, 20 to 30 minutes.

11. Unroll the roulade. Spread it generously with the walnut filling, and then roll it up again. Place the roulade in the refrigerator, and chill it until the filling has set, 1 to 2 hours. (The roulade can be made 1 day ahead; cover it with a towel and plastic wrap and refrigerate.)

12. To serve, sprinkle the roulade with confectioners' sugar, and cut it on an angle into 10 slices. Place the Hot Fudge Sauce in a bowl. Serve each slice of the roulade ladled with some of the fudge sauce.

Serves 10

HOT FUDGE SAUCE

4 tablespoons (½ stick) unsalted butter
4 ounces unsweetened chocolate
1½ cups sugar
¼ cup light corn syrup
1 can (13 ounces) evaporated milk

In a medium-size heavy saucepan, melt the butter and chocolate over medium heat. Stir in the sugar and corn syrup. Slowly add the evaporated milk. Cook, stirring often, until the sugar has dissolved and the mixture is thick, about 20 minutes. Serve warm. (The sauce can be made 4 to 5 days in advance. Cool, cover, and refrigerate; reheat before using.)

Makes about 2 cups

Walnut Orange Cake with Orange Peel Confetti

This tall stately cake stands almost six inches high. Flavored with ground nuts and orange zest, it is extremely moist and light. My students tell me that this dessert reminds them of carrot cake in texture, appearance, and popularity.

Special equipment: Three 9-inch straight-sided round cake pans

Cake
8 tablespoons (1 stick) unsalted butter, at room temperature
½ cup vegetable oil
2 cups sugar
5 large eggs, separated, at room temperature
1 teaspoon baking soda
2 cups all-purpose flour
1 cup buttermilk
1 teaspoon vanilla extract
1¾ cups ground walnuts
2 tablespoons grated orange zest

Icing
1 package (8 ounces) cream cheese, at room temperature
6 tablespoons (¾ stick) unsalted butter, at room temperature
3 cups confectioners' sugar
1 tablespoon fresh orange juice
2 teaspoons grated orange zest
1 cup chopped walnuts

Garnish
8 walnut halves
Candied Orange Peel (see Index)

1. Position a rack in the center of the oven and preheat the oven to 350° F.

THE RIGHT EQUIPMENT
For this cake to look its best, it is important to use cake pans with straight sides. Most cake pans have sides that slant outward slightly. Professional cake pans have perfectly straight sides. They are usually available in shops that sell cake decorating supplies and in restaurant supply stores.

A COOK'S REFLECTIONS

This cake travels well and feeds a
crowd. I especially like to take it
on summer picnics or autumn tailgates.

2. Prepare the cake: Butter and flour three 9-inch round cake pans. Line the bottom of each with a round of waxed paper. Butter and flour the paper.

3. With an electric mixer, cream the butter and oil until smooth. Gradually beat in the sugar until smooth. Add the egg yolks and beat well to incorporate.

4. On slow speed, add the baking soda and flour. Then add the buttermilk, vanilla, walnuts, and orange zest.

5. Beat the egg whites until they form stiff peaks but are still moist. Fold the whites into the batter in three equal but separate additions.

6. Divide the batter evenly among the prepared pans. Bake the cake layers until they are golden and the cake springs back when touched gently, about 25 minutes. Remove the pans from the oven, run a knife around the edge of each cake, and unmold the layers immediately onto racks to cool.

7. Prepare the icing: With an electric mixer, cream together the cream cheese and butter until softened. Gradually add the confectioners' sugar, beating until smooth. Add the orange juice and orange zest, and mix well.

8. Place a cake layer on a large sheet of aluminum foil. Spread the layer evenly with ½ cup of the icing. Then sprinkle half the chopped walnuts over the icing. Repeat with the second layer. Then top with the final layer flat side down, and using an icing spatula, spread the remaining icing evenly and smoothly over the sides and top of the cake.

9. Place the walnut halves evenly around the top edge of the cake. Arrange the orange peel between the walnuts. Keep refrigerated until ready to serve. (The cake can be prepared to this point 1 to 2 days in advance; tent loosely with aluminum foil and refrigerate.)

Serves 12

FIVE FAVORITE CHEESECAKES

AT THE MARKET

Chestnut purée and whole chestnuts packed in water are available
in specialty food stores and in
some grocery stores. Faugier, a
French brand that is widely available, packages both chestnut
purée and whole chestnuts of good
quality.

Chocolate-Glazed Chestnut Rum Cheesecake

This unusual cheesecake—lightly flavored with chestnut purée and covered with a rich dark chocolate glaze—is not as sweet as most cheesecakes. It is a dessert I use for very special occasions.

Special equipment: 9-inch springform pan; pastry bag fitted with a medium star tip; small ovenproof dish such as a custard cup or ramekin; toothpicks

Crust
1 cup graham cracker crumbs
5 tablespoons unsalted butter, melted

Filling
1½ pounds (3 large packages) cream cheese, at room temperature
¾ cup sugar
1 can (15½ ounces) sweetened chestnut purée
3 tablespoons dark rum
4 large eggs, lightly beaten

Glaze and Garnish
6 ounces semisweet chocolate
4 tablespoons (½ stick) unsalted butter, cut into small pieces
1¼ cups heavy or whipping cream
6 canned whole chestnuts in water, drained and patted dry

1. Prepare the crust: Place the graham cracker crumbs in the bottom of a 9-inch springform pan. Pour in the melted butter and mix well with a fork until all the crumbs are thoroughly moistened. Use your fingers to firmly pack the crumbs evenly on the bottom of the pan. Set the pan aside.

2. Position a rack in the center of the oven and preheat the oven to 325° F.

3. Prepare the filling: Place the cream cheese in the bowl of an electric mixer, and with the mixer on medium speed, cream the

cheese, then gradually pour in the sugar. Add the chestnut purée and continue to mix until the mixture is smooth. Beat in the rum. Finally add the eggs, and mix only until incorporated.

4. Pour the filling into the prepared springform pan, and place it in the oven. Fill a small ovenproof ramekin three-quarters full with water and place it on a shelf below the cheesecake. (This helps prevent cracking during the baking process.) Bake for 45 minutes. Then turn the oven off but leave the cheesecake in the oven with the door shut for 30 minutes more. Remove the cheesecake and let it cool to room temperature. Cover and refrigerate for 6 hours or overnight. When it has chilled, run a knife around the edge of the cheesecake and remove the rim. (Do not remove the bottom of the pan.)

5. To glaze the cooled cheesecake, melt 4 ounces of the chocolate along with the butter and ¼ cup of the cream in the top of a double boiler placed over simmering water. Stir until the mixture is smooth and shiny, 4 to 5 minutes. Remove the pan from the heat and let the glaze cool until it is still warm to the touch but not hot, 5 to 10 minutes. Carefully pour the glaze over the cheesecake, and tipping the cake back and forth, coat the top and sides of the cake. Use a spatula to smooth the glaze around the sides of the cake.

6. Refrigerate until the glaze is set, 30 to 45 minutes. (The cheesecake can be made to this point up to 2 days ahead. Keep it covered and refrigerated.)

7. One hour before serving, remove the cheesecake from the refrigerator. (This brings out the flavor more.)

8. To decorate the cake, melt the remaining 2 ounces of chocolate in the top of a double boiler placed over simmering water. Stick a toothpick into a chestnut. Tip the pan and swirl the chestnut in the chocolate so that half of it is coated. Place the chestnut on a plate covered with a sheet of waxed paper. Coat the remaining chestnuts in this way, and refrigerate until the chocolate is firm, 30 minutes or less.

9. Several minutes before serving, whip the remaining 1 cup cream until firm. Place it in a pastry bag fitted with a star tip, and pipe a border of rosettes on top of the cake. Then arrange the chestnuts evenly on the whipped-cream border.

Serves 10

THE RIGHT EQUIPMENT

You can create all kinds of great designs by using a pastry bag. A good one, plus two pastry tips should cost under $10. I always encourage my students to buy a 14- to 16-inch pastry bag lined in plastic, and one medium and one large star tip.

The best way to become familiar with using a pastry bag is to practice. Drop one of the star tips into the bag so it protrudes from the opening. Fill a bag half full with solid vegetable shortening. Twist the top of the bag so it presses all the shortening to the bottom. Practice piping onto a sheet of wax paper. Pipe straight lines to get the feel of the bag; make circular swirls to form rosettes. Refill the bag with shortening as needed.

When you have completed your practice session, just scoop all the shortening back into the can. Rinse out the bag with hot water and detergent.

Pumpkin Cheesecake

My family likes this dessert so well that it has replaced pumpkin pie at our Thanksgiving table!

Special equipment: 9-inch springform pan; pastry bag fitted with a small star tip

Crust
1 cup finely ground graham cracker crumbs
½ cup finely ground gingersnap crumbs
5 tablespoons unsalted butter, melted

Filling
1 pound cream cheese, at room temperature
1 cup sour cream
1 cup sugar
1 can (1 pound) unsweetened, unseasoned pumpkin purée
¾ teaspoon ground cinnamon
¼ teaspoon ground cloves
2 tablespoons bourbon
4 large eggs, lightly beaten

Garnish
1 cup heavy or whipping cream
⅓ cup pecan halves, preferably small pecans

1. Prepare the crust: Toss the graham cracker crumbs and the gingersnap crumbs together in a medium-size bowl. Transfer the crumbs to a 9-inch springform pan and pour in the melted butter. Mix well with a fork until the crumbs are thoroughly moistened. Use your fingers to firmly pack the crumbs evenly on the bottom and halfway up the sides of the pan. Set the pan aside.

2. Position a rack in the center of the oven and preheat the oven to 350° F.

3. Prepare the filling: In the bowl of an electric mixer on medium speed, cream the cream cheese, sour cream, and sugar until smooth. Add the pumpkin, cinnamon, cloves, and bourbon, and beat until well incorporated, 1 minute. Add the eggs and beat just until mixed.

4. Pour the filling into the prepared pan. Bake 35 minutes, then turn off the oven but leave the cheesecake in the oven with the door shut 30 minutes more.

AS A VARIATION

Being a Southerner, I like to use bourbon in this dessert, but an equal amount of dark rum or cognac could be substituted.

AT THE MARKET

Ground espresso (not instant) is necessary for this recipe. Medaglia d'Oro is a good brand that is widely available.

5. Remove the cheesecake from the oven and let it cool at room temperature. Cover and refrigerate for 6 hours or overnight. (The cheesecake can be made 1 day in advance and kept refrigerated.)

6. When you are ready to serve it, run a sharp knife around the edge of the cheesecake and remove the rim. (Do not remove the bottom.) Whip the cream until stiff, and place it in a pastry bag fitted with a star tip. Pipe a border of whipped cream around the top of the cake. Then pipe a lattice design within the border of whipped cream. Place a pecan half at each point where the rows of cream intersect.

Serves 10

Espresso Cheesecake with a Chocolate Almond Crust

Flavored with freshly brewed espresso and semisweet chocolate, this cheesecake is a good dessert to offer when you are planning an Italian menu. A large platter of homemade pasta, a salad, hot crusty Italian bread, and this cheesecake would make a wonderful buffet.

Special equipment: 9½-inch springform pan; pastry bag fitted with a large star tip

Crust
1 cup finely ground plain chocolate cookie wafers
1 cup ground toasted almonds (see Index)
4 tablespoons (½ stick) unsalted butter, melted

Filling
6 tablespoons finely ground espresso coffee beans
½ cup water
1 pound cream cheese, at room temperature
1 cup sugar
3 ounces semisweet chocolate, melted
1¼ cups sour cream
4 large eggs, lightly beaten
1 cup heavy or whipping cream

Garnish
3 ounces semisweet chocolate
Confectioners' sugar

A COOK'S REFLECTIONS

I have a small box of 1½-inch cutters in heart, diamond, leaf, triangle, and other shapes that I use for cutting decorative shapes from chocolate. The box is labeled Hors d'Oeuvre and Canape Cutters, but they work well for chocolate, too. If you don't have special cutters, a sharp paring knife will do. Outline, then cut all the way through the chocolate to make a design.

1. Prepare the crust: Toss the wafer crumbs and ground almonds together in a medium-size bowl. Transfer the mixture to a 9½-inch springform pan and pour in the melted butter. Mix well with a fork until the crumb mixture is thoroughly moistened. Use your fingers to firmly pack the crumb mixture evenly on the bottom and halfway up the sides of the pan. Set the pan aside.

2. Position a rack in the center of the oven and preheat the oven to 350° F.

3. Prepare the filling: Brew the espresso with the water. (You can use an automatic drip coffee maker. Place the ground coffee in a filter-lined chamber and then add the water to the water chamber and process.) You should have ⅓ cup brewed coffee; add more water to make this amount if you do not have enough, or pour off any excess.

4. Place the cream cheese in the bowl of an electric mixer, and with the mixer on medium speed, add the sugar in a thin stream, beating until the mixture is smooth and creamy. On slow speed add the brewed coffee, and mix until just incorporated. Then add the melted chocolate and mix until smooth. Finally beat in the sour cream until smooth.

5. Add the eggs and beat only until well incorporated. Pour the mixture into the prepared pan and bake 45 minutes. Then turn off the oven and leave the cheesecake in the oven with the door shut for 30 minutes. Remove the cheesecake from the oven and let it cool to room temperature. Cover and refrigerate it for 6 hours or overnight. (The cheesecake can be made 1 day ahead and kept refrigerated.)

6. One hour before serving, run a knife around the edge of the cheesecake and remove the rim. (Do not remove the bottom). Whip the cream until it is firm. Using a pastry bag fitted with a large star tip, pipe a decorative cream border around the top of the cake. Tent loosely with aluminum foil and refrigerate.

7. To garnish the cheesecake, melt the chocolate in the top of a double boiler placed over simmering water. When it is smooth and shiny, pour the chocolate onto a baking sheet and spread it out to form a thin layer about $1/16$ to ⅛ inch thick. Refrigerate until firm and no longer shiny, 10 to 15 minutes.

8. Remove the chocolate from the refrigerator, and using a small paring knife, cut out six decorative leaf shapes (or heart, triangle, or diamond shapes, if desired). Arrange the chocolate leaves on the whipped cream border. Sprinkle a little confectioners' sugar on the center of the cake just before serving.

Serves 10

AS A VARIATION

Although the peach brandy adds a nice touch to this cheesecake, if you don't have any on hand you can substitute 1 tablespoon of lemon juice.

Peaches and Cream Cheesecake

Mimi Sheraton once wrote in one of her *New York Times* columns that "certain foods complement each other so well that the mention of one automatically suggests the other." One combination that falls into that category is peaches and cream. Nothing could be better than a cheesecake with these two great flavors!

It is essential that this cheesecake have a long chilling period because the filling is so creamy. It is best made a day in advance.

Special equipment: 8½-inch springform pan; pastry bag fitted with a medium star tip

Crust
1 cup graham cracker crumbs
4 tablespoons (½ stick) unsalted butter, melted

Filling
1 jar (10 ounces) peach preserves
1 teaspoon grated lemon zest
2 tablespoons peach brandy
1½ pounds (3 large packages) cream cheese, at room temperature
¾ cup sugar
1 tablespoon all-purpose flour
2 large whole eggs
2 large egg yolks
¾ cup sour cream

Garnish
¾ cup heavy or whipping cream
1 pound peaches
2 teaspoons fresh lemon juice
2 tablespoons confectioners' sugar

1. Prepare the crust: Place the graham cracker crumbs in the bottom of an 8½-inch springform pan. Pour in the melted butter and mix well with a fork until the crumbs are thoroughly moistened. Use

your fingers to firmly pack the crumbs evenly on the bottom of the pan. Set the pan aside.

2. Position a rack in the center of the oven and preheat the oven to 375° F.

3. Prepare the filling: Combine the peach preserves, lemon zest, and peach brandy in a medium-size saucepan and place over medium heat. Heat, stirring, just until the mixture has liquified. Set aside.

4. With an electric mixer on medium speed, beat the cream cheese in a large bowl until fluffy. Then gradually add the sugar and the flour, and beat until well incorporated.

5. Combine the whole eggs and the yolks in a small bowl, and beat lightly. With the mixer on slow speed, add the sour cream and the reserved peach flavoring to the cream cheese. Then add the eggs, and beat just until well incorporated.

6. Pour the filling into the prepared pan, and bake for 40 minutes. Then turn the oven off and leave the cheesecake in the oven with the door shut for an additional 30 minutes. Remove the cheesecake, let it cool to room temperature, and then refrigerate it overnight. (The cheesecake can be made 1 day ahead and kept refrigerated.)

7. When you are ready to serve the cheesecake, run a knife around the edge of the cheesecake and remove the rim. (Do not remove the bottom.) To garnish the cheesecake, beat the cream until firm, and using a pastry bag fitted with a star tip, pipe a border of rosettes around the top of the cake.

8. Peel the peaches and slice them very thin. Toss the peaches in a mixing bowl with the lemon juice and the sugar. Using a slotted spoon, mound the peaches in the center of the cheesecake.

Serves 10

Christmas Cheesecake

This is a large cheesecake made with a pecan and graham cracker crumb crust. The cream cheese filling is baked with candied fruits and raisins. It is a wonderful make-ahead dessert to serve during the holidays—in fact, it works best if you make this cheesecake a day or two in advance.

A COOK'S REFLECTIONS

This dessert travels well and is nice to take to potlucks or family dinners during the holidays.

Special equipment: 10-inch springform pan; rimmed baking sheet

Crust

1 cup finely ground pecans
1 cup graham cracker crumbs
1 cup confectioners' sugar
8 tablespoons (1 stick) unsalted butter, melted

Filling

½ cup coarsely chopped mixed candied fruits
½ cup raisins
½ cup kirsch
1½ pounds (3 large packages) cream cheese, at room temperature
1 cup sugar
4 large eggs

Topping and Garnish

16 ounces sour cream
½ cup sugar
Pecan halves
Candied cherries

1. Prepare the crust: Toss the pecans, graham cracker crumbs, and confectioners' sugar in a medium-size bowl. Transfer the mixture to a 10-inch springform pan and pour in the melted butter. Mix well with a fork until the pecan mixture is thoroughly moistened. Use your fingers to firmly pack the crust evenly on the bottom and halfway up the sides of the pan. Set the pan aside.

2. Prepare the filling: Place the candied fruits and raisins in a small mixing bowl, and cover with the kirsch. Let the fruit marinate 1 hour or longer.

3. Position a shelf in the center of the oven and preheat the oven to 300° F.

4. In the bowl of an electric mixer, beat the cream cheese and sugar together until the mixture is smooth. Then beat in the eggs just until incorporated.

5. Drain the fruits, and fold them into the cream cheese mixture. Then pour the filling into the prepared pan.

6. Bake the cheesecake until firm, 50 to 55 minutes. (Place a rimmed baking sheet on the shelf below the cheesecake while it is baking to catch any batter drippings.) Remove the cheesecake from the oven, but leave the oven on.

7. Prepare the topping: Whisk the sour cream and sugar together in a small bowl. Then, using an icing spatula, spread the topping over the warm cheesecake. Return the cheesecake to the oven, and bake until the topping is set, about 10 minutes.

8. Remove the cheesecake from the oven and let it cool to room temperature. Then cover the cheesecake with plastic wrap, and refrigerate overnight. (The cheesecake is best made 1 to 2 days in advance and kept covered and refrigerated.)

9. To decorate the cheesecake, make a border of pecan flowers: Place a candied cherry 1 inch in from the top edge, and surround it with pecan halves. Continue until the border is complete.

Serves 12 to 14

TARTS, PIES & STRUDELS

I had far too many recipes in this category for inclusion in this book, and when it came time to make the final choices, I selected entries for one of two reasons. A dish had to be as unusual as the dramatic Cassis Walnut Tart or the delectable Raspberry Mousse Pie with a Brownie Fudge Crust, or it had to be a variation on a familiar theme, such as the Coconut Cream Mousse Pie in a delicate chocolate pecan crust or the Blueberry Strudels served with a tempting Cassis blueberry sauce. Making the selections was a challenge, but these recipes will ensure a stellar finale to any meal, no matter which one *you* choose.

TARTS AND PIES

Puff Pastry Heart Tarts

These golden flaky tarts are filled with fresh strawberries and whipped cream and then served on a bed of raspberry sauce. Beautiful and elegant, they make an impressive conclusion for a special dinner.

Pastry

1 recipe Quick Puff Pastry (see Index) or a good commercial
    brand
1 large egg
1 tablespoon water

Sauce

1 package (10 ounces) frozen raspberries in heavy syrup, thawed
1½ tablespoons fresh lemon juice
2 tablespoons sugar, or to taste

Filling

1 cup heavy or whipping cream
1½ tablespoons Grand Marnier
1½ tablespoons confectioners' sugar, plus extra for garnish
2 pints strawberries, rinsed, hulled, and cut into ½-inch pieces

1. Cut out a paper heart pattern measuring 5 inches across at the broadest point and 3¾ inches from the center indentation to the bottom tip.

2. Position a rack in the center of the oven and preheat the oven to 450° F.

3. Prepare the pastry hearts: Roll the dough out to form a 12-inch square about ¼ inch thick. Using the paper pattern as a guide, cut out six hearts. (Make one in each corner of the dough and two in the center.) With a small paring knife, make tiny ¼-inch slits around the outside edge of each heart to create a decorative border.

4. Place the pastries on a baking sheet. Blend the egg with the water, and brush the top and sides of the hearts with the egg mixture. Bake until puffed and golden, 15 to 20 minutes.

AT THE MARKET

If you do not have the time to make homemade puff pastry, try a good commercial variety. Just make certain you roll the dough out to a thickness of ¼ inch for the best results.

5. Remove the pastries from the oven and let them cool 5 minutes. Then split the hearts horizontally with a serrated knife. Scrape away and discard any uncooked dough from the inside of the pastry halves. (The pastry hearts can be baked early on the day they are to be used. Cool, cover with plastic wrap, and keep at room temperature.)

6. Prepare the sauce: Purée the berries and their syrup in a food processor or blender. Strain through a sieve to remove the seeds. Add the lemon juice and sugar to the sauce. (The sauce can be made 2 to 3 days in advance; cover and refrigerate. Bring to room temperature before using.)

7. Prepare the filling: Whip the cream until soft peaks form. Then gradually add the Grand Marnier and 1½ tablespoons confectioners' sugar, continuing to beat. Fold in the strawberries.

8. To serve, ladle the raspberry sauce onto six dessert plates. Place a pastry base on each plate, and spread it with filling. Place the pastry tops over the filling, and sprinkle with confectioners' sugar.

Serves 6

Hot Apricot Almond Tart

I like to serve this glazed apricot tart while it is still warm from the oven. Just to gild the lily, I top each slice with whipped cream.

Special equipment: 9-inch tart pan with removable bottom

Pastry Crust
1½ cups all-purpose flour
2 tablespoons confectioners' sugar
Pinch of salt
5 tablespoons unsalted butter, well chilled and cut into small pieces
2½ tablespoons solid vegetable shortening, well chilled
3 to 4½ tablespoons ice water

Filling
12 ounces dried apricots
¼ cup apricot preserves
½ teaspoon grated lemon zest
3 tablespoons unsalted butter
¼ cup sugar

Topping and Garnish

2 tablespoons unsalted butter
2 tablespoons sugar
1 tablespoon milk
¾ cup (2½ ounces) sliced almonds

1. Prepare the crust: Combine the flour, confectioners' sugar, and salt in a bowl. Cut in the butter and shortening with a pastry blender or two knives until the mixture resembles oatmeal flakes. Gradually add the water, mixing just until the dough holds together. Transfer the dough to a lightly floured surface. Using the heel of your hand, smear ¼ cup of dough at a time across the surface to form a 6-inch strip. Gather the dough together and repeat two more times. Gather the dough into a ball, and flatten it out to form a disk. Wrap it with plastic wrap and refrigerate it at least 1 hour or overnight.

The pastry dough can also be made in a food processor: Place the dry ingredients in the bowl, then add the butter and shortening. Process until the mixture resembles oatmeal flakes. With the machine still running, add the water slowly through the feed tube until a ball of dough forms. Wrap the dough and refrigerate as in the hand method.

The dough can be made 1 day in advance, or it can be frozen.

2. Roll the dough out on a lightly floured surface to form a circle 12 inches in diameter and ¼ inch thick. Mold the dough into a 9-inch tart pan. Trim the edge so you have ½ inch of dough extending over the sides of the pan. Fold the overhang in, and push it against the edge of the shell to reinforce the sides. Prick the bottom of the shell with a fork, and refrigerate the shell, covered, for 30 minutes.

3. Position a rack in the center of the oven and preheat the oven to 375° F.

4. Mold a sheet of aluminum foil inside the tart shell. Fill the foil with pie weights or dried beans, and bake for 8 minutes. Then remove the foil and weights and bake 10 minutes more. Remove the tart shell and set it aside, but leave the oven on.

5. Prepare the filling: Slice the apricots into halves if they are whole, and place them in a medium-size saucepan. Add enough water to cover by ½ inch, bring to a boil over medium heat, and simmer until the apricots are softened, 20 to 30 minutes. Drain well.

6. Heat the apricot preserves in a small saucepan over medium heat just to liquify. Stir in the lemon zest. Brush the bottom of the

AT THE MARKET

Try to buy dried apricots that are soft and moist for this recipe. Packaged commercial varieties are often very dry and discolored. I have the best luck purchasing good-quality apricots in bulk at health food stores or specialty food shops.

precooked tart shell with 2 tablespoons of this mixture. Then arrange the apricot halves, smooth side up, in overlapping circles in the tart shell.

7. Cut the butter into small pieces and place them over the filling. Sprinkle the sugar on top.

8. Bake the tart for 20 minutes.

9. While the tart is baking, prepare the almond topping: Combine the butter, sugar, milk, and almonds in a small saucepan over medium-high heat. Bring to a boil and boil until the sugar has dissolved, only 1 minute. Remove and reserve.

10. Remove the tart from the oven, and arrange the topping in a 1½-inch border around the top of the tart. Return the tart to the oven, and bake until the almonds are golden, about 10 minutes.

11. Remove the tart from the oven and let it cool for 10 minutes. Brush the apricots with the remaining 2 tablespoons of apricot preserves. Serve the tart warm.

Serves 6 to 8

Cassis Walnut Tart

Every time I'm in Paris I go to Fauchon, the celebrated food store on the Place de la Madeleine. With notebook in hand I walk through the store, sketching food presentations and taking notes on unusual dishes. On one such visit, I discovered their fabulous Cassis walnut tarts. When I returned home, I spent several weeks working in my own kitchen to reproduce them. The result was this recipe.

Special equipment: 9-inch tart pan with removable bottom

Pastry Crust
1¼ cups all-purpose flour
2 tablespoons confectioners' sugar
Pinch of salt
*5 tablespoons unsalted butter, well chilled and cut into small
     pieces*
*2½ tablespoons solid vegetable shortening, well chilled and cut
     into small pieces*
1 large egg yolk
3 tablespoons ice water

AT THE MARKET

Cassis is a liqueur made from black currants and produced in France. It is a rich deep purple color and has a slightly sweet taste.

Filling

5½ tablespoons unsalted butter
½ cup sugar
3 large eggs, separated, at room temperature
1 teaspoon vanilla extract
1 cup finely ground walnuts
2 tablespoons all-purpose flour
Pinch of cream of tartar

Glaze

1 cup crème de Cassis
2 tablespoons sugar
2 tablespoons cornstarch
2 tablespoons cold water
1½ tablespoons fresh lemon juice
1 cup walnut halves

1. Prepare the crust: Combine the flour, confectioners' sugar, and salt in a bowl. Cut in the butter and shortening with a pastry blender or two knives until the mixture resembles oatmeal flakes. Gradually add the egg yolk and ice water, mixing just until the dough holds together. Transfer the dough to a lightly floured surface. Using the heel of your hand, smear ¼ cup of the dough at a time across the surface to form a 6-inch-long strip. Gather the dough together and repeat two more times. Gather the dough into a ball, and flatten it to form a disk. Wrap it with plastic wrap and refrigerate it at least 1 hour or overnight.

The pastry dough can also be made in a food processor: Place the dry ingredients in the bowl, then add the butter and shortening. Process until the mixture resembles oatmeal flakes. With the machine still running, add the egg yolk and the water slowly through the feed tube until a ball of dough forms. Wrap the dough and refrigerate as in the hand method.

The dough can be made 1 day in advance, or it can be frozen.

2. Position a rack in the center of the oven and preheat the oven to 375° F.

3. Roll the dough out on a lightly floured surface to form a circle 12 inches in diameter and ¼ inch thick. Mold the dough into a 9-inch tart pan, and trim the edge so you have ½ inch of dough extending over the sides of the pan. Fold the overhang in, and push it against the edge of the shell to reinforce the sides. Pierce the bottom of the crust with a fork. Line the shell with aluminum foil and fill the foil

with pie weights or dried beans. Bake 10 minutes. Remove the foil and weights, and continue baking until the crust is golden brown, about 15 minutes more. Remove the shell from the oven, but leave the oven on.

4. Prepare the filling: Cream the butter in an electric mixer. Gradually beat in the sugar, egg yolks, and vanilla. Combine the walnuts and flour in a small bowl, and add them to the butter mixture. Using a clean dry beater, beat the egg whites and cream of tartar together in another bowl until stiff but not dry. Gently fold the whites into the walnut mixture.

5. Spread the filling in the crust. Bake until the filling is brown and slightly puffed, about 20 minutes. Cool the tart on a rack.

6. Make the glaze: Heat the crème de Cassis and sugar in the top of a double boiler placed over simmering water, stirring until the sugar dissolves. Combine the cornstarch, water, and lemon juice in a small bowl, stirring until the cornstarch dissolves. Add the cornstarch mixture to the Cassis. Cook, stirring, until the mixture thickens and coats the back of a spoon, about 8 minutes. Remove the glaze from the heat and let it cool for 5 minutes. Pour half the glaze over the top of the tart and set it aside to cool until the glaze thickens, about 1½ hours. Reheat the remaining glaze, stirring until it is of pouring consistency. Pour it over the tart, and let it stand 1½ hours more. (The tart can be prepared 1 day ahead. Store at room temperature.) Arrange the walnut halves around the top edge of the tart before serving.

Serves 6 to 8

AS A VARIATION

This tart can be made with pecans or almonds as well as walnuts. I use coarsely chopped pecans or almond slivers when I make these variations.

Chocolate Walnut Caramel Tart

This dessert is the creation of talented chef Joan Wyner. The tart is made with a butter crust that is baked until golden and then spread with a thin bittersweet chocolate filling. A creamy caramel walnut mixture is mounded over the chocolate layer. Served garnished with whipped cream, this pie is absolutely irresistible!

Special equipment: 9-inch tart pan with removable bottom; pastry bag fitted with a medium star tip; candy thermometer

Pastry Crust

1½ cups all-purpose flour

½ teaspoon salt

7½ tablespoons unsalted butter, well chilled and cut into small
  pieces

1 large egg, lightly beaten

1 tablespoon heavy or whipping cream

Filling

5 ounces bittersweet chocolate, broken into small chunks

1 tablespoon unsalted butter

Topping

2 ounces cream cheese, at room temperature

¼ cup sour cream

¾ cup sugar

6 tablespoons water

¼ teaspoon fresh lemon juice

3 tablespoons unsalted butter, cut into small pieces

2 cups very coarsely chopped walnuts

Garnish

1 cup heavy or whipping cream

1. Prepare the crust: Place the flour and salt in a bowl and cut in
the butter with a pastry blender or two knives until the mixture
resembles oatmeal flakes. Gradually work in the egg and cream,
mixing just until the dough holds together. Transfer the dough to a
lightly floured surface. Using the heel of your hand, smear ¼ cup of
the dough at a time across the work surface to form a 6-inch-long
strip. Gather the dough together and repeat two more times. Gather
the dough into a ball, and flatten it to form a disk. Wrap the dough
with plastic wrap, and refrigerate it at least 1 hour or overnight.

  The dough can also be made in a food processor: Place the dry
ingredients in the bowl and add the butter. Process until the mixture
resembles oatmeal flakes. With the machine still running, slowly add
the egg and cream through the feed tube until a ball of dough forms.
Wrap the dough and refrigerate it as in the hand method.

  The dough can be made 1 day in advance, or it can be frozen.

2. Position a rack in the center of the oven and preheat the oven to
375° F.

3. Roll the dough out on a floured work surface to form a circle 12
inches in diameter and ¼ inch thick. Mold the dough into a 9-inch

tart pan, leaving ½ inch of dough extending over the edge of the pan. Fold the overhang toward the inside edge of the pastry shell and push it against the shell to reinforce the sides. Line the crust with parchment or aluminum foil, and fill it with pie weights or dried beans. Bake the crust until it is set, about 10 minutes. Remove the lining and weights. Continue baking until the crust is brown, about 20 minutes. Remove the crust from the oven and let it cool to room temperature.

4. Prepare the chocolate filling: Melt the chocolate and butter together in the top of a double boiler over medium-high heat until the mixture is smooth and shiny. Pour the chocolate into the baked tart shell, and use a spatula to spread it evenly. Chill the shell in the freezer until the chocolate is firm, about 20 minutes.

5. Prepare the topping: Combine the cream cheese and sour cream in a bowl, and whisk until the mixture is smooth. Set aside.

6. Place the sugar, water, and lemon juice in a medium-size heavy saucepan over medium-high heat. Stir with a wooden spoon until the sugar has dissolved. Then continue to cook, without stirring, until the mixture caramelizes and reaches 300° F on a candy thermometer. Remove the pan from the heat, and stir in the cream cheese mixture with a wooden spoon. The mixture will bubble. Then add the butter all at once, and stir until the mixture is smooth and creamy. Add the walnuts, and pour the caramel mixture into the tart shell. Let it sit at room temperature until firm, 2 to 3 hours. (The tart can be made early in the morning on the day to be served.)

7. When you are ready to serve the tart, whip the cream until firm. Spoon it into a pastry bag fitted with a star tip, and pipe a 2-inch border of whipped cream around the top of the tart.

Serves 6 to 8

Deep-Dish Nectarine Pie

This deep-dish nectarine pie, made with a tender, flaky pastry, is served with lemon-flavored whipped cream. It is wonderful!

Special equipment: 8-inch square glass baking dish

AS A VARIATION

If nectarines are not available, you can make this pie with the same amount of peaches.

Pastry

2 cups all-purpose flour
1 teaspoon salt
1 cup (2 sticks) unsalted butter, chilled and cut into small pieces
2 large eggs
1 tablespoon heavy or whipping cream
1 teaspoon water

Filling

7 packed cups peeled and sliced nectarines (about 4½ pounds)
1 cup sugar
½ teaspoon grated lemon zest
4 tablespoons cornstarch

Garnish

1½ cups heavy or whipping cream
4 tablespoons confectioners' sugar
¼ teaspoon grated lemon zest

1. Prepare the pastry: Place the flour and salt in a mixing bowl. Cut in the butter with a pastry blender or two knives until the mixture resembles oatmeal flakes. Then mix in 1 of the eggs and the cream. Using the heel of your hand, smear 2 to 3 tablespoons of dough across a lightly floured work surface to form a 4- to 5-inch strip. Continue with the remaining dough until all the dough has been spread in this manner. Then gather the dough into a ball, flatten it to form a disk, wrap it in plastic wrap, and refrigerate for 30 minutes.

To make the dough in a processor, place the flour, salt, butter, 1 egg, and the cream in the bowl. Process, turning the machine on and off, until the mixture is crumbly and resembles oatmeal flakes. Then turn the dough out onto a lightly floured work surface and continue by spreading and smearing the dough as in the hand method.

2. After the dough has been chilled, roll it out on a lightly floured work surface to form a 12 x 8-inch rectangle. With a short side nearest you, fold the dough into thirds as for a business letter. Lift the dough off the work surface, scrape the surface clean, and reflour. Return the dough to the work surface with a short side nearest you. Repeat rolling and folding two more times. Wrap the dough tightly and refrigerate it at least 1 hour or overnight. (The dough can be made 1 to 2 days in advance to this point or it can be frozen.)

3. Prepare the filling: Combine the nectarine slices with the sugar and lemon zest in a large mixing bowl, and mix well. Let the mixture

marinate 15 minutes. Then pour off all the juices that have collected in the bowl. Add the cornstarch to the nectarines, and stir well to incorporate. Place the nectarine mixture in an 8-inch glass baking dish and spread it out evenly.

4. Lightly flour a 15-inch-long sheet of waxed paper and place the dough in the center of it. Cover the dough with another sheet of lightly floured waxed paper. Roll the dough out to form a 10-inch square about ¼ inch thick. Remove the top sheet of waxed paper, and then invert the dough over the dish with the nectarines. Carefully peel off the remaining sheet of waxed paper.

5. Using a pastry brush, moisten the rim of the baking dish with water. Press the edges of the dough over the rim, making certain the dough adheres well. Use the tines of a fork to make a crimped border.

6. Roll out the leftover dough and cut out decorative shapes (hearts, leaves, triangles). Garnish the top of the pie with the cutouts. Make four 1-inch slits in the top of the pastry to allow steam to escape. Beat the remaining egg and 1 teaspoon water together, and brush the pastry with the mixture. (The pie may be made several hours ahead to this point; keep covered and refrigerated.)

7. Position a rack in the center of the oven and preheat the oven to 425° F.

8. Bake the pie until the crust is a rich golden color, about 25 minutes. Remove it from the oven and allow it to cool 15 minutes or longer.

9. While the pie is cooling, whip the cream until it starts to mound. Then, continuing to beat, add the confectioners' sugar, a little at a time, and then the lemon zest. Beat until firm but not stiff.

10. Serve the pie while it is still warm, with a bowl of the whipped cream.

Serves 8

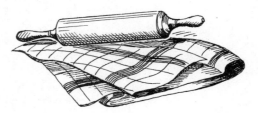

Old-Fashioned Peach Custard Pie

As a food writer, nothing pleases me more than the discovery of an old family recipe. One of my aunts, a talented cook herself, gave me this recipe, which has been in our family since the nineteenth century. Nothing could be simpler or more delicious than this dessert. Almost a hundred years old, it has endured the test of time!

Special equipment: Pastry bag fitted with a medium star tip

Pastry Crust
1½ cups all-purpose flour
3 tablespoons confectioners' sugar
¼ teaspoon salt
6 tablespoons (¾ stick) unsalted butter, chilled and cut into small pieces
2½ tablespoons solid vegetable shortening, chilled and cut into small pieces
About 4 tablespoons ice water

Filling
1 cup sugar
2 tablespoons all-purpose flour
½ teaspoon vanilla extract
2 tablespoons fresh lemon juice
4 tablespoons (½ stick) unsalted butter, melted
2 large eggs, lightly beaten
6 to 7 (about 1¾ pounds) ripe peaches, preferably freestone

Garnish
1 cup heavy or whipping cream (optional)

1. Prepare the crust: Combine the flour, confectioners' sugar, and salt in a bowl. Cut in the butter and shortening with a pastry blender or two knives until the mixture resembles oatmeal flakes. Gradually add the water, mixing just until the dough holds together. Transfer the dough to a lightly floured surface. Using the heel of your hand, smear ¼ cup of dough at a time across the surface to form a 6-inch-long strip. Gather the dough together and repeat two more times. Gather the dough into a ball and flatten it to a disk. Wrap it with plastic wrap and refrigerate at least 1 hour or overnight.

The pastry dough can also be made in a food processor: Place the dry ingredients in the bowl; then add the butter and shortening.

Process until the mixture resembles oatmeal flakes. With the machine still running, slowly add the water through the feed tube until a ball of dough forms. Wrap the dough and refrigerate as in the hand method.

The dough can be made a day in advance, or it can be frozen.

2. Roll the dough out between two pieces of floured waxed paper to form a circle 12 inches in diameter and ¼ inch thick. Remove one sheet of paper and invert the dough into a 9-inch pie plate. Mold it to fit the plate, then remove the second sheet of paper. Trim the dough, leaving a ½-inch overhang. Fold the overhang in and push it against the edge of the shell to reinforce the sides. Flute the edges. Refrigerate the pie shell while you prepare the filling.

3. Position a shelf in the center of the oven and preheat the oven to 325° F.

4. Prepare the filling: Combine the sugar, flour, vanilla, lemon juice, butter, and eggs in a mixing bowl, and mix just until smooth. Set aside.

5. Peel five of the peaches and cut them in half lengthwise. Remove the pits. Arrange the peach halves, pitted sides down, in the unbaked pie shell. Peel the remaining peaches and cut them into ½-inch slices. Place the peach slices in the crevices between the peach halves. Pour the egg mixture over the peaches. (If freestone peaches are not available, cut all peaches into ½-inch slices to make 3 cups. Fill the shell with sliced peaches and pour the egg mixture into the shell.)

6. Bake the pie for 1 hour. Then raise the heat to 350° F and bake until the custard is firm, 20 to 25 minutes. Remove the pie from the oven, and let it cool 30 minutes or longer. (The pie may be made several hours in advance to this point. Cover loosely with aluminum foil or plastic wrap and keep at room temperature.)

7. If you are using the cream, whip it until firm. Spoon the cream into a pastry bag fitted with a star tip, and pipe a border of whipped cream on top of the pie. Serve slightly warm or at room temperature. (This pie is best made and served on the same day.)

Serves 6 to 8

A COOK'S REFLECTIONS

In preparing the filling for this pie, you must use scalded milk. Scalding simply means heating the milk until bubbles form around the edge of the pan. Milk that is scalded should be warm, not hot.

This is a rich pie, so when I offer it as dessert at the end of a meal I cut it into smaller portions. Often, however, I will invite friends over just for dessert and serve this pie alone with cups of coffee. Then I offer larger portions.

Best-Ever Banana Cream Pie

The name of this recipe says it all. My students tell me that this pie is addictive.

Special equipment: 9-inch glass pie plate; pastry bag fitted with a small or medium star tip

Pastry Crust
1 cup sifted all-purpose flour
2 tablespoons confectioners' sugar
3 tablespoons unsalted butter, well chilled and cut into pieces
2½ tablespoons solid vegetable shortening, well chilled and cut into small pieces
About 3 tablespoons ice water

Filling
1 cup milk
4 large egg yolks
1 cup sugar
5 tablespoons all-purpose flour
3 tablespoons unsalted butter
Scant ¼ teaspoon ground cinnamon
1 tablespoon dark rum
2 bananas
Juice of ½ lemon
1 cup heavy or whipping cream

Garnish
1 cup heavy or whipping cream
2 tablespoons confectioners' sugar
1 tablespoon dark rum

1. Prepare the crust: Combine the flour and confectioners' sugar in a bowl. Cut in the butter and shortening with a pastry blender or two knives until the mixture resembles oatmeal flakes. Gradually add the water, mixing just until the dough holds together. Transfer the dough to a lightly floured surface. Using the heel of your hand, smear ¼ cup of dough at a time across the surface to form a 6-inch-long strip. Gather the dough together and repeat two more times. Gather the dough into a ball, and flatten it to form a disk. Wrap the dough with plastic wrap and refrigerate it at least 1 hour or overnight.

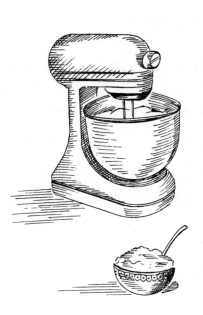

The pastry dough can also be made in a food processor: Place the dry ingredients in the bowl, then add the butter and shortening. Process until the mixture resembles oatmeal flakes. With the machine still running, slowly add the water through the feed tube until a ball of dough forms. Wrap the dough and refrigerate as in the hand method.

The dough can be made 1 day in advance, or it can be frozen.

2. Position a rack in the center of the oven and preheat the oven to 400° F.

3. On a lightly floured surface, roll out the dough to form a circle 12 inches in diameter and ¼ inch thick. Mold the dough into a 9-inch glass pie plate. Trim the dough, leaving a ½-inch overhang. Fold the overhang in and push it against the edge of the shell to reinforce the sides. Crimp to form a border. Prick the bottom of the dough with a fork. Mold a sheet of aluminum foil against the bottom and sides of the crust, and fill it with dried beans or pie weights.

4. Bake the pie shell for 10 minutes. Remove the foil and weights, and bake until the crust is a light golden color, 12 to 15 minutes more. Remove the crust and set it aside to cool.

5. Prepare the filling: Heat the milk in a medium-size saucepan over medium heat just until scalded. Remove from the heat. Beat the egg yolks in the bowl of an electric mixer on medium speed, and gradually add the sugar. Continue to beat until the mixture is thick and pale yellow, 3 to 4 minutes. Then beat in the flour. On slow speed, gradually pour in the hot milk.

6. Transfer the mixture to a medium-size heavy saucepan, and cook, stirring constantly, over medium-high heat. The mixture will start to thicken and appear to be lumpy. Bring the mixture to a boil, and boil, stirring the entire time, for 1 minute. Remove the pan from the heat, and continue to stir until the mixture is smooth. Then beat in the butter, a few pieces at a time. Stir in the cinnamon and rum. Let the mixture cool to room temperature.

7. Peel the bananas, slice them paper-thin, and toss them with the lemon juice. Whip the cream until it is firm but not stiff. Mix about one fourth of the whipped cream into the cooled egg mixture to lighten it, then fold the remaining cream into the egg mixture. Finally, drain the bananas and fold them into the mixture.

8. Fill the pastry shell with the banana cream mixture, and spread it out evenly.

9. To garnish the pie, whip the cream until it starts to mound, and then gradually add the confectioners' sugar and the rum. Using a pastry bag fitted with a star tip, pipe a lattice design on top of the pie. (The pie is best prepared early on the day it is to be served. Tent with aluminum foil and refrigerate until serving time.)

Serves 6 to 8

Raspberry Mousse Pie with a Brownie Fudge Crust

My husband thinks that every dessert should include raspberries, while I prefer chocolate as the quintessential flavor for sweet confections. This scrumptious pie satisfies both our cravings!

Special equipment: 9-inch metal pie plate

Crust
8 tablespoons (1 stick) unsalted butter, at room temperature
2 ounces unsweetened chocolate
½ teaspoon instant coffee powder
1 cup sugar
2 large eggs
½ teaspoon vanilla extract
½ cup all-purpose flour
¼ teaspoon salt
½ cup chopped walnuts

Filling
1 package (10 ounces) frozen raspberries in heavy syrup, thawed
2 large egg whites, at room temperature
2 tablespoons granulated sugar
1¼ cups heavy or whipping cream
3 tablespoons confectioners' sugar
2 teaspoons kirsch
1¼ cups fresh raspberries, rinsed and patted dry

Garnish
2-ounce piece of semisweet chocolate

1. Position a rack in the center of the oven and preheat the oven to 350° F. Butter a 9-inch metal pie plate, and line the bottom and sides of the plate with a sheet of aluminum foil. Butter the foil.

AS A VARIATION

When fresh raspberries are not available, I make this pie without them—the mousse is strongly flavored with the raspberry purée.

This brownie fudge crust is very versatile. It can be filled with scoops of coffee ice cream topped with Hot Fudge Sauce, or you could fill the shell with vanilla ice cream and top it with fresh strawberries. Let your imagination be your inspiration!

2. Prepare the crust: Combine 4 tablespoons of the butter, the chocolate, and coffee powder in the top of a double boiler placed over lightly boiling water. Stir constantly until the mixture is smooth and shiny, 4 to 5 minutes. Set the mixture aside to cool.

3. In an electric mixer (or by hand), cream the remaining 4 tablespoons butter and the sugar together until light and fluffy. Then add the eggs, and continue to beat until well incorporated. On slow speed, add the vanilla and the chocolate mixture. Combine the flour and salt in a small bowl, and slowly add to the batter.

4. Fold the nuts into the batter, and pour it into the prepared pie plate. Bake the crust until a toothpick inserted in the center comes out clean, 30 to 35 minutes. Remove the brownie crust from the oven, and while it is still hot, protecting your fingers with a clean kitchen towel or hot pad, gently press down against the center of the crust and then push out toward the edges to form a pie shell. Repeat the process several times, always pressing gently, until you have a shell about 1 inch deep.

5. Cool the pie shell completely, 40 minutes to 1 hour. Then, using the foil as an aid, lift the pie shell from the plate and peel off the foil. (The pie shell can be made 1 day in advance, covered with plastic wrap, and refrigerated until needed.)

6. Prepare the filling: Purée the raspberries and their syrup in a blender or food processor. Then strain the purée through a fine-mesh sieve into a heavy saucepan to remove the seeds. Reduce the purée over medium heat to ½ cup. This will take about 10 minutes. Watch carefully so the purée does not burn. Cool the reduced purée to room temperature, about 20 minutes.

7. Beat the egg whites until they begin to mound. Then gradually add the granulated sugar and continue to beat until the whites are just firm but still moist. Set them aside.

8. In another bowl, whip the cream until it starts to mound. Then slowly add the confectioners' sugar and the kirsch, and beat until the cream is quite firm. Fold in the cooled raspberry purée, and then fold in the egg whites and the fresh raspberries. Mound the raspberry mousse in the prepared crust. Use a spatula to make a swirl pattern in the mousse. (The pie may be prepared to this point several hours before serving; keep refrigerated.)

9. To garnish, shave some chocolate over the top of the pie.

Serves 8

Coconut Cream Mousse Pie

I have always loved coconut pies—in any way, shape, or form—but
this one made with a rich chocolate pecan crust is the ultimate!

Special equipment: 9-inch glass pie plate; pastry bag fitted with a
small or medium star tip

Crust
1 cup finely ground plain chocolate wafers
½ cup very finely chopped pecans
4 tablespoons (½ stick) butter, melted

Filling and Garnish
1 cup flaked sweetened coconut
2 teaspoons unflavored gelatin
2 tablespoons cold water
5 large egg yolks
¼ cup sugar
1 cup cream of coconut (see Index)
2 cups heavy or whipping cream
2 teaspoons vanilla extract

1. Position a rack in the center of the oven and preheat the oven to
350° F.

2. Prepare the crust: Toss the wafer crumbs and the pecans in a
medium-size bowl. Transfer the mixture to a 9-inch glass pie plate
and pour in the melted butter. Mix well with a fork until the crumb
mixture is thoroughly moistened. Use your fingers to firmly pack the
crumb mixture evenly on the bottom and sides of the pan. Bake the
crust 10 minutes, then cool on wire rack. Reduce the oven temperature to 250° F.

3. Prepare the filling: Spread the coconut out in a jelly roll pan or
on a baking sheet. Place it in the oven to dry, about 25 minutes. Set
the coconut aside to cool.

4. Combine the gelatin and cold water in a small bowl; set aside.

5. In a small mixing bowl, beat the egg yolks on medium speed.
Gradually add the sugar, and continue to beat until the mixture is
thick and lemon colored, 5 to 10 minutes. Reduce the speed to low,
and gradually add the cream of coconut. Transfer the mixture to the
top of a double boiler. Add the softened gelatin and cook, stirring

constantly, over simmering water until the mixture feels hot when tested on the inside of your wrist. Then chill the mixture in the refrigerator, stirring it occasionally, until it mounds when dropped from a spoon, about 1 hour.

6. Whip the cream until slightly thickened. Add the vanilla, and beat until soft peaks form.

7. With a whisk, beat the chilled egg mixture to soften. Reserve 1 cup of the whipped cream for the garnish, and fold the remaining cream, and then the cooled coconut, into the egg mixture. Spoon the filling into the prepared crust.

8. Spoon the reserved whipped cream into a pastry bag with a star tip, and pipe a lattice design over the top of the pie. Tent the pie with aluminum foil and refrigerate at least 5 hours or overnight.

Serves 8

STRUDELS

Apricot, Pear, and Almond Strudels

I love the combination of dried apricots, sliced fresh pears, and toasted almonds in this dessert. Baked to a rich golden brown, these strudels are garnished with almonds and powdered sugar and served with apricot-flavored whipped cream.

Special equipment: Jelly roll pan or rimmed baking sheet

1 cup dried apricots
4 to 5 moderately ripe pears
1 cup sliced toasted almonds (see Index)
4 teaspoons grated lemon zest
¾ cup sugar
9 thick phyllo sheets, 18 x 14 inches (see Index)
¾ cup (1½ sticks) unsalted butter, melted
½ cup dry bread crumbs
3 tablespoons apricot jam or preserves
1½ cups heavy or whipping cream
Confectioners' sugar, for garnish

AT THE MARKET

Phyllo. **Packages of phyllo dough are sometimes labeled ''thick'' or ''thin.'' I always buy the thick kind, which is easier to use. If you can find only thin phyllo sheets, use 4 sheets of phyllo per strudel. To store the dough, I freeze it in the package and then defrost it in the refrigerator overnight, or at room temperature for 2 hours. Leftover phyllo sheets can be re-wrapped tightly with plastic wrap, covered with foil, and refrozen for another use.**

You can use any variety of pear for this strudel. Anjou or Bosc, for example, are good choices when in season. Bartletts are available year-round, however, and are the ones I use most frequently.

1. Cover the apricots with water in a small saucepan, bring to a boil, then lower the heat and simmer until softened, about 20 minutes. Drain, cool, and chop the apricots. Place them in a large mixing bowl.

2. Peel and core the pears, and cut them lengthwise into ¼-inch slices. You should have 4 cups. Add the pear slices to the apricots.

3. Add ½ cup of the toasted almonds, the lemon zest, and the sugar to the bowl with the apricots. Toss well to mix, then set aside.

4. Place a phyllo sheet on a clean kitchen towel on a work surface, with a short end facing you. (Cover the remaining phyllo sheets with a lightly dampened kitchen towel so they do not dry out.) Brush the sheet generously with butter, and sprinkle with 1 tablespoon of the bread crumbs. Repeat the process with a second sheet, then place a third sheet on top, and butter, but do not sprinkle the third sheet with bread crumbs.

5. Drain the apricot and pear filling well. Place a third of the filling on the end of the phyllo sheet nearest you, and spread the filling horizontally to form a 3-inch-wide strip going almost to the edges. Fold the two long sides of the dough over about 1 inch, to enclose some of the filling. Then, starting at the end with the filling, roll the dough into a log shape. Use the kitchen towel as an aid to help turn the strudel over.

6. Butter a jelly roll pan or rimmed baking sheet. Using two spatulas, transfer the strudel to the pan. Brush the strudel with melted butter.

7. Repeat the process to make the second and third strudels. (The strudels may be made 1 day in advance to this point. Keep them covered with a lightly dampened kitchen towel and plastic wrap, and refrigerate.)

8. When you are ready to bake the strudels, position a rack in the center of the oven and preheat the oven to 375° F.

9. Bake the strudels until a rich golden brown, about 18 minutes. Remove the strudels from the oven and let them cool 5 to 10 minutes.

10. Heat the apricot jam just until liquified. Strain out any remaining pieces of fruit. Whip the cream until soft peaks form, and then gradually beat the jam into the whipped cream.

11. Transfer the strudels to a serving platter, and brush with melted butter. Sprinkle each strudel with some of the remaining ½ cup toasted almonds, then with confectioners' sugar. Serve the strudels warm, with a bowl of the apricot whipped cream. Cut each strudel into 5 slices with a serrated knife.

Serves 15

Cranberry Walnut Strudels

M y students are crazy about this dessert. It can be assembled a day in advance and makes a festive addition to a Thanksgiving or Christmas dinner.

Special equipment: Jelly roll pan or rimmed baking sheet

1 ¼ cups plus 2 tablespoons granulated sugar
½ cup plus 1 ½ tablespoons water
4 cups (12-ounce package) cranberries
½ cup raisins
1 teaspoon finely chopped, peeled fresh ginger
1 tablespoon cornstarch
1 cup coarsely chopped walnuts
6 thick phyllo sheets, 18 x 14 inches (see Index)
8 tablespoons (1 stick) unsalted butter, melted
¼ cup dry bread crumbs
1 ½ cups heavy or whipping cream
1 ½ teaspoons vanilla extract
2 tablespoons confectioners' sugar, plus more for garnish

1. Combine 1 cup plus 2 tablespoons of the granulated sugar with ½ cup of the water in a large heavy saucepan. Place over medium heat and stir to dissolve the sugar. Add 2 cups of the cranberries, the raisins, and the ginger. Cook, stirring, until the berries pop, 5 to 6 minutes. Remove the pan from the heat. Combine the cornstarch with the remaining 1½ tablespoons water, and stir the cornstarch mixture and remaining 2 cups of berries into the cooked berries. Return the pan to the heat and cook, stirring, until the mixture has thickened, 2 to 3 minutes. Remove from the heat and stir in the walnuts. Set aside.

2. Place a phyllo sheet on a clean kitchen towel on a work surface, with a short end facing you. (Cover the remaining phyllo sheets with a lightly dampened kitchen towel so they do not dry out.) Brush the sheet generously with butter, and sprinkle with 1 tablespoon each of bread crumbs and granulated sugar. Repeat the process with a second sheet, then place a third sheet on top, and butter, but do not sprinkle the third sheet with the bread crumbs or sugar.

3. Place half of the cranberry mixture on the end of the phyllo sheet nearest you, and spread the filling horizontally to form a 3-inch-wide strip, going almost to the edges. Fold the two long sides of the dough over about 1½ inches to enclose some of the filling, and then, starting at the end with the filling, roll the dough into a log shape. Use the kitchen towel as an aid to help turn the strudel over.

4. Butter a jelly roll pan or rimmed baking sheet. Use two spatulas to transfer the strudel to the pan. Brush the strudel with melted butter.

5. Repeat the process with the second strudel. (The strudels may be made a day in advance to this point. Keep them covered with a lightly dampened kitchen towel and plastic wrap, and refrigerate.)

6. When you are ready to serve the strudels, position a rack in the center of the oven and preheat the oven to 375° F.

7. Bake the strudels until golden, 18 to 20 minutes. Allow them to cool 5 to 10 minutes. Strudels may be served warm or at room temperature.

8. Whip the cream until soft mounds form. Add the vanilla and 2 tablespoons confectioners' sugar, and whip just until firm.

9. Slice the strudels into 5 to 6 servings with a serrated knife. Sprinkle them generously with confectioners' sugar. Serve the strudels with a bowl of the whipped cream.

Serves 10 to 12

Blueberry Strudels

These strudels, served garnished with whipped cream, mint leaves, and a light blueberry Cassis sauce, make a striking presentation. They make a good dessert to serve at brunches.

Special equipment: Jelly roll pan or rimmed baking sheet

4 cups fresh blueberries, rinsed and patted dry, or frozen
*   unsweetened blueberries, thawed and well drained*
2 teaspoons grated lemon zest
1 cup sugar
¼ cup cornstarch
6 thick phyllo sheets, 18 x 14 inches (see Index)
¾ cup (1½ sticks) unsalted butter, melted
¼ cup dry bread crumbs
1 cup heavy or whipping cream
Confectioners' sugar, for garnish
Mint sprigs, for garnish
Blueberry Cassis Sauce (recipe follows)

1. Combine the blueberries and lemon zest in a mixing bowl, and toss together. In another bowl mix the sugar and cornstarch well. Then add the sugar mixture to the blueberries and mix well. Set aside.

2. Place a phyllo sheet on a clean kitchen towel on a work surface, with a short end facing you. (Cover the remaining phyllo sheets with a lightly dampened kitchen towel so they do not dry out.) Brush the sheet generously with melted butter and sprinkle it with 1 table-spoon of the bread crumbs. Repeat the process with a second sheet, then place a third sheet on top and butter, but do not sprinkle the third sheet with bread crumbs.

3. Place half the blueberry mixture on the end of the phyllo sheet nearest you, and spread the filling horizontally to form a 3-inch-wide strip going almost to the edges. Fold the two long sides of the dough over about 1½ inches to enclose some of the filling, and then, starting at the end with the filling, roll the dough into a log shape. Use the kitchen towel as an aid to help turn the strudel over.

4. Butter a jelly roll pan or rimmed baking sheet. Use two spatulas to transfer the strudel to the pan. Brush the strudel with melted butter.

AT THE MARKET

Frozen blueberries work very well in this recipe when fresh ones are not available. However, it is important to thaw and drain them well, as the recipe indicates.

5. Repeat the process to make the second strudel. (The strudels may be made 1 day in advance to this point. Keep covered with a lightly dampened kitchen towel and plastic wrap and refrigerate.)

6. When you are ready to bake the strudels, position a rack in the center of the oven and preheat the oven to 375° F.

7. Bake the strudels until golden, 18 to 20 minutes. Remove them from the oven, and allow them to cool 5 to 10 minutes.

8. Whip the cream until it is firm but not stiff.

9. To serve, cut each strudel into five pieces with a serrated knife. Serve each piece sprinkled with confectioners' sugar, and garnished with a sprig of mint and a dollop of whipped cream. Pass the Blueberry Cassis Sauce separately.

Serves 10

BLUEBERRY CASSIS SAUCE

½ cup water
½ cup crème de Cassis
3 tablespoons fresh lemon juice
2 tablespoons cornstarch
2 cups fresh blueberries, rinsed and patted dry, or frozen
*   unsweetened blueberries, thawed, drained, and patted dry*
2 to 3 tablespoons sugar (optional)

1. Combine the water, cassis, lemon juice, and cornstarch in a heavy 3-quart saucepan. Stir over low heat until the cornstarch dissolves. Then add the blueberries and raise the heat to medium. Cook, stirring, until the sauce thickens and coats a spoon, about 5 minutes. Let the sauce cool 5 to 10 minutes.

2. Purée the sauce in a food processor, blender, or food mill until smooth. Strain the puréed sauce through a fine-mesh sieve. Taste, and add sugar if desired. Reserve in a covered bowl in the refrigerator. (The sauce may be made 1 to 2 days in advance and kept refrigerated.) Reheat the sauce until warm, not hot, before serving.

Makes about 2 cups

FROZEN & FRUIT DESSERTS

Icy cold or satisfyingly warm—take your pick. Each of the desserts in this chapter is one or the other. My students love to serve the Red Grape and Green Grape Sorbets and the Frozen Chocolate Marbled Mousse when entertaining, because they can assemble these dishes long before the day of their party. However, on the first crisp days of autumn or for a cold wintry night, they are just as enthusiastic about serving the Hazelnut Hot Fudge Sauce and the Rum Caramel Pecan Sauce over poached pears or a slice of pound cake. And on a night when the thermometer is hovering around zero, nothing could be simpler or more welcome than the Marinated Hot Fruit.

CHILLED DESSERTS & TOPPINGS

Red Grape and Green Grape Sorbets with Frosted Grapes

When Lazarus Department Stores planned a week-long extravaganza featuring products from Italy, they invited chefs from the celebrated Ciga hotel chain to participate. As part of their agenda, these talented Italian cooks taught classes at La Belle Pomme. This is one of the fabulous desserts they demonstrated for our students.

Special equipment: Food processor; ice cream maker (optional)

Sugar Syrup
2½ cups water
1¼ cups sugar

Red Grape Sorbet
½ pound seedless red grapes
1¼ cups sugar syrup
½ cup dry red wine, such as Cabernet Sauvignon

Green Grape Sorbet
½ pound seedless green grapes
1¼ cups sugar syrup
½ cup dry white wine, such as Chenin Blanc

Frosted Grape Garnish
2 large egg whites
6 small clusters seedless red grapes
6 small clusters seedless green grapes
Sugar
Grape leaves (optional)

1. Prepare the sugar syrup: Combine the water and sugar in a medium-size heavy saucepan over medium-high heat, swirling the pan occasionally until the sugar dissolves. Then increase the heat and bring the syrup to a boil. Boil without stirring for 5 minutes. Cool the syrup completely, then cover, and refrigerate until needed. (Sugar syrup can be made several weeks in advance. Keep it covered and refrigerated.)

AS A VARIATION

Although these two sorbets make an interesting presentation served together, I often serve only one, garnished with the appropriate color grapes.

2. Prepare the red grape sorbet: Purée the red grapes in a food processor. Transfer the purée to a non-aluminum bowl, and mix in the sugar syrup and wine. Let the sorbet stand at room temperature for 4 hours.

3. Strain the grape mixture, discarding the skins. Then process the mixture in an ice cream maker according to the manufacturer's instructions. Freeze the sorbet in a covered container to mellow the flavors, 3 to 4 hours.

   The sorbet can also be made in the freezer: Pour the strained grape mixture into a shallow pan and freeze until firm, stirring occasionally. Transfer to a food processor and purée until smooth. Freeze until almost firm.

4. Prepare the green grape sorbet: Follow the directions for the red grape sorbet, using the green grapes, sugar syrup, and dry white wine. (Both these sorbets can be made several days in advance and kept in the freezer. However, if they harden, you will need to whip them in a food processor until smooth and then refreeze for 1 to 2 hours before using.)

5. To prepare the frosted grapes, beat the egg whites in a large bowl until they are frothy. Dip the clusters of grapes in the egg whites, then place them on a rack. Sift sugar over the grapes, turning the grapes to coat the entire surface. Place the grapes on a plate and freeze, uncovered, 1 to 2 hours. Use them straight from the freezer.

6. Let both sorbets soften slightly in the refrigerator if necessary before serving. Garnish each serving with frosted grapes.

Serves 6

Left Bank Coconut Sorbet

In 1983 Paris had one of the hottest summers on record, with temperatures soaring to the nineties daily. My family and I were there for several weeks that year, and our only respite was a regular trip to a little *sorbet* stand on the Rue de Buci on the Left Bank. We tried just about every flavor they offered, and decided that the *noix de coco* was the best.

Special equipment: Ice cream maker

Sugar Syrup
3 cups water
¾ cup sugar

Sorbet
3 cups cream of coconut (see Index)
3 cups sugar syrup
3 tablespoons fresh lemon juice

1. Prepare the sugar syrup: Combine the water and sugar in a medium-size heavy saucepan over medium-high heat, swirling the pan occasionally until the sugar dissolves. Then increase the heat and bring the syrup to a boil. Boil without stirring for 5 minutes. Cool the syrup completely, then cover, and refrigerate until needed. (Sugar syrup can be made several weeks in advance. Keep it covered and refrigerated.)

2. Combine the cream of coconut, sugar syrup, and lemon juice in a large mixing bowl, and stir to mix well.

3. Transfer the mixture to an ice cream maker and prepare according to the manufacturer's directions. Process until the sorbet is very white in color and of a solid but fluffy texture.

4. Store the sorbet in a covered container in the freezer to firm it up, 2 to 3 hours. (The sorbet can be made several days in advance. It stays remarkably smooth and usually does not need to be whipped in a food processor to be softened.)

Serves 6 to 8

AS A VARIATION

Sometimes I serve a scoop of Apricot Sorbet, a scoop of Left Bank Coconut Sorbet, and a scoop of Honeydew Sorbet all together for a striking presentation. Since all the sorbets can be made in advance, you only need to arrange the sorbets in dishes at serving time.

Honeydew Sorbet

Going into the market one hot summer day, I couldn't resist buying some beautiful and perfectly ripened honeydew melons. I wasn't sure how I would use them, but when I got home, I decided they would be perfect in an ice-cold sorbet. This easy recipe is the result, and one of my favorites.

Special equipment: Ice cream maker; food processor

Sugar Syrup
½ cup water
1 cup sugar

Sorbet
1 large (about 6 pounds) ripe honeydew melon
½ cup sugar syrup
6 tablespoons fresh lime juice
6 thin lime slices, for garnish
6 sprigs fresh mint, for garnish

1. Prepare the sugar syrup: Combine the water and sugar in a medium-size heavy saucepan over medium-high heat, swirling the pan occasionally until the sugar dissolves. Then increase the heat and bring the syrup to a boil. Boil without stirring for 5 minutes. Cool the syrup completely, then cover, and refrigerate until needed. (Sugar syrup can be made several weeks in advance. Keep it covered and refrigerated.)

2. Peel, seed, and chop the melon. Transfer the chopped melon to a food processor and purée. You should have 4 cups of purée.

3. Combine the purée, sugar syrup, and lime juice in a bowl, and mix well. Place the mixture in an ice cream maker and process according to the manufacturer's directions. Store the sorbet in a covered container in the freezer to firm it up, 2 to 3 hours. (This sorbet can be made several days in advance; store it covered in the freezer. If the sorbet hardens, whip it in a food processor until smooth, and then refreeze for 1 to 2 hours before using.)

4. To serve, fill six bowls or wide-mouth wine glasses with scoops of sorbet. Garnish each serving with a slice of lime and a mint sprig.

Serves 6

A COOK'S REFLECTIONS

Most sorbets that are processed in any kind of home ice cream maker come out soft, but could be eaten at that moment. I like mine frozen a little longer, as do most cooks, so that they are slightly firm and icy cold. That's why I call for additional freezing in my recipes.

Apricot Sorbet

This is a tart, delicate sorbet flavored subtly with raspberry vinegar. It was created by one of our teachers, Tom Johnson, a talented chef and generous colleague.

Special equipment: Ice cream maker; food processor

Sugar Syrup
2½ cups water
1¼ cups sugar

Sorbet
2 cans (1 pound each) apricot halves in heavy syrup
2½ cups sugar syrup
¼ cup raspberry vinegar
8 sprigs fresh mint, for garnish

1. Prepare the sugar syrup: Combine the water and sugar in a medium-size heavy saucepan over medium-high heat, swirling the pan occasionally until the sugar dissolves. Then increase the heat and bring the syrup to a boil. Boil without stirring for 5 minutes. Cool the syrup completely, then cover, and refrigerate until needed. (Sugar syrup can be made several weeks in advance. Keep it covered and refrigerated.)

2. Drain the apricots, discarding the syrup, and place the apricots in the bowl of a food processor. Process until they are well puréed, 30 to 60 seconds. Add the sugar syrup and the raspberry vinegar, and process until well incorporated, several seconds more.

3. Transfer the apricot mixture to an ice cream maker and process according to the manufacturer's directions. Store the sorbet in a covered container in the freezer to firm it up, 2 to 3 hours. (The sorbet can be prepared several days ahead to this point. Cover and freeze. If the sorbet hardens, whip it in a food processor until smooth, and then refreeze it for 1 to 2 hours before using.)

4. To serve, fill eight bowls or wide-mouth wine goblets with scoops of sorbet. Garnish with mint sprigs.

Serves 8

Pink Grapefruit Sorbet with Campari Sauce

I am often asked to attend tasting meals to critique the food that will be served at large social events in Columbus. At one such tasting at the Hyatt Hotel on Capitol Square, I sampled this unusual grapefruit sorbet served with a delicious Campari sauce. It was obvious that this sorbet needed no improvement! I couldn't get to the phone fast enough the next day to see if I could get the recipe. Chef Doni Schoendinger, the inventor of this unique dish, could not have been more generous in sharing the directions with me.

Special equipment: Ice cream maker

Sugar Syrup
4 cups water
2 cups sugar

Sorbet
4 cups sugar syrup
1½ cups fresh pink grapefruit juice, strained
2 teaspoons fresh lemon juice
2 teaspoons Campari

Campari Sauce and Garnish
1 cup sugar
½ cup water
½ cup dry white wine
6 to 8 whole cloves
2 cinnamon sticks
5 to 6 strips lemon zest, about ½ by 4 inches
½ cup Campari
8 cinnamon sticks, for garnish
8 sprigs mint, for garnish

1. Prepare the sugar syrup: Combine the water and sugar in a medium-size heavy saucepan over medium-high heat, swirling the pan occasionally until the sugar dissolves. Then increase the heat and bring the syrup to a boil. Boil without stirring for 5 minutes. Cool the syrup completely, then cover, and refrigerate until needed. (Sugar syrup can be made several weeks in advance. Keep it covered and refrigerated.)

2. Prepare the sorbet: Combine the sugar syrup, grapefruit juice, lemon juice, and Campari in a saucepan. Bring to a boil, reduce the heat, and simmer about 5 minutes. Cool to room temperature.

3. Pour the sorbet mixture into an ice cream machine and process according to the manufacturer's directions. Store the sorbet in a covered container in the freezer to firm it up, 2 to 3 hours. (The sorbet can be made several days in advance to this point. Cover and freeze. If the sorbet hardens, whip it in a food processor until smooth, and then refreeze 1 to 2 hours before using.)

4. Prepare the Campari sauce: Combine the sugar, water, white wine, whole cloves, cinnamon sticks, and lemon strips in a saucepan over medium-high heat. Stir until the sugar has dissolved. Bring to a boil, reduce the heat, and simmer about 5 minutes. Do not stir once the syrup boils. Remove the pan from the heat and let the syrup cool to room temperature. Strain the syrup and discard the cloves, cinnamon, and lemon zest. Stir in the Campari, cover, and refrigerate until well chilled. (The sauce can be made 2 to 3 days in advance to this point; cover and refrigerate.)

5. To serve, place several scoops of sorbet into eight bowls or wide-mouth wine goblets. Ladle some Campari sauce over the sorbet, and garnish each serving with a cinnamon stick and a mint sprig.

Serves 8

AT THE MARKET

Red Delicious and Winesap are good apples to use for this dessert.

Apple Cinnamon Ice Cream with Apple Wedges

The recipe for this ice cream was given to me by my very first culinary assistant, Loretta Umbaugh. When I first read her directions for the dessert, I was certain that something so easy could not taste so good, but I was wrong. Made simply by flavoring a good-quality store-bought vanilla ice cream with cinnamon, nutmeg, lemon, and apple brandy, this frozen confection is delectable. Serving the ice cream surrounded by apple wedges and with a garnish of lemon leaves makes a striking presentation.

GREAT ACCOMPANIMENTS

A plate of Orange and Ginger Butter Cookies is nice to serve with this apple ice cream.

6 red apples
1 quart best-quality vanilla ice cream, slightly softened
1 teaspoon ground cinnamon
Generous grating of fresh nutmeg
¼ cup sugar
1 tablespoon fresh lemon juice
4 teaspoons Calvados or applejack
Several lemon leaves, for garnish

1. Peel, core, and grate 2 of the apples. Combine them with the softened ice cream, cinnamon, nutmeg, sugar, and lemon juice in a large mixing bowl. Mix well, and then stir in the Calvados or applejack. Freeze, covered, until firm, about 6 hours or overnight. (The ice cream can be made 2 days in advance and kept covered and frozen.)

2. To serve, quarter and core the remaining 4 apples. Cut each of the quarters in half lengthwise. On each dessert plate arrange four apple slices in a half-circle on the lefthand side; then place two to three lemon leaves opposite the apple wedges. Place a generous scoop of ice cream in the center of the dish. Serve immediately.

Serves 8

Frozen Chocolate Marbled Mousse

This is creamy, smooth, and rich—a great dessert for chocoholics. One of my students told me that her husband likes this creation so much that he now requests it in place of cake for his birthday.

Special equipment: 6-cup ring mold or 9- or 10-inch springform pan with a ring insert

6 ounces sweet chocolate
3 ounces unsweetened chocolate
10 large egg yolks
1 cup sugar
1 teaspoon vanilla extract
3 tablespoons dark rum
3½ cups heavy or whipping cream
¾ cup chopped toasted hazelnuts (see Index)
2 ounces semisweet chocolate, for garnish

1. Melt the chocolates together in the top of a double boiler placed over simmering water until smooth. Set aside to cool slightly.

2. Place the egg yolks in the bowl of an electric mixer and beat at medium speed. Gradually add the sugar, and continue to beat until the mixture is very thick and pale yellow, 4 to 5 minutes. On slow speed, add the vanilla and the rum to the mixture. Mix a few seconds more. Remove half (approximately 2 cups) of this egg yolk mixture and place it in a medium-size bowl. Add the melted chocolate to the egg yolk mixture in the mixing bowl, and beat on medium speed until just incorporated.

3. Whip 2 cups of the heavy cream until firm but not stiff.

4. Fold half the whipped cream gently into the plain egg yolk mixture in the medium-size bowl. Then fold the remaining whipped cream into the chocolate mixture in the mixing bowl. (If you can't push a wooden spoon easily through the chocolate mixture, before you fold in the whipped cream, add ½ to ¾ cup of the whipped cream to the mixture. Mix on slow speed with an electric mixer until the mixture is smooth and loose. Then fold the remaining whipped cream into the chocolate.) Fold the hazelnuts into the chocolate mixture.

5. Alternately drop heaping tablespoons of the chocolate mixture and of the plain mixture around the bottom of a 6-cup ring mold or a 9- or 10-inch springform ring. Then take a table knife and slowly run it through the two mixtures, twisting the knife and touching the bottom of the pan as you go to produce a swirl pattern in the mousse. Continue filling the mold in this manner—dropping alternating mixtures in the pan and swirling the mixtures with a knife—until all the chocolate and plain mixtures have been added. Cover the top of the mousse with plastic wrap and freeze until firm, 6 hours or overnight. (The mousse can be made several days or a week in advance and kept tightly covered and frozen until needed.)

6. When you are ready to unmold the mousse, spread a large sheet of aluminum foil on a work surface. Remove the mold from the freezer, and run a thin flexible knife around the sides of the pan. Then dip the mold in hot water for 20 to 30 seconds. Invert the mold over the aluminum foil, and rap the bottom. The mousse should drop out. If it does not, tap the mold several times with the handle of a knife to help release it. After the mousse is unmolded, you may see that some of the chocolate has melted. Use a spatula to smooth the surface of the mousse, using a circular motion to reproduce the

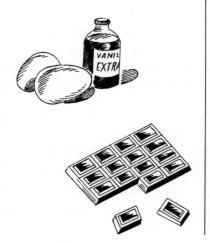

swirled pattern. The mousse can be replaced in the freezer, uncovered, to firm up for 2 to 3 hours before serving.

7. When you are ready to serve the mousse, whip the remaining 1½ cups of cream until firm and mound it in the center of the mousse. Shave the semisweet chocolate over the cream.

Serves 10 to 12

A COOK'S REFLECTIONS

It is important to be careful when grating the grapefruit peel. Grate only the color portion of the rind; the white section underneath the skin will leave a bitter aftertaste if it is included.

Sometimes students ask me what to do if the chilled gelatin mixture gets too hard. You can gently reheat it, preferably in the top of a double boiler set over simmering water, and whisk it just until the mixture is pliable again. Do not let the mixture get warm. Use it as soon as it is loose enough to fold in the egg whites and cream.

Grapefruit Mousse with Berries and Mint

This is a good dessert to serve for a brunch. It is feather-light and can be made completely in advance.

Special equipment: Pastry bag with a large star tip (optional)

2 envelopes unflavored gelatin
1 cup sugar
¼ teaspoon salt
4 large eggs, separated
½ cup fresh grapefruit juice, strained (4 to 5 white grapefruit)
½ teaspoon grated grapefruit zest
1 teaspoon finely chopped crystallized ginger
1½ cups heavy or whipping cream
2 cups fresh strawberries (hulled), blueberries, or raspberries, or any combination
8 mint sprigs, for garnish

1. In a medium-size heavy saucepan, combine the gelatin, ⅔ cup of the sugar, and the salt. In a bowl, combine the egg yolks and grapefruit juice, and whisk together until well mixed. Add the grapefruit mixture to the gelatin mixture.

2. Place the saucepan over low heat and cook, whisking constantly, until the gelatin has dissolved and the mixture has thickened slightly, about 5 minutes. Remove from the heat; stir in the grapefruit zest and the chopped ginger.

3. Chill the mixture in the refrigerator until it starts to set, 1 hour or longer. (Stir the mixture several times during the chilling process to prevent it from getting too hard or lumpy.)

4. When the chilled mixture is quite thick but not set, beat the egg whites until they start to mound. Then gradually beat in the remaining ⅓ cup sugar, and continue to beat only until soft peaks form. Gently fold the whites into the chilled grapefruit mixture.

5. Beat 1 cup of the cream until it is firm but not stiff, and fold it carefully into the mousse mixture. Divide the mousse mixture among eight small dessert bowls. (The mousse can be made a day in advance to this point, covered tightly with plastic wrap, and refrigerated.)

6. When you are ready to serve the mousse, garnish the top of each serving with fresh berries. Whip the remaining ½ cup cream until it is firm. If you are using a pastry bag, fit it with a star tip and pipe rosettes on top of the berries. Or simply top each serving with a generous dollop of the whipped cream. Garnish each serving with a mint sprig.

Serves 8

Hazelnut Hot Fudge Sauce

Dense, dark, delicious, decadent! That is the way my students describe this rich chocolate sauce flavored with toasted hazelnuts.

4 tablespoons (½ stick) unsalted butter
4 ounces unsweetened chocolate, broken into small pieces
1 cup sugar
¾ cup light corn syrup
1½ cups heavy or whipping cream
1 teaspoon vanilla extract
1 cup hazelnuts, toasted and coarsely chopped (see Index)

1. Place the butter, chocolate, sugar, and corn syrup in a medium-size heavy saucepan over low heat. Stir constantly until the chocolate and butter have melted. Then pour in the cream while continuing to stir. Cook the chocolate sauce over low heat, stirring often, until the mixture is thickened and smooth, 15 to 20 minutes.

2. Remove the pan from the heat and stir in the vanilla and hazelnuts. Serve hot. (The sauce will hold well, covered, in the refrigerator for 5 to 7 days. Reheat, in a heavy saucepan over very low heat, stirring constantly before using.)

Makes 3 cups

AS A VARIATION

Of course you can vary the nuts in this recipe; toasted slivered almonds and walnut halves both work well.

Dark Caramel Pecan Rum Sauce

Thick, rich, and creamy, this dessert sauce takes only a few minutes to prepare and can be made well in advance. I like to serve the sauce over scoops of vanilla ice cream all year round, and in the summer for a fancier presentation I mound vanilla or peach ice cream on fresh peach halves and ladle the warm caramel mixture over the top.

Special equipment: Candy thermometer (optional)

1 package (3 ounces) cream cheese, at room temperature
⅓ cup heavy or whipping cream
1 cup sugar
⅓ cup water
2 tablespoons dark rum
1 cup pecans, toasted and coarsely chopped (see Index)

1. Place the cream cheese and heavy cream in a mixing bowl, and beat with a whisk until smooth. Set aside.

2. Place the sugar and water in a heavy saucepan over medium-high heat. Stir just to dissolve the sugar, then let the mixture cook without stirring until it caramelizes (300° F on a candy thermometer), 8 to 10 minutes. Remove the pan from the heat, and pour in the cream mixture; it will sputter. Then, over low heat, whisk the mixture just until smooth. Stir in the rum and pecans. (The sauce will hold well, covered, in the refrigerator for 5 to 7 days. Reheat over very low heat, stirring often.)

Makes 1½ to 2 cups

FRUITS AND A FLAN

Peach Halves with Blueberries and Lemon Custard Sauce

This is a dessert I like to make in midsummer, when peaches and blueberries are familiar offerings in the market. The icy-cold custard sauce is best made a day ahead, and the peaches and blueberries can be readied in advance. The only work required at the last minute is a quick assembly of the dessert.

Sauce
1½ cups milk
1 cup heavy or whipping cream
6 large egg yolks
½ cup plus 1 tablespoon sugar
3 tablespoons cornstarch
2 tablespoons fresh lemon juice
2 teaspoons grated lemon zest

Fruit
6 large ripe peaches, preferably freestone
6 tablespoons fresh lemon juice
2 cups blueberries, rinsed
8 sprigs mint, for garnish

1. Prepare the sauce: Combine the milk and cream in a medium-size saucepan and bring just to a boil. Remove from the heat. Place the egg yolks in a mixing bowl. Combine the sugar and cornstarch in a small bowl, and gradually beat the mixture into the yolks. Continue to beat until the mixture is pale yellow and has thickened, 4 to 5 minutes. Then stir in the warm milk mixture. The sauce will be thin at this point.

2. Transfer the mixture to the top of a double boiler, placed over simmering water. Whisk constantly, until the mixture thickens, 3 to 4 minutes.

3. Remove the sauce from the heat and let it cool. Stir in the lemon juice and zest, cover with plastic wrap, and refrigerate until very

---

A COOK'S REFLECTIONS

Peeling peaches. Peaches are usually hard to peel unless you blanch them first. Drop whole peaches into boiling water for 15 to 30 seconds. Remove them from the water with a slotted spoon, and peel off the skin with a sharp paring knife.

AS A VARIATION

If blueberries are not available, either raspberries or strawberries are a delicious substitute.

One of my students likes to make this dessert with the following changes: She places ¼ cup of the sauce on a dessert plate, lays a slice of pound cake over the sauce, then mounds sliced peaches and blueberries over the cake and garnishes the dessert with additional sauce and a sprig of mint.

A COOK'S REFLECTIONS

The proportions of fruits here are just a suggestion. Use your imagination and take advantage of whatever is available in the market to create new combinations. You should have a total of 8 cups of prepared fruit.

cold. (The sauce may be made 1 day in advance; keep covered and refrigerated.)

4. To prepare the fruit, peel the peaches. Cut 4 of the peaches in half and remove the pits. Thinly slice the remaining 2 peaches. Toss the peaches with the lemon juice to prevent discoloring. (Peaches can be peeled 1 hour or more before serving. Refrigerate until needed.)

5. To serve, ladle ¼ cup of the cold sauce into each of eight wide-mouth wine glasses or dessert bowls. Place a peach half, cut side up, on the sauce. Mound ¼ cup blueberries over the peach half, and strew several peach slices over the berries. Then ladle 1 tablespoon of the sauce over the fruit and garnish with a sprig of fresh mint.

Serves 8

Marinated Hot Fruit

In the Midwest, where I live, the winter is a time when we see only apples, oranges, grapes, bananas, and, occasionally, early strawberries in our markets. This is a dessert in which these common fruits are elevated to new heights.

2 oranges, peeled and sectioned
2 bananas, peeled and sliced
1 cup red seedless grapes
1 cup green seedless grapes
1 Granny Smith apple, cored and cut into bite-size wedges
1 Red Delicious apple, cored and cut into bite-size wedges
1 pint strawberries, hulled
Juice of 1 lemon
1½ cups water
¾ cups sugar
1 cup dry white wine
¾ tablespoon grated peeled fresh ginger

1. Place the prepared fruit in a large attractive serving bowl. (The fruit may be prepared 30 minutes to 1 hour before serving time. Toss the fruit with the juice of a lemon to prevent discoloring.)

2. Combine the water and sugar in a medium-size heavy saucepan. Heat, stirring, until the sugar has dissolved and the mixture comes to

GREAT ACCOMPANIMENTS

I like to serve a basket of warm Spiced Madeleines with this fruit.

a boil, about 5 minutes. Remove from the heat and stir in the wine and ginger. Return the pan to the heat long enough to warm the wine.

3. Pour the hot wine mixture over the fruit, and serve immediately.

Serves 8

Poached Pears with Blueberry-Cassis Sauce

These pears are sleek and elegant. Poached in a red wine sugar syrup until they are deep burgundy hued, they are napped with a dark blueberry-Cassis sauce and garnished with a swirl of whipped cream and a sprig of mint. I like to serve this dessert (which can be made a day ahead) at fall and winter dinner parties.

Special equipment: Pastry bag fitted with a medium star tip

6 cups dry red wine
3 cups sugar
6 tablespoons fresh lemon juice
2 teaspoons grated lemon zest
8 large firm Bosc pears, peeled, stems left on
2 cups Blueberry-Cassis Sauce (see Index)
1 cup heavy or whipping cream
Mint sprigs, for garnish

1. Poach the pears: Heat the wine, sugar, lemon juice, and lemon zest in a heavy 3- to 4-quart saucepan over low heat, swirling the pan occasionally until the sugar dissolves. Then increase the heat and bring the mixture to a simmer. Cut a small slice off the bottom of each pear so it can stand upright.

2. Add the pears to the wine mixture, and adjust the heat so the liquid barely simmers. Cook the pears until they are just tender when pierced with a knife, 30 to 50 minutes, depending on the ripeness of the pears.

3. Using a slotted spoon, transfer the pears to a large bowl. Cool the pears and poaching liquid separately. Then pour the cool poaching liquid over the pears, cover, and refrigerate overnight.

AT THE MARKET

Bosc pears—the slender, russet-skinned variety—are my favorite choice for this dessert, but Bartletts or Anjous could also be used.

4. When you are ready to serve them, drain the pears. If necessary, stir the Blueberry-Cassis Sauce over low heat until it is thin enough to pour.

5. Whip the cream until firm, and spoon it into a pastry bag fitted with a star tip.

Ladle 2 tablespoons of sauce onto each dessert plate, swirling the plate to coat it evenly. Stand a pear on each plate, and nap it with some sauce. Pipe a swirl of whipped cream around the stem of each pear. Garnish with mint and serve immediately. Pass any remaining blueberry sauce separately.

Serves 8

Coconut Caramel Flan

A good variation of the classic *crème caramel renversée,* this velvety coconut custard is garnished festively with sliced almonds, toasted coconut, and candied orange peel. This is a great dessert to serve at large buffets, especially during the Christmas holidays.

Special equipment: 2-quart soufflé dish

1 cup sweetened flaked coconut
1½ cups sugar
½ cup water
2¼ cups heavy or whipping cream
¾ cup cream of coconut (see Index)
3 large whole eggs
3 large egg yolks
1 teaspoon almond extract
24 pieces sliced almonds, toasted, for garnish (see Index)
3 tablespoons Candied Orange Peel (recipe follows), for garnish

1. Position a rack in the center of the oven and preheat the oven to 250° F.

2. Spread ¼ cup of the coconut on a jelly roll pan or cookie sheet and bake until golden and dry, 15 to 20 minutes. Remove, and set aside for the garnish. Raise the oven temperature to 350° F.

3. Prepare the caramel: Heat the sugar and water in a medium-size heavy saucepan over low heat, swirling the pan occasionally until

A COOK'S REFLECTIONS

Some of my students tell me they are nervous about making caramel. They have either burned it or haven't let it cook long enough. I always offer the following hints:

• Use a good heavy saucepan—one that is a light color inside so that you will be able to see the mixture turn caramel color.

• Swirl the sugar and water together so that there are as few sugar grains as possible on the sides of the pan.

• Once the sugar has dissolved in the water, do not stir again.

• Watch the mixture carefully during the caramelization process. First you will begin to smell the "burnt" caramel, and then, usually within seconds, the mixture will start to change color, starting with a light golden hue. Cook a few seconds longer until the caramel is a rich tea brown. Do not let it get dark brown; then the caramel will taste burned.

• Once the caramel is the right color, remove it from the heat and use immediately.

• Finally, always be extremely careful when working with caramel. The mixture reaches over 300° F and can give you a bad burn.

the sugar dissolves. Increase the heat and boil, without stirring, until caramelized, 7 to 10 minutes. Immediately pour the caramel into a 2-quart soufflé dish, tilting and swirling the dish to coat the bottom and sides well. Set the dish aside.

4. Scald the cream and the cream of coconut together in a heavy saucepan. Remove from the heat.

5. Using an electric mixer on medium speed, beat the eggs and yolks until they are thick and light in color. On slow speed, gradually mix in the scalded cream. Fold in ¾ cup of the flaked coconut and the almond extract. Pour the mixture into the caramel-lined dish.

6. Place the soufflé dish in a large baking pan. Pour enough hot water into the baking pan to reach halfway up the sides of the soufflé dish. Bake the flan until a knife inserted in the center comes out clean, about 55 minutes.

7. Cool the flan to room temperature, then cover and refrigerate until well chilled. (Coconut flan can be prepared up to 1 day ahead; keep well covered and refrigerated.)

8. Just before serving, run a knife around the sides of the dish and invert the flan over a rimmed platter. Tap the bottom of the dish gently to release the flan. Arrange the almonds in eight fleur-de-lis patterns around the edge of the flan, using three slices for each pattern. Sprinkle the remaining ¼ cup toasted coconut between the almond patterns. Top with the Candied Orange Peel.

Serves 6

CANDIED ORANGE PEEL

1 large thick-skinned orange
1 cup water
¼ cup sugar

1. Using a vegetable peeler, cut the peel from the orange in 1-inch-wide strips. Cut out any white membrane, and cut the peel into thin strips, 2 inches by ⅛ inch.

2. Blanch the orange strips in a small saucepan of boiling water to cover for 1 minute. Drain, then rinse under cold water. Repeat the blanching and rinsing two more times.

3. Heat the water and the sugar in a heavy 8-inch skillet over low heat, swirling the pan occasionally until the sugar dissolves. Increase the heat to medium and bring to a simmer.

4. Add the orange peel and simmer, swirling the pan occasionally, until the peel is glazed and most of the liquid has evaporated, about 20 minutes. Cool the peel on a plate. (The orange peel can be made 1 day in advance and kept loosely covered at room temperature.)

Makes about ¼ cup

COOKIES &
BROWNIES

Everyone loves the aroma of just-baked cookies, and for most of us a plate of homemade brownies is one of life's most irresistible sights. All the recipes in this chapter were created for classes at La Belle Pomme. The Chestnut Brownies with rich chestnut buttercream icing, the Amaretto Brownies baked in miniature muffin tins (so that they resemble tiny cupcakes), and the triple-layered Nanaimo Bars are some of the most popular morsels I have brought before my students. Three special cookies, elegant Chocolate and Almond Crisps, fragrant Spiced Madeleines, and simple Orange and Butter Cookies, are good as snacks, not to mention as an offering with sorbets, ice creams, or a bowl of fresh fruit.

AT THE MARKET

Although regular semisweet chocolate is called for in this recipe, I
often buy semisweet compound
coating chocolate, which is usually
available in specialty food shops
and in some wholesale bakery supply stores. The compound coating
chocolate will not discolor or
bloom over a long period of time
and will keep its dark sheen.

Chocolate Almond Crisps

These thin round almond meringue cookies are baked until crisp
and then elegantly decorated with a dark chocolate glaze and
garnished with slivers of toasted almonds. They are sophisticated-
looking fare, ideal for serving with fresh fruit sorbets or ice creams.
At the end of a special dinner party, I often pass a silver tray
arranged with an assortment of sweets, including these crisps,
Orange and Ginger Butter Cookies, and Lucy's Nanaimo Bars, to
have with liqueurs.

3 large egg whites, at room temperature
⅛ teaspoon cream of tartar
⅛ teaspoon salt
2½ cups confectioners' sugar
1 teaspoon almond extract
1 cup toasted almonds (whole, sliced, or slivered), finely ground
*   (see Index)*
8 ounces semisweet chocolate
¾ cup slivered almonds, toasted (see Index)

1. Preheat the oven to 325° F.

2. Line two baking sheets with aluminum foil, and set aside.

3. Beat the egg whites in the bowl of an electric mixer on high
speed until foamy, and then add the cream of tartar and the salt.
Lower the speed to medium and continue to beat the whites until
they hold a peak when the beater is lifted from the mixture, 4
minutes or longer. Continue to beat, gradually adding the confectioners' sugar by tablespoons, making certain that all sugar has been
incorporated before adding the next. Beat until all the sugar has
been added and the meringue is stiff and glossy, at least 5 minutes.

4. Fold in the almond extract and the ground almonds.

5. Drop heaping teaspoonfuls of the meringue onto the prepared
baking sheets, leaving 2 inches between them. Flatten each meringue drop into a round cookie, using a knife to spread it evenly.
The cookies should be approximately 2½ to 3 inches in diameter.
Make certain the cookies are as round as possible to ensure that they
will be attractive. If all the meringue will not fit on two baking
sheets, reserve the rest and repeat the process when the first batch
has been cooked.

6. Bake the cookies in the oven for 20 minutes, then lower the heat to 275° F and bake 20 minutes more. Turn off the oven and leave the cookies in the oven with the door closed until completely cool.

7. Remove the cookies from the foil and place them on a cake rack. Melt the chocolate in a small heavy saucepan over low heat, stirring until it is smooth and shiny, 3 to 5 minutes. Then, using a teaspoon, drizzle a small amount of melted chocolate on each cookie. Use a knife or icing spatula to spread the chocolate evenly over the top of the cookies. Place a single toasted almond sliver in the center of each cookie, or if desired, use the almond slivers to make a pattern. Let the cookies rest until the chocolate is set, about 45 minutes. Store in a tightly covered container. (Cookies will keep 1 week or more tightly covered.)

Makes approximately 36 cookies

Spiced Madeleines

Marcel Proust made madeleines famous around the world. However, the ones that he dipped into his tea were lemon flavored. These are richly aromatic—baked with cardamom, nutmeg, and allspice—and I am sure they, too, could jar his memory!

Special equipment: 2 standard-size madeleine pans with 12 molds each

3 large eggs, at room temperature
⅔ cup sugar
1 cup bleached all-purpose flour
½ teaspoon baking powder
½ teaspoon cardamom seeds, crushed (see "A Cook's Reflections,"
*   page 364)*
½ teaspoon freshly grated nutmeg
¼ teaspoon ground allspice
1 teaspoon vanilla extract
10 tablespoons (1¼ sticks) unsalted butter, melted

1. Position a rack in the center of the oven and preheat the oven to 400° F.

2. Generously butter the madeleine molds. Place the eggs in a mixing bowl and beat with an electric mixer on medium speed.

THE RIGHT EQUIPMENT

Most gourmet stores sell madeleine pans. I like the standard-size ones made of tin. Always wash and then thoroughly dry the molds after using them, to prevent rusting.

GREAT ACCOMPANIMENTS

The madeleines are, of course, delicious served with tea and coffee, or you could offer them with ice cream, sorbets, or fresh fruit. They are also good with the Marinated Hot Fruit.

Gradually add the sugar in a thin stream, then continue beating until the mixture is very thick, pale yellow in color, and increased in volume, 5 to 8 minutes. Set aside.

3. Combine the flour, baking powder, and spices in a mixing bowl, and stir to mix. Then sift half of these dry ingredients over the beaten egg mixture and gently fold them in. Repeat with the remaining flour mixture. Fold in the vanilla. Pour one third of the melted butter over the batter and fold it in. Repeat with the remaining butter.

4. Fill each mold with 1 tablespoon of batter. The molds should be three-quarters full. (If you fill the molds too full, the madeleines will be difficult to unmold.) You may have a little batter left over after filling the pans. Either discard the extra batter or refill the pans after the first batch of madeleines has been baked.

5. Bake the madeleines until golden, 10 to 15 minutes. Watch carefully so the cakes do not overbrown. Serve warm.

Makes 24 madeleines

Orange and Ginger Butter Cookies

These are old-fashioned butter cookies flavored generously with orange and subtly with ginger. They are the type of cookies I love to dip in a cup of hot tea while curled up with a good book in front of a fire. They are as easy to make as they are good, and they keep well if stored tightly covered.

Special equipment: 2-inch cookie cutter

2 cups all-purpose flour
¼ teaspoon baking powder
¾ teaspoon ground ginger
8 tablespoons (1 stick) unsalted butter, at room temperature
½ cup sugar
1 teaspoon grated orange zest
1 tablespoon thawed orange juice concentrate
1 tablespoon water

AS A VARIATION

If you want a stronger ginger flavor, increase the ginger to 1 teaspoon. For a slightly sweeter flavor, sprinkle the cookies generously with granulated sugar before baking.

GREAT ACCOMPANIMENTS

These cookies are delicious with the Left Bank Coconut Sorbet, the Honeydew Melon Sorbet, and the Red and Green Grape Sorbets.

1. Sift together the flour, baking powder, and ginger in a bowl, and set aside.

2. Place the butter in a mixing bowl, and with an electric mixer on medium speed, cream the butter while gradually adding the sugar. Beat until the mixture is smooth and the sugar is well dissolved, 3 to 4 minutes. Then add the orange zest. Blend the orange juice concentrate and the water, and beat to incorporate.

3. Lower the mixer speed and add the flour mixture. Beat only until well mixed, scraping the sides of the bowl with a spatula, if necessary, to make certain the flour is well incorporated.

4. Gather the dough into a ball, flatten it slightly, and cover it tightly with plastic wrap. Chill the dough in the refrigerator until firm, 45 minutes or longer.

5. When you are ready to roll out the cookies, preheat the oven to 375° F.

6. Divide the dough in half. Place one half on a lightly floured work surface and roll it out ¼ inch thick. Cut out cookies with a 2-inch cookie cutter, and transfer them, using a metal spatula, to two baking sheets, leaving 1 inch space around each cookie. Repeat with the remaining dough. (If you cannot get all the cookies on the two sheets, repeat the process when the first batch has been cooked.)

7. Bake the cookies on two racks in the oven, reversing the sheets top to bottom and front to back once during baking to ensure even cooking, about 10 minutes. Watch carefully. The cookies should be just lightly browned around the edges when done.

8. With a metal spatula, transfer the cookies to a wire rack to cool. Store the cooled cookies in an airtight container. (These cookies can be made 3 to 4 days ahead if stored properly.)

Makes 30 to 36 cookies

Chestnut Brownies

These rich, moist brownies frosted with a chocolate chestnut icing can be made in advance and are nice to take to potlucks and picnics.

Brownies
12 tablespoons (1½ sticks) unsalted butter
3 ounces semisweet chocolate, broken into chunks
2 ounces unsweetened chocolate, broken into chunks
4 large eggs, at room temperature
Pinch of salt
1½ cups sugar
1 teaspoon vanilla extract
1 cup all-purpose flour

Icing
2 tablespoons plus 2 teaspoons water
3½ tablespoons sugar
2 large egg yolks
8 tablespoons (1 stick) unsalted butter, at room temperature
3 ounces semisweet chocolate, melted and cooled
2½ tablespoons sweetened chestnut purée

1. Preheat the oven to 350° F. Butter a 9-inch square baking pan and line the bottom with a sheet of waxed paper. Butter the paper, and dust the paper and pan with flour, shaking out any excess flour.

2. Prepare the brownies: Melt the butter and both chocolates in the top of a double boiler placed over simmering water. Stir until smooth, then remove from the heat and set aside to cool.

3. In a mixing bowl, beat the eggs with the salt until they start to foam. Then gradually add the sugar, beating until the mixture is thick and pale yellow. Stir in the vanilla, and fold in the cooled chocolate mixture. Sift half the flour over the mixture, and fold it in. Repeat with the remaining flour.

4. Pour the brownie mixture into the prepared pan and bake until a toothpick inserted in the center comes out clean, 30 to 35 minutes. Remove from the oven and let the brownies cool in the pan.

5. Run a knife around the edges of the brownies, and invert the pan onto a work surface. Remove the waxed paper. Refrigerate the brownies, covered, until ready to ice.

6. Prepare the icing: Combine the water and sugar in a small saucepan, and stir to dissolve the sugar. Bring the mixture to a boil, and boil for 2 minutes. Remove the pan from the heat.

7. Place the egg yolks in a mixing bowl, and beating with an electric mixer on medium speed, gradually pour in the sugar mixture. Continue to beat until the mixture is thick and pale yellow, 5 minutes. Add the butter, 1 tablespoon at a time, with the mixer on low to medium speed. On low speed add the melted chocolate and the chestnut purée, and mix only a few seconds until smooth. If the icing seems soft, refrigerate it until firm but not hard, about 10 minutes.

8. Spread the icing on the exposed flat side of the brownies in an even layer, but do not ice the sides. Cut into sixteen squares. Place the brownies on a serving plate, cover, and refrigerate. (Brownies can be made 1 day in advance; keep covered and refrigerated.) Let the brownies stand at room temperature 30 to 45 minutes before serving.

Makes 16 brownies

Amaretto Brownies

I like the look of these brownies. Baked in miniature muffin tins, then unmolded and decorated with a dark chocolate glaze and a garnish of toasted almond slices, they are chic little cupcakes.

Special equipment: Two 12-cup miniature (1¾-inch) muffin pans, preferably nonstick

Brownies
½ cup sliced or slivered almonds, toasted (see Index)
8 tablespoons (1 stick) unsalted butter at room temperature
2 ounces unsweetened chocolate
¾ cup sugar
2 large eggs
½ cup all-purpose flour
¼ cup amaretto liqueur

Glaze
4 ounces sweet chocolate, broken into small chunks
4 tablespoons heavy or whipping cream
⅓ cup sliced almonds, toasted (see Index)

THE RIGHT EQUIPMENT

Miniature muffin pans are essential for this recipe. The nonstick variety are the best to use and should still be well buttered.

1. Position a rack in the center of the oven and preheat the oven to 350° F. Butter the muffin molds generously.

2. Prepare the brownies: Process the almonds in a food processor or blender until finely ground. Set aside.

3. Melt 4 tablespoons of the butter and the unsweetened chocolate in the top of a double boiler placed over simmering water. Stir until the mixture is smooth and shiny, 3 to 4 minutes. Set aside.

4. Place the remaining butter and the sugar in the bowl of an electric mixer, and beat on medium speed until the mixture is light and fluffy, about 3 minutes. Then add the eggs, and continue to beat 2 to 3 minutes more. Reduce the speed and add the melted chocolate mixture, flour, amaretto, and ground almonds. Mix only until all ingredients are well incorporated.

5. Fill each muffin cup almost up to the edge with batter.

6. Bake the brownies until they spring back when touched, about 15 minutes. Remove them from the heat and let the brownies cool for 5 minutes; then remove them from the pans and cool to room temperature.

7. While the brownies are cooling, prepare the glaze: Combine the chocolate and cream in a heavy 8- to 10-inch skillet over low heat, and stir until the mixture is smooth and shiny, 3 to 4 minutes. Remove the pan from the heat. Then, one at a time, dip the top of each brownie into the chocolate mixture to coat lightly. Lift the brownie over the skillet and swirl it to let any excess chocolate drip back into the skillet. Use a spatula to smooth the chocolate icing on the brownie. Garnish the top of each glazed brownie with two toasted almond slices. Continue until all the brownies are glazed and decorated. If the chocolate in the skillet gets too thick to use easily, reheat it over low heat just to thin.

8. Let the brownies rest at room temperature until the glaze is set, 30 to 40 minutes. Then cover them with plastic wrap. (The brownies can be stored, covered tightly, at room temperature for 1 to 2 days. They can also be frozen; thaw in the refrigerator and bring to room temperature before using.)

Makes 24 brownies

Lemon Mousse Squares with Date Walnut Crust

I like these tart lemony confections so much and have made them so many times that I've lost track. My students love them because they are simple to prepare and can be made a day in advance.

Special equipment: Pastry bag fitted with a small star tip; food processor

Crust
½ cup chopped walnuts
½ cup chopped dates
¼ cup firmly packed dark brown sugar
4 tablespoons (½ stick) unsalted butter, cut into small pieces
¾ cup all-purpose flour
1 teaspoon vanilla extract

Mousse
1 tablespoon gelatin
1 tablespoon water
5 large eggs, separated
½ cup plus 2 tablespoons fresh lemon juice
2 teaspoons grated lemon zest
⅔ cup sugar
1 cup heavy or whipping cream

Garnish
¾ cup heavy or whipping cream
16 fresh strawberries, rinsed, hulled, and sliced lengthwise
Mint leaves (optional)

1. Position a rack in the center of the oven and preheat the oven to 375° F. Generously butter the sides and bottom of an 8-inch square baking pan.

2. Prepare the crust: Process the walnuts, dates, brown sugar, butter, flour, and vanilla in the bowl of a food processor, using a pulsing action, until the mixture is crumbly. Press the mixture firmly into the bottom of the prepared baking pan. Bake the crust for 8 to 10 minutes. The edges will be browned, but not the center, and the crust will still be somewhat soft to the touch. Remove the pan from the oven and let the crust cool.

AS A VARIATION

For the garnish, any seasonal berry works well. I have used raspberries, blueberries, and blackberries when available, and sometimes a combination of berries. In the winter months, I use a walnut half as a garnish.

3. Prepare the mousse: Combine the gelatin and water in a small bowl and set aside. Place the egg yolks in the top of a double boiler placed over simmering water. Stir, then add the lemon juice and lemon zest. Add ⅓ cup of the sugar and stir until it has dissolved. Cook until the mixture thickens enough to coat the back of a spoon, 4 to 5 minutes. Remove it from the heat and add the softened gelatin, stirring thoroughly. Set the mixture aside to cool.

4. Whip the egg whites with an electric mixer, slowly adding the remaining ⅓ cup sugar, until the whites hold a soft peak. Whip the cream with an electric mixer until it holds soft peaks. Fold the egg whites into the cooled lemon mixture, and then fold in the cream. Spread the mixture evenly over the prepared crust. Cover with plastic wrap and refrigerate for 3 to 4 hours until firm. (The bars may be made a day ahead; keep covered and refrigerated.)

5. To serve the bars, cut the mousse into sixteen squares with a sharp knife, making sure to cut completely through the crust. Remove the squares from the pan. Place the whipped cream in a pastry bag fitted with a small star tip, and pipe a border around the edges of each square. Garnish the center of each square with two strawberry halves and a mint leaf. These are best served on a plate and eaten with a fork.

Makes 16 squares

Lucy's Nanaimo Bars

Neither brownie nor cookie nor candy, these triple-layered chocolate creations are delicious. I first sampled these addictive bars in Toronto, where I was attending an annual meeting of the International Association of Cooking Professionals. As part of the agenda, out-of-town members were invited to sample a Canadian dinner in the homes of Toronto colleagues. The Nanaimo bars were one of the most popular offerings of the evening. The version we tasted was the work of Lucy Waverman, a Toronto cooking teacher, who willingly shared the recipe and the history of the dish. As the story goes, a woman from Nanaimo, British Columbia, invented and entered this confection in a recipe contest and won. The bars became an instant success, and as their fame spread throughout Canada, they became known as Nanaimo bars.

A COOK'S REFLECTIONS

I use these bars in many ways. They are terrific for eating as a snack, and they are nice to serve as an accompaniment to home-made sorbets or ice creams. On many occasions, I have packaged a box of these sweets and taken them as host and hostess presents when I am invited to dinner. During the holidays, I offer baskets of these bars as special gifts for good friends.

Special equipment: 9-inch square metal baking pan

Bottom Layer
2 cups graham cracker crumbs
1 cup sweetened coconut flakes
½ cup chopped walnuts
8 tablespoons (1 stick) unsalted butter, cut into small pieces
6 tablespoons unsweetened cocoa powder
¼ cup sugar
1 large egg, lightly beaten

Middle Layer
2 cups confectioners' sugar
3 tablespoons milk
4 tablespoons (½ stick) unsalted butter, melted
½ teaspoon vanilla extract
2 teaspoons grated lemon zest

Top Layer
6 ounces semisweet chocolate, cut into small chunks
1 tablespoon unsalted butter

1. Position a rack in the center of the oven and preheat the oven to 350° F. Butter a 9-inch square metal baking pan generously, and set it aside.

2. Prepare the bottom layer: Toss the graham cracker crumbs, coconut, and walnuts together in a large bowl. Transfer the crumb mixture to the baking pan.

3. In a small heavy saucepan over low heat, combine the butter, cocoa powder, sugar, and egg, and stir until the butter has melted and the mixture is blended and smooth, 2 to 3 minutes.

4. Pour the butter mixture onto the crumb mixture. Mix well with a fork until the crumb mixture is thoroughly moistened. Use your fingers to firmly pack the crumb mixture evenly on the bottom of the pan. Bake until the layer is just firm to the touch, 10 to 12 minutes.

5. Remove the pan from the oven and let the bottom layer cool completely.

6. Prepare the middle layer: Mix the sugar, milk, butter, vanilla, and lemon zest together in a mixing bowl until icing-like and smooth. Spread this icing evenly over the cooled baked layer in the pan. Refrigerate until the icing is firm, 30 minutes or longer.

7. Prepare the top layer: Melt the chocolate and butter together in the top of a double boiler placed over simmering water. Stir until the mixture is smooth and shiny, 3 to 4 minutes. Let it cool a few minutes, and then spread the chocolate evenly, using an icing spatula or a knife, over the icing layer. Refrigerate just until the chocolate is set, about 15 minutes. Then cut it into 16 large or 32 smaller squares. It is important to cut the squares while the chocolate is firm but not hard; otherwise the chocolate cracks when cut. (These bars can be made 3 to 4 days in advance; keep them covered lightly and refrigerated until needed.)

Makes 16 large or 32 small squares

FROM DAWN
TO DUSK

It's never too early or too late in the day to serve something special from the kitchen. Students remind me of this often, when they ask for new recipes for weekend breakfasts or request an interesting way to serve coffee, the traditional end of an evening meal. The foods in this section are for such occasions. Morning people who like to cook and entertain early in the day will find innovative dishes ideal for breakfast or brunch menus. For lunch, supper, or a late-night feast, the collection of chic sandwiches provides inspiration for delicious yet unusual fare. There is also a collection of drinks—some hot, others cold, a few plain, a handful spirited—which will brighten one's mood no matter what hour of day they are served.

BRUNCHES

As a cooking teacher always devising new offerings for my classes, I find that students often suggest the best ideas. Frequently they ask me to suggest menus for interesting breakfasts or brunches. And when a special early-morning meal class is listed in the school's brochure, these enthusiastic fans promptly fill it to capacity. Some of the best-received recipes from these courses have been the Individual Breakfast Strudels and the Eggs Baked with Chèvre and Artichoke Hearts, two make-ahead creations perfect for large gatherings. For smaller groups the Sour Cream Apple Pancakes, Jenny's Pecan Waffles with Praline Butter, and the Breakfast Tart have received great reviews.

Sour Cream Apple Pancakes with Apricot Butter

When we were renovating our kitchen several years ago, I never knew what to expect on arriving home from work. For a while I had no ceiling, then no lights, then no floors. According to my contractor's whims, I had water on some days, none on others, and I never knew whether to expect electricity or not. After weeks of this chaos, the workmen finally installed a new cooktop, and my family pleaded for some home-cooked meals. These simple apple pancakes are one of the dishes I created one evening in my Spartan kitchen. Everyone, including the electricians who were working late that night, loved the taste of these hotcakes. Since then I have made this recipe often for weekend breakfasts and brunches.

1 Granny Smith apple, peeled, cored, and coarsely grated
2 tablespoons sugar
½ teaspoon ground cinnamon
⅛ teaspoon ground cloves
¼ teaspoon grated lemon zest
½ cup all-purpose flour
¼ teaspoon salt
1 teaspoon baking soda
1 cup sour cream
2 large eggs
2 tablespoons unsalted butter, melted
Vegetable oil
Apricot Butter (recipe follows)

1. Combine the grated apple, sugar, cinnamon, cloves, and lemon zest in a small bowl and mix well. Set aside.

2. Sift the flour, salt, and baking soda together into a mixing bowl. In another bowl whisk together the sour cream and eggs. Add this to the flour mixture, and mix lightly to form a batter. Stir the melted butter into the batter. Then add the prepared apple mixture and any juices that have collected in the bowl, and stir only to mix. Cover and refrigerate the batter for 15 minutes.

3. To cook the pancakes, lightly oil a large heavy skillet or griddle, and place it over medium-high heat. When the pan is hot, spoon 2 tablespoons batter per pancake onto the hot surface. Flatten each

AS A VARIATION

*Although the Apricot Butter is deli-
cious with these hotcakes, some of
my students like to offer them
topped with their favorite apple
butter.*

pancake slightly with a spatula to make a uniformly thin pancake, 3
to 4 inches in diameter. Cook the pancakes until bubbles form on top,
about 3 minutes, and then turn carefully and cook until brown on
the bottom, 1 to 2 minutes more. As the pancakes get done, cover
them with aluminum foil and keep in a preheated 250° F oven. Serve
the pancakes with warm Apricot Butter.

Serves 4

APRICOT BUTTER

*8 tablespoons (1 stick) unsalted butter, cut into small pieces
½ cup apricot jam or preserves
½ teaspoon grated lemon zest*

Melt the butter in a medium-size heavy saucepan over medium-high
heat. Stir in the jam and lemon zest, and continue stirring until just
hot. Remove from the heat. (The Apricot Butter can be made a day
in advance; keep covered and refrigerated, and reheat when
needed.)

Makes about 1 cup

Jenny's Pecan Waffles with Praline Butter

Jenny Workman created these scrumptious waffles for a brunch
class at the school. She explained to the students that she had gotten
the idea while making breakfast one morning. She decided to add
chopped pecans and bourbon to her usual batter, and then, as an
accompaniment, whipped some butter and stirred morsels of crushed
caramelized pecans into it. The result: light golden waffles topped
with swirls of flavorful praline butter, perfect to serve for a special
morning meal.

Special equipment: Waffle iron; pastry bag with a large star tip
(optional); candy thermometer (optional)

3 large eggs, separated
¼ cup firmly packed brown sugar
6 tablespoons (¾ stick) unsalted butter, melted
3 tablespoons bourbon
1 tablespoon vanilla extract
1½ cups milk
2¼ cups sifted all-purpose flour
1 tablespoon baking powder
½ cup chopped pecans
Pinch of salt
Praline Butter, softened (recipe follows)

1. Preheat a waffle iron.

2. With an electric mixer beat the egg yolks and brown sugar until the mixture is thick and pale yellow, 3 to 4 minutes. Set aside.

3. Combine the melted butter, bourbon, vanilla, and milk in a mixing bowl and stir well. Add the milk mixture to the egg/sugar mixture, and stir the batter well.

4. Sift the flour and baking powder together and add to the batter, along with the chopped pecans. Stir well to incorporate.

5. Beat the egg whites with the pinch of salt until firm but not dry, and then gently fold them into the batter. Cook the waffles on the waffle iron until golden and crisp. Place the cooked waffles, loosely covered with aluminum foil, in a preheated 250° F oven to keep warm.

6. Fit a pastry bag with a large star tip and fill it with the softened Praline Butter. Decorate each waffle with a large rosette of praline butter in the center. If you do not have a pastry bag, place a large scoop of the butter on top of each waffle.

Serves 4 to 6

PRALINE BUTTER

½ cup sugar
⅓ cup water
¼ cup pecan halves
¾ cup (1½ sticks) unsalted butter, softened

1. Butter a baking sheet generously.

GREAT ACCOMPANIMENTS

These waffles are delicious served with fried sausage links and a bowl of Marinated Hot Fruit.

2. Place the sugar and water in a medium-size heavy saucepan over medium heat. Stir to dissolve the sugar, and then cook without stirring until the mixture turns rich amber and begins to smell like burning sugar, 8 to 10 minutes. On a candy thermometer this will be just a little over 300° F. Watch carefully, as the sugar will start to caramelize as soon as it reaches the right temperature and will burn quickly if not removed from the heat.

3. Take the caramel mixture off the heat and add the pecans. Quickly pour it onto the buttered baking sheet and let it cool, 10 to 15 minutes. When it has cooled, break up the hardened caramel and grind it into a coarse powder in a food processor, chop it finely with a large knife, or pound it with a mortar and pestle. Stir the praline into the softened butter. (The butter can be made several days in advance; keep covered and refrigerated. Bring to room temperature before using.)

Makes about 1 cup

Breakfast Tart

Several years ago I created a new way to serve the typical bacon, eggs, and toast—in a breakfast tart. I mold white sandwich bread in a springform pan. Brushed with butter and baked, the result is a lightly toasted shell, which I fill with diced Brie, crumbled bacon, and sautéed leeks. After the shell is baked again to melt the Brie, creamy scrambled eggs are spread over the cheese layer.

Special equipment: 8-inch springform pan

Toast Shell
8 slices good-quality white sandwich bread
5 tablespoons unsalted butter, melted, plus more if needed

Filling
8 ounces good-quality Brie cheese, well chilled
5 slices (about 4 ounces) bacon
1 cup finely chopped leeks (white parts only)
8 large eggs
Salt and freshly ground pepper to taste
2 tablespoons unsalted butter
¼ cup heavy or whipping cream
2 tablespoons chopped fresh chives or parsley, for garnish

AS A VARIATION

This tart can be varied to suit your own taste. For example, the Brie and bacon could be replaced with crumbled Roquefort and breakfast sausage, or with sharp Cheddar and chopped baked ham. You might even like to try cream cheese and smoked salmon for a sophisticated version. For a garnish to any of these fillings, you could surround the tart with fresh cooked asparagus or another vegetable of your choice.

1. Preheat the oven to 350° F.

2. Prepare the toast shell: Cut away the crust from the bread, and roll each piece of bread with a rolling pin until it is quite flat. Brush the bottom and sides of an 8-inch springform pan with about 1 tablespoon of the melted butter. Place a slice of bread so that a point reaches just up to the middle of the side of the pan. Gently press the bread against the side of the pan and along the bottom. The bread will not quite reach the center point of the bottom of the pan. Brush the bread generously with melted butter. Place another piece of bread slightly overlapping the first piece and mold it in the same way. Brush with butter. Continue in this manner, using seven slices of bread to make the shell. Cut a 3-inch circle from the eighth slice and place it in the center of the pan. Brush it with butter.

3. Line the toast shell with a sheet of aluminum foil, pressing the foil firmly against the sides and the bottom. Fill the foil with 2 cups dried beans or pie weights, and bake for 12 to 15 minutes. The points of the bread should have just begun to darken, and the bread should be dry to the touch but not golden. Remove the foil and beans and cook 5 minutes more. Remove the pan from the oven but leave the oven on.

4. Prepare the filling: Cut the Brie, including the rind, into ½-inch dice and set aside.

5. Sauté the bacon until crisp in a large skillet. Remove the bacon but reserve the fat. Drain the bacon on paper towels, and crumble. Using 1 tablespoon of the reserved bacon fat, sauté the leeks over medium heat until softened, about 5 minutes.

6. Mix the Brie, bacon, and leeks together in a bowl, and spread evenly in the toast shell. Cover the top of the springform pan loosely with a piece of aluminum foil. Bake until the Brie is melted and hot, 10 minutes. Remove the pan from the oven and set it aside for a few minutes.

7. Meanwhile, mix the eggs lightly with salt and pepper. Melt the butter in a medium-size heavy skillet over medium-high heat. When it is quite hot, add the eggs. Cook, stirring, until the eggs are scrambled to a soft, creamy consistency. Then stir in the cream. Fill the tart with the egg mixture, and sprinkle with chopped chives or parsley. Serve by cutting into wedges.

Serves 6

AS A VARIATION

In place of sausage I have used crumbled fried bacon or good country ham cut into ¼-inch dice. And you can use a favorite Cheddar cheese in place of the Gruyère and Parmesan.

GREAT ACCOMPANIMENTS

For a brunch menu I serve these strudels along with buttered asparagus, Cucumber and Watercress Salad, and Lemon Date Pecan Muffins.

Individual Breakfast Strudels

These unique strudels consist of crisply baked phyllo dough wrapped around a filling of scrambled eggs, cooked crumbled sausage, and fresh herbs in a Mornay sauce. I have made these individual strudels time and again when entertaining, because they can be completely prepared in advance and need only to be baked before serving.

Special equipment: Rimmed baking sheet

10½ tablespoons unsalted butter, melted
1½ tablespoons all-purpose flour
¾ cup milk
6 tablespoons grated Gruyère cheese
2 tablespoons grated imported Parmesan cheese
½ teaspoon salt
Pinch of cayenne pepper
Freshly grated nutmeg to taste
¼ pound bulk pork sausage
5 large eggs
1½ teaspoons minced fresh thyme or ½ teaspoon crumbled dried
Freshly ground black pepper to taste
1 tablespoon minced fresh parsley
6 thick sheets phyllo pastry (see Index)
6 tablespoons dry bread crumbs
Fresh thyme sprigs, for garnish

1. Combine 1½ tablespoons of the butter and the flour in a heavy medium-size saucepan over medium-high heat and stir 3 minutes. Gradually whisk in the milk. Continue whisking until the mixture comes to a boil and thickens, 2 to 3 minutes. Remove the pan from the heat and stir in both cheeses, a little at a time. When all the cheese has been incorporated, add ¼ teaspoon of the salt and the cayenne pepper. Season generously with nutmeg. Pour into a medium-size bowl.

2. Cook the sausage in a medium-size heavy skillet over medium-high heat until no longer pink, breaking the meat into small pieces with a fork, 4 to 5 minutes. Drain on paper towels.

3. Mix the eggs, thyme, remaining ¼ teaspoon salt, and black pepper in a medium-size bowl. Add the sausage. Heat 1 tablespoon of

the melted butter in a large heavy skillet over medium-high heat. Add the eggs, and stir with a fork until just set and scrambled, but still moist. Mix the eggs into the cheese sauce. Add the parsley, and adjust the seasonings. Cool completely.

4. Brush a rimmed baking sheet with some of the remaining melted butter. Arrange one phyllo pastry sheet on a towel on a work surface. (Keep the remaining pastry sheets covered with a damp towel.) Generously brush the pastry sheet with melted butter, and sprinkle with 1 tablespoon of the bread crumbs. Fold the sheet in half lengthwise and brush the surface with butter.

5. Spoon ⅓ cup of the filling on the short end of the phyllo nearest you. Spread the filling horizontally in a 3-inch-wide strip, leaving a ¾-inch border on the long edges. Fold the edges of the two long sides of the pastry over the filling. Starting at the end with the filling, fold the dough up to form a package. Place the package seam side down on the prepared baking sheet. Brush the top with butter. Repeat with the remaining pastry. (The strudels can be prepared 1 day ahead to this point. Wrap them tightly in plastic wrap and refrigerate. Let them stand at room temperature while preheating the oven.)

6. Position a rack in the center of the oven, and preheat the oven to 375° F.

7. Bake the strudels until they are golden brown, about 15 minutes. Allow them to cool for 5 minutes before serving. Garnish each strudel with fresh thyme springs.

Serves 6

Eggs Baked with Chèvre and Artichoke Hearts

Nothing could be more delicious or simpler to assemble than this irresistible combination of eggs baked with marinated artichoke hearts, sweet red peppers, and chèvre. I like to serve this dish for large brunches because the recipe can be doubled or tripled easily and the eggs can be baked and kept warm in a low oven for half an hour before serving.

GREAT ACCOMPANIMENTS

Grilled sausages, a seasonal green salad, and a dessert such as the Poached Pears taste delicious with these eggs.

2 tablespoons olive oil
1 cup finely chopped scallions (green onions), including 1 inch of green stems
⅔ cup finely chopped red bell pepper
2 teaspoons finely chopped garlic
2 jars (6 to 6½ ounces each) marinated artichoke hearts, drained, patted dry, and coarsely chopped
8 ounces good-quality chèvre, such as Montrachet without the ash coating or Bucheron, at room temperature
5 large whole eggs
3 large egg yolks
1 cup heavy or whipping cream
1 cup milk
¼ cup plus 2 tablespoons grated imported Parmesan cheese
Salt and white pepper to taste

1. Preheat the oven to 400° F. Grease a 12 x 8-inch baking dish generously with butter.

2. Heat the oil in a medium-size heavy skillet over medium-high heat. When it is hot, add the scallions and sauté 2 minutes. Add the red peppers and sauté 3 to 4 minutes. Then add the garlic and cook 1 minute more. Remove the skillet from the heat and stir in the chopped artichoke hearts. Drain the mixture on paper towels.

3. Using an electric mixer or a whisk, cream the chèvre until smooth. Beat in the eggs and yolks one by one. On slow speed add the cream and milk, and mix just until incorporated. By hand stir in ¼ cup of the Parmesan cheese. Add the reserved vegetable mixture and stir well. Taste, and if desired, add salt and white pepper.

4. Pour the mixture into the baking dish, and sprinkle the remaining 2 tablespoons Parmesan cheese on top. Bake until the top is browned and a knife inserted in the center comes out clean, 30 to 45 minutes. Serve hot or at room temperature. (This dish holds very well. It can be baked, then covered loosely with foil and left in a 150° F oven for 15 to 20 minutes before serving.)

Serves 6

AT THE MARKET

Fontina cheese is made in Scandinavia and in Italy. For this recipe, the Italian variety is more desirable.

Souffléed Omelet with Porcini and Fontina

I remember the first meal I had in France many years ago as clearly as if it were yesterday. Along with a group of college friends, I ate a fabulous souffléed omelet in Mont St. Michel in Normandy. Never had I tasted an omelet quite so light and airy. This omelet with porcini mushrooms and Fontina cheese is a variation on that memorable dish. It too has a delicate texture and rises an inch off the plate. Served with a hearty tomato sauce, it is perfect to offer for a special-occasion breakfast or brunch.

Special equipment: 10-inch black cast iron skillet with an ovenproof handle and a lid

10 grams (⅓ ounce) dried porcini mushrooms
1 cup boiling water
6 large eggs, separated
¼ cup heavy or whipping cream
¼ teaspoon plus a pinch of salt
Freshly ground pepper to taste
2 tablespoons unsalted butter
¾ cup grated Italian Fontina cheese
Tomato Sauce (recipe follows)
Fresh basil or parsley sprigs, for garnish

1. Place the dried mushrooms in a small mixing bowl and cover them with the boiling water. Let them soak until they are soft, 30 minutes. Drain the mushrooms but reserve the soaking liquid. Rinse the mushrooms under running water, pat dry, and cut into small pieces and set aside. Strain the soaking liquid through a sieve lined with a coffee filter, and set aside to use in the Tomato Sauce.

2. Whisk the egg yolks with the cream, and add the ¼ teaspoon salt and a generous grinding of black pepper. In a separate bowl, beat the egg whites with a pinch of salt until they hold their shape in soft peaks. Fold the whites into the yolk mixture.

3. Set a broiler rack 4 inches from the heat and preheat the broiler.

4. Melt the butter in a black cast iron 10-inch skillet over medium-high heat. When it is melted and foaming, but not browning, pour in half the omelet mixture and spread it evenly in the pan. Quickly

GREAT ACCOMPANIMENTS

*For a brunch or light supper, I like
to serve this omelet with a tossed
green salad in vinaigrette and hot
buttered French or Italian bread.
The Red Grape and Green Grape Sorbets are a good light dessert.*

sprinkle the mushrooms and ½ cup of the cheese over the omelet,
and then spread the remaining omelet mixture over this filling.
Cover, and reduce the heat to medium. Cook for 4 minutes, then
lower the heat to low and cook until the top of the omelet is set but
still a little moist, 3 minutes more. Watch carefully and lift occasionally with a spatula to check that the underside of the omelet is not
browning too rapidly.

5. Uncover the omelet, sprinkle it with the remaining ¼ cup cheese,
and place it under the broiler until the cheese melts and the omelet
puffs, 1 to 2 minutes. Watch carefully. Have ready a plate that is
larger than the skillet. Remove the skillet and immediately invert the
omelet onto the plate. Garnish with several basil or parsley sprigs.
Slice into wedges and serve each slice with a generous amount of
warm Tomato Sauce.

Serves 4

TOMATO SAUCE

2½ tablespoons olive oil
*2½ cups peeled, seeded, chopped fresh tomatoes or chopped,
    drained canned plum tomatoes*
2 teaspoons chopped garlic
*3 tablespoons chopped fresh basil, or 1 tablespoon finely chopped
    fresh parsley and 1 teaspoon dried basil*
⅔ cup strained mushroom soaking liquid from Souffléed Omelet
Salt and freshly ground pepper to taste
Sugar to taste

Heat the olive oil in a heavy skillet over medium heat. When it is
hot, add the tomatoes and garlic. Stir, and add the basil and the
mushroom liquid. Cook over medium heat, uncovered, until the
mixture resembles a purée, about 15 minutes. Taste, and add salt,
pepper, and a pinch of sugar as desired. (This sauce can be made 1
day ahead; cover with plastic wrap and refrigerate. Reheat before
using.)

Makes 1½ to 2 cups

SANDWICHES & SIPS

Twice a month I give an hour-long course called "A Touch of Class." The food, which must be quick and uncomplicated to prepare due to the time restriction, often consists of a bowl of hot homemade soup, a freshly tossed seasonal salad, a "chic" sandwich, and a light dessert. Students have come to appreciate the simplicity of the menus and have especially savored the unusual sandwiches. No matter whether it's the Hot Pita Sandwiches with Corned Beef, Cheese, and Creamy Horseradish or the "Something Special" BLTs, perfect for summer dining, people tell me repeatedly how much they enjoy using these creations for entertaining.

Occasionally it is a drink more than the food that is the star attraction in a class. On cold blustery evenings, for example, the Hot Buttered Cider with Rum has certainly been the *pièce de résistance*. In summer classes, chilled Fresh Fruit Spritzers have given students cause for celebration.

CHIC SANDWICHES

Hot Baguettes with Onions, Pancetta, and Two Cheeses

My friend Jim Budros willingly shared this recipe with me, and I have been offering these baguettes as special luncheon or informal late-night sandwiches ever since.

2 large onions
2 leeks
8 tablespoons (1 stick) unsalted butter
2 teaspoons sugar
12 ounces pancetta, sliced ¼ inch thick
2 French baguettes, 2½ to 3 inches in diameter and 18 inches long
¾ cup olive oil, plus more if needed
12 ounces chèvre cheese, at room temperature
8 ounces Monterey Jack cheese, grated (about 2 cups)
Freshly ground pepper to taste

1. Peel the onions, cut them in half, then cut them into ¼-inch-thick slices. You should have 4 cups. Trim the leeks, slice them in half lengthwise, and rinse them well under cold water and pat dry. Cut the leeks into strips 2 inches long and ¼ inch wide. You should have 1½ cups.

2. Melt the butter in a heavy 10- to 11-inch skillet over medium heat. When it is hot, add the onions and leeks and cook over low heat, stirring, 4 to 5 minutes.

3. Sprinkle the mixture with the sugar, and continue to cook slowly, stirring, until the onions and leeks are well browned, about 30 minutes. Remove the mixture and drain on paper towels.

4. Meanwhile, cut the pancetta into ¼-inch dice. In another heavy 10- to 11-inch skillet, sauté the pancetta cubes very slowly over medium heat until they are golden and just crisp, about 15 minutes. Remove, and drain on paper towels. (The recipe may be prepared

AS A VARIATION

To serve these baguettes as hors d'oeuvres, simply slice each cooked baguette into 2-inch pieces and arrange them on a warm serving plate garnished with fresh lemon leaves.

several hours in advance to this point. Cover both the onion mixture and the pancetta loosely with plastic wrap and leave at room temperature.)

5. Position a rack in the center of the oven and preheat the oven to 350° F.

6. Split each baguette in half lengthwise. Drizzle olive oil generously over the cut surface of each half. Using a pastry brush, brush the oil evenly over each baguette, using additional oil if necessary. Spread each bread half with one quarter of the chèvre. Then divide the onion mixture into fourths, and place some on top of each chèvre layer. Sprinkle each baguette with one quarter of the fried pancetta and one quarter of the grated Monterey Jack. Finally, sprinkle the baguettes with pepper.

7. Arrange the assembled baguettes on a baking sheet, and place it on the center shelf of the oven. Bake, uncovered, until the sandwiches are hot and the cheese has melted, about 15 minutes.

8. Remove the baguettes from the oven and let them rest before slicing, 3 to 4 minutes. Cut each baguette into four equal pieces. Serve hot.

Serves 8

Hot Pitas with Corned Beef, Cheese, and Creamy Horseradish

These unusual sandwiches go well with bowls of hearty soup for easy, informal meals. The horseradish sauce can be made ahead and the pita pockets assembled in advance, so all that is necessary at the last minute is to heat the sandwiches in the oven.

6 pita breads (6- to 7-inch rounds)
6 tablespoons (¾ stick) unsalted butter, at room temperature
2 pounds best-quality corned beef, very thinly sliced
12 ounces thinly sliced Baby Swiss or Gruyère cheese
1 cup sour cream
2 tablespoons mayonnaise
1½ teaspoons prepared horseradish
Salt to taste
Paprika to taste

GREAT ACCOMPANIMENTS

Tomato Soup without the Avocado Cream Garnish, and served warm rather than chilled, is delicious with these sandwiches. A plate of Amaretto Brownies is nice to offer for a sweet ending.

1. Slice the pita breads in half so you have two half-moon-shaped pockets. Spread some softened butter on the inside of each half. Then fill each half evenly with alternating slices of corned beef and cheese. Wrap each half tightly in foil. Place them on a baking sheet and set aside. (The sandwiches can be assembled 1 hour in advance and kept at a cool room temperature.)

2. To prepare the sauce, combine the sour cream, mayonnaise, and horseradish, stirring until well incorporated. Season the sauce with salt and sprinkle with paprika. (The sauce can be prepared several hours in advance; keep covered and refrigerated. Bring to room temperature before serving.)

3. When you are ready to cook the sandwiches, preheat the oven to 400° F.

4. Bake the sandwiches until the cheese has melted and is bubbling, about 10 minutes. Remove the foil and serve the sandwiches hot. Pass the horseradish sauce separately.

Serves 6

A Fanciful Foursome

Here are four sandwiches, all made with familiar staples—chicken, ham, pork, and roast beef—but with innovative seasonings. I like to make this quartet as an ensemble to serve at tailgates, picnics, or any special informal gathering.

PIG IN A POKE

2 slices dark pumpernickel bread
1 to 2 tablespoons unsalted butter, at room temperature
2 ounces baked ham, thinly sliced
3 thin slices Vermont Cheddar cheese
2 tablespoons good-quality mango chutney

Spread both slices of bread generously with butter. Place the ham slices on one piece of buttered bread; top with the cheese slices. Spread chutney on top of the cheese, and cover with the remaining slice of bread. Slice in half.

Serves 1

CHICKEN LITTLE

¼ cup homemade mayonnaise (see Index) or good-quality
 commercial brand
¼ teaspoon best-quality curry powder
2 slices best-quality white bread
2 ounces sliced cooked chicken
6 paper-thin slices peeled cucumber
3 sprigs watercress

1. Combine the mayonnaise and curry powder in a small bowl and mix well. (This will make ¼ cup curried mayonnaise, enough for four sandwiches.)

2. Spread each slice of bread generously with ½ tablespoon or more of the curried mayonnaise. Place the sliced chicken on one piece of bread, and cover it with cucumber slices. Top it with watercress and the remaining slice of bread. Slice in half.

Serves 1

SPECTACULAR BID

1½ ounces cream cheese, at room temperature
1 tablespoon sour cream
1½ tablespoons chopped fresh dill, or 1½ teaspoons dried
1½ tablespoons coarsely chopped kosher dill pickle
Salt to taste
2 slices rye bread
2½ ounces thinly sliced roast beef

1. Combine the cream cheese, sour cream, dill, and pickle in a small bowl and mix well. Taste, and add salt if needed. (This sauce can be made several hours in advance; keep covered and refrigerated.)

2. Spread each slice of bread generously with the cream cheese dill sauce. Then place the roast beef on one slice of bread and top it with the other. Slice in half.

Serves 1

GREAT ACCOMPANIMENTS

Sometimes I cut each of these sand-
wiches into quarters and arrange
them attractively on a large platter
with a border of whole scallions and
cherry tomatoes. They go well with
the Tomato and Corn Bisque and, as
dessert, the Chestnut Brownies or
Lucy's Nanaimo Bars.

THE CHINA CONNECTION

2 ounces cold roast pork, thinly sliced
2 slices whole wheat bread
1 tablespoon hoisin sauce
1½ tablespoons coarsely chopped scallions (green onions)
2 tablespoons shredded iceberg lettuce

Place the slices of roast pork on one slice of bread. Spread the hoisin sauce over the pork. Sprinkle the scallions over the sauce, and then add the shredded lettuce. Top with the remaining slice of bread, and slice in half.

Serves 1

"Something Special" BLTs

I think just about everybody loves a good BLT—the quintessential American sandwich. Certainly of all the sandwich recipes we have tested for this book, the response to these special bacon, lettuce, and tomato creations was among the most enthusiastic. Made with lightly toasted sourdough bread and fresh basil mayonnaise, these sandwiches are indeed something special.

12 slices bacon
2 round loaves sourdough bread, each about 5½ inches in
*   diameter*
Basil Mayonnaise (recipe follows)
2 large ripe tomatoes, thinly sliced
Boston or Bibb lettuce greens, coarsely shredded
Basil sprigs, for garnish

1. Fry the bacon in a large skillet until crisp. Drain it well on paper towels.

2. Preheat the broiler.

3. Cut each bread in half horizontally and scoop out the soft center, leaving two shells. Toast the halves, cut side up, under the broiler until crisp but not colored, 3 to 4 minutes. Allow the bread to cool.

4. Spread each toasted half generously with about ¼ cup Basil Mayonnaise.

GREAT ACCOMPANIMENTS

My idea of a wonderful, easy summer lunch or light supper is to serve these sandwiches along with tall glasses of freshly made minted iced tea and a bowl of crisp potato chips. For dessert either the Peaches and Cream Cheesecake or the Coconut Cream Mousse Pie is scrumptious.

5. Place the tomatoes over the two bottom halves of the bread. Top with bacon strips and lettuce. Replace the top halves. Place each sandwich on a serving plate and cut into quarters; garnish each sandwich with a basil sprig. Serve immediately.

Serves 2 to 4

BASIL MAYONNAISE

1 large egg, at room temperature
1 tablespoon fresh lemon juice
1 teaspoon Dijon mustard
¼ teaspoon salt
½ cup vegetable oil
½ cup olive oil
1 cup coarsely chopped fresh basil leaves

1. Place the egg, lemon juice, mustard, and salt in the bowl of a food processor or blender. Process several seconds to mix well.

2. With the machine running, add the oils in a thin stream through the feed tube until all of the oil has been incorporated and the mayonnaise is thickened and smooth.

3. Add the basil leaves and process about 1 minute more, until the basil is finely minced and well blended into the mayonnaise. Refrigerate the mayonnaise, covered. (The mayonnaise can be made 1 day in advance. Cover with plastic wrap and refrigerate.)

Makes about 1 cup

DRINKS

AT THE MARKET

Fresh cider, without preservatives, tastes best in this drink. Myers's dark rum is the one I always use to flavor the cider. You can omit the rum for a nonalcoholic preparation; it will still taste good.

Hot Buttered Cider with Rum

For me, visions of winter in Ohio include a snow-covered landscape, a glowing fire warming the hearth, and a warm spirited drink in my hand to stave off the Midwestern cold. Seasoned with oranges, cinnamon, and rum, this hot buttered cider, with its robust flavor and alluring aroma, is a drink I make every year when the temperature starts to plunge.

GREAT ACCOMPANIMENTS

I often serve the Chestnut Brownies or the Spiced Madeleines along with this warm cider.

1 gallon fresh, untreated cider
8 tablespoons (1 stick) unsalted butter
1 cup firmly packed dark brown sugar
28 thin orange slices (about 5 oranges)
¼ teaspoon ground cloves
4 cinnamon sticks, 2 to 3 inches long
1 cup dark rum
20 cinnamon sticks, for garnish (optional)

1. Heat the cider in a large saucepan until it is warmed through.

2. While the cider is being heated, melt the butter in a large heavy pot over medium heat. When the butter has melted, add the brown sugar and stir 2 to 3 minutes. Add the warm cider and continue to stir until all the sugar has dissolved. Add 8 of the orange slices, the ground cloves, 4 cinnamon sticks, and the rum. Stir, and cook at a simmer for about 10 minutes.

3. To serve, ladle the cider into cups or mugs. Garnish each serving with a slice of orange and a cinnamon stick. (You can make this drink several hours in advance. Let it cool, uncovered, at room temperature. Reheat, stirring constantly, when ready to serve.)

Serves 20

AT THE MARKET

Use cardamom pods, not ground cardamom. The pods should be crushed gently with your hand or a pounder and added directly to the wine mixture.

GREAT ACCOMPANIMENTS

I often serve this hot mulled wine at Christmastime with a generous offering of sweets such as the Christmas Cheesecake, Lucy's Nanaimo Bars, and the Apricot, Pear, and Almond Strudels.

Warm Spiced Zinfandel with Cranberries and Orange

This hot zinfandel combined with cranberry juice and orange peel and simmered with cloves, cinnamon, and cardamom is enticing and easy to assemble, and its wonderful fragrance permeates the kitchen.

2 cups water
1 cup sugar
3 cups red zinfandel wine
1½ cups cranberry juice
4 cinnamon sticks, 3 to 4 inches long, broken in half
12 whole cardamom pods, crushed
12 whole cloves
8 strips orange zest, 3 inches long and ½ inch wide

1. Combine the water and sugar in a medium-size heavy saucepan over medium-high heat, swirling the pan occasionally until the sugar dissolves. Then increase the heat and bring the syrup to a boil. Boil without stirring for 5 minutes. Cool the syrup completely, then cover, and refrigerate until needed.

2. Add the zinfandel, cranberry juice, cinnamon sticks, crushed cardamom pods, cloves, and orange zest to the sugar syrup, and bring the mixture to a simmer over medium heat. Cook at a simmer for 10 to 15 minutes. Strain, and serve in cups or mugs. (This drink can be made several hours in advance. Let it cool, uncovered, at room temperature. Reheat, stirring constantly.)

Serves 8

Aunt Susan's Lemonade

I discovered this recipe tucked away in one of my relative's files. Nobody recalls an "Aunt Susan," but her lemonade is our favorite.

2½ cups water
2 cups sugar
1 cup fresh lemon juice (6 lemons)
¼ cup fresh orange juice (½ orange)
¾ cup loosely packed fresh mint leaves, rinsed and patted dry
Fresh mint sprigs, for garnish
Thin lemon slices, for garnish

1. Place the water and sugar in a medium-size saucepan over medium heat. Stir until the sugar has dissolved, and cook 5 minutes. Remove from the heat and let cool about 20 minutes.

2. Add the lemon juice and orange juice to the sugar syrup. Place the mint leaves in a mixing bowl, and pour the lemon-orange mixture over them. Let the mixture stand for 1 hour. Strain the lemonade into a jar, and keep it covered in the refrigerator. (The base can be stored in the refrigerator for several days.)

3. To serve, place ⅓ cup lemonade in a glass. Stir in ⅔ cup water. Fill the glass with ice cubes, and garnish it with a sprig of mint and a lemon slice.

Serves 12

A COOK'S REFLECTIONS

Legend has it that lemonade was invented by the Arabs around the time of Omar Khayyám—at the end of the eleventh and beginning of the twelfth century. They used the juice of lemons to create a drink to quench their thirst.

Today there are many variations on classic chilled lemonade. For example, you can add a scoop of lemon sherbet to a glass of lemonade to make a lemonade float, or you can use carbonated water to produce a lemon fizz. Some people serve hot lemonade, made with boiling water and often spiked with a dash of rum or whiskey, as a cold remedy.

For a tarter lemonade, you can increase the amount of lemon juice in this recipe as desired.

Fresh Fruit Spritzers

The idea for this drink came about during a trip I made to Italy one year. I was in Florence during one of the hottest summers on record, and when I stopped in *trattorie* and cafés to quench my thirst, I discovered *macedonia di frutta,* a glass of chilled fruit covered with a cold, slightly sweet liquid. Upon returning home I developed this interesting variation made with a combination of white wine, soda water, and a light sugar syrup along with fresh fruit.

Special equipment: Six 8-ounce wine glasses; drinking straws (optional)

1 cup water
½ cup sugar
1 cup dry white wine
1 cup club soda
6 cups mixed fruit (any combination of sliced peaches or
nectarines, sliced strawberries, raspberries, blueberries,
cantaloupe cubes, honeydew melon cubes, watermelon cubes,
and seedless grapes)
6 sprigs mint, for garnish

1. Combine the water and sugar in a medium-size heavy saucepan over medium-high heat, swirling the pan occasionally until the sugar dissolves. Then increase the heat and bring the syrup to a boil. Boil without stirring for 5 minutes. Cool the syrup completely, then cover, and refrigerate until needed. (Sugar syrup can be made several weeks in advance. Keep it covered and refrigerated.)

2. Combine the sugar syrup with the wine and club soda in a large non-aluminum bowl, and set aside. Fill each of six 8-ounce wine glasses with 1 cup of the mixed fruit, and pour ½ cup of the wine mixture over the fruit. Place the filled wine glasses in the freezer until they are chilled and the fruit is very cold, about 45 minutes to 1 hour.

3. Garnish each glass with a sprig of mint, and if desired, a straw. Sip the liquid, then eat the fruit.

Serves 6

A COOK'S REFLECTIONS

The origin of the name "mint julep" is interesting. "Julep" is from the Persian *julab* or *gulab,* meaning a sweet concoction made with rosewater. The word came into usage in our country in the eighteenth century and of course today is widely used to describe the Kentucky cocktail made with sugar, whiskey, and mint leaves.

Louisiana Mint Juleps

My husband, who was born and raised in the South, rarely does any cooking, but he does fancy himself accomplished in one culinary area—and that is in making mint juleps. He needs little excuse to roll up his sleeves and whip up a batch of these potent libations.

Special equipment: 10-ounce glass (or mint julep cup, if available), well chilled; drinking straw

1½ tablespoons sugar
3 sprigs fresh mint
Shaved or crushed ice
3 ounces bourbon

Place the sugar in the bottom of a chilled 10-ounce glass or cup, and moisten it with just enough water to dissolve the sugar. Rub two of the mint sprigs between your fingers, then rub the inside of the glass or cup with the mint. Leave the mint in the bottom of the cup, and pack the cup with crushed ice up to the rim. Fill the cup with bourbon until the liquor is just visible at the top of the cup. Stir. Serve immediately, garnished with the remaining sprig of fresh mint and a straw.

Serves 1

A COOK'S REFLECTIONS

According to Stan Delaplane, a writer for the *San Francisco Chronicle,* Irish coffee was first served by Joe Sheridan, a chef at the Shannon Airport in Ireland. Delaplane claims to have been among a group of passengers who, during a flight delay in 1950, tried "gaelic coffee," as it was called on the menu. Intrigued, the writer brought the recipe back to the States and in 1952 shared it with one of the owners of the Buena Vista Bar in San Francisco. The rest is history. The bar is known here as the home of Irish coffee.

Murray's Irish Coffee

Murray Beja, chairman of the English department at Ohio State University and a specialist in twentieth-century Irish literature, makes the best Irish coffee I have ever sampled. Having spent several sabbaticals in Ireland, Murray has perfected his technique for making this celebrated drink and shared the recipe with me.

Special equipment: Irish coffee glass or sturdy 8-ounce wine glass or cup

2 tablespoons Jameson's or other good-quality Irish whiskey
2 teaspoons sugar
⅓ cup freshly brewed hot coffee (preferably strong, dark French roast)
2 to 3 tablespoons softly whipped cream

1. Place the whiskey and sugar in an 8-ounce glass or cup, and stir with a spoon until the sugar has dissolved. Pour in the hot coffee so that it fills the glass or cup three-quarters full, and stir again.

2. Hold a tablespoon with the back facing you over the cup, and ladle the whipped cream onto the back of the spoon so that it gently falls onto the coffee. (This method causes the whipped cream to float on the coffee rather than sink to the bottom.)

Serves 1

GREAT ACCOMPANIMENTS

Since this coffee is filling, I offer it either alone or with something light, such as Spiced Madeleines, at the end of a meal.

Amaretto Chocolate Coffee

Chocolate, whipped cream, and amaretto make wonderful additions to a cup of well-brewed coffee. Rich and warm, this could easily replace dessert at an informal meal.

Special equipment: Drip coffee pot

1 cup heavy or whipping cream
¼ cup finely ground French roast or other strong, dark coffee
*   beans*
1 cinnamon stick, 3 to 4 inches long, split lengthwise
5 cups cold water
1½ tablespoons sugar
2 tablespoons unsweetened cocoa powder
¼ to ⅓ cup amaretto liqueur

1. Whip the cream until it is just firm. Set it aside in the refrigerator.

2. Place the freshly ground coffee and the cinnamon pieces in a paper filter fitted into a drip coffee pot. If your pot is electric, add cold water and process. If you are using a manual drip pot, bring the water to a rapid boil and process. Keep the coffee warm.

3. Combine the sugar and cocoa powder in a saucepan. Add the brewed coffee and amaretto to taste, and stir to dissolve. Place the pan over very low heat and stir until the mixture is warmed but not boiling. Remove the pan from the heat.

4. Fill four coffee cups with the coffee mixture, and garnish each with a generous dollop of whipped cream.

Serves 4

AT THE MARKET

This tea really tastes best made with orange pekoe tea. I tried several other varieties and none worked as well as Twinings blend.

Spiced Indian Tea

On a trip to London I sampled a delicious hot tea at an Indian restaurant called The Last Days of the Raj. It was one of those cold, damp London nights and my husband and I were having a quick meal before going to the theater. After a hearty dinner we ordered cups of tea—expecting, of course, English tea. But instead our waiter arrived with a pot of aromatic tea prepared with Indian spices. Nothing could have been more satisfying on that chilly evening. After my second cup I asked the waiter how it was made and jotted down his directions. When I got home I did some experimenting and came up with this very close facsimile.

2 orange pekoe tea bags
8 bay leaves
8 whole cardamom pods, crushed gently until just cracked
1 stick cinnamon, 3 to 4 inches long, cut or broken in half
    lengthwise
2 cups boiling water

Place the tea bags, bay leaves, crushed cardamom pods, and cinnamon sticks in a teapot. Pour in the boiling water, and let the mixture steep about 2 minutes. Remove the tea bags but let the spices steep 5 minutes more. Strain and serve hot. An additional 1 to 1½ cups boiling water can be added to the spice mixture in the teapot as the tea is drunk.

Serves 2

AT THE MARKET

Use a good-quality sweet chocolate in this drink for the best results. Maillard's Eagle Chocolate, which is available in many specialty food shops, has a terrific flavor and works very well.

Hot Chocolate à la Angelina

Angelina's is a large tearoom on the Rue de Rivoli in Paris. Always crowded, it is best known for its fabulous hot chocolate. On one trip to Paris I went to the restaurant five days in a row to sip their ethereal concoction and to try to get the secret recipe. The waitresses were like tombs—silent and unwilling to divulge the establishment's directions for making this special brew. Finally, one of them confided in me that the hot drink was made with milk and chocolate bars broken into pieces, heated together, and stirred for a long time. Back home I spent the better part of a Saturday making pots of hot

chocolate until I had duplicated the Parisian original. The following recipe was the winning combination.

½ cup heavy or whipping cream
2 teaspoons confectioners' sugar
1 bar (4 ounces) best-quality sweet chocolate
2 cups milk

1. Whip the cream until it just starts to mound, then add the confectioners' sugar and continue whipping until the cream is just firm. Set aside in the refrigerator.

2. Break the chocolate bar into coarse chunks. Place the chocolate and the milk in the top of a double boiler placed over simmering water. Stir the mixture constantly until all the chocolate has melted. Continue to stir with a wooden spoon until the mixture is very smooth and slightly thickened, 10 to 15 minutes. When stirring the mixture, make certain that you scrape the bottom of the pan well, because the chocolate tends to collect there.

3. When you are ready to serve the chocolate, pour it into a small pitcher. Serve with a bowl of whipped cream.

Serves 2 to 4

Strawberry Yogurt Milkshake

When my son, Michael, was twelve he suffered a broken leg. I created this calcium-rich, strawberry-flavored milkshake, to help speed his recovery. Many years later, with bones all mended, he still enjoys this special drink.

1 cup milk
½ cup heavy or whipping cream
1 package (10 ounces) frozen strawberries, partially thawed
½ cup plain yogurt
3 generous scoops best-quality vanilla ice cream

Combine all the ingredients in a blender, mixer, or food processor, and process until the mixture is smooth and frothy. Pour into glasses and serve immediately.

Serves 2

BASICS

A COOK'S REFLECTIONS

Chicken or beef that has been simmered slowly for several hours in the preparation of stock usually retains little flavor by the end of the cooking time. More often than not I discard these meats, along with the vegetables, when I strain the stocks. Occasionally, however, I have added the cooked beef to a pot of well-seasoned chili or have combined the pieces of cooked poultry with a curried mayonnaise to make chicken salad with satisfactory results.

Homemade Chicken Stock

A good chicken stock has to simmer for several hours, but it's one of the best investments a cook can make. If not used right away, it can be covered and frozen until needed.

1 chicken (3 pounds)
2 onions, quartered
2 carrots, cut into 1-inch slices
2 ribs celery, cut into 1-inch slices
3 sprigs parsley
½ teaspoon dried thyme
2 cloves garlic, crushed
1½ teaspoons salt, or to taste
3 quarts water, plus more if needed

1. Combine all the ingredients in a large saucepan or stockpot, and add 3 quarts of water. Bring the mixture to a simmer over medium-high heat. Lower the heat and simmer, uncovered, until the stock has developed a good flavor, 2½ to 3 hours or longer. Spoon off any scum that rises to the top during the cooking. If the water cooks down below the level of the ingredients, add more water.

2. When the stock is done, remove it from the heat and strain it through a fine-mesh strainer or sieve. Discard the vegetables and either discard the chicken or save it for another use. Remove the grease from the stock before using. (The easiest way to degrease the stock is to refrigerate it for several hours; the grease will solidify on top and then you can remove it easily with a spoon.) Taste the stock, and add more salt if desired. (Stock can be made 1 to 2 days in advance and refrigerated, or it can be frozen.)

Makes about 2 quarts

Homemade Beef Stock

Beef stock takes more time than poultry stock, but it too is a very wise investment of a cook's time.

2 pounds lean beef, cut into 1- to 2-inch cubes
2 pounds beef soup bones
2 carrots, cut into ½-inch slices
2 large onions, cut into ½-inch slices
2 celery stalks, leaves included, cut into ½-inch slices
1 clove garlic, crushed
½ teaspoon dried thyme
1 bay leaf, broken in half
3 sprigs parsley
1 cup dry white wine
2 tablespoons tomato paste
Salt to taste
4 quarts cold water, plus more if needed

1. Preheat the oven to 450° F.

2. Place the beef cubes and bones, carrots, onions, and celery in a roasting pan. Brown them in the oven for about 15 minutes. If the vegetables start to burn, remove them.

3. Place the browned beef and vegetables in a large stockpot or deep-sided pot (at least 8-quart size). Add the garlic, thyme, bay leaf, parsley sprigs, wine, tomato paste, and salt. Stir in 4 quarts cold water. Place the pot over medium heat, and very slowly bring the water to a boil. When the mixture reaches a boil, lower the heat and simmer the stock, 3½ to 4 hours. Add water if the liquid cooks down below the level of the meat and vegetables. Remove any scum that accumulates in the pot during cooking.

4. When the stock is done, remove the pot from the heat and strain the stock through a fine-mesh strainer or sieve. Discard the meat, bones, and vegetables. Remove the grease from the stock. (The easiest way to degrease the stock is to refrigerate it for several hours. The grease will solidify on top, and then you can remove it easily with a spoon.) Taste the stock, and add more salt if desired. (Stock can be made 1 to 2 days in advance and refrigerated, or it can be frozen.)

Makes about 2 quarts

Classic Mayonnaise

Homemade mayonnaise is far superior to any commercial product and is easy to make either by hand or in a food processor. If you remember to have all the ingredients at room temperature and to add the oil very slowly, you should have no problems producing excellent mayonnaise.

3 large egg yolks if making recipe by hand; 2 large egg yolks plus
*   1 large whole egg if making it in a food processor*
½ teaspoon salt
Generous pinch of cayenne pepper
2 tablespoons plus 1 teaspoon fresh lemon juice
1 teaspoon Dijon mustard
¾ cup olive oil
¾ cup vegetable or corn oil

1. Have all the ingredients at room temperature.

2. To prepare the mayonnaise by hand, rinse a mixing bowl with hot water and dry it thoroughly. Place the egg yolks in the bowl and add the salt, cayenne pepper, lemon juice, and mustard and whisk until incorporated. Combine the oils in a measuring cup with a spout. Very slowly, whisking by hand or using medium speed on a mixer, add the oil a drop or two at a time. After about ½ cup has been added in this manner, start adding the oil in a very thin stream, and continue until all the oil has been incorporated. It is important to add the oil slowly so the mixture does not separate or curdle. (The mayonnaise can be kept covered and refrigerated for 2 to 3 days. Always store mayonnaise in the refrigerator.)

To prepare the mayonnaise in a food processor, place 2 egg yolks and 1 whole egg in the bowl of the processor. Add the salt, cayenne pepper, lemon juice, and mustard. Turn the machine on, and process several seconds until all the ingredients are well blended. Then combine the oils in a measuring cup with a spout, and with the processor running, slowly add the oil in a very thin stream through the feed tube until all the oil has been added and the mixture is thick and smooth. Remove the mayonnaise from the processor and store it in the same way as for the hand method.

Makes 1¾ to 2 cups

Crème Fraîche

There are many ways to make crème fraîche, the classic French cream that is thicker and less sweet than our American heavy cream. This is the way that always works best at my school.

1 cup heavy or whipping cream
⅓ cup sour cream

Combine the heavy cream and the sour cream in a medium-size bowl and mix well. Let it stand, uncovered, in a warm spot for 6 to 7 hours or overnight, until thickened. (Crème fraîche can be covered and stored in the refrigerator for up to 1 week.)

Makes 1⅓ cups

Basic Pasta Dough

This is my favorite pasta recipe, the one I use over and over again. Just remember that when making pasta, just as when making bread, the amount of liquid needed will depend on the dryness of the flour. If the flour is very dry, you will need to add more eggs.

Special equipment: Food processor; pasta machine

3 cups flour (see Step 1)
½ teaspoon salt
5 large eggs
1 tablespoon vegetable oil

1. Measure the flour by lightly spooning it into a measuring cup.

2. Place the flour, salt, 4 of the eggs, and the oil in the work bowl of a food processor. Turn the machine on and off several times; then process for 45 to 60 seconds. Check the dough by pinching a bit of it between your fingers. It should be slightly moist and should hold together easily. If it appears to be dry, lightly beat the extra egg. Process the mixture again, adding half the beaten egg through the feed tube. Stop the machine and check the texture again. If needed, add the remaining half of the beaten egg. The dough will be slightly lumpy.

3. Remove the dough from the machine and knead it by hand for 3 to 4 minutes, until it is smooth. (The dough should have the texture of an ear lobe.) Divide the dough into six portions and cover them with a lightly moistened kitchen towel.

4. Place a pasta machine (hand cranked or electric) on the widest setting and run a piece of dough through once. Fold the dough in half and run it through again. Repeat this process several times until the dough is very smooth. Then roll the piece of dough through each setting, only once and without folding, until the dough is paper thin. For lasagne noodles, cut the dough into the desired lengths. For specific noodle shapes, run the dough through the attachment that cuts the shape you desire—linguine, fettuccine, and so on.

5. Spread the noodles out on a lightly floured surface to dry, 30 minutes. While they dry, repeat this process with the remaining dough. (The noodles can be used right away, or they can be stored in a sealed plastic bag at room temperature and kept for several weeks.)

Makes about 1¼ pounds

Quick Puff Pastry

When I first saw a recipe for quick puff pastry I couldn't believe that this classic dough, which usually takes at least six hours to make, could be prepared from start to finish in under two hours. This is my variation on this easy technique.

Special equipment: Heavy-duty electric mixer, preferably with a flat beater attachment; dough scraper

1½ cups unbleached all-purpose flour
½ cup cake flour
1½ cups plus 2 tablespoons (3¼ sticks) unsalted butter
½ teaspoon salt
¼ to ½ cup ice water, plus more if needed

1. Refrigerate both flours for 1 hour. Freeze the butter for 15 minutes. Then cut the butter into paper-thin slices.

2. Combine the chilled flours and the salt in the bowl of an electric mixer fitted with a flat or paddle attachment. Place the sliced butter on top, and mix on slow speed until the butter is broken into very small pieces and well coated with flour. Add the water gradually, adding just enough to make the mixture form a mass of dough. Some of the butter will still be in lumps. (If the flour is extremely dry, you may need to use additional water. Add extra water slowly, 1 to 2 tablespoons at a time.)

3. On a lightly floured surface, roll the lumpy dough out to form a rectangle 12 to 14 inches long and 8 inches wide. The lumps of butter will show through the dough. With the short side nearest you, fold the dough into thirds as for a business letter. This process of rolling and folding the dough into thirds is called a "turn."

4. Lift the dough off the work surface, scrape the surface clean, and reflour. Return the folded dough to the work surface with a short side nearest you. Repeat this rolling and folding process three more times, for a total of four turns. With the ball of your finger, make four depressions in the dough to indicate that four turns have been made. Wrap the dough tightly in plastic wrap, and refrigerate it for 40 minutes to 1 hour.

5. Remove the dough from the refrigerator and roll, fold, and turn the dough two more times. Wrap it in plastic again, and refrigerate it for 30 minutes or longer. The dough can now be rolled and used as needed. (The puff pastry can be made 2 days ahead and kept covered and refrigerated, or it can be frozen. Bring frozen dough to refrigerator temperature at least a day before it is needed.)

Makes 1¾ pounds

Toasted Nuts and Seeds

A few minutes spent toasting certain nuts and seeds reaps great dividends. Baking them until they are golden or lightly browned brings out their flavor.

Special equipment: Rimmed baking sheet

ALMONDS

1. Preheat the oven to 350° F.

2. Spread the almonds (blanched whole, slivers, or slices) on a rimmed baking sheet, and bake on the center shelf of the oven until golden, 8 to 10 minutes. Watch carefully and stir once or twice.

A COOK'S REFLECTIONS

Nuts can be kept a long time if stored properly. I package shelled nuts in thick airtight plastic bags and keep them in the freezer until needed.

3. Remove the baking sheet from the oven and transfer the nuts to a work surface to cool.

HAZELNUTS

1. Preheat the oven to 350° F.

2. Spread the hazelnuts (shelled but with the skins left on) on a rimmed baking sheet, and bake on the center shelf of the oven approximately 10 minutes. Watch carefully and stir once or twice.

3. Remove the baking sheet from the oven, and while the nuts are still hot, place a handful at a time in a clean kitchen towel and rub them together to remove as much of the skin as possible.

PECANS

1. Preheat the oven to 350° F.

2. Spread the pecan halves on a rimmed baking sheet, and bake on the center shelf of the oven until just lightly browned, 5 to 8 minutes.

3. Remove the baking sheet from the oven and transfer the nuts to a work surface to cool.

PINE NUTS

1. Preheat the oven to 350° F.

2. Spread the pine nuts on a rimmed baking sheet, and bake on the center shelf of the oven until lightly browned, about 5 minutes. Pine nuts toast quickly and can burn easily, so watch very carefully.

3. Remove the baking sheet from the oven and transfer the nuts to a work surface to cool.

SESAME SEEDS

1. Preheat the oven to 350° F.

2. Spread the sesame seeds on a rimmed baking sheet, and bake on the center shelf of the oven until golden, 10 to 15 minutes. Stir several times and watch carefully.

3. Remove the baking sheet from the oven and transfer the nuts to a work surface to cool.

INDEX